THE TRAP

**WHAT IT IS,
HOW IT WORKS,
AND HOW WE ESCAPE ITS ILLUSIONS**

First published in August 2022.

ickonic
publishing

New Enterprise House
St Helens Street
Derby
DE1 3GY
UK

email: gareth.icke@davidicke.com

Cover Design: Gareth Icke
Book Design: Neil Hague

British Library Cataloguing-in
Publication Data
A catalogue record for this book is
available from the British Library

ISBN 978-1-8384153-2-7

THE TRAP

WHAT IT IS, HOW IT WORKS, AND HOW WE ESCAPE ITS ILLUSIONS

DAVID ICKE

Dedication:

To all those unbowed by tyranny and with open minds
they can call their own.

To all those who could do the same if they made that choice.

To Christianne van Wijk for all our fascinating conversations.

Life is what happens to you

while you're busy making other plans.

John Lennon

Is this the real life? Is this just fantasy?

Caught in a landslide, no escape from reality.

Open your eyes, look up to the skies and see.

Freddie Mercury

Contents

CHAPTER ONE

We Are Here to *Remember*

David Icke is a visionary genius. Anyone who doesn't realise this at this late stage of the game is deluded, ignorant or foolish
James Delingpole

Who would have thought amid the decades of ridicule and abuse that those words would have been written one day by a respected proper journalist about that nutter David Icke? Very close to no one.

I hope that my life experience has shown how important it is to speak your truth whatever that may be no matter what the actions and reactions of others. Humanity has been manipulated into a reality bubble through thousands of years of what we call 'time' to see self and life in a myopia so small, so microscopic, that only the basic functions of survival constitute the perception of 'living'. This is changing as ever more minds awaken from the trance, but it remains the case for great swathes of the human family. Therefore anyone exposing, thinking, feeling, knowing, beyond those walls of myopic perception is going to face ridicule, abuse, and dismissal from those who literally cannot compute or process the expanded sense of reality being communicated. We must speak our truth nevertheless. We *must*. Without that unwavering determination to challenge the holding-pattern of convention nothing can change. Perception-eddies continue to spin while the rest of the river – Infinite Possibility – flows by unseen and unacknowledged. I decided when my mind awakened in 1990 and then crashed open early the following year that I was going to speak my truth. No level of abuse was going to stop me. To put this in human terms – I am a stubborn bastard. So stubborn, in fact, that like the keystone of an archway the more pressure you apply the stronger I get. This strength is not 'human'; it is beyond human. I am not human. Neither are you. 'Human' is the Great Illusion and the foundation of our mass servitude. We are *NOT* human. We are consciousness having a brief *experience* called 'human'. Here lies the revelation that will set us free.

I am living an amazing life … *amazing* … and I would not change a

day of it – the good, bad, or the bits in between. If I did I would break
the interconnectedness that has shown me so much on so many levels
and in so many facets that have conjured the magic that has led me to
where I am today. I love where I am today so why would I want to
change the incredible tapestry of experience that got me here? I would,
however, like to change many of the things I have been made aware of in
a life of extraordinary synchronicity since my consciousness exploded
awake in 1990 and 91 and I was launched into a blaze of mass ridicule
and abuse and ultimately, three decades later, to vindication. Possibly
hundreds of millions around the world have acknowledged my
vindication and more all the time while there are still many who seek to
avoid the blatant truth that I *have* been vindicated. They can do so only
through self-deception. I have said for those more than 30 years that
current events were coming and here they are. The question is how –
how did I know? Why are things that I said which are most far out
increasingly being supported by mainstream scientists? After all I left
school at 15 to play professional football with no exam certificates. To
the intellectual mind that is a paradox. How could I know without a
proper 'education'? I could know because the 'world' is not what people
think it is or, more to the point, are *told* it is. The intellectual mind must
be the servant of expanded states of consciousness. Instead the intellect
has long been the master and not the servant. When that happens the
cell door slams shut on wisdom, on knowing, and our 'world' is the
result. I am going to outline key moments in my life in the opening
chapters to provide a 'human' life-blueprint with which to compare the
seriously deep levels of reality which we will explore later. My life
experience will also give you the background to where my information
has come from these last 32 years as I pass my 70th 'year' 'on' mad-
house Earth.

I arrived 'here' in earth-year 1952 and like many today I had a
mission to wrest control of human perception from the clutches of a
deeply evil (inverted) force that manifests in countless different ways
that I will be exposing. I didn't consciously know this of course as I grew
up on a council estate in Leicester, England, went to school and pursued
a career in professional football. Nor did I know this when that career
ended with arthritis and when I went on to be a newspaper, radio and
television journalist and nationally-known sports presenter with the
BBC. I didn't know when out of nowhere I became a national
spokesman for the British Green Party in the late 1980s. But I *did* know
after a visit to a psychic in 1990 and when my sense of reality was blown
apart on a hill in Peru in 1991. They talk about life-changing moments.
That doesn't even begin to tell the story of what happened to me that
day. I will describe all of these experiences and so many more as we go
along. They are essential background to how I could call current events

and be way ahead of mainstream 'science' many times over three decades.

I have learned (the real term should be 'remembered' as we'll see) so many things including the fact that there is no death and what we *call* death is only a transition between different expressions of life. Far from being pawns in someone else's game we can control our experienced reality *if* we know how to do so. If we don't then we *are* pawns in someone else's game and that's the stark situation that almost everyone faces. I have learned (remembered) the nature of the psychopathic force behind all this, how it operates through its hidden networks, and to what end. Knowing the 'what end' has allowed me to predict current events. I have also been shown – to allow me to *remember* – that what we call the human world is a massively-advanced version of a virtual reality computer system created to entrap our sense of reality and imprison our lower consciousness in an ever-recycling feedback loop between different levels of this simulation or 'Matrix'. This process has become known as 'reincarnation'. The physics of our reality and computer games are the same as highlighted by physicist and cosmologist Max Tegmark at the Massachusetts Institute of Technology (MIT). Who would have thought amid the frenzy of ridicule that once descended upon me that they would read a headline that said: 'We owe David Icke … an apology if quantum experiment proves we are living in a Matrix.' Or that the article would start with the line: 'Whisper it, but many respected scientists and academics are becoming increasingly convinced by left-field provocateur David Icke's assertion that our reality is an artificial simulation.' Who would have believed when I said soon after the millennium that we live in a simulation and its 'walls' are the speed of light that 20 years later an article in the mainstream *Scientific American* would come to the same conclusion? How I could know this so much earlier with no exam passes or academic instruction beyond the basics. That will become clear and this is the point: The ability to do that is open to *everyone*. It should be our natural state. To understand the simulation is to understand human society and to understand human society is to understand … *perception*. We shall see that perception is both the foundation of human control and the means that can set us free of that control. The simulation or Matrix is a manipulator of perception because that which is behind the simulation knows that from perception everything – *everything* – else comes. Every last fine detail of experience.

Hello world

I was born on April 29th, 1952, in an inner-city area of Leicester in the English East Midlands (Figs 1 and 2 overleaf). Our terraced house was in Lead Street which ran into Wharf Street so you get the picture (Fig 3 overleaf). Lead Street was demolished in a slum clearance scheme pretty

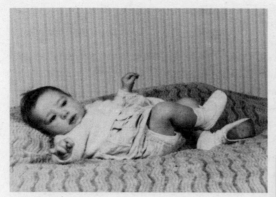

Figure 1: Hello world – did I volunteer for this?

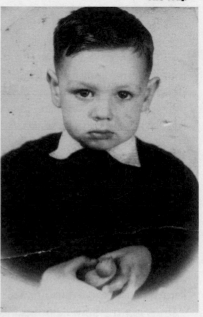

Figure 2: I'm not sure I like it here.

Figure 3: Lead Street, Leicester, in 1952 – my first home before it was all swept away by slum clearance.

soon after I was born. My earliest memory is sitting in an austere room at a grim empty table except for a bottle of sterilised milk which came with a top like you get with a bottle of beer. This lasted longer than regular milk which meant it was cheaper and that was rather vital given that we were skint. I mean *skint*. My second memory – just a flash – was heading for the bus to move to a new council estate which was built in the 1950s on the outskirts of Leicester. This would be my home until I left to play professional football in 1967. I lived there for short periods later, too, and my younger brother Paul still lives there. I also have an older brother, Trevor. Paul and I shared the same little bedroom after he arrived and thankfully the same sense of humour to this day. It's never long before we're laughing. My father Beric was born in 1907 and lived a challenging life growing up through the First World War and then struggling to survive the Great Depression of the 1930s (Fig 4). During the Depression he walked 250 miles from London to Blackpool in the English North West and slept rough every night as he sought summer work on the 'Golden Mile' of Blackpool's seafront area. He couldn't find a job even then and walked a further 18 miles to Preston where he secured work in a factory. Soon came World War Two when he

Figure 4: My father Beric. A thoroughly-decent man with a short fuse.

volunteered for the Medical Corp. He always wanted to be a doctor, but his financial and social background made this impossible in class-ridden Britain. Nevertheless he was a brilliant self-taught 'physician'. We had a doctor called Redizch or something like that which, whether right or wrong, we pronounced Rediski. He was always writing a prescription before you finished saying how you felt. Time and again I would tell my father about Redizch's diagnosis and he would say he was wrong. Beric's medical conclusion invariably turned out to be correct. He served in the Middle East and North Africa during the war and then up through Italy into Northern Europe and this had a profound effect on him for the rest of his life. He would recount all the stories to me many times and how he was turned away from religion for life by seeing families and children living in abject poverty in places like Naples surrounded by magnificent churches where clergy still asked the poor for money.

Beric was a rebel at heart and very suspicious of authority. He found it very difficult to walk away from injustice and lost many jobs by not accepting it. He was fired from a London pub for punching the owner who was badly treating a young employee and this led to his trek to Blackpool in search of work. Later he was urged by fellow workers in a shoe factory to represent them over poor treatment by the bosses and when he did he was sacked on the spot. He told me how he picked up some possessions from his work spot and all those who urged him to represent them – because they daren't – sat with their heads down refusing to make eye-contact as he walked out with another income gone. It taught him as my own experiences have taught me never to do anything with the motivation of helping people. If you do that you will be disappointed and hurt when those same people turn on you despite what you did for them. Instead do what you know to be *right* and by doing so people are helped as a result. When they turn against you the dynamic is different. You didn't do it for them. You did it because you knew it was the *right* thing to do. Your relationship is not with individuals; it is with doing what is right and just and fair *because* it is right and just and fair irrespective of the people involved. That is how I live my life to this day.

My father was a rebel in the military, too, and got away with a lot. He was willing to do things that others wouldn't do which included picking up body parts of those blown to pieces and sending them home in coffins weighed down with ballast so their families believed it contained a full body when it was only a few pieces. The authorities needed him and he took full advantage of that. He was part of a plan to falsely diagnose with tuberculous a highly dangerous officer whose idiocy was getting many killed. The move ensured the officer would be sent home to England and no longer able to cause his deadly mayhem. When Beric won the British Empire Medal for pulling pilots and crew from a crash-landed blazing plane at Chipping Warden airfield in Oxfordshire he became pretty much untouchable. He would be picked up from local pubs in the evening, poured into a truck, poured into bed, and be ready for work the next morning. No action was ever taken against him. He was too invaluable and the medal was his protection. The Icke family has rebel in its DNA. Beric's challenges and life experiences didn't make him the easiest man to live with. He was angry and frustrated at the world and he could have a short fuse. Behind that was a sense of decency and he cried easily at the sight of injustice. By contrast I am the opposite. Injustice doesn't make me cry. My response is to want to put it right. What makes me cry (very easily) is to see kindness and people joyful and happy. I am a sucker for a weepy movie with a happy ending. I was brought up in an atmosphere of questioning authority and never giving up. My father told me at a young age: 'You are never finished until you tell yourself you're finished. It doesn't matter what anyone else says.' That came in handy when the deluge of ridicule was turned upon me in 1991.

Rent man radar

My mother Barbara was very different. She was dragged around from place to place and home to home by my grandfather as she was growing up. She never had what you would call an education. My father said to me once: 'You've got your mother's looks and your father's brains and thank god it wasn't the other way round.' In fact, while not being in any sense an academic, Barbara was very streetwise about many things. My father needed her more than vice-versa. She was incredibly loyal and the kind of woman you want next to you when the going gets tough which during my childhood was pretty much all the time (Fig 5). I would go with her on a Thursday lunchtime to the Gents clock factory in Leicester's St Saviour's Road where my father would slip out with his pay packet so we could eat that night. Barbara never complained and just got on with it. We kids didn't complain either. It was all we knew. You didn't miss what you'd never had in the days before mass marketing and desire-manipulation to which subsequent generations have been subjected.

Figure 5: My mother and my mate. Always looking out for me.

When I was still in a pram she would walk the streets to deliver to shops the toys my father made at Christmas to bring in a few more pennies. He would use round pie tins to make toy banjos and the first Christmas present I remember was a big wooden bus that he made for me. My mother would tell the shops that she was delivering on my pram because the van had broken down – a van we never had. Then there were the many times council rent men knocked on the door and my mother would go '*Shhhhh*! to me and pull me behind the settee. I didn't know what was happening at first, but I learned that when the rent man got no answer (he often didn't from people who couldn't pay the rent that week) he would peer through the front window. Hence if we were in the front room at the time we hid behind the settee. Beric and Barbara were a great balance, if not always in harmony to say the least. He was very much the angry man who could be very aggressive and she was the feminine calm that he so badly needed. She was always singing when I was small as she cleaned the stone floor or polished the front door step which seemed to be an obsession with working class women of the time. One of her regular songs around Christmas was 'The Little Boy That Santa Claus Forgot' most famously sung by wartime singing legend Vera Lynn. The song described how a little boy had no toys at Christmas while everyone else did. I would follow her round the house telling her that he could have mine! It still brings tears to my eyes remembering that and don't play the song to me whatever you do.

One other point about my childhood is how it almost ended soon after it began. I was still very small when I was paddling in the North Sea at Caister near Great Yarmouth in Norfolk. I fell over and went under the water. I can clearly remember as I write this lying on my back looking through the water to the sky. I made no effort to get up. Everything was so calm and I was fine with just experiencing how lovely it all was. Then I saw the face of my brother Trevor appear above me and his arm dipped in and pulled me out. The next thing I knew was lying on my belly on the beach coughing up water. I have wondered if I would have just stayed there, but thanks to Trevor I didn't find out. What a good job he was looking and saw what I had done. Funny, even though I was not fazed by the experience in the moment, the coughing up of water and the struggle to breathe made me frightened of water for much of my childhood. I would claim I had forgot my swimming trunks to avoid school swimming lessons and didn't learn to swim until I was in my 30s. Another fear of mine as a kid was dogs and when I walked anywhere they always seemed to make me their target for attention and barking. Once I realised how reality works I understood why. They were picking up the energy I was giving off. I love dogs today. Their eyes and faces are magical.

Looking back at my life and all that has happened I came out of the womb symbolically wearing running shoes as I sprinted from experience to experience and emotion to emotion to glean as much knowledge as possible as quickly as possible. This related to what it is like and what it means to be 'human' and how the 'human' world is controlled. Obviously, I didn't know then why these experiences were happening. They were, however, essential to what my higher levels of consciousness knew was coming. Others who have clearly come here to roll back human control will no doubt recognise my rollercoaster life-experience. To understand how the game is played you have to experience all significant parts of the game. I was sitting in a circle of people from all ages and walks of life one time and as they told their personal stories I was thinking 'Wow, that happened to me'; 'Yes, I know exactly how that feels'; and 'Crikey, I did that, too'. This is what I mean by the running shoes.

Diffident Dave. Never, surely?

I talk and write a lot about the 'Little Me' mentality in which people consider themselves powerless to impact on life. They are followers and reactors, not leaders and impactors. 'Little me' is the foundation mentality of the Matrix simulation and utterly essential to the few controlling the many. I understand Little Me. I was there myself once. Through my early years and when I first went to school I kept myself to myself with my head down and lived life as the also-ran I thought that it was my destiny to be. It never occurred to me that anything special would ever happen. Special, different and successful were only for others. My hand-to-mouth life experience in the 1950s and early 1960s just confirmed that my present would be my future. Keeping myself to myself, spending time alone and enjoying my privacy has been a life-long trait which is rather ironic given that almost everything I have done since I was 15 has been in the public eye in some way. The reason I seek out solitude has changed, however. Subsequently this has been to withdraw from the public stage between public things that I do. As a kid I was simply hiding from the world. I was shy in the extreme, had little to say, and my mother would laugh at me crossing the street to avoid even saying hello to someone. When I say shy I mean it. I know what it's like and I know how Little Me feels. I was frightened of everything. My first day at Whitehall Infant School was a nightmare for me. I ran home at lunchtime to tell my mother I didn't like school and didn't want to go back again. My heart sank when she said that I had to. I was frightened every day.

I was especially terrified of the dentist and I remember going with my mother to have a tooth out at a school dental clinic. If I was going to the dentist I would ask my mother if I could have something to eat on our walk there. I knew that if she said 'no' I was going to have a tooth pulled with 'the gas' to knock me out. She used to keep that from me. She knew I might run for it and this particular day I did. The dentist lowered the gas mask to my face and at the last second I banged him in the chest, jumped up, did a body serve around him and ran full-pelt out of the surgery, through the waiting room and into the street. I kept running with my mother, shopping bag on arm as always, shouting in the distance 'David!, David! – come back'. I turned around to see her running towards me some way behind and it dawned on me that there was nowhere to run. I had toothache and it would not go away if I

didn't return. The next day one of the kids at school told me he was in the waiting room when I sped past. Another one of endless bad days for my self-esteem. In the years after we moved from slum clearance Lead Street to a new council house on a new estate the road to Whitehall school was a dirt track. It was known locally I seem to recall as 'Cut-Throat Lane'. My father ran a campaign to get it paved and decades later I found a picture from the local paper of the time reporting his efforts. The picture included my mother with me in my school cap as I was at Whitehall Infants (Fig 6).

I had an experience at infant school about the

Figure 6: The mud-track to school holding my mother's hand. We're just behind the first three to the left with me in my dark coat, cap and wellies. The picture was taken in 1957 when I was 5 and I'd only just started at Whitehall Infants.

same time – maybe 1958 – that both typified me in that period and gave me a spooky precursor of where my life was much later to go. I was in a school play (school plays have been significant in my life as we'll see!) and of course I played the starring role. I was a tree. Teacher's pet Graham Glover was the prince in our rendition of Sleeping Beauty and good luck to him. The thought of saying lines in public would have been catastrophic for me. I was with a group of others dressed in brown trousers, green tops and something on our heads supposed to symbolise branches. The idea was that the prince would cut down the trees with his make-believe scythe and we would fall down as he passed. I was playing it for real and Graham Glover never came near me so I thought how can I fall when he's so far away? That would be silly. All the other trees fell down no matter where he was and I was left standing on my own. The audience of parents and teachers started to titter and then to belly-laugh. I stood there thinking: 'Why are they laughing? He didn't come near me so how could I fall?' The symbolism of refusing to fall down while everyone laughed at me was a sign of things to come. The next day I was called out of class by the headmistress, Miss Wilkinson. Think of a classic headmistress of the 1950s and you got her. Tall, wide, tweed skirt and jacket, and her shoulders so big she pre-dated shoulder pads without any need to have them. She leaned over me like Cruella De Vil and launched into a rant about how I had made the play look foolish, the school look foolish and myself look foolish. It was like that old joke about an inflatable boy who stabbed an inflatable headmaster, an inflatable school, and then stabbed himself. The headmaster said: 'You've let me down, you've let the school down, and worst of all you've let yourself down.' Well, I laughed anyway. Miss Wilkinson and the play were yet more blows for my self-esteem, but what a precursor and preparation for what was to come.

Uppers and downers

I moved to Whitehall Junior School next door and my life and demeanour eventually began to change thanks to football. The tarmac playground was on a slight incline and we used to play a game we called uppers and downers. Someone kicked a plastic football in the air, shouted 'uppers and downers' and everyone chose which team they wanted to play for – the ups or the downs. The teams could be seriously uneven as a result, but it sort of worked. I was attracted from the start by the position of goalkeeper which was rare. Most kids wanted to score goals while I wanted to stop them. The playground is still there, as is the infant school hall where my tree refused to fall. I was walking into the school one day when I saw a notice on the door asking for anyone interested in a trial for the school third year football team to add their name. I didn't think for a second to do so. Play for the school team? I would never get in, so what's the point? I was walking home alone shortly afterwards when a boy ran after me shouting for me to stop. He said the football teacher Mr Rickard (that's how you pronounced it anyway) wanted me to go to the trial for the team the next day. He said he had seen me playing in goal in the playground. I ran home so excited to tell my father. Then it dawned on me that I had no football boots. We had no money for boots and I had no need for them till now. Anyway, the shops were closed by the time my father came back from work. Shops then had strict opening hours, There were no supermarkets open all day and night. There *were* no supermarkets, period. I went with him to the nearest shops where there was any chance of finding football boots in the hope that one was still open by chance. It was a forlorn hope. Then we found a tiny shop in Leicester's Green Lane Road that sold bric-a-brac. There in the window was a pair of *football boots* and it was *still open*. The problem comes with my description of them as 'football boots'. Yes, they were boots and yes you could kick a ball in them. That's where the comparison ended. First of all they were colossal adult boots far too big for me and they would have been state-of-the-art in about 1915. By this time you were more likely to see a diver in a big metal helmet wearing them to aid his submersion. They had an enormous toecap and cost seven shillings and sixpence, the equivalent today a converter tells me of 38 pence. Even then they were overpriced.

I went for the trial the next day as a goalkeeper with my boots attracting great hilarity. Another boy was picked in goal and I had to somehow get into the team playing outfield. It came down to me and one other kid for the last position and Mr Rickard decided to have us both take a shot at goal and the one with the most powerful shot would get in. Well, this was going to be a no-contest. I had boots with toecaps that could have launched missiles. I kicked the ball toecap-first and it begged for mercy when contact was made. I was in!! I can't tell you the rush of self-esteem this gave a little boy without any up to that point. My eyes still water thinking about it even today. My god, I *can* achieve things. I scored in my first game for the school, a goal my father missed. He tended to leave home just when he was supposed to arrive somewhere else. When he did come I ran over to him shouting 'I scored, I scored.' Mind you, that was not such a great achievement given that we won 16-nil against a Catholic school called The Newry who were to football what Bill Gates is to human decency. Soon afterwards the goalkeeper picked in front of me went to play for the fourth year team and I was now in goal (Fig 7 overleaf). I decided immediately what I wanted to be – a *professional footballer*. What an ambition for the kid who two weeks earlier thought he would never amount to anything. I played for the fourth year team the next season and we won a cup in which all the schools in Leicester could enter. It was an incredible achievement –

hey this Icke kid might not be an also-ran after all (Fig 8). I should mention something else, though, with regard to all this. While I had low self-esteem up to this point and didn't expect to amount to much there was actually a big contradiction running alongside that. From

Figure 7: My first football team with Mr 'Rickard'. I'm fourth from the left at the back.

Figure 8: Whitehall School all-Leicester cup-winners in 1963. I'm fourth from the left at the back.

somewhere deep inside from an early age I felt I had come to 'do something'. Like a destiny if you like. It was coming from a different place to my conscious lack of belief in myself. It was there as a feeling more than a thought. The feeling would just come and go here and there. When I set my sights on being a footballer I thought that might be this 'destiny' I had the feeling about.

Pre-planned 'random'

There were another couple of incidents that stick in the memory at Whitehall Junior School and when I look back they were not random. They were me being guided through the human maze and activating traits that would be essential in my future life which I had no idea was coming. Other levels of me did, though. What I call Body-Mind – the five-senses basically – are only a part of our multi-dimensional consciousness. We are much more than that if we open our minds to expanded states of consciousness. If we don't, our perception becomes entrapped in five-sense myopia and we are a manipulator's dream. Body-Mind is like a guy paddling down the river in a canoe. The limit of his vision and awareness is the next turn in the river. Our expanded awareness beyond the simulation, beyond the perception of the five senses, can view the whole river from source to sea. What means one thing to Body-Mind means something very different to expanded awareness. For example the canoe might spring a leak and you paddle to the shore furious at your 'bad luck'. Then someone comes over to you and says: 'My god you are lucky there's a big waterfall around that next corner.' These situations have happened to me throughout my life and not only since my initial conscious awakening in 1990. I began to recognise them after that, but they had been happening since I was a young kid. They appeared to be just coincidences and 'bits of luck' until I became aware enough to see the pattern and realise something strange was happening that could not be explained by mere 'coincidence'. This revelation would be decades away, however, as I made my way through the school system.

In the third year at Whitehall I was told by the fourth year football teacher to ask my own class teacher for permission to take part in the weekly football training afternoon which fourth year boys had written into the curriculum. I asked the first week and he said yes and then the second week when I was out playing in goal a kid from my class came over and said I had to return immediately. When I did I was humiliated in front of everyone by a morose, arsehole of a teacher. I thought permission had been given to go to football every week. He didn't. Something inexplicable followed. I sat down at my desk and he set a class spelling test. Now I'm not bad at spelling these days – through decades of repetition – and there's always spell-check. In my schooldays I was useless. At the end of the class the teacher announced the spelling test results. Somehow – *somehow* – I had come *top*. What? *Me?* At spelling? I must say I enjoyed his embarrassment amid my own incredulity when he had to reveal that the boy he had just lambasted in front of everyone and didn't think was very bright had won his test. It was from here that I began to develop a 'fuck you' attitude to anyone who sought to belittle me and put me down. It came in handy after 1990.

That same year with that same teacher I came top of the class in the end of year exams for the single time in my life. It was the only point in my school career that I had really tried. I was going to be a professional footballer – I *knew* it – and so why did I need all this school crap? There was, in fact, another reason unknown to me: Why do I need all this perception programming?

The other incident I recall was in my final year at Whitehall when I had a teacher that showed me some respect. He sent a very fragile piece of slate around the class and when it was given to me by the boy in front I broke it in two by accident testing how strong it was. Oh, no! I watched the now two pieces continuing their journey back to the teacher who was furious when he was given two pieces instead of one. 'Who broke the slate'? came the cry. Silence followed. Could I get away with it? I thought that I had until he went around the class asking each child in turn if it was broken when it got to them. I could see that the only way I was going to survive was to say it was broken when it came to me so blaming the boy in front. I could never do that and so I was left to my fate. In fact, the teacher, a decent man, didn't fume. He said how disappointed he was that I didn't own up immediately. That hurt more than any rollicking. The good thing was that I refused to protect myself by blaming someone else which I could have done. That attitude has stayed with me ever since and it is amazing how apparently random 'little' incidents and choices especially in childhood can have a profound impact on you for life (Fig 9).

Figure 9: My final year class at Whitehall Junior School with the 'slate' teacher. I'm fourth from the left at the back – my usual position!

Four wonderful years

Being a professional footballer was all that mattered to me as I moved on from Whitehall to a senior school, Crown Hills Secondary Modern, in 1963. Whitehall is still there pretty much as it was while Crown Hills has a school of the same name on the same site, but with a ferociously ugly building replacing the unique one that I knew. I was supposed to go from Whitehall to another school called Spencefield where they played rugby not football and a group of us got permission instead to go to Crown Hills which was fantastic on so many fronts. There was a big staff change at the same time I arrived and while school work was never my priority (to say the least) I had an amazing four years (Fig 10). The great majority of the teaching staff were brilliant and I can still recall their names, Mr Danvers, Stone, Jay, Hartley, Duggan, Woodcock and Jones. The state curriculum was of course designed to mould young minds in ways that suited the state, but not even close to the scale of perceptual programming that we see today. Those teachers at Crown Hills allowed a freedom of thought and expression that the young of current generations would hardly believe. They were also great characters, often very funny, and went the extra mile to help and support the kids when they didn't have to. It was a different age and a far better one.

I was getting a bit rebellious by now. School work bored me and I couldn't see how much of it would ever be of use in the life I had in mind. At the same time being at the school with my mates and in that teaching atmosphere was a joy I have never forgotten. My French teacher, a lovely lady called 'Madame Barwood', would often make it her first priority at the start of each lesson – especially the late Friday one for some reason – to find an excuse to eject me to

Figure 10: Crown Hills School on Gwendolen Road in the 1960s. (Courtesy of Tony Danvers.)

the corridor. She knew I wasn't interested in learning French so what was the point in me being there I guess was her conclusion. I still liked her, though, and when I met her in the street years after I left we had a good laugh about it. To this day the only phrase in French I remember is

'Quelle heure est-il?' If you are ever in Paris and want to know the time I'm your man. The headmaster, a guy called Oldfield, and a rare one I didn't really take to, would teach a class next door on Fridays and would often come out to take a phone call and give me the double-take as I stood alone in the corridor. What, you *again*? I wasn't a surly rebel – a rebel in search of a cause – it was just that I wasn't interested in most of what they tried to teach me. I instinctively knew that I would never have a need for much of it and so it has proved. Most of what interested me – like history – I have spent decades *un*learning because it simply wasn't true or at the very least only partly so.

At the start of each school year I would be near the front of the queue for new classrooms so I could get my seat for the year next to the windows which looked out on the sports field. I spent many hours daydreaming out of the window as I spend so much of my life still daydreaming today (Fig 11). Daydreaming is my form of meditation letting the mind go where it wants without limitation. 'Icke, look this way', and 'Icke, stop daydreaming' was a regular response from the teachers trying to fill my head with maths (ugh!) or whatever. My mind was only on the job with English (writing not the rest of it), history and geography. The rest passed me by. Oh, yes, and there was also art with a top teacher, Tony Danvers. He encouraged kids to be creative even if you couldn't draw or paint (guilty!). I did a symbolic representation with Tony's encouragement of the great England goalkeeper Gordon

Figure 11: Crown Hills school photograph when I was 14 in 1966. I'm the one nodding off (daydreaming).

Banks, my hero at the time, made from plaster and wire. Tony entered the work in an art exhibition – the one and only time that would ever happen in my life given I was crap. 'Gordon' wasn't very good, to be honest, and made Banks look like the winner in a pie-eating competition. Tony was one outstanding teacher and made art what it should be – fun. It was a delight to make contact with him again before I began writing this book and he provided some of the pictures (Fig 12).

Figure 12: Playing someone or other in a Crown Hills play in my last year at school. I'm second from the left with me spear. (Courtesy of Tony Danvers.)

I remember so much about my time at Crown Hills, almost all of it with affection, but again there were key moments with hindsight that affected me deeply in terms of preparing me for what was to come. There was a school bully who like all bullies frightened people into submission with the fear of the consequences of not doing what he said. The consequences didn't have to be delivered – the thought of them was enough (see humanity for thousands of years and more). One day he and the group of boys around him, all of them cowards, stopped speaking to me and the verbal bullying started which went on for weeks. I was 13 at the time. The bully would often threaten to beat me up. My father saw that I was not happy and asked me what was wrong. When I told him he said: 'Right, go to school, pick out the main one, and tell him you'll take him on.' The message was that if you have a problem look it in the eye and deal with it. If you have a bully don't be cowered into compliance. The next school day the bully came to me with his gang behind him and told me to wait after school in the boys' toilets. He was going to, yes, 'beat me up'. I can still see his face when I replied: 'Okay, I'll be there.' That wasn't the response he was expecting. I was alone in the toilets after all the other kids went home and in walked the bully with his 'gang'. He then spent the next fifteen minutes or so trying to hit me and never did once. Whatever he threw I blocked. It was a slowed down version of Neo in *The Matrix*! When I went towards him and appeared to be trying to hit him (I wasn't, but he didn't know) he backed off like a frightened moggy. Oh, so this was the big, bad bully when his bluff was called. He swept out, his gang trailing behind, still yet to land a single punch. The next day they all started talking to me again and the bullying stopped. To this day I will not stand aside in the face of a bully no matter who it may be from an official in a luminous jacket to the psychopaths behind mass human control. This was another apparently passing childhood experience that had a profound effect on me from then on.

From big boots to football pro

I played for Crown Hills football teams for three years – many times outfield in the first two – and my chances to be a footballer were disappearing. To be seen by scouts of professional clubs you had to be playing for your city representative team. The thought was that if you couldn't get into your city team you couldn't be good enough to be of interest to football clubs. I was nowhere near doing that. Then came the break that set me on the road to the ambition that began with those giant boots years earlier. There was a trial for the Leicester Schools under-14 team and my sports teacher, a great guy called Mr Stone, sent me along with a few others. The catch was that he sent me an as outfield player. It was taken for granted that the goalkeeper selected would be a boy called Dave Vallance. He was already playing a year up for the under-15 Leicester Schools team and naturally he would be picked for his own age group as well. I turned up on a cold and misty morning with the grass dripping with dew in an area now known as Ellis Meadows and I think connected at the time to the old John Ellis School. They played games of half an hour with different groups of trialists and I was pretty useless outfield at this level. My heart wasn't in it. I was a goalkeeper and that's all I wanted to be. The teacher in charge told about four of us to go and kick a ball around on an area away from the pitch and he would call us back if he needed us again. It was clearly thanks, but no thanks. I walked away pondering on where my ambition could possibly go from here. About five minutes later I heard a shout from the teacher in the distance – 'Hey, any of you lads play in goal?' I was running towards him in a flash – 'Yes – I do'!' The other goalkeeper with Vallance had been injured and I took over. I did okay and the teacher told me afterwards that I should come to the next trial because 'We need a reserve goalkeeper to Dave Vallance'. Well …

The next trial took the form of a full game between two teams of the surviving trialists and the selection produced one team far more talented than the other with me in the other. I was bombarded with shots from all

angles for the totality of game and it was one of those days when if I had
dived the wrong way the ball would have hit me somehow and stayed
out. I was inspired, My goal was battered throughout and only one shot
went past me. Talk about the performance of my life at exactly the right
time. The teacher-manager to be fair said that as I had played so well in
the trial he had to pick me for the team. We had a strange situation in
which Vallance was playing for the Under-15 team and yet couldn't get
in the Under-14s. A scout from Arsenal Football Club saw me play for
the team a few weeks later and I went on trial there during the week that
England won the World Cup in 1966 for the only time. The whole
England squad came over to the Arsenal training ground in the week
before the final at Wembley when the players not in the main team
played a training game against Arsenal. I stood on the touchline
alongside these world famous players including the captain Bobby
Moore and my hero, the then Leicester City goalkeeper Gordon Banks.
What a dream for a kid who loved football. I had learned the skills of
goalkeeping by watching Banks week after week from behind the goal at
Leicester's former ground, Filbert Street. Arsenal asked me to sign what
were called schoolboy forms with them, but my father wanted to hold
on. Another famous goalkeeper that I knew in schools football in
Leicester was Peter Shilton who played for the Leicester City first team
at just 16 and went on to play more games for England than any other
player (125) and holds the all-time record for the most competitive
appearances in world football – 1,390. I could have signed for Leicester,
but at the time
Gordon Banks
was in the first
team and Peter
Shilton was his
reserve and I
thought it best
to go
somewhere else!
I was picked
ahead of Dave
Vallance for the
under-15
Leicester Boys
team the next
season and for

Figure 13: Leicester schools under-15 team in 1967 when professional
club scouts were getting interested. Third from the left at the back this time.

the Leicestershire County Schools team. Everything took off (Fig 13).

I was recommended for trials by scouts for Liverpool. Nottingham
Forest, Blackpool, Millwall and others. My father was adamant that he
wanted me to have a trial first with Coventry City, then managed by a

flamboyant character called Jimmy Hill. He had taken them from Third Division obscurity to the top division in the season that I joined them in 1967. I played only half an hour in the trial game before they offered me a full-time contract. Coventry was 25 miles from Leicester and it meant that I could get home at weekends after matches. Here I was six years after my 'big boots' trial at Whitehall leaving school behind to be a professional footballer. Would that have happened without the goalkeeper getting injured at the Leicester under-14 trial after I had at first been rejected? A great deal less likely it is fair to say. These are the 'coincidences' and 'bits of luck' which have peppered my life throughout. Success in football had saved me. God knows what I would have done otherwise. Even as a kid the thought of working in a factory or office – where most from my school ended up – was excruciating. I did not have the mind for that. Where would we be without people working in factories and offices in terms of production and organisation? I *know that* and I am not knocking those that take that path. It's just that I would have died of boredom and I knew that from a very early age. Thank goodness for football which gave me a way out.

Leaving Crown Hills was still a big blow despite where I was going. I had loved my four years there when I could dream about being a footballer and all that I wanted to do. Now I had to make that happen in a very different environment. In the last year at school I only had to turn up for a trial to know I would be picked as my confidence and ability blossomed, Here I was going away to another city to compete with people older and better or just as good. My relationship with football was bound to change and it did. I left Crown Hills to pursue my ambition with a heavy heart. Bye, bye, Crown Hills, thanks for the memories. There was also a girl still at the school in the year below me that I wanted to stay in touch with. I was extremely attracted to her and she to me. I was in love with her actually or as much as a 15-year-old can know what that means. We wrote every week for a few months when I went to Coventry before she dropped me suddenly and without explanation out of the blue. I have never known why, but bizarrely – and I do mean bizarrely – she came back into my life 52 years later. Well, not 'her' in the literal sense, but you'll see what I mean later in the book.

I was about to live my dream and I now knew why since I was a kid that I had the feeling of being 'here to do something'. I was here to be a footballer. Yes, that was it. Right?

CHAPTER TWO

Guided Through The Maze

There is no need to build a labyrinth when the entire universe is one
Jorge Luis Borges

Coventry City manager Jimmy Hill resigned three weeks after I moved into 'digs' in the city and started my professional career. Noel Cantwell, a lovely guy, replaced him. I had watched Noel from the crowd playing for Manchester United at Leicester only a short time before and now here he was my club manager.

Jimmy Hill went into television where I would meet and work with him a lot of years later while Noel had the job of keeping a Coventry City team in the top division with a playing staff of limited ability at that level. The fact that he did with some very close shaves is testament to him. Noel had a big heart and was a great support to me. What the Coventry first team lacked in top-class talent it more than made up for in characters. Laughs were never far apart with that group including the excellent goalkeeper Bill Glazier who always talked extreme-posh when he was pissed. You knew he'd had too many when he stopped dropping his h's and g's and put them in all the wrong places. Then there were two players that Cantwell brought in – Maurice Setters who played with him at Manchester United and Ernie Hunt from Everton. Both were hysterical. Ernie was one of the most skilful players I ever saw at close range and certainly the funniest. He would launch into one of his stories or songs in his broad West Country accent and you were crying. Maurice was a defender who couldn't run, had bow legs, carried too much weight and was much smaller than most of the forwards he was marking. Despite all of this he was rarely bettered. He knew all the tricks, little push here, little kick there, just at the right moment. I learned so much from his long experience in the many games we would play together. Cantwell's job was not helped early on when the main wooden stand at the Highfield Road ground burned down one night. I was called early next day by youth player Graham Paddon who went on to win the FA Cup with West Ham to tell me there had been a fire. We

met up and walked round the corner of the terraced street to see fire
engines everywhere and a big hole in the stand. We went inside one end
that was still intact and there was Cantwell. He sent us in to get the
boots out of all the first team players and firefighters were still inside
with big wooden rafters continuing to burn. We were ankle deep in
water. The next day I read in the paper that Cantwell had rushed into
the burning stand to 'save the boots'. Well, not quite. I was wearing a
black jumper and the smell of smoke never did wash out. Imagine
getting past the clipboard bloke to enter a still-burning building today.

The footballer

I was 15 and weeks out of school when I began to play for Coventry's
under-18 youth team with and against people who were often bigger,
stronger and certainly older and more experienced (Figs 14 and 15).
Some were even playing in the first teams of top division clubs and

Figure 14: This was me when I joined Coventry –
just a kid of 15 and I would have to grow up fast.

Figure 15: Footballer collector's card in my
early days at Coventry City.

came into the youth team only in big cup matches. The game was so
much faster than I knew, the shooting harder and the physical side of
things much tougher, even sometimes brutal. I had to grow up real quick
and get up to speed in every way mentally and physically. No account
was taken of your age – 15 or otherwise – you had to perform or you
were out. It was a real challenge. I also had to cope with the blow a few
months into my professional career of being dumped by the girl at
Crown Hills which took a lot of getting over emotionally with the

hormones still in a state of transition. I was not helped by an older cousin from Leicester who I had never met before I joined Coventry. He played central defender in the youth team. He was three years older and one of the most truly arrogant people I had experienced at that time. Every conceded goal caused by his mistake had him pointing at the kid behind him, in other words me. He went on to become a first team player with a few clubs and then sank without trace. I'm sure in his whole career (in his own mind) he never conceded a single goal that wasn't someone else's fault. What I was in those days was super-fit. I would win cross country runs by a mile – often literally – against much older first team players even though I was just out of school. I could run like the wind, as they say, and what an irony that fitness would plague my career. I also obsessively wanted to learn and improve. I would still be on the training pitch working on some skill or other when official training was over. The top competition in professional youth football was the FA Youth Cup, the youth equivalent of the FA Cup, in which every professional club competed and many that weren't. In that first season, when I was still 15, we progressed through the rounds to the semi-final. This was a serious achievement in the light of the competition we had to overcome (Fig 16). I played in the first game of a two-legged semi-final away at Crystal Palace. We got a one-all draw which was good with the second leg to come at home. Then *crash*. My life was about to change in so many ways in a matter of minutes.

I was sitting on the grass at Coventry's Ryton training ground in the spring of 1968 the day before the second leg when the youth team manager, Pat Saward, a former player with Aston Villa, read out the

Figure 16: The 1967-68 season Coventry City youth team from which I was dropped with no warning. I was 15. Third from the right at the back.

team he had selected. He prefaced his announcement with the words: 'Some of you are going to be disappointed when they hear this.' Saward then read out the team and I wasn't in it. *What?* I had played in every game this far. I had never really liked or trusted Saward and I liked him even less now. I always felt he lacked integrity and I wasn't wrong on that one. I was 15, I had played in every round of the competition including the first leg of the semi-final, and he dropped me without even having a word beforehand, trying to soften the blow, or at least giving me a warning. The first I knew was when he read the team out. Even worse he then said that all the players in the team should go with him for a training session and the rest of us should grab a ball and have a kick around. The teacher's words at the Leicester schools trial were repeated only this time there was going to be no happy ending. Quite the opposite. I was in a daze as I watched the team I had played in all season (they would go on to lose the final) disappear into the distance leaving a handful of us to our own devices. The dark day, actually the dark 20 minutes, was not over, however. We set up a practice exercise with someone crossing the ball into goal area and I would come out to catch it under pressure from other players. Soon after we started a big lad jumped at me and buried his knee into my left thigh. I went down like I'd been hit with sniper fire. Agony was not the word and it was turning out to be a really great day, or 20 minutes. I was helped to the club physiotherapist, Norman Pilgrim, who was a real nice chap. He diagnosed a haematoma – 'an abnormal collection of blood outside of a blood vessel' – which can follow a blow of the kind that I had. It looked like an egg sticking out of my thigh. We called them week-at-homers at Coventry. Norman would send us home to rest for a week before starting treatment. In a single day I had gone from looking forward to playing the following night in the semi-final, second leg, in front of a big crowd at Coventry's Highfield Road stadium to sitting alone at the guest house where I lived in Westminster Road in Coventry with my thigh strapped and my heart broken.

A vital preparation for where my life would go was to become incredibly emotionally strong. I wouldn't otherwise survive where my path would take me. Anyone who couldn't deal with an unyielding emotional onslaught, let alone mere disappointment, would go under fast in the wake of what was to come for me. Life so often gives you your greatest gifts brilliantly disguised as your worst nightmare. Look at your own life and you'll see how the bad times gave you the chance to become wiser, more empathetic and emotionally strong. I have had many emotional blows and disappointments in my life (with many great moments, too) to give me the emotional strength to keep going no matter what is thrown my way. These experiences can destroy you or make you emotionally unbreakable. It's your choice. I chose the latter.

You only survived my father's short-fuse personality if you had
emotional strength and it started early for me – exactly as pre-planned.
My life has confirmed the words of German philosopher Friedrich
Nietzsche (1844-1900): 'One must *need* to be strong, otherwise one will
never become strong.'

I would like to say that things improved after those 20 minutes that
changed my life, but honesty prevents me. They were about to get worse
– much worse. When the strapping was removed my left knee was
clearly very swollen. I was told that blood and debris from the blow had
gathered in my knee. My body systems would soon absorb it and I
would be fine was the inaccurate medical conclusion. The knee remains
swollen to this day and yet not once have I had any pain in all that time.
Norman Pilgrim and the club surgeon at the local hospital were
increasingly bewildered when the swelling wouldn't go away. I didn't
play for about six months while everyone tried to work it out. Given
there was no pain they advised that I start playing again and see what
happened. I did, the knee was fine despite being swollen, and the most
successful period of my Coventry career began. The following season,
when I was 17, I played in a youth team full of highly talented players
and captained by Dennis Mortimer who would go on to captain Aston
Villa when they won the European Cup in 1982. By now I was super
confident both as a goalkeeper and an individual. The diffident little kid
at Whitehall was like another life. My best mate was Coventry player
Bob Stockley who would play for Wimbledon in a memorable FA Cup
run in the 1970s. People in the UK who remember the famous television
series *The Likely Lads* will get the feel for our relationship. We would go
out to night clubs and discotheques full of hope of meeting girls and
always go home alone! We had so many laughs, though. He was a great
kid, a great bloke, and I hope he's well.

Every summer Coventry would play football tournaments in the
Netherlands, one time France, against the top teams in Europe including
Barcelona and Real Madrid. My experience, horizons, and sense of
individuality and personality were fast developing (Fig 17 overleaf). We
once again progressed through the rounds of the FA Youth Cup in the
1969-70 season and beat Manchester United one-nil at Old Trafford to
reach the final against a Tottenham Hotspur team that included top-
players-to-be Graeme Souness and Steve Perryman (Fig 18 overleaf). I
say top players 'to be'. They were already outstanding and Souness was
a right character even at 16. He was every bit the 'fuck you' player,
manager, and now TV football pundit that he went on to be. I liked him.
He was an arrogant bugger full of himself to be sure. He was also a one-
off. I like one-offs. The final was over two legs, but the teams were so
close in ability that it went to four games before they beat us one-nil at
the famous White Hart Lane to take the trophy (Figs 19 and 20 overleaf).

Figure 17: Playing abroad with Coventry – Pat Saward standing far left at the back with Bob Stockley at the front on the right. You know me by now!

Figure 18: A programme featuring Dennis Mortimer for one of the fantastic Coventry-Spurs games. So many of those players went on to play professional first team football including myself.

Figures 19 and 20: Playing for Coventry City against Tottenham Hotspur at White Hart Lane in 1970.

It had been a fantastic season although, as it turned out, a brief respite from reality.

The next season I was too old for the youth team and Coventry loaned me to other clubs to get experience playing at a higher level. I spent three months at Oxford United, then in the Second Division, now the Championship, and captained by Ron Atkinson or 'Big Ron' (he was) who went on to make his name as a football manager at clubs including Manchester United and then as a brilliant football pundit with his 'Ronism' phrases that set him apart. There was 'early doors' as in 'get at them early doors' which means to get at them from the start. I have no idea where the doors come in. He was already using that phrase back at Oxford. His TV career was destroyed by the political correctness mob when he made an apparently racist remark when he thought the microphone was off. PC tyranny has no forgiveness and no mistake is allowed. They have to destroy you. It's what they do. I say the remark was 'apparently racist'. While it was not at all nice to say the least, I knew Ron Atkinson in a number of football and TV situations here and there over the years and the last thing he was is a racist. It was he who gave black players their big break when he managed West Bromwich Albion and built a team around them. None of this mattered. The PC mob is consumed by its deluded sense of self-righteousness and once it smells blood it has to taste it, too. Lift the mask from the self-righteous and you always find they are everything they rail against. I remember Oxford United for breaking my thumb and for my right ankle swelling for no reason. This time, unlike my left knee, it was *painful* – very. What the hell? What was going on? The swelling wouldn't go down and I headed back to Coventry for treatment. I tried to keep going and I was picked as substitute goalkeeper when the Coventry first team played away at Bayern Munich in a European competition with football legends in their team like Franz Beckenbauer and Gerd Müller. Coventry lost six-nil and it would have been 20 had I been on the pitch. My ankle was heavily strapped and I was in serious pain. It settled down a bit, although still swollen, and I went on loan to Northampton Town where I felt weakness in my left knee although still not pain. Back again I went to Coventry and they thought it must be a damaged cartilage, I had an operation to have one removed and it wasn't the cartilage. By now my left elbow was swollen, too, for no apparent reason.

'It's over, son' (Hey, not so fast)

The inevitable happened when I was given the news that I probably had rheumatoid arthritis and my career was over. I was just 19. What had started with those big boots at Whitehall had run its course or so it seemed. Obviously I was gutted. The worst part was driving back to Leicester to tell my father. He had lived a very challenging life and I

Figure 21: Marrying Linda on September 30th,1971, only four months after we met.

knew what a buzz it gave him to have me break the mould in a way. He walked out to meet me from the Gents clock factory where I went with my mother as a kid to get that week's pay on a Thursday lunchtime. It was a horrible moment. My father did have a trait that led him in the wake of disappointment to take his anger and frustration out on someone and this time it was me. Our relationship broke down for years after this as a result and even when it was patched up it was never really the same again. In this period, I had met Linda who I married within months of our first meeting and she would be my wife for the next 29 years (Fig 21). She's still a great friend, lives down the road, and helps me in many ways that allow me to focus 100 percent on what I do. We had three children, Kerry, Gareth and Jaymie, who are all stalwarts of freedom and give me tremendous support. I needed a friend in Linda and some warmth and love at that time for sure. My football career was over, I'd been effectively thrown out of home by my father and I had nowhere to sleep. Linda lived in Leamington Spa not far from Coventry and she was a Coventry City supporter who watched for those FA Youth Cup games at Highfield Road. She helped me find a guest house in Leamington to live for a week and then a flat. Funnily enough, our family doctor in Leamington was to be Vernon Coleman who nearly 50 years later was one of the leading voices in the UK exposing the 'Covid' scam and we shared a stage at a big public rally in London's Trafalgar Square in 2021.

So what now? I was called around this time by John Camkin, a director of Coventry City and owner of a chain of travel agents with their headquarters in of all places, Leamington Spa. He asked me what I was going to do and I said I still hadn't given up on continuing to play if my joints settled down. John was a former sports journalist on national newspapers, did some television commentary and had a lot of contacts in football. He offered me a job at his travel agency – I was *terrible* – and said he would ask around a few football clubs. What came back was an offer from a football great, John Charles, who was manager of a then semi-professional club, Hereford United (Fig 22 overleaf). Big (no, *colossal*) John was known as the 'Gentle Giant' and he was a legend in Italy where he played for Juventus. I played against him for Hereford

Figure 22: The Hereford United team when I first joined in an attempt to save my career despite the arthritis. The great John Charles on the far left in the front row.

when he moved on to manage and play for another club and he was a handful even at over 40. John Charles was a terrific bloke, far too nice to be a football manager, although he did sell me a wreck of a 'car' once from which bits periodically dropped off like a clown car in a circus. Rust was holding it together, well, most of the time. Hereford played in the Southern League which was outside the fully-professional leagues and involved playing a couple of times a week with a training session where possible. Players had other jobs like I did at the travel agent until my uselessness led to me leaving. That job sure confirmed my instincts that I could never do a 'proper job'. My boredom threshold was far too low. John Charles would leave Hereford a few months after I joined to be replaced by Colin Addison who would make his name as the player-manager who led the club on an historic FA Cup run that included a

Figure 23: At Hereford United aged 20 when we won promotion in our first season in the professional Football League.

Figure 24: Cartoon image in the Hereford local paper.

David Icke

Former Coventry City. Played in the 1969-70 F.A. Youth Cup final against Spurs.

famous victory over top division Newcastle United in 1972. I had been in the team at the start of the season and lost my place with a month-long injury. I couldn't get my place back for the cup run. The following season Hereford were promoted into the professional leagues and I became a full-time professional again. My joints had settled down. The swelling was still there but not much pain – for now. The season was a reverse of the previous one. I started out of the team and then regained my place early on to stay there to the end when we won promotion in our first professional season. When I look back I always seemed to play in successful teams from the first one at Whitehall through to Hereford. We were playing in wonderful atmospheres at home where ground-full signs went up every week and in those days the football club was the focus of

Figure 25: Turning the ball over the bar for Hereford United. So many came to Hereford matches they had to sit around the edge of the pitch as you can see in the background. Imagine that being allowed today.

attention for pretty much the whole town. 'Hereford United we all love you' was not only a club song – it was the way things were (Figs 23 and 24). My career had been resurrected after all seemed lost. I was just 20, playing in goal for a professional first team which was rare for a goalkeeper so young. I had conceded the second least number of goals that year in the entire four divisions of the Football League in England. I had also by then conceded the least number of goals per game of any goalkeeper in Hereford United history, a record the local paper tells me still stands (Fig 25). All was well in my world. I was on my way again. Well, not quite.

There was a sub-text that only Linda and I knew about. Hereford is the home of the SAS, the elite Special Air Services of the British army which had a base just outside the town at a place called Credenhill. They had first class sports facilities and pitches for the time and we used to train there every day. Imagine that being allowed now, but this was long before 9/11 and the fake 'war on terror'. As the season progressed, the cold mornings came and my arthritis returned with a vengeance. I couldn't tell the club or they would have looked for a new goalkeeper and I was playing well so it wasn't obvious there was a problem except every morning at Credenhill during the warm up. My joints would be stiff and agony until they were warm. Every day I awoke with the knowledge that I would soon face at least half an hour of sometimes excruciating pain. I made every excuse for the limps – 'Oh, I've got a bit of a pull' or 'I think I've got a blister coming'. It was always the same cause – the arthritis in my knees (both by now) and my ankles. 'There's always something wrong with you, Ickey', other players would say and I would laugh while thinking 'if you only knew'. Amazingly, I never felt pain in the actual games which seemed inexplicable. I can tell you that if you want to bring out a fierce determination in someone not to give in then make them warm up with rheumatoid arthritis on cold or freezing English mornings if they want to remain a professional footballer. That'll do it.

There was one incident that season that gave me a powerful insight into the fact that the reality we think we see is not all there is. I have been open to that all my life although this was my first direct experience. We were playing a cup game at Barnet at the old Underhill ground in North London. It was packed that night and one hell of an atmosphere. Newcastle 'giant-killing' Hereford United were quite a draw at the time. I remember the ball falling to a Barnet player about 15 yards from goal and he hit it first time with terrific power. Often as a goalkeeper you think 'this is in' when the ball is hit and then somehow you keep it out. This was one such occasion. I saw the ball leave his foot in real time, but then everything went into slow-motion. Sound became silence as I moved across to my left towards the direction of the ball. I launched myself from the ground as the ball headed to the top left-hand corner – all in slow motion to my experience and with no sound. I arched my head back and I saw my right hand touch the ball and divert it just enough to go an inch or so over the bar. The moment I touched the ball everything surged back into normal speed and the sound of the crowd crashed back in like pressing the unmute button. As I landed and team-mates ran over to say 'Great save, Ickey', I lay there thinking: 'What on earth just happened?' Well, perhaps not 'what on earth'. That experience never left me and I can still see it now as I write. It was the best save I ever made. Blimey, I thought, there is more to the world than we think. Oh, yes.

Getting the needle

I was looking for anything to ease the pain and swelling and with mainstream medicine giving up on me I had to search elsewhere. I had been given a big jar of pills called Indocin after the end-your-career verdict at Coventry and warned that I could be in a wheelchair in my thirties given the young age at which the arthritis began. I had one reply to that: No way is that going to happen. I also asked if the Indocin would cure the arthritis. No, I was told, it would just ease the pain. Right, you can stick that then, I thought. Even at this early age I was extremely sceptical about drug companies and their products thanks to my father. This was just as well. I later read that Indocin and the same nonsteroidal anti-inflammatory drugs under other trade names are rather less than good for your health:

> Nonsteroidal anti-inflammatory drugs (NSAIDs) cause an increased risk of serious cardiovascular thrombotic events, including myocardial infarction and stroke, which can be fatal. This risk may occur early in treatment and may increase with duration of use … NSAIDs cause an increased risk of serious gastrointestinal adverse events, including bleeding, ulceration, and perforation of the stomach or intestines, which can be fatal. These events can occur at any time during use and without warning symptoms.

I was prescribed these at *19* and told nothing about those potential effects or a list of other adverse consequences which is so long it's shocking. If I had taken them I would have been dead long ago, actually murdered by Big Pharma and the doctor who advised me to take them without regard to the effects or even warning me about them. Linda told me soon after we met in 1971 that she'd read an article about a man in Kenilworth, just down the road from Leamington Spa, who was healing people with something called acupuncture. I went to see him and it turned out he had read about my arthritis story in the local paper. I had not just found an acupuncture practitioner – I'd found Professor J. R. Worsley who is described today as being 'universally acknowledged as the father and master teacher of Five-Element acupuncture in the modern world who brought this system of medicine to the West'. He and others at his practice basically kept me playing football in the Hereford years against all the odds. I remember hurting my wrist in training one Thursday morning two days before a game and I was told I would never be fit in time to play. I left training and drove the 70 miles to Kenilworth for some needles in the wrist and I trained the next morning with the wrist no problem. I have always been open to other ways of doing things and suspicious of authority in all its forms. I became very interested in acupuncture which clearly helped me when mainstream medicine could not. I read about why it worked and listened to the explanations of Professor Worsley during the treatments.

The body is a field of energy (information) and acupuncture is balancing the flow with its hair-like needles and other techniques. My mind was already opening to other ways of seeing the world. While the arthritis was painful it also gave me many gifts and not least in unleashing unbreakable determination. Acupuncture is a perfect example of how the suppression of knowledge makes you ignorant of what is possible. People say that you can't put a needle in the foot to cure a headache. Their five-sense Body-Mind myopia perceives only dots and cannot see how the foot and the head can be connected. Well, they can if the body field is interpenetrated by energy flows of information called meridians and these operate in circuits with some passing through the foot and the head. If a blockage or disturbance in the flow of that line in the foot leads to a headache further along the circuit what's the point of putting the needle in the head? Oh, says the five-senses, I didn't know that. No. You know next to nothing about anything, that's the trouble.

'It's over, son' (Okay, agreed this time)

The end of my football career ironically came between seasons in the summer of 1973. In the last few weeks of the previous season the pain had gone and I could actually warm up almost normally every morning. The spring temperatures helped, but it was more than that. I had just turned 21 and signed a new contract with Hereford as we headed into Division Three when the end finally came. I was getting into bed one night and I looked down at my left knee to see that it wasn't swollen for the first time since that blow in the thigh in 1968. My god, I've cracked it, I thought, it's gone. The next morning I woke up in a half-sleep and realised that I couldn't breathe or move. I tried to knock Linda lying beside me. Nothing happened. I was like frozen rigid. I was sure I was going to die until eventually I gasped a breath and immediately feeling surged back through my body – a feeling that knives were being thrust into every joint. I went to bed a professional footballer and woke up never to play again. Linda had to help me even to the toilet for the first three days. No lower joint would work and when I tried it was excruciating. I hoped that it would settle down again before the next season started in a couple of months. While it improved it was never enough to play. The club hospital doctor advised me to stop playing, not that I needed to be told that when I simply *couldn't* play by then. When I tried to start pre-season training the pain was too much and I couldn't hide it any more. The manager Colin Addison asked to meet me in his office one lunchtime and the hour before I got the verdict from the hospital. What followed was a bizarre interaction in which he was telling me he didn't think I was trying hard enough in training (I was in agony) and I was telling him my career was over. It took a while for him to hear me.

I would later look back on my life and see that doors were opening and closing. When one closed another opened, when one thing stopped something else would start, with no lag-time in between. It seemed for years like mere coincidence. Later I would realise there was something else going on. The local Hereford paper ran a front-page lead story about the end of my career and I was asked to be interviewed live on the television show *ATV Today* in Birmingham which covered the Hereford area. The interviewer was a well-known sports presenter, Gary Newbon, and he was talking to me with my career just ended and to cricketer Mike Hendrick who was starting a career as an England bowler. The interview was a segment in the early evening news magazine show and the three of us tip-toed into the studio as the news was being read. Newbon was pacing up and down and I looked around at the presenters, cameras and lights, and felt the tension in the atmosphere. I remember thinking 'Ickey, this is for you, son.' I did the interview and asked Newbon afterwards how I could get into television. He said it normally happened through newspapers and radio. As we drove home I told Linda that I was going to work in television and I set my ambition to present a BBC sports programme called *Grandstand* which spanned the whole of Saturday afternoon and later Sunday, too. The two main hosts were Frank Bough and David Coleman and I'd first watched Coleman present the show as a kid in the late 1950s. It seemed to most people to be a ridiculous goal. I had set out as a ten-year-old to be a professional goalkeeper which at that time was confined to just 92 people in professional first teams each Saturday. Now I wanted to present a TV show that only a handful of people ever did in its entire run between 1958 and 2007.

Village store journalist

Enter once again at just the right time Coventry City director John Camkin, who called to ask me what I planned to do now. I told him I wanted to be a journalist with a view to getting into television and he said he would talk to a few people he knew from his own time in newspapers and TV. I always had journalism in my mind as a second string as I devoured news and sports papers from quite an early age especially the coverage of Leicester City games by a writer on the local *Leicester Mercury*, Laurie Simpkin. He would later give me a job on the paper in another remarkable synchronicity. John Camkin came back to me with an offer from an old friend of his on the London *Daily Mail* who was head of a journalism college in Harlow, Essex, to which newspapers in the Midlands and the south of England sent their young journalists to be trained. His name was Bill Hicks, namesake of the brilliant and spiritually profound American comedian, and he said that if I came down and passed the entrance exam for acceptance into his college he would recommend me to all the newspapers he worked with. I did pass and he kept his word. Only two papers responded, the *Kent Messenger* and, more synchronicity, the *Leicester Advertiser* which was part of the *Leicester Mercury* group. The lack of interest was two-fold. All footballers in those days were considered to be thick (see 'journalists' today) and I had no educational qualifications whatsoever after leaving school at 15 to play football. The nearest I came to university was playing for Oxford United and would-be journalists were invariably expected to be university graduates as if that somehow ensured basic intelligence. It doesn't. It means you have a good enough memory to take what you have been told and repeat that on an exam paper. Innate intelligence which can't be taught is something very different and today's excuse for 'journalism' is almost entirely devoid of that in the mainstream. The industry demands compliant clones not innately intelligent people who will pursue the truth for the truth's sake.

The basics of journalism, as with writing in general, are not difficult. Writing books, for example, is simply having a conversation via the written word with the reader and proper journalism is telling people what they need to know and asking the questions the public would like to ask, but can't. These questions include: What happened?; Why?; How?; When?; and who was involved? Today's fake journalism might sometimes tell you what happened (if you are really lucky and there is not the usual spin). What it does not tell you is *why* it happened in terms of the real context and implications. Nor will it tell you most of the time, especially with crucial subjects and societal changes, who is really responsible for what is happening behind the scenes. To our fake journalists there is no 'behind the scenes' or manipulation from the shadows. That is always a 'conspiracy theory' no matter what the scale of evidence to support it. Journalism today is a propaganda machine, a mass perceptual manipulation operation, and nothing more. The 'Covid' era has proved this beyond doubt. More than that this journalistic fakery seeks to demonise and dismiss those in the alternative and independent media who do still work to uncover the truth. How the fakes sleep at night is beyond me although given their lack of integrity and self-awareness I suspect 'like a baby' would be the answer.

The *Leicester Advertiser* offered me the job on the basis that no one else wanted it. The paper covered every area of Leicestershire where hardly anyone lived. All the urban areas had their own paper and the *Advertiser* covered everywhere else. There were more sheep on my patch than people. I would go to village stores, post offices and the local vicar to find 'news' to report. Oh, you've got a bring and buy sale? There's a concert at the village hall? Quick – hold the front page. We had a three-day working week in Britain soon after I started to preserve coal stocks in response to a miners' strike. I attended a village parish council meeting in which the main hall was closed and everyone sat around a gas fire in the tiny kitchen discussing village happenings. A few months earlier I had run into my goal at Hereford United with the crowd chanting my name and now I was sitting in a village hall kitchen listening to discussions about street lamps. I'm not knocking journalism at this level. It is necessary in any democracy and many local papers have since sadly been systematically destroyed. The experience just did not fit my vision of a campaigning journalist. Still, hey, it was a start. My eyes were on *Grandstand* which seemed such a long way off. My visits to post offices, vicars and local grocery stores were more Cow and Gate than Watergate and if the *Leicester Advertiser's* circulation had been human it would have been on a life-support machine. The *Advertiser* was a tax write-off for the *Leicester Mercury* and little more. This was the bottom rung of bottom rungs and I had to get out of here!

I began to do radio reports of Leicester City matches on Saturdays for a local news agency owned by a real character, Roland Orton. Pretty soon he offered me a job at his office on the same floor as BBC Radio Leicester. My close proximity and football background led to me becoming their Leicester City match reporter – my first work, albeit minor, with the BBC. This was alongside all my news work with Roland's Leicester news agency which sold its news and sports reports to local and national papers and radio stations. It was a big-step up from the village store. My first football report with Roland was for BRMB Radio in Birmingham who within a few years I would be working for. News agency work put you on call pretty much 24/7 and I was its only regular reporter with only one or two others coming and going. I wanted the more predictable hours of working defined shifts on a newspaper and my eye was on the *Leicester Mercury*. They couldn't offer me anything on the main paper, but there was a job going on one of their other papers, the *Loughborough Monitor*. I took it in the hope that something would come up eventually on the *Mercury* which it did. Loughborough is in the north of Leicestershire and I lived south of Leicester in the village of Croft. Linda and I were pretty much skint trying to pay a mortgage and when our car literally fell apart (like the one John Charles sold me) my time at the *Monitor* consisted of getting up before the sun, walking half a mile for a bus to the nearest railway station, getting a train into Leicester, changing trains for one to

Loughborough, and then walking right across the town to the *Monitor* offices all before 9am. I would work through my lunchtime to leave an hour early to do the reverse trip. Happy days. The *Mercury* job came at last, and was offered by Laurie Simpkin. I spent two great years there learning the trade. What I found strange is that despite spending all that time living and working in and around Leicester between the *Advertiser* and the *Mercury* I never once came across any of the kids that I knew at three separate schools, even though the *Mercury* job took me constantly all around the city. I continued to live in Croft and spent lots of time in Leicester when I took my next job with BRMB in Birmingham. Still I met no one

Driving force

Throughout my pre-1990 life I had an unquenchable inner drive pushing me on. First to be a footballer despite the arthritis and then to reach the goal of *Grandstand*. The drive was relentless which stopped me settling anywhere for long and much as I liked working on the *Mercury* I successfully applied to BRMB to work as a radio journalist in their newsroom in Birmingham at the old ATV television studios in Aston next to the Ansells beer and HP sauce factories. If you haven't experienced the aromatic combination of beer and brown sauce at 6am in the morning after a good night out you have not lived. I worked there for yet another two years learning to be a broadcaster with a break in the middle after the intervention again of John Camkin and also Jimmy Hill who was my brief first manager at Coventry City and now a famous football broadcaster and pundit. They had been given the contract to improve football in Saudi Arabia and John wanted me as part of the team. The money was way more than I was earning as a journalist with a big catch. The contract I was offered lasted two years with no wife or family allowed in the light of the lunatic Saudi anti-women laws. By this time Kerry was born and that was obviously a big consideration. I was sick of being skint and having old cars that didn't work which was a constant theme from the time I left school. Here was a chance to end all that and I took the job. I lasted not two years, but eight weeks. I was trying to come home almost from the first day. Saudi Arabia was a crazy country with crazy laws imposed by crazy people. Some that I met were lovely, if utterly controlled by their religion, while the authorities and their minions were head cases. Even more so today under the psychopath 'Crown Prince' Mohammed bin Salman. All that oil money stolen from the people by the fascist fake 'royal' families did not shield the country from being utterly chaotic. I missed my family and sod the money. It didn't matter to me anymore. I wanted out. John Camkin could see I wasn't happy and suggested I go back home for a week and think it through. He knew as I did that once I was on that plane to

Heathrow there would be no return flight. Those two months, however, gave me a later very useful front seat experience of Saudi Arabia and its hypocrisies like alcohol shipped in secretly for the royals through fronts like furniture importers while strict and extreme Islamic laws were enforced by those same hand-chopping, head-chopping ,'royals' who are not 'royals' at all. They are non-Islamic interlopers as they are in all the other 'royal'-controlled Arab countries including the United Arab Emirates, Bahrain, and Qatar (see my comprehensive 9/11 exposé book *The Trigger*).

The TV reporter

More synchronicity followed when I returned to the UK. My old job at BRMB was now filled, but a guy I had worked with was just leaving and there was a perfectly-timed space for me to return. We had a lot of laughs especially surrounding a character in often bright used-care-salesman suits called Tony Butler who presented sport for the station. He was wary of me. I think he believed I wanted his job when that was absolutely the last thing on my mind. *Grandstand* was on my mind, nothing else. I remember Tony coming on the phone furious when I was reporting on a game from Coventry City's ground. I was a news journalist while covering football at the weekend. Coventry's ground was sparsely attended that day with spectators only dotted around the concrete terrace. I described the ground as looking like concrete spotted-dick which is a suet pudding dotted with dried fruit. Its delights had obviously eluded Tony Butler who came on the phone to tell me I could not say 'dick' on the radio. Nevertheless the word did come to mind as I put the phone down. I stayed another year at BRMB before I saw an ad for a 'regional journalist' at the BBC's Birmingham studio on a show called *Midlands Today* which I'd watched since I was a kid. Its presenters and reporters like Tom Coyne, Alan Towers and Geoffrey Green were household names in the Midlands and now I was about to join them as I was offered the job. The term 'regional journalist' was defined in the job description as writing news scripts with 'occasional appearances in vision'. I thought sod that. I was not going to be that close to my goal of television and sit in the background. I was now working for the BBC that produced *Grandstand*. This was no time to slacken the pace. I spent my spare time while working my notice at BRMB in the *Midlands Today* newsroom learning as much as I could before I started and on the Saturday of my first week when I had my BBC pass to get into any building I was down to London to watch *Grandstand* go out. In doing so I would meet many of the people I would be working with a few years later. They included the presenter Frank Bough whose charm and easy style made him rightly a television legend. He was very nice to me that day. Wow, I had now made it to the *Grandstand* studio and I wasn't leaving it there.

Back at *Midlands Today* I noticed that when the designated reporters had been sent out on diary jobs in the morning – events we knew were happening – any news story that broke would have to be covered by one of the group of regional journalists. I also noticed that these stories would often come to our attention during the lunchbreak and I began taking sandwiches and sitting in the newsroom on my

Figure 26: In the newsroom at *Midlands Today* – I was always at it. Gotta, gotta, gotta.

own while everyone else headed for the BBC bar. Day after day the producer would put his head round the door to find me alone in the newsroom: 'David, grab a crew, there's a story to cover'. Very soon 'occasional appearances in vision' became on the programme every night and I was redesignated to be a full-time reporter (Fig 26). I would volunteer for the weekend jobs and spent several nights after work with the between-programme continuity presenter, the lovely David Stevens, fine-tuning my presentation skills. It reminded me of all those extra hours on the training pitch that I chose to do at Coventry City. I was asked what I wanted to achieve when I first joined Coventry. I could have said a top player or first team player. I said that I wanted to be the best goalkeeper that ever lived. That was me. Limited horizons were not my style once the little boy in the big boots became history. Something was always driving me to be the best that I could be at whatever I did. This didn't apply to the rest of my life. I wasn't obsessive in that way, but if I wanted to achieve something I went for it with everything I had. This has remained so ever since although these days in a much more laid-back way. The drive is still there, but the 'gotta, gotta, gotta,' has subsided with age and experience.

Again the established presenters and reporters on *Midland's Today* who I had watched as a kid thought I was trying to usurp them. This was especially true of Tom Coyne who feared the next cleaner was going to replace him as presenter of the show. His demeanour on and off camera couldn't have been more different and I was to find the same with so many in television. Geoffrey Green, then at an advanced age, was especially wary of this young whipper-snapper as he perceived me. He was a miserable old bugger, but I liked him for all that. Once again they had all misread me. I didn't want their jobs or to override them. I wanted to go through *Midlands Today* as fast as possible and head for London and *Grandstand*. I stayed a couple of years (a recurring theme that happened many times). Two years at Hereford United, the *Leicester Advertiser*, *Leicester News Agency*, *Leicester Mercury*, *BRMB*, *Midlands Today* and the same with my next job presenting sport for the national London-based BBC current affairs show, *Newsnight*, which still continues today. I was offered that job in the same period as another with the *Midlands Today* rival *ATV Today* which became *Central News*. What synchronicity that would have been had I taken the ATV job and presented the same show in the same studio where I was interviewed by Gary Newbon (who was still there) when my football career ended. The studio where I decided that TV was my new goal. *ATV Today*, however, was based in Birmingham and *Newsnight* was at the main BBC Television Centre in London where I saw that edition of *Grandstand* go out. ATV was offering significantly more money to leave the BBC and yet that was not going to influence my choice at all. The BBC = *Grandstand* and that meant more to me than money. It was a good choice to turn down ATV with the *Newsnight* offer coming shortly afterwards that would soon lead to *Grandstand*.

The TV presenter

I had specialised in news since I became a journalist, with sport as an add-on here and there, and for the first time with *Newsnight* it was going to be full-time sport. Events now began to move very fast. Within a few months of moving from regional television to *Newsnight*, where national TV producers could see me, I had a call in the *Newsnight* office: 'Hello, David, this is Martin Hopkins at *Grandstand*.' My mouth went dry. *Grandstand!* At the end of the show as the football results came in at 5.45 and the audience was at its peak there was a spot when a presenter named Tony Gubba would round up all the games not covered by reporters from the grounds and go through the new league positions as they were after the day's results. Martin Hopkins, a long-time *Grandstand* stalwart, said Gubba would be away for two weeks soon and would I be interested in filling in. It took me 0.1 of a second to say yes and he said he would check with a few people and come back to me in an hour or so. I paced the floor waiting for the call and when it came he said: 'Okay, you're on'. I did a jig around the office in some disbelief at what had just happened. I went to the *Grandstand* studio for the next two weeks to follow Tony through his afternoon to see what was required and then the day came of my first *Grandstand* appearance. The slot was maybe five minutes long, but very intense and almost entirely ad-lib apart from a written opening with endless crossings out and added words when games changed with very late goals. There were pictures of relevant players to include, too, and it was always bordering on disaster because it was so rushed. The slot was delivered literally minutes after the games ended and information about changes in the league tables was often slipped to you while you were live on air and given that it was handwritten you hoped you could make sense of it. Frank Bough handed over to me and I just about got through the first one with the brilliant Martin Hopkins speaking in my ear. I was shattered afterwards by the sheer intensity of the concentration. If I cocked it up that would be the end of me with *Grandstand*. Anything less than quality and they were not interested.

The following week I was back and compiled my opening script with the usual late changes and went across to sit next to Frank. A football report was being delivered on the phone and when it was finished I knew I would be on live. I sat down and looked at my papers to see nothing but a blank sheet. My heart went walkabout. I sifted through the papers and no opening script. 'I haven't got my script' I said out loud. Seconds, I mean *seconds,* before I was on air John Tidy, who oversaw all the graphics and captions for the show, came over and said: 'Is this what you want?' It was the script. I could have kissed him. The next thing I hear is Frank Bough saying: 'And now here's David Icke with the rest of the football'. The end of my *Grandstand* career was that close. I was so relieved that my whole body relaxed and I delivered the slot with the supreme confidence that surviving near-disaster can give you. 'You read that well', Frank said to me afterwards confirming the finest of lines between success and disaster. Within a few weeks I was given the spot permanently. I was now part of the *Grandstand* team. The experience also introduced me to the joys of 'open-talkback'. Presenters wear earpieces so the gallery can talk to them while live on air. Up to this point you heard silence unless the producer pressed a button to speak. With open talkback, which is what I had for the rest of my television career from hereon, the connection was always open and you heard everything happening in the gallery and everything being said. You had to pick out and respond to what was relevant to you while you were speaking to camera and leave the rest. Live sports shows tended to change so quickly that producers could not be burdened with pressing a button every time they wanted to speak with you. Instead you heard the lot.

I continued working for *Newsnight* with *Grandstand* on Saturdays watching and learning at close range from legendary presenters Frank Bough and David Coleman both of whom I had watched as a kid in Leicester. I got on well with them both. Coleman had a reputation for being hard to work with and super-critical. I saw through that bullshit to a man who had a big heart behind it all. Like so many people he had a vulnerability and insecurity that the apparently arrogant side was designed to cover. I was offered a full-time contract in 1982 with the BBC Sports Department after being given leave from *Newsnight* to work on the World Cup that year in Spain. I was designated to cover the Northern Ireland team which was expected to play only the initial group games before being eliminated. Instead they became one of the biggest stories of the tournament as they qualified for the next stage after beating the host country Spain in Valencia where we were based. I sat next to an advertising board directly behind the Spanish goalkeeper in the first half when the Irish scored the game's only goal. Alongside me was producer Brian Barwick who would go on to be Head of BBC Sport and Chief Executive of the Football Association. Brian was a brash Liverpudlian then (maybe still is). Once he saw that I don't take shit from anybody we got on well and I liked him a lot as I did the Welsh rugby great Cliff Morgan who headed the BBC department of sport and outside broadcasts. He asked to meet me after the World Cup to congratulate me on my work and we had a wonderful chat. Cliff was an emotional man who loved language and had the gifts of a Welsh orator. I remember he said to me that day: 'David – never lose your sense of wonder.' I never have.

A national face – overnight

My full-time arrival at BBC Sport coincided with the 1982 Commonwealth Games in Brisbane when virtually every presenter and reporter headed for Australia and the few of us left behind had to host all the UK-based shows. Suddenly, almost in an instant, I was all over national TV as part of the early-morning Commonwealth Games programmes, then grabbed a few hours' sleep before presenting the prime time *Horse of the Year Show* from Wembley Arena in the evening while knowing absolutely nothing about horses. I was running on fumes by the end of the week but it was the start of a phenomenal few years in which my face was constantly on the British TV screen working on all the shows I had watched so intently as a boy including the main football programme, *Match of the Day*. This was famously presented by Jimmy Hill, my first manager at Coventry and the man ultimately behind the operation in Saudi Arabia. Jimmy was an intense man when it came to football and very funny with a sharp sense of humour and fun. I found myself by far the youngest presenter at BBC Sport – I was only 30 in 1982 – working with the legends of sports broadcasting history. They have never been surpassed and in the often bland world of broadcasting today they never will be. All of them were unique broke-the-mould characters. Apart from Jimmy Hill there were presenters Coleman, Bough, later Des Lynam, and commentators Coleman (football and athletics); Harry Carpenter (boxing); Peter O'Sullevan (horse racing); Richie Benaud (cricket); John Arlott (cricket); Peter Allis (golf); Ron Pickering (athletics); Brendan Foster (athletics); Murray Walker (motor racing); Ted Lowe (snooker); Eddie Waring (rugby league); Bill McLaren (rugby union); Dan 'Oh, I say' Maskell (tennis); David Vine (snooker, skiing, anything that moved); Sid Waddell (darts); and John Motson (football). I first met Motson with more synchronicity at the pre-match lunch before Hereford United beat Newcastle in that FA Cup shocker in 1972. His commentary on the game would launch his career. Another famous voice, if not so much face, was Len Martin who read the football results on *Grandstand* from the first edition in 1958 to his death in 1995. It may not seem such a big deal today to read the soccer scores, but everyone alive in Britain at that time knew the unique voice and delivery of Len Martin. I was there in the halcyon days of BBC Sport before sport broadcasting contracts were lost to pay-to-view channels and the department became the comparative rump that it is today. I regard my time there as an absolute privilege.

I also worked alongside some of Britain's most famous, and again legendary, newsreaders when I was asked to present the sport on *BBC News* every Saturday night in a slot that had one of the highest national audiences of the week as it followed the also legendary BBC Saturday night entertainment line-up now long gone. Two of the news presenters were Moira Stewart, one of the nicest people I worked with in television, and the lovely Jill Dando who would later be murdered on her doorstep by a still-unknown assassin. My most poignant memory of those *BBC News* days came on April 15th, 1989. *Match of the Day* was covering the FA Cup semi-final at Hillsborough, Sheffield, between Liverpool and Nottingham Forest. The game was not aired live, but I could watch it live as the coverage came into Television Centre in London to be recorded. I watched as something unpleasant was clearly unfolding early in the game and I shouted across to the news desk to switch to the football – 'Something bad is happening here'. It was bad – *real bad*. I was watching the Hillsborough Disaster in which 96 Liverpool supporters died, children and adults, in the crush that followed the South Yorkshire Police decision to allow far too many people to enter an already tightly-packed area behind one of the goals. A disgusting police cover-up began and it took tenacious families decades to eventually secure a verdict that the police and not the fans were responsible for the tragedy. But don't worry. Conspiracies never happen, right? That's just a theory.

My television career included presenting a Friday evening slot on *Nationwide*, a major show of the day, and I was in the original presenting team, led by Frank Bough and Selina Scott, on *Breakfast Time*, the UK's first breakfast TV show launched amid huge publicity and fanfare in 1983 (Fig 27). Princess Diana came on a 'royal' visit in the early weeks

Figure 27: A presenter on Britain's first breakfast show – BBC Breakfast Time with Selina Scott in the front centre and Frank Bough to her right.

some two years after she married Prince Charles and I was introduced to her. I was taken aback by how tall she was and by the look of sheer fear in her eyes which I didn't understand until events later played out. Fifteen years later I would be exposing the background to her assassination in a Paris road tunnel in *The Biggest Secret*. I particularly liked Selina Scott in my *Breakfast Time* years. She was a genuine woman untouched by all the fame hysteria that surrounded her at the time and which clearly irked Frank Bough who saw himself as the show's 'star'. Selina interviewed me much later when she worked for *Sky News* and I was in the middle of mass ridicule. She was just as warm and friendly as

Figure 28: The Saturday Superstore team with John Craven, Mike Read, Keith Chegwin and Sarah Greene.

I remembered her and she treated me with rare respect in the mainstream media. I was also a presenter on a young people's programme, *Saturday Superstore*, which began in 1982 presented by disc jockey Mike Read and Sarah Greene, alongside one of the stars of children's TV at the time, Keith Chegwin (Fig 28). Keith was a great bloke. I met him a lot of years later in a motorway service area car park and although I was portrayed as the national 'nutter' by then he, like Selina Scott, was warm, friendly and respectful. I'll always remember Keith for that and his endless laughter. *Saturday Superstore* allowed me to meet all the famous people and popstars of the day as I did on *Breakfast Time*. Talking of which, I met the *Monkees* singer Davy Jones on a train to London once. He came into my compartment as I headed for the BBC and he went to his West End show. Davy has got to be one of the nicest people I ever chatted with and like Selina and Keith there was not a hint of showbiz me, me, me. My focus was always on the next ambition and I never really savoured and enjoyed what I had achieved. The next goal was always in my mind. Okay, done that – now what? These were the 'running shoes' I came out of the womb already wearing. Writing this brief biography section – and my god, there's so much more – has made me look at my life anew. I was everywhere on TV in those years and experienced so much even before the top of my head blew off in 1990/91.

Made it!

And so back to *Grandstand*. This had been the incessant ambition since the end of my football career and it was secured in the mid-1980s when I was asked to present a run of the Sunday version. All those years – well, only about twelve in fact – and all that effort and here I was driving into London from my then home in Oakley, Buckinghamshire, to do my first

show. There were tears in my eyes at the thought of picking myself off the ground with my football dreams in tatters, my body racked in pain, and immediately setting another target in that Birmingham TV studio.

Figure 29: At last came the magic day when I presented *Grandstand* for the first time.

Now here I was about to achieve it (Fig 29). The *Grandstands* went very well, but something strange began to happen. With my ambition secured, I lost interest in television. The fire in my belly that drove me forward towards *Grandstand* dramatically waned and while I still did my best my heart was no longer in it. Television is a very vacuous world of backstabbing, inward-looking myopia, and the BBC Sports Department was run by many people who would be a therapist's life's work. I was never a mixer away from the studio setting and that became ever more pronounced as my heart retreated from the TV world. I would prepare my scripts at home on the Isle of Wight where I moved in 1982, travel to London as late as I could to do a show, and have a taxi with the engine running outside Television Centre timed for the closing titles. I was on the train home at London's Waterloo railway station before the rest of the crew were in the BBC bar. Mike Murphy, the *Grandstand* editor who gave me those shows and promised many more, left the BBC and he was replaced by one of those people for whom a therapist would need no other clients. *Grandstand* and me were parting company and in the greater scheme of my life it was, with hindsight, exactly what needed to happen.

I was increasingly marginalised by the London end of BBC Sport, but I had a final and glorious Indian summer with the far more humane Manchester operation headed by a proper decent bloke, Nick Hunter. He has never been given the credit he deserves for taking a marginal game in snooker and making it a global television phenomenon in the 1980s. Nick hired me as a snooker presenter as my London career was waning and put me before TV audiences that the London people could only dream about. Snooker simply exploded as a focus of national interest and the players were amazing one-off characters including Cliff Thorburn, Bill Werbeniuk, Kirk Stevens, the brilliant Jimmy White, Ray Reardon, John Virgo, Terry Griffiths, John Spencer, Dennis Taylor and the mercurial genius turned always-destined tragedy, Alex 'Hurricane' Higgins. Alex could be the nicest man and the worst in the same few minutes. Snooker reached its peak audience with the 1985 World Championship final presented by my colleague David Vine between the world's top player Steve Davis and Irish underdog Dennis Taylor which went to the last ball of the best-of-35 frame match before Taylor won. The audience reached 18.5 million – close to a third of the UK population at the time – and remains to this day both the record viewing figure for the BBC-2 channel and the biggest past-midnight audience in British television history. With today's multi-channel dilution of audiences it will never be beaten. That was snooker in those days. It was a wonderful time and again a privilege to be part of that (Fig 30 overleaf). I did my last snooker world championship with Nick in the spring of 1990 at the Crucible Theatre in Sheffield. My BBC and entire television career was only two months from reaching its conclusion.

The 'politician'

As my interest in television faded from the mid-1980s my mind turned

to other things
and primarily
what human
economic
activity was
doing to what
I then
perceived as
the natural
world (much
more later). I
don't mean
the global
warming
hoax (see
Covid hoax

Figure 30: Snooker – my television highlight and Indian summer.

sprung by the same people) which was starting to emerge. This was far
from the dominating factor in the so-called 'green movement' as it has
become today. 'Greens' then cared about all aspects of environmental
assault and that would have included the extraordinary impact of mass
mask-wearing which greens in general have encouraged, even
demanded, no matter what the environmental consequence. My
concerns involved the way beautiful landscapes were being destroyed
by inappropriate building and how the environment was being deluged
by pollution at all levels, air, food, water, the lot. My interest began on
the Isle of Wight when I saw landscapes and unique urban and village
areas destroyed by buildings that a child could have designed and in no
way sympathetic to what was already there. It wasn't a case of stop all
development; it was rather what kind of development and where? I
came to realise that these decisions were being made by a network of
Freemasons and Satanists on the island collectively referred to as the
Island Mafia which controlled the local councils – a single council today
– and in particular the planning department that had the major say in
what was built or not. In other words who could make fantastic profits
from developments that the council sanctioned. When you can vastly
increase the value of land by giving planning permission for
development, corruption will always be rife. The Isle of Wight was – *is* –
awash with it. The island is still widely beautiful despite the best efforts
of the Mafia, but it has a very dark and satanic underbelly which
understandably has contempt for me. I take that as an honour and a
compliment. I helped to create Island Watch, an organisation pledged to
campaign against inappropriate development and the corruption
involved. It was now that I began to appreciate the influence of
Freemasons and other secret societies as I realised that decisions the

council apparently made in public in the evening were actually being decided at the Freemasons' lodge in the afternoon. 'Public debate' was therefore a farce.

I pondered about going into politics to challenge this and the increasing centralisation of power fast emerging known as 'globalisation'. I looked first at the Liberal Party (now the Liberal Democrats) in the mid-1980s which returned the island Member of Parliament and I was in for a crash course in political hypocrisy, mendacity and deceit. God, it was horrible and the people appalling. This is how bad. Soon after I joined the Liberal – note *Liberal* – Party I made a cash contribution to a local council-run school for the disabled after being shown little kids so brain-damaged that all they could do was lie on a plastic flat-top vehicle with wheels and do their best to use their feet to make it move. Looking at their faces wouldn't fail to break your heart. Well, if you had one, I mean. Staggeringly the head of the school told me they were short of these vehicles due to lack of funds. I was dumbstruck at the callous injustice and I handed over the money they needed for some more. My donation was never publicised and nor was it meant to be, but it got back to leading members of the local Liberal Party which ran the council at the time. This led to the most prominent of them, a guy called Morris Barton, telling me that I should not have made the donation. He said that it left them open to being condemned by the political opposition for not funding the school adequately enough to the point where a member of the party had to give money himself. I was very new to politics and I was dumbstruck and gutted to the core at what I was hearing. The Liberal Party and me parted company with swift effect. Morris Barton was the most classic politician and if he had ever told the truth his body would have genetically-imploded from the shock. He was not an exception, however, just an example of the worldwide breed.

I then turned my attention to the Green Party that had recently changed its name from the Ecology Party. It was intellectually headed by what I found to be an incredibly arrogant man, Jonathan Porritt. It's policy material, however, included so much that I could support. The party was campaigning for environmental sanity and also justice and fairness for all. It was *then*, anyway. Don't start me on the 'Woke' green movement of today which believes freedom of speech and opinion is not a right but a crime. I wrote to the head office to ask if they had a contact on the Isle of Wight and they replied that there was no Green Party on the island, which I knew, and not even a contact. This would be 1988. The reply encouraged me to start an island branch and I organised a few public meetings and away we went. What happened next was utterly ridiculous and made me wonder for the first time about a force guiding my life. A couple of weeks after starting the Isle of Wight branch we had

Figure 31: Elected national speaker for the Green Party.

a letter from the regional party inviting us to send a delegate to its quarterly meeting of all the local parties in the south of central England at Winchester in Hampshire. I went along and after hours of meaningless navel contemplating the chair lady said that the regional party's representative on national party council was stepping down that day and they needed nominations for a replacement. No one volunteered and so I did on the basis of someone's got to do it. I had been a member of the Green Party for a matter of weeks and now I was on the national party council. *What?* There was a meeting of the council in a couple of weeks and I arrived at a building near Regents Park in London where there was more navel contemplating at a higher level. Just before the lunch break the man chairing said they needed to elect 'speakers' to represent the party in the media for the coming year and he would take nominations when the meeting resumed. During lunch a man came over and said 'You're on the television aren't you?' Yes, I replied. 'So you would be confident in the media then?' he continued. Yes, I guess so. 'If you put your name forward as a speaker I will second you' came the punchline. Okay, why not? I'm up for anything. A short time later I was elected a national speaker for the Green Party – again just a matter of weeks after I joined (Fig 31). It was crazy.

Bye, bye, Maggie

I didn't think that being officially a national politician would mean much given the tiny Green Party support and the almost total lack of interest by the media. Events would prove otherwise and move fast. Pollution and other environmental concerns began to appear in the mainstream and public attention turned to the subject ahead of the European elections in the summer of 1989. What followed were two million votes for the Green Party in Britain and we were suddenly a player, albeit briefly, on the political stage until the party tore itself apart in a war between the 'Fundies' and the 'Realos'. These were groups represented by those that wanted to keep the core policies and principles and those that wanted to change them to win more votes and be more acceptable to the mainstream. I was caught in the middle as what I called a Fundie-Realo. I wanted to retain the core principles while presenting them in a clearer and more accessible and professional way. In the wake of the European election success I was in the national media talking about politics and this didn't go down well with the BBC Sport people and the BBC hierarchy in general. Apparently there was a conflict between presenting sport and saying the economic system was destroying the environment. I could understand if I was reporting news, but I hadn't done that since I joined *Newsnight* in 1980. The crunch came when I refused to pay the Poll Tax or 'Community Charge' introduced by Prime Minister Margaret Thatcher in 1989 and another remarkable series of synchronistic events followed. The tax in effect had people on small and large incomes paying the same which was obviously unfair and large numbers of people refused to pay in protest. The first court cases for non-payers could have been held anywhere in Britain and yet it happened in the small town of Newport on ... the *Isle of Wight* ... where my case was to be heard. The hearings attracted national and wider-world attention. I arrived on the bus from Ryde with Linda to find an extraordinary number of photographers surrounding me and moving in unison like a single entity. It was akin to the scene in the movie *Notting Hill* when a guy opens the door to find a mass of cameras pointing at him. It's happened a few times to me in different situations and it's quite a sight to experience.

There were so many appearing in court that day that they were processing six to eight at a time instead of one. It came to my turn and in the line with me was a young chap I had seen at a number of protest meetings. He was very forensic in studying the rules and regulations. As the magistrates were going through what they believed was another group to rubber stamp he put his hand up and asked to speak. He asked the magistrates when the prosecution summonses to court were sent out to people and how that compared with the time between non-payment and a summons being issued as dictated by the law. The magistrates consulted with the court clerk. The atmosphere around them and their demeanour visibly changed. They announced an adjournment. When they returned they said that all the summonses to court that day had been sent out too early and therefore all the prosecutions delivered were invalid. Everyone was free to go. I put up my hand and pointed out that those summoned to court that day had lost a day's pay plus their travel costs and these needed to be reimbursed. The magistrates agreed and I would eventually receive my £2.50 bus fare. Margaret Thatcher's Poll Tax never recovered from that humiliation at the first legal hurdle and nor did she. The tax would be replaced and so would Thatcher the following year when her own party conspired to remove her. The 'Iron Lady' was not so 'iron' after all when people stood up to her.

The next day I had a meeting scheduled at Television Centre in London with the Head of Sport Jonathan Martin. He was a system-man claiming to have socialist tendencies and I never really trusted him as I did Cliff Morgan. In fact by then Cliff was the only one that I did trust at the BBC in London. I walked into Martin's office and the morning papers were all over his table with my picture on the front of most of them after the Poll Tax debacle in Newport the day before. 'What I have to say is nothing to do with those', he said confirming that it was, at least in part. He said the BBC was not renewing my contract which had only a few weeks to run. He and they didn't even have the decency to give me longer warning so I could have time to make arrangements for another income. I'd already lost the weekend job on *BBC News* in a bizarre conversation with the then Head of News Tony Hall, later BBC Director General as the by-then Baron Hall of Birkenhead. The fancy titles are so pathetic. Hall rang to tell me that I could no longer work on the Saturday news programme given my political activities. The problem was he couldn't quite blurt out the words. He went round and round the houses. I saved him from his stuttering by saying I thought it would be best if I stood down. 'Oh, do you, really?' he said, the relief in his voice almost hilariously obvious. So that was it, the end of my television career. Was I gutted? Nope. I had concerns about how to earn a living, but it wasn't only Baron Hall that was relieved. Relief surged through my body. I was free of the nonsense I had come to loathe – Nick Hunter and the Manchester team apart – and by then another life was revealing itself in the most extraordinary way.

Guiding hand

I had believed that my progress in pursuit of multiple ambitions was down to good luck, hard work, and focus. I was now to realise that my entire life had been heading in a particular direction in many and various ways and expressions. There was never a time in my life when the 'journey' started. There was only the moment when it became conscious. My whole life was the 'journey'. When I became a national spokesman for the British Green Party in a matter of weeks I began to reconsider and look back at the pattern. I would set a goal and then achieve it with 'lucky' breaks happening at precisely the right time and once the ambition was achieved something would happen to move me on with a period of around two years often the ball-park time involved. My 'luck' included, but was far from limited to:

- The big toe-cap boots that let me kick the ball much harder than the other kid and get into my first school team.

- The goalkeeper getting injured at the Leicester schoolboys trial after I had been rejected as an outfield player.

- The game of my life in the second trial that put me in the team against all the odds and on the road to being a professional footballer.

- The perfectly-timed interventions of John Camkin with exactly the right contacts in football and media to get me to Hereford United through his friend John Charles and then into journalism through his friend Bill Hicks.

- How John Camkin was based in Leamington Spa where I'd moved shortly before because it was the home town of Linda who I had only just met.

- Finding down the road the world-renowned acupuncturist Professor J. R. Worsley, who kept my career going for two years at Hereford when I should never have been playing.

- Being invited on the *ATV Today* show two days after my career ended which immediately triggered my TV ambitions that drove me through the disappointment and on to the next target.

- How I was recommended by John Camkin's friend, Bill Hicks, to all those newspapers across the south and Midlands of England and one of only two that responded was back in my home city (with all that came from that in Leicester).

- The *Grandstand* break out of nowhere from the programme that had been my target from that day at ATV and the John Tidy incident when seconds saved me from *Grandstand* disaster that would have ended that ambition immediately.

- The never-expected Northern Ireland success at the 1982 World Cup that earned me a contract with BBC Sport and how I joined just in time for the staff exodus to the 1982 Commonwealth Games in Australia which immediately gave me the opportunity back home to quickly become a national face.

- The snooker opportunity at the right time to relaunch my career as it faded in London.

- The ridiculous speed that I went from joining the Green Party to becoming a national spokesman less than a year before the one big election success which gave me national exposure as a politician, albeit briefly.

- Newport, Isle of Wight, of all the towns and cities in the UK, was the first to hold Poll Tax court cases and a man in my line of defendants stopped the prosecutions and made the Poll Tax and Margaret Thatcher a laughing stock.

On and on the list continues with synchronicities, 'coincidences' and 'luck' at the right moment. By the time of the Green Party and Poll Tax court cases I didn't believe that it was 'luck' anymore. Yes, I was focussed and worked hard, but sorry, that no longer told the whole story. Something strange was happening. The question was – *what?*
I was about to find out.

CHAPTER THREE

A Kind of Magic

Permanence, perseverance and persistence in spite of all obstacles, discouragements, and impossibilities: It is this that in all things distinguishes the strong soul from the weak
Thomas Carlyle

The 'something strange' theme gathered pace as 1988 became 1989. I began to feel a presence around me. When I was in a room alone it was like I was not alone. I kept this to myself as I continued to work for the BBC and the Green Party. Months passed and the presence became ever more tangible and obvious to me.

I had never experienced anything like this before and now it was becoming a part of my life and increasingly undeniable. In March, 1990, while working for the BBC in London, I went back to my room at the Kensington Hilton Hotel in Holland Park a less than 20 minute walk from the BBC Television Centre. As I sat on the bed the presence was so strong I said out into the room: 'If there's something there would you please contact me because you are driving me up the wall.' A few days later I was with a then nine-year-old Gareth heading for lunch at a café at the Ryde seafront railway station near our home, but it was packed. As we walked away a railway worker stopped me to talk about football and when the conversation ended I couldn't see Gaz. I knew he would be in the tourist and newspaper shop on the station looking at books they sold about Isle of Wight stream trains. He always did at every opportunity. Gareth and Jaymie both inherited my love for steam trains even though they were long gone on public railways by the time they were born.

I stood at the door to the shop (which is still there with the door in a slightly different place) and there he was with a stream train book in his hand. I said: 'Come on, Gaz, we'll go and get some lunch in the town.' As I was about to turn and leave I felt the atmosphere change around me which I now know was an electromagnetic field. It was the same feeling I had with the presence although way more powerful. My feet felt like two magnets were pulling them to the floor and then I heard words pass through my mind: 'Go and look at the books on the far side.' It was not so much a voice as a very strong thought-form that was absolutely not consciously generated by me. Obviously bewildered, and with Gaz still with his nose in his book, I walked across to the other side of the shop where I knew they kept a few paperback books dominated by romantic novels for tourists to read while sitting on the beach. My bewilderment included both what was happening and the fact that I could not understand how the type of books they sold there would be of any relevance to me. In among the romantic novels by writer Barbara Cartland and a publisher called Mills and Boon I saw a book

Figure 32: The Betty Shine book in among the romantic novels.

with a woman's face on the front called *Mind to Mind* (Fig 32). I picked it up because it was so different to the others and turned it over to read the blurb. That's when I saw the word 'psychic'. The book was a sort of autobiography written by professional British psychic, Betty Shine. I wondered immediately if she would pick up the presence around me. I read the book in 24 hours and contacted her to arrange a visit. I told her nothing about what had been happening to me with the presence for the past year. Instead I said that I had arthritis and maybe the Reiki energy healing she did through her hands might be helpful. That would have been a bonus. My real interest was would she sense anything around me?

My new life begins

I went to see Betty a couple of times at her home in the village of Ditchling near Brighton on the English south coast. She performed her healing while we had an interesting chat about levels of reality that we cannot see. I had always been fascinated by this. Even more so after my strange experience with the slow-motion save in the Hereford game at Barnet and what I learned about the energetic basis of acupuncture thanks to Professor Worsley. Then, on my third of four visits, my life changed forever. I was on a medical-type bench in her front room while

she worked on my left knee when I felt like a spider's web on my face.
My mind immediately went to her book where she said that when other
levels of reality are trying to lock into you it sometimes feels like a
spider's web on your face. It did. What I didn't know at the time is that
I was feeling an electromagnetic field through which other realities
communicate with this one. It's the same phenomenon as the hairs on
your neck or arm standing up in a place that feels spooky (the 'spook' or
ghost entity affects the electromagnetic field) and when you are among
an excited crowd generating electromagnetism with their emotions. No
more than 15 seconds after I felt the spider's web, and without me
saying a word, Betty threw her head back and said: 'Wow! This is
powerful. I'll have to close my eyes for this one.' She said she was seeing
an ancient Chinese-type figure in her mind who gave a name and said
'Socrates is with me.' I had no idea who Socrates was except that
someone of that name once played football for Brazil. 'The' Socrates was
an ancient Greek philosopher who was condemned to death for
'corrupting the youth' by telling them the truth that the authorities
didn't want them to know. Psychics would later tell me that in 'previous
lives' I had been Socrates and Italian philosopher Giordano Bruno.
Socrates died basically laughing at authority by drinking hemlock in 399
BC and Bruno did the same as he was burned at the stake for 'heresy'
(telling the truth) by the Roman Church in 1600. I am *not* saying that I
was these people, only that this is what I was told and nothing more.
Betty Shine said that the Chinese-type communicator was asking her to
pass information to me and as I sat there, still a BBC presenter and
Green Party spokesman, she communicated the following:

- We know he wanted us to contact him, but the time was not right (Betty
  knew nothing of my words in the hotel room).

- He was led here to be contacted, not to be cured. But one day he will be
  completely cured.

- He is a healer who is here to heal the Earth and he will be world famous.
  He will face enormous opposition but we will always be there to protect
  him.

- He is still a child, spiritually, but he will be given the spiritual riches.

- Sometimes he will say things and wonder where they came from. They
  will be our words.

- Knowledge will be put into his mind and at other times he will be led to
  knowledge.

- He was chosen as a youngster for his courage. He has been tested and has passed all the tests.

- He was led into football to learn discipline, but when that was learned it was time to move on. He also had to learn how to cope with disappointment, experience all the emotions, and how to get up and get on with it. The spiritual way is tough and no one makes it easy.

- He will always have what he needs, but no more.

I was stunned, of course, in one way, and the 'normal' reaction would have been to dismiss what I was told as ridiculous. I'm a healer and I was here to heal the Earth? I present the snooker! I was going to be world famous? For what? But in fact I didn't dismiss it. There was something vaguely familiar about the whole thing. I got on the train in a daze at the nearby Hassocks station and headed to London to present a programme at the BBC. I watched the world go by from the carriage window as I tried to make sense of what had just happened. This line in particular made so much sense of my earlier life:

> He was led into football to learn discipline, but when that was learned it was time to move on. He also had to learn how to cope with disappointment, experience all the emotions, and how to get up and get on with it.

My life had indeed been like walking through a maze with some force opening and closing doors – do this, experience that, okay, move on. Now do this next, experience that, okay, move on. These were the 'running shoes' at work. I had most certainly learned how to cope with disappointment, experienced all the emotions, and how to get up and get on with it. Before long my new life would require every last smear of my emotional strength to get up and get on with it and 'the spiritual way is tough and no one makes it easy' would be confirmed with a vengeance over and over. I would see that my life up to this point had been preparation for what I really came to do and why I had felt from an early age that I had some sort of 'destiny'. No, it would now turn out, it was not to be a footballer. As my life moved on I saw that my years in journalism and television had shown me how the media and 'the system' worked and how television had given me a famous public face so that when I came out with my 'revelations' they would not be ignored. When eventually I did speak out at the start of 1991 it was met with fantastic publicity and historic levels of ridicule. No matter. It wasn't ignored and at that stage this was the main thing. My god, I thought, as I arrived at Waterloo station that Betty Shine day: Who am I?

What am I? Why me? Where was this all going? A week later I returned to Betty and these messages came through:

- One man cannot change the world, but one man can communicate the message that will change the world.

- Don't try to do it all alone. Go hand in hand with others, so you can pick each other up as you fall.

- He will write five books in three years. The written word will be there forever. The spoken word disappears on the wind.

- Politics is not for him. He is too spiritual. Politics is anti-spiritual and will make him very unhappy.

- He will leave politics. He doesn't have to do anything. It will happen gradually over a year.

- There will be a different kind of flying machine, very different from the aircraft of today (there was also a line about the coming of electric cars).

- Time will have no meaning. Where you want to be, you will be.

All these messages relating to me in early 1990 have happened or are in the process of happening. I did, for example, write five books in three years although I didn't realise that until after the fifth one was published and I counted back the months. Any author will tell you that writing one book a year is a challenge never mind five in three. To think with now 23 books to my name – some of them mega works – that I once said to Linda that I'd never write a book because I didn't have enough to say. Even this message has to a large extent come true: 'One day he will be completely cured.' My arthritis continued to progress after I left football and it was in both knees, ankles and wrists, my toes, neck, hips, lower back, and later my hands. The spiritual way is tough and no one makes it easy! Ha, ha. Walking was at times extremely painful in my journalism days in Leicester and I was often in back pain. I had no idea what life without pain was like. If I wanted to open a train carriage door which had a twist action on the handle in those days I would have to wait for someone else to come along. If I tried, the pain was excruciating. This was all happening while I was in television. Hence my pain threshold today is extremely high. I am used to it.

The low point came in around 2007 when I went on a trip to India. The arthritis was so bad that I walked through Heathrow Airport in my socks so I could shuffle my feet along the ground. I couldn't even lift my legs to walk properly. Fortunately it was Terminal 5 that had a slippery floor without carpet. I sat at the departure gate until everyone else was on the plane so I didn't have to stand in the queue. I wondered how I was going to survive the more than eight-hour flight cooped up in cattle class. I handed my boarding pass to the steward and when he passed it through the machine there was a beep. What's up now? I thought. 'Oh, you've been upgraded to business class, sir' he said. I actually started to quietly cry as I headed for the plane so relieved was I and comforted in the knowledge that someone 'out there' was looking after me. Such little 'signs' and bits of 'luck' have been a constant in my life. I spent the whole flight to India horizontal in business class and most of it asleep exhausted by the pain. When I got to my hotel near Tiruvannamalai below Arunachala Mountain, which is sacred to Hindus, I slept for virtually 48 hours with the curtains closed and there were times when I didn't know if it was day or night. My joints improved after that although when I visited the temples the attendees were all in the lotus position (forget it) while I sat in my foldable garden chair that I had brought with me in the knowledge that sitting on the floor would be out of the question. People looked at me very strange while I laughed at the ridiculousness of it all which always appeals to me. The India trip was the lowest point of my arthritis pain and it faded from hereon. When it should be getting worse and putting me in that wheelchair it has faded. Today it doesn't trouble me at all and I have not been in pain with it for years.

Starting over

My life was about to change dramatically in the wake of those visits to Betty Shine. Within weeks the BBC failed to renew my contract and I was out of work with no income. I was set free to follow where events were taking me. I began to withdraw from working with the Green Party. I wanted to distance myself in the knowledge that the time would come when I would speak about what was happening and it would generate much scepticism and ridicule. Just how much I would find out in early 1991. I wanted to protect the party from that as much as I could. In line with the Betty Shine communications it took the best part of a year to withdraw from politics completely. I did confide to a couple of Green Party insiders a little about what I was experiencing and soon the rumours were circulating in the party that national speaker David Icke was going a little crazy. If you want to experience a closed mind that thinks it's open find yourself a Green and even more so today as the Green mind has coagulated into the all-encompassing concreted-encased insanity known as 'Woke'. My time in the Green Party had given me both an insight into the Green mind – now far more extreme – and also into politics at close range that would be very useful later on. Politics is going to change nothing I concluded and no matter what the party name, colour of rosette, or claim to be 'different', the political mind blueprint is common to them all. Caroline Lucas, who became Britain's first Green Party Member of Parliament, worked in the national office when I was involved. Almost every time she opens her mouth she supports the agenda of a global multi-billionaire elite while thinking she's 'anti-Establishment'. The global Green movement and the Green Parties that represent its political wing have degenerated into little more than a fascistic tyranny and a free speech-deleting mob promoting the coordinated sinister agenda of billionaires and corporations that I have now been exposing for more than three decades.

I had one or two minor offers for TV work when I left the BBC, but I wasn't interested. I had made the decision that I was going with this, whatever 'this' actually was. By now I could see that life is forever and that we are eternal expressions of consciousness having a brief experience called human. The worst thing I could do was to completely mess up one human life and I could handle that. Bring it on and let's see where this goes. My family was not having my strange experiences as the upheavals began in my life and their own. Why should they understand what was happening to Dave and dad? I didn't understand never mind them. To their eternal credit they continued to stand by me even through the tidal wave of ridicule that was soon to be unleashed (Fig 33). Fortunately I had always lived below my income in terms of spending and there was a bit of money to get us through a year or so without paid work. The idea of getting up to your neck in debt (thus dependency) to live some expensive lifestyle in a big house never appealed to me. I guess

Figure 33: The family in my television days – little did we know what was coming. There's a young Kerry, baby Gareth, with my brother Paul, now another campaigner for freedom, in the middle at the back.

being brought up in my early years – and many after – with a pay packet lasting only to the end of the week or month left its mark that way. There was also the message that said 'He will always have what he needs' and I always have.

The communications through Betty Shine were as good as their word as my life became an extraordinary series of 'coincidences' and happenings. I was indeed led to knowledge and knowledge was put into my mind. This happened through the synchronistic 'coincidence' of people I met and through books, documents, and personal experiences, first at home and later abroad. I never read a book from start to finish until I was in my 20s and not many after that. Now I read ferociously. One book finished and I was on to the next for year after year. I didn't bother with education at school and suddenly I was seeking knowledge from every source possible on my own terms in my own way. In the early years of the 1990s I would be led to information and make conclusions from that about what was going on. Pretty soon that flipped and I would conclude what was happening first and then the names, dates, places, detail would follow supporting that conclusion. This is how I have worked ever since: 'Knowledge will be put into his mind and at other times he will be led to knowledge.' Then there was this line: 'Sometimes he will say things and wonder where they came from. They will be our words.' My goodness, the times that has happened – as in constantly.

I would go on to present a stream of public talks every year with many lasting up to 11 hours such was the information I had compiled and been led to by then. Again and again I would say things in those talks and also interviews and think 'Blimey, that's interesting, where did that come from?' This continues to this day and led to my out-of-nowhere conclusion soon after the turn of the millennium that we live in a simulated reality limited by the speed of light which has since been supported by gathering evidence even in the scientific mainstream. If you wanted to meet a psychic or medium in the post-Betty Shine months of 1990 then all you needed was to follow me. Betty was the only one I consciously decided to visit and synchronicity brought the rest. Hello, what do you do? I'm a psychic. My god, not another one! A communication that later proved very accurate said:

The diamonds can be found even in the mud – the waters wash them clean … Seek diamonds, sparkling truth, the clarity, perfection of the Word. The whirlpools of life carry you to where the diamonds are. Resonate to the perfection of the crystals. Arduous seeking is not necessary. The path is already mapped out. You only have to follow the clues …

… We are guiding you along a set path. You are learning according to our teaching of you. It was all organised before you incarnated.

A few months later I was in Canada one night on the banks of the Oldman River about 134 miles from Calgary in Alberta. The light of the torch picked out a mass of bright diamond-shaped white stones lying in the mud and washed clean by the receding river. I could clearly see by now that my whole life had been mapped out from the moment I was born to do what I am doing. How true it has proved to be that all I had to do was 'follow the clues'. That's exactly what has happened as they have been put before me. The challenge has been to go with those clues and communicate what they say in the knowledge of what that would mean in terms of public reaction. This, you may have noticed, has never been a problem for me.

Through the rest of 1990 I was compiling my first book on these subjects and what had happened to my life. I called it *Truth Vibrations*. The title was inspired by an amalgamation of information through the psychics about an energetic frequency that was going to be infused into our reality to awaken humanity from its slumber induced by forces that I would subsequently expose. I was told that this frequency or vibrational change would have two main effects. It would open closed minds to a greater reality of self and the 'world' with the most open affected first and eventually even those at the time with padlocks on their minds would be teased awake. The other effect – hence the book title – was that the vibrational change would bring to the surface all that had been hidden from us. When I was told all this in 1990 there was no evidence that any of it was true. If you observed global society there was no evidence that people were waking up from their induced perceptual coma or that the hidden was being revealed. This continued to be the case for many years, a fact I can seriously confirm from my own direct experience of dismissal and ridicule. Then came the millennium with 9/11 and the Western wars of conquest and destruction in the Middle East. I began to observe how minds were beginning to stir and view the world differently. This has continued to expand until a tsunami of awakeness has been triggered by the 'Covid' era. In terms of all that has been hidden would be shown to us – are you kidding? Look at what those with opening minds know about the world and the forces behind events that they didn't know in 1990, 1995, 2000, 2005, 2010, 2015 and so on. It is fantastic what has come to light as my previous books and this book clearly show.

Message to mind: You are about to be blown

Truth Vibrations went into production at the end of 1990 for publication the following May when what was left of my old life would be torched. From before Christmas as the book was finished I began to have the urge to go to Peru. I had no idea why. I knew nothing about Peru. In the same period I would turn on the television and there would be a documentary about Peru or I would pass the local travel agent to see holidays to Peru featured in the window. Purely on intuition – my constant guide now – I booked a flight I could not really afford to Lima, Peru. Intuition comes to

Figure 34: The heart vortex in the 'chakra' system that interpenetrates the human energetic field is our prime connection to expanded awareness beyond the simulation.

us through the heart vortex in the centre of the chest which is one of many vortexes known as chakras or 'wheels of light' that interpenetrate the human energy field (more later). We feel intuition in the chest for this reason (Fig 34). Another chakra vortex relating to emotion connects with the belly area and that's why we feel emotion there and people 'get the shits' when they are emotionally nervous and fearful. Watch the body language of someone saying they intuitively *know* – 'I just *know*' – and their hands will invariably go to their chest. When people say they are thinking their hand goes to their head. These are indications of where the source of the perception, knowing or thinking, is coming from. Thinking is very much the act of perceiving within the strict limitations of human simulation awareness while intuitive knowing comes from expressions of reality way beyond the human realm and its phenomenal levels of illusion. Thought perception results from a sequence of thinking leading to a conclusion while intuition comes as one complete

Figure 35: Thinking and knowing come from very different sources.

package with no run-up sequence. The heart *knows* because it is connected to that level of awareness that *does* know. The head/mind *thinks* because it *doesn't* know and has to try to work it out with that sequence of thought (Fig 35). My conclusions come to me first through the heart and then the detailed evidence to support them comes to the mind in the form of dates, places, people, and such like. Heart awareness and brain awareness are connected, or they are meant to be. They are not, however, the same. Much more on this as we go along.

My planned two weeks in Peru became three amid an incredible series of synchronicities and experiences. I landed in Lima early in the morning not knowing what I would do next. Events moved fast the moment I entered the luggage hall and within an hour of arriving I was on another plane to Cusco in the Andes mountains with a hotel secured and waiting. I tell that story in other books. I sat on the bed at the hotel thinking, okay, what now? Another hour of 'coincidences' passed and I was connected with a Peruvian guide and a two-week itinerary. I went to all the major tourist sites including the extraordinary and breathtaking Machu Picchu and the guide took me to the city of Puno on the shores of Lake Titicaca which, at some 13,000 feet above sea level, is billed as the highest navigable lake in the world. He booked us into a hotel called the Sillustani named after an Inca site a 40 minute drive away. There were pictures of Sillustani all over the hotel and as I looked at one of them I had the overwhelming feeling – heart again – that I had to go there. I went the next day in a minibus/taxi with the guide and a driver and spent an hour walking around the ruins. It was beautiful looking out from the highpoint across the land to a lake and distant mountains, but I went back to the bus feeling quite disappointed. What I had experienced did not match the powerful urge I'd had to go there the night before. That was to change rather dramatically.

A few minutes down the road on the way back to Puno, as I daydreamed out of the window, I saw a hill to my right. Words began repeating in my mind – 'Come to me, come to me, come to me'. Could my life get any stranger? Nine months earlier I was presenting the snooker for the BBC and I was a national representative for the Green Party. Now I was in Peru purely on intuition and a bloody hill was talking to me. I asked the driver to stop and climbed the hill to find a stone circle. I have never mentioned this before because I have been trying to establish how it could be possible and now I have. I found the stone circle at the top of the hill – a stone circle that wasn't 'physically' there. Yeah, yeah, Icke's crazy. Well, with the hindsight of 32 years, maybe not. I experienced a stone circle at that time and I'll explain what followed in a moment. The circle had some stones with memorable shapes which made it easy to remember. I went back to Sillustani with a group of people in 2012 to mark my 60th birthday and returned to the hill to show them the circle. *It wasn't there.* The hill was, of course, just not the circle. Instead it was in the main area of the Sillustani site looking exactly how I experienced it on that hill a mile or so from where it was 'physically'. I recognised some of those stones that so registered with me at the time. The discrepancy was not faded memory. I was telling the story of the circle on the hill immediately after it happened and the story never changed. A whole stone circle had been *'moved'??* Ugh?? Not exactly, not 'physically' anyway. I'll explain later how this could be done when we consider the illusory nature of 'physical' reality. There is no 'physical' as we perceive it and you only have to study quantum physics to see that. Many people have told me, especially in the last year or so, that objects in their homes have disappeared. They remember exactly where they left them and sometimes they will reappear exactly where they left them. The stories are far too numerous to dismiss and anyway I have experienced the phenomena myself. I live in a tiny flat where things cannot go missing, but they have when I knew precisely where they were. If you think this is all too crazy and far out (it is from the perspective of 'normal') then strap in for the next bit.

I walked to the centre of the circle and experienced a repeat of what happened in the newspaper shop in Ryde. The soles of my feet began to burn and tingle with a sort of magnetism and I couldn't move them. I felt energy pulsating into the top of my head (where the 'crown chakra' vortex is located) and flowing through me into the ground. Another flow was coming the other way. My arms spontaneously stretched out at 45 degrees. I made no conscious decision to do that. It just happened. I

Figure 36: My return to Sillustani in 2012.

re-enacted the moment on my return to Sillustani in 2012 (Fig 36). I heard a thought-form 'voice' clearly in my mind which said: 'They will be talking about this a hundred years from now' and 'It will be over when you feel the rain.' I was standing under a fierce Peruvian sun

Figure 37: A symbolic representation of what happened to me at Sillustani.

looking into a brilliant blue sky with not a cloud to be seen. *What rain? Where?* The energy passing through me became ever more powerful until my whole body was shaking (Fig 37). Time disappeared as I entered a realm of consciousness where there is no time which is only an illusion of the simulation as I will explain. I was mostly 'out there' while all this was going on and in another realm of awareness. I returned to my conscious mind every now and then like when you drive your car and can't remember the last few miles. Your conscious mind has been elsewhere and your subconscious has been doing the driving. In one of these conscious periods I saw a light grey mist over the mountains way in the distance. The mist became progressively darker very quickly and I could see that it was now raining heavily far away. I watched the storm come towards me ridiculously quickly until dark clouds covered the sun and a wall of stair-rod rain came across the hill and struck me with such power that I was instantly drenched.

The front of the storm was a straight line you could have drawn with a ruler and hence my term 'wall of rain'. If you put that scene in a movie people would laugh at the very idea that this could ever happen, but it *did* happen. As the rain struck, the energy passing through me for most of an hour immediately stopped. My arms had been in the air all this time and I felt nothing. Now my shoulders were stiff and very painful and my legs so weak I struggled to stand. Energy was still pouring from my feet and hands and my feet were like that for the next 24 hours. I couldn't sleep that night because of it.

What just happened?

I had no idea what had happened or its soon-to-be-experienced implications and it was years before I fully understood the process. I had my perceptual bubble shattered and I was plugged in to a much higher and more expanded state of awareness. This transformation in terms of impact on my life would soon be played out in newspaper headlines and mass public ridicule. Information, concepts, perceptions, poured into my conscious and subconscious mind and my ability to process it all was overwhelmed through sheer volume. It was akin to delivering too many instructions to a computer too quickly. It freezes. It can't process it all. I symbolically froze in just the same way and it lasted about three months by which time I became one of the most ridiculed people in British history. As I 'unfroze' people would say they thought I was supposed to have 'gone mad' when to them I was the same person they always knew. Yes, 'David' had come back although not the same one in the sense that while I acted the same and had the same outward personality I was seeing the world through very different eyes. I was still okay when I headed for home from Peru and then soon after I arrived back in England the consequences of that experience on the hill began to manifest. I didn't know where I was. I'd stayed on another week in Peru and I had to change my flight. I was out of money thanks to a credit card that so few would accept in Peru at the time. I had to barter my radio to get a taxi to the airport. I was only on standby even then and if I didn't get on the flight I had no idea where I was going from there. A thought-form 'voice' kept saying don't worry you'll get on the flight and at one point that 'they' had found me a seat with plenty of leg room. You write it off as wishful thinking. With all the passengers checked-in and the flight soon to leave I was called across to the desk. I was on the flight and when I went on board my seat was next to the emergency door and with a serious amount of leg room. These things are often done to give you both confidence in what is being communicated and to say 'don't worry, we're looking after you and we always will'. 'They' have certainly looked after me. Israeli-American scientist Itzhak Bentov writes in his 1988 book, *Stalking the Wild Pendulum*, about experiences like mine:

It is ironic that persons in whom the evolutionary processes of Nature have begun to operate more rapidly, and who can be considered as advanced mutants of the human race, are institutionalised as subnormal by their 'normal' peers. I dare to guess, on the basis of discussions with my psychiatrist-friends, that this process is not as exotic and rare as one would like us to believe, and possibly 25 to 30 percent of all institutionalised schizophrenics belong to this category – a tremendous waste of human potential.

The reason for this is that they have been catapulted suddenly into a situation in which they are functioning in more than one reality. They can see and hear things occurring in our neighbouring realities, that is the astral or other higher realities, because their 'frequency responses' have been broadened ... The onslaught of information may be overwhelming, and they begin to mix and confuse two or three realities.

That is exactly what happened to me and I am still functioning in more than one reality – many more than one. The difference is that I have integrated them all into one unified interconnecting whole. In the aftermath of Peru I was all over the place switching between realities and trying desperately to make sense of it. For three months after my return from Sillustani if you asked me my name I would have had to check and I had no idea what was going on. It was like being in a permanent waking dream. I was invited in the middle of all that to

appear on a live prime time BBC chat show hosted by the then mega-famous Irishman, Terry Wogan. What followed became television folklore. The audience were laughing at me within minutes egged on in many ways by Wogan who would publicly apologise years later for the way he handled it (Fig 38). He would interview me again

Figure 38: On the now legendary Wogan Show.

in 2006 in a retrospective of his shows and the interchange went very differently with Wogan looking out of his depth with my information that was well received by the audience in a turning of the tables that I understandably found very cathartic. In a little over 15 minutes that first interview in 1991 burned every bridge to my previous life. There was no going back. There was nothing to go back to. I couldn't walk down any street in Britain without being pointed out and laughed at. I was the focus of years of unceasing ridicule in an onslaught that few will ever have experienced. It was historic in scale and nature.

Kerry and Gareth were followed to school by 'journalists' and mercilessly ridiculed when they got there every day over their mad father. If you wanted to see an endless flow of humanity at its very worst, in all the depths of its empathy-deleted ignorance and density, you should have been with the Ickes in those years between 1991 and at least a decade later. Even today after all that I said was coming is happening there are still legions of people so locked away in their programmed self-delusion that 'Icke's a nutter' is still the reflex action response to my name. By self-delusion I mean how they repeat the narratives of authority as their own opinions when they are simply believing what authority wants them to believe to benefit authority. Given that authority wants them to believe that 'Icke's a nutter' that's what they do. It's me that should be laughing at what is truly pathetic to behold. How such people function between 'Covid' jab and 'Covid' jab I have no idea. What appears to be one thing, however, can be very much another when viewed from a different angle and perspective. Life doesn't always give you what you want so much as what you need. A communication to me through a psychic in those early years said:

> True love does not always give the receiver what it would like to receive, but it will always give that which is best for it. So welcome everything you receive whether you like it or not. Ponder on anything you do not like and see if you can see why it was necessary. Acceptance will then be very much easier.

No more prison cell

Those years of unceasing ridicule were actually setting me free from the prison that most people live in which is the fear of what other people think. My life was going to uncover secrets and truths so fantastic that anyone still concerned with how they were perceived by others would never have spoken about them never mind so publicly. My conscious mind didn't know what was coming while other levels of me did. I was being prepared for this just as my whole life up to this point had been preparation for what I had come here to do. You don't talk about shape-

shifting Reptilians if you have a smear of concern about how others see you. When you are faced with the years of unyielding and merciless ridicule and abuse that I experienced you either withdraw from the world and hide away or you stick your chin up, your chest out, and allow the fire to hone you into unbreakable steel. I chose the latter (Fig 39). I was going to speak my truth and no level of ridicule and abuse was going to stop me (Fig 40).

Amid the hysteria of ridicule I embarked on a speaking tour of university student unions organised by my old television agent Paul Vaughan who stuck with me through it all and proved himself to be a real genuine friend.

Figure 39: Throw all the ridicule and abuse that you like. You will not break me. I cannot be broken.

Figure 40: Freedom.

Can you imagine what happened at those universities? I remember driving home through the night after my first university event at Bangor in North Wales in the early 1990s. I had been ridiculed all evening by the packed student audience and instead of staying overnight I just wanted to get home. What was the point of going on? Everywhere I went was abuse and ridicule. Outside of my own front door I couldn't get away from it wherever there were people. The sun was just appearing as I drove along a deserted one-track country road. A psychic had told me a year earlier to pick a symbol that 'they' could show me to communicate answers to questions. Behind her right ear on a shelf was a pot fish. 'I'll make it a fish', I said. As the darkness lifted in that early morning on the isolated and deserted country road, I said 'show me a fish' if what I am doing is going somewhere – if it is worth keeping on. At that very moment – and I mean the *very* moment – that I asked the question a big blue van appeared over the rise in the distance. It was the first vehicle I had seen in ages through the night. As the vehicle got closer I saw that it was a fish and chip van with the word 'fish' blazed above the cab windscreen. The 'coincidence' was so fantastic that I thought, okay, I'll carry on a bit longer and see where it goes.

Students were booking me to speak at universities in the knowledge that I was being set up to be ridiculed for their entertainment. They were not self-aware enough, as most people aren't, to see that what we do and say is a statement about *us* and not those we think we are making a statement about. I remember walking out to a packed audience of students at one university and the laughter, ridicule and abuse was so loud and long that it was minutes before I could speak. I stood patiently looking at them in despair that these were potentially influential figures of tomorrow. Eventually they calmed down and the room became quiet. I said: 'You think I'm mentally ill, don't you?' More uproar followed as they shouted their agreement. I let the noise disperse back once again to silence. 'So what does that say about you?', I said. 'You have come here tonight to ridicule someone you think is mentally ill.' You could have heard a pin drop as that realisation sank in and I was treated with respectful silence for the rest of the night except for about four young blokes at the back near the bar who continued to heckle. The room was in darkness so I couldn't see them. When I took questions in the second half I asked for the lights to be turned on and for the microphone to be handed for the first question to these prats at the back. They recoiled as if the microphone was on fire and that's the last we heard of them. Shouting ridicule from the darkness is the modus operandi of cowards and like all bullies they have balls the size of nanotechnology when someone faces them up. My experience in the Crown Hills school toilets with the bully and his gang showed me that and the lesson would now be mighty handy. Indeed my whole life up to this point gave me the emotional and stoical tools I needed and that's why it happened as it did.

Fear of what others think of you is the prison that enslaves almost everyone. It is the foundation of group-think when people fuse into the belief system of the group and stay quiet about their own unique take on life even if they have one. When you seek the approval of others instead of expressing your uniqueness you are no longer 'you', unique 'you'. Instead you become *them* by couching your views and behaviour in ways that are acceptable to the group which is precisely how cults operate. Well, sod that for a game of soldiers as they say. I am me and if anyone doesn't like that, well, fine, that's their right, but I am me and I am not going to be otherwise because of what others may think. They can think what they choose – *so can I* and I will thank you. The 'Covid' era has been all about molding group-think (authority-think) and turning that coagulated psyche against the individual-think of those that pushback against the lies and won't have the fake 'vaccine' that isn't actually a vaccine. Kerry, Gareth, and Linda were subject to ridicule by association although I think a lot of people felt more sorry for Linda that she lived with a crackpot like me. Kerry, Gareth and later Jaymie were all strengthened in their personalities by using the experience of their dad's ridicule to ditch their concern with what others think of them. What hurt me so much over the years about the effect of my actions on them has turned out to be exactly what they needed to experience. The spiritual way is tough and no one makes it easy. It's worth it, though. Look at what they are doing now – building platforms and groups to challenge tyranny and defend freedom. To think they could have had some other mind-numbing life working in a bank or something instead of expressing their uniqueness every minute of every day.

While the world was laughing at me almost wherever I went in public, amazing things continued to happen as I travelled increasingly further afield. I was gathering ever more detailed information about how those that appeared to be running the world were actually pawns of those *really* in control. Later I came across the non-human force behind it all and later still the illusory nature of our apparently 'physical' world and the simulation that holds humanity in perceptual servitude. I'll cover all these aspects and put them together in a coherent whole as we proceed. Information would come from whistleblowers, people inside government-military-intelligence networks, researchers in specialist fields, books, documents, direct personal experience, the sources were many. An extraordinary picture emerged that is still expanding into ever greater knowledge to this day. A new subject would come into my life and suddenly information on that subject would be coming at me from all angles. This recurring process has taken me deeper and deeper in the rabbit hole as I have been led to knowledge and knowledge has been put into my mind. This book is the latest instalment. The constant flow of information into my life for the last 32 years would be incredible by itself, but there is more. The incredible 'paranormal' experience on the hill in Peru was only one example of happenings that cannot be explained by the official and 'normal', 'scientific', take on reality which is provably flawed and fundamentally so. The 'para'-normal has become part of life to me and in fact there is nothing 'para' about it. Myopic 'science' simply adds 'para' to anything that its closed minds can't explain.

Eagle tales

I'll describe one sequence of happenings as an example of the experiences I have had which 'science' can't explain, but absolutely can be explained, and will be later in the book. The sequence has a theme of Native Americans and Canadians which was in my life a lot between 1991 and 1993. I remember the first time I spoke abroad on these conspiracy subjects in Houston, Texas, in 1993 at a 'New Age' event at a local hotel so off-the-wall (even for me!) that I went for a walk before I spoke to get away from what I was seeing. The 'turn' before me involved people running on and off the stage dressed as planets. I travelled to Texas with 'Yeva' who looked appropriately like a Native American grandmother with her long grey hair. We met just over a year earlier in Glastonbury in Somerset in a house next to the famous Glastonbury Tor. Yeva was a godsend to me at that time (Fig

Figure 41: The lovely Yeva – a great lady and a great friend.

41). I was still trying to understand what on earth was happening to my life and she had long experience in esoteric circles and had considerable psychic abilities. We began to travel together and arrange talks to which nobody came. Anyway, she went with me to Houston and while I was speaking for my 90 minutes I saw that she was talking intently with a Native American-looking guy. When I finished she came over to say 'You have to talk with this man'. I did and he was indeed a Native American. He said that he never came to New Age events. He found them nonsensical, but something told him he should come to this one. He had a little stall selling his wares. The man said that when I started to speak he knew why he had felt so strongly to be there. 'We have a legend', he said, 'about a white man who would come to Turtle Island [America] and change everything – you are that man.' He handed me a beautiful eagle feather which I have beside my bed to this day. I knew nothing of the legend. I read when I searched out the story that the Hopi people in Arizona await the return of Pahana, their 'lost white brother', who will come from the east and bring peace and a new religion. I am all for the peace, but not a new, or any, religion although the term is used in this context in the widest sense. The legend says that Pahana will return dressed in red and bring a missing section of a sacred Hopi tablet. An Internet article says:

> Many of the Hopi believe we are living in the 'End Times', and therefore they expect Pahana to return soon. The lost white brother should arrive before the time of the 'Great Purification' of Hopi prophecy. The belief in the lost white brother is so strong that the Hopi even bury their dead facing east in expectation of the Pahana who will come from that direction.

I would make many visits to the Hopi reservation when I lived for months on end in Arizona and also to the Navajo lands across the Utah border in the extraordinary Monument Valley. The strangest thing happened as I was speaking with the Native American outside the Houston hotel. He said what he did and I looked away at something quite briefly to find when I looked back that he was gone. I'm not claiming that I am 'Pahana', by the way. I'm just recalling what happened. The Native American/Canadian theme had been with me for a couple of years by then and the following sequence began in Calgary, Canada, when I went to the Glenbow Museum where a whole floor was dedicated to Native Canadian history and culture. I saw a picture on the wall of Sitting On An Eagle Tail, one-time chief of the Peigan tribe, also called Piikani. They were forced onto a reservation in Alberta in the late 19th century. I stared at the picture for a while and something attracted me to it very strongly.

Later that day I was on indigenous land and went into a shop selling books on Native Canadian history. As I leafed through one of them I saw the name again Sitting On An Eagle Tail also known as Zaotze Tapitapiw. He was a friend of Crowfoot, the famous chief of the Blackfoot. The Peigan/Piikani were and are part of a tribal grouping sometimes known as the Blackfoot Confederacy. There was great controversy at the time I was there over flooding sacred indigenous lands with the building of the Oldman River Dam a more than two-hour drive south of Calgary. I went to the site to see what was happening and it was on this trip that I had the 'diamonds in the mud' experience. I took the scenic route off the main highway and stopped at one point where the land made my heart sing. I got out the car and looked across the landscape. It felt like home somehow. I would later find out that this was the land that Eagle Tail chose for the Peigan/Piikani reservation and it remains so today. I also went to the Blackfoot reservation to visit Crowfoot's grave high on a bleak ridge, well, it was bleak that day anyway, and then headed to the nearby Blackfoot museum. When I arrived a sign said 'museum closed' and I thought I'd missed out. I walked up the stairs of the building which housed the little museum on the first floor in the hope that someone was still there and they would let me in. Better than that I found the museum door ajar with no one around and I could just walk in. There in front of me among a very few exhibits was the original medicine bag of Zaotze Tapitapiw – Eagle Tail.

Feathers from the sky

Sometime later I went with Yeva to the Pitt Rivers Museum in Oxford where lots of Native American artefacts were on show stolen during what was the near-genocide of indigenous peoples in North America and certainly the genocide of their culture and way of life. When I parked the car in the city centre a student recognised me and came over for a chat. I asked him for directions to the Pitt Rivers, but he sent us the wrong way it turned out. As I walked with Yeva in the wrong direction and began to recount the story of what had happened to me in Canada I mentioned the name Sitting On An Eagle Tail and immediately looked up to see a pub sign portraying a baby flying with an eagle. The pub was called the Eagle and Child and I would later read that this was a regular meeting place for Oxford writers J. R. R. Tolkien who wrote *Lord of the Rings* and C. S. Lewis, author of the *Narnia* books who had handed out proofs of his *The Lion, the Witch and the Wardrobe* at a meeting in the pub in 1950. They both explored the nature of reality. That night Yeva and I had arranged to go into Stonehenge on a private visit which you could do in those days. I would be banned from the stones on a later night visit for playing music. The guard said there might be complaints. I looked around in all directions to see no other building from horizon to horizon and asked: 'What – from the neighbours?' I told an alleged 'spiritual' woman about this and she called a national newspaper to tell them the story. It was reported that I was in a group dancing naked in Stonehenge. If only it was true. That would have been fun.

Yeva was a visual psychic and as we sat among the stones in the darkness she said she was seeing the whole of the surrounding Salisbury Plain covered in Native American tepees. She then said that a long line of Native American spirits were coming towards us and the chief at the front was holding a long headdress which he was handing to me saying 'It's time to give you your feathers' or something close to that. The next morning I wanted to see an abbey building in Amesbury, the nearest village to Stonehenge, which is now the Amesbury Abbey Care Home. Yeva stayed at the nearby church and I walked down the path to the abbey to find it closed off. I came back to see Yeva on the far side of the churchyard stooping down constantly picking up something from the grass over and over again. *What the* ...? I walked towards her to see that she was picking up feathers as literally hundreds of them were appearing out of 'nowhere' at about 50 feet and falling all over the grass. It was raining feathers. The few trees in the churchyard were not very tall and there were certainly no birds around. Even if there had been how would they produce hundreds of feathers that literally manifested out of the ether 50 feet or so above us? I stood there watching them manifest and fall. We were there for ages picking up as many as we could carry and it was well over 300 before we gave up with more still falling. I took them home and kept them for years. Once again that's impossible, right? We will see not. I have spoken to many people around the world who have seen objects appearing 'out of nowhere' including coins, crystals, many different things, which they have kept. We are 'in' a *simulation*. A virtual reality game creator could not insert a program in which feathers fall out of the sky? Or a storm comes out of the mountains super-fast? Or a stone circle ... You get what I'm saying and we'll be going much deeper.

Talking to myself

Extraordinary experiences like this were not happening all the time – as in every day – but they were far from rare. What *was* an almost daily experience was the synchronicity of my life leading me to information. In the early years it was mainly about how those apparently running the world were not the ones actually running it. Then, from 1996 when I first embarked on 'speaking tours' of America, the non-human and Reptilian dimension appeared followed after the turn of the millennium with the key to everything – the illusory nature of 'physical' reality. The revelations about the simulation came next and now for this book another level of knowledge about the human plight and how we escape to eternity. I put the term 'speaking tours' in quotes because yes, I was speaking, but next to no one was listening. You could hardly claim them to be a 'tour' except in the literal travelling sense. A freedom organisation in California helped me embark on my first 'speaking tour' of the United States in 1996 as they also supported the long-time researcher Jordan Maxwell who I first met that year. I would speak night after night to tiny audiences, sometimes five in someone's front room as I did in New England one evening. I spoke in Portland, Oregon, where the organiser said at the start how pleased he was to see so many people there. There were 40. Blimey, what was he expecting then? It was heart-aching and sometimes heart-breaking to wake-travel-speak-sleep day after day, week after week for three months at a time when interest in my information was almost non-existent. 'What's the point?' crossed my mind so many times. Something deep inside drove me on and just when I was at my lowest something would happen to give me a lift and keep me going. On the 1996 'tour' the pointlessness of it all was almost overwhelming me when I arrived in Vancouver, Canada, to a one-off event organised by a great man, Joseph Duggan. He was a vociferous campaigner for freedom despite the serious debilitating consequences of Parkinson's. Joseph had hired a hotel conference room. I expected another night talking to empty chairs and found the place to be full with 250 people. What a lift that gave me to carry on and the next year it was 350, the next 750, then 1,000, and it would have been thousands after that had venues not cancelled bookings through the efforts of ultra-Zionist organisations and a bloke called Richard Warman, a government employee in Ottawa, who seemed obsessed with preventing me from speaking in public. There is a UK Channel 4 documentary about his efforts to stop me produced by a guy called John Ronson which is still around on the Internet. All that effort Warman put in to stop me and ultimately in terms of global attention to no avail. His determination against mine was always going to be a no-contest.

It was the same story back home in the UK. Yeva would travel around Britain with me. I would so often put the chairs out, talk to them, and then put them away again poorer than when I arrived. At the same time people were saying 'where's the money going?' Out of my life was the answer. I recall one 'tour' talking to empty venues when my hopes were on the talk in Manchester where there seemed a lot more interest and a decent crowd was likely. That afternoon we went on a visit to the old set at Granada studios in the city of legendary television soap *Coronation Street*. I had watched the first episode in black and white in 1960 at home in Leicester when I was eight. Some 60 years later I would meet and have a long chat with an actor in that first show and still there today, William Roache, who plays Ken Barlow. Bill is really spiritually awake and the youngest-looking 88-year-old I had ever seen. It was extraordinary. Whatever he's on I want some. It was interesting to see

the '*Street*' set with most of the public tour indoors and I was looking
forward to speaking to a decent number of people that evening. Then as
Yeva and me came outside again to head for the venue we were met
with a massive snowstorm. It came in so fast and with such depth and
ferocity that when we drove – slowly – to the venue the radio weather
reports were warning people not to go out unless absolutely necessary. It
was to be another night of empty seats and it was the same story the
next night at a theatre in Forres, Scotland, which had I think 325 seats
with only the front row with any bums on them. Yet another 'speaking
tour' had been a gut-wrenching, spirit-sapping, nightmare, and with
only one venue left in the Scottish capital Edinburgh thoughts of calling
it a day swirled around my mind. What happened next became a theme
in those early years as hundreds came to the Edinburgh event just as my
heart was struggling to go on.

Perhaps the lowest point was that trip to Houston when money was
pouring out of my life with none coming in. I was not paid for the
Houston talk, but I did sell a lot of books that I had brought with me
from England. A lot for me then, anyway. On the journey to the airport I
was asked do an interview with a local community radio station and I
took off my jacket to do so. At the airport I realised I'd left the jacket
behind and the talk organiser drove back to find it. She did, minus all
the book money in the pocket. The long flight home followed with my
spirit in the hold. Yeva and I would eat in roadside cafes called Little
Chefs and Happy Eaters. We would stare into the distance trying to
make sense of it all. 'What's it all about, Yeve?', I would say. 'I dunno,
Dave', would come the reply and we'd drive on to the next empty

Figure 42: What's it all about Yeve? I dunno, Dave.

Figure 43: Neil, Ayem, and me after a talk event I did in Amsterdam. I may have had enormous challenges, but there have been so many laughs.

venue. We had that exchange so often it became a joke between us (Fig 42). Two other great friends who stepped forward to support me from around 1994 were artist Neil Hague, who is still with me today with his art work and publishing skills, and a one-off character from Liverpool known simply as 'Ayem' who passed in 2019. She perfectly shared my sense of humour and we laughed so much (Fig 43).

The tide turns (at last)

This was pretty much the story throughout the entire 1990s although there was a visible increase in interest with the publication of my book, *The Biggest Secret*, in 1998 which has been called the Rosetta Stone of the conspiracy research movement. The movement didn't exist except as a few individuals when I started out and now it's a worldwide phenomenon despite desperate ongoing efforts by global authorities to censor it out of existence. Two thousand years after its creation the Rosetta Stone was found that helped scholars to crack the code of the long-lost language of hieroglyphics. I have been working to crack the code of a global conspiracy to enslave the entire human race. Interest in my work expanded rapidly after the blatantly-staged 9/11 attacks which were not the work of '19 Arab hijackers' (see my mega-9/11 exposure book *The Trigger*). This increased further when George Bush and Tony Blair lied for their masters about weapons of mass destruction to justify a catastrophic invasion of Iraq. The momentum has continued to gather and grow ever since with two all-day events at the Wembley Arena in London where I had once played in a televised national five-aside tournament for Coventry City in 1967 and later presented sports programmes there including that BBC *Horse of the Year Show*. To walk out on stage and see all those thousands of people in 2012 and 2014 was

Figure 44: On stage at the Wembley Arena – the tide was turning.

Figure 45: What great moments the two Wembley shows were for a family that had come through so much for the crime of seeking the truth. Jaymie organised the 2014 event as his business and organisational skills were coming to the fore and led to the outstanding Ickonic media platform that was his creation.

testament to the fact that the waters were breaking (Figs 44 and 45). With the 'Covid' era has come global recognition for my work with my stream of books since the early 1990s warning that what is happening today was coming unless humanity awoke to its real controllers and the agenda being pursued for global technologically-imposed fascism. I have lived alone for the best part of two decades to focus my mind totally on the job in hand and not once have I felt lonely. There is too much to do and every minute of that focus has been worth it now. Funny, I am known for talking – and talking and talking – but in fact 95 percent of my life is spent listening and quietly looking. Talking and writing communicate information. Listening and looking uncover it.

From being ridiculed by the mainstream media I am now ignored – don't let anyone know what he's saying because it will make too much sense to them. I was banned from YouTube, Facebook, Twitter and anything that moved on the mainstream Internet in the spring of 2020 when I exposed that 'Covid' was a gigantic scam to turn the world fascist – exactly what then happened. Once I was ridiculed wherever I went. Now I am stopped in the street by people all over the world who support what I am doing and want to know more. I have spoken to 40,000 people in London's Trafalgar Square (Fig 46). Davidicke.com is visited by millions every week while Jaymie has built a fantastic team, including Gareth, an outstanding presenter, at Ickonic media. This is like an alternative Netflix, with news programmes, series, original documentaries, and films galore added to every week. I do my own

Figure 46: Freedom rally in Trafalgar Square in 2020.
(Photo: Alan Ball)

show dot-connecting the news every Saturday and I have presented a 13-part series on the nature of reality as well as many other contributions. All my talks at Wembley and in many other locations and countries since the 1990s are also there. Jaymie and Gareth have both become major figures in the freedom movement with the different and complementary skills they bring to the table (Figs 47 and 48). Multi-talented Gaz also oversees all my book publishing and distribution. A psychic communication in 1990 said of my daughter Kerry: 'One day your daughter will see her star and go for it.' She has done just that and has developed, again through hard and challenging experience, into an exceptional human being – or rather consciousness – and a leading light in the freedom movement on the Isle of Wight where a community is being formed of like-minded awakening people. We always go to the London freedom marches and rallies together. Those words communicated through Betty Shine in 1990 have proved stupendously prophetic about where my life would go and I couldn't be more proud of how everything has turned out. Now we have the

Figures 47 and 48: Gareth and Jaymie ... so proud of them. (Photo: Alan Ball)

epic challenge of finishing the job and thwarting global fascism just when it thinks the game is won.

An extraordinary aspect of what my children have gone on to do is that I never encouraged them to listen to me, accept my information, or walk my path. I don't believe in that. The best thing parents can do for their kids in my view is set them free to go their own unique way. Support them and guide them from your own experience, yes, but never force or manipulate them into what you think they should do. They are their unique self and they must be allowed to express that. Both my sons became goalkeepers even though I never encouraged them to play in that position. They chose it. Gareth went on to play for the England beach soccer team around Europe, Jaymie played for Portsmouth FC youth teams and had trials with Manchester United and Aston Villa. Gareth looked like making a full-time career as a singer-songwriter and Kerry, a brilliant middle distance runner in her school days, became an outstanding mother and highly-intelligent campaigner for freedom with a backbone of steel. The flow of life and circumstance brought all of them into this arena focused on the defence of freedom. I didn't encourage it. I would not impose on their choices. It just happened.

Ambition is fine, but only if it does not block out all other possibility. If one ambition is pursued and it is not happening it is no good banging your head against that padlocked door while other doors are wide open and saying 'over here' – this is for you. Look at my own experience and you see that again and again. Life if you are awake to it has a flow. You can go with that flow and surf the wave, or you can battle against it with a mono-ambition that leads only to a mono-mind, frustration and sense of failure. You have not failed. You have simply picked a course that is not for you. Maybe societal-programming chose it. Maybe your parents did. I have met many people at advanced age still feeling guilty at not doing what their parents wanted for them. *Sod that.* It's none of their business. Parents should be supporters, not dictators.

Another thing I didn't do with my children was protect them from every experience and emotional challenge. That does them no favours. I had seen by then what my own challenges in life had given me in mental and emotional strength. Protect children from all unpleasant life experience and when they go out into the world as adults they will be crushed. They will have no emotional tools to cope. What we become is the sum total of the experience that we have *learned* from and other people's experience that we have learned from. If someone acts in a way that teaches us not to do the same we should thank them and not condemn them for their 'error'. They have to deal with that, but their 'error' and consequence has given us a gift of knowledge. The problem is not having challenging experience; it is not learning from that, gaining wisdom from that, which means you are destined to repeat the

challenging experience maybe over and over. A 'mistake' is only
negative if you don't learn from what it shows you and so you do it
again. There are no 'mistakes' only learning from experience – or not.
'Mistakes' are either wonderful opportunities to learn and gain wisdom,
or disasters to be repeated. We make the choice that dictates which they
are. I love what I call 'lived in' people who have developed the strength
of personality that comes from overcoming adversity. They are the wise
ones with something to say that is not taken directly from a daily news
show. Those who have had easy lives protected from challenge have so
little to say, so little to engage you, because they have experienced so
little that engaged them and gave them *life*.

I have outlined some of the basic pillars and happenings in my 70
years so far which can serve as examples for later explanations for why
the 'world' is as it is – or seems to be. For those new to my work it also
gives a feel for where the information comes from with multiple sources
synchronistically coming my way to be weaved together in a dot-
connected whole. I have not lived a 'normal' life I think it is fair to say,
but then what is 'normal'? It is simulation 'normal'; It is human program
'normal'. It is how you are supposed to live your life according to that
programmed 'normal'. What is 'normal' except that which is 'normally'
done? 'Normal' is merely what most people do, it is the familiar, that's
all. It doesn't make it the right way or, most importantly, the only way.
We learn from experience and if you censor what can be experienced

© Alan Ball 2020

Figure 49: Still crazy after all these years – and just as fiercely determined.
(Photo: Alan Ball)

you censor learning. You censor the means to enlightenment. If we use the linear 'time' of the five senses – what we *were* is what made us what we *are*. Without the were, there is no are. The 'were', the 'have been', the 'have done', are only experiences in the exploration of forever. What is 'yesterday' except an experience that made us what we are 'today'? Intelligent awake people learn from experience. Asleep people repeat it. That's the only real difference.

My life has been guided to experience whatever I needed to experience, go wherever I needed to go, in pursuit both of expanding awareness and understanding the human plight. On that basis my life was never going to be 'normal'. How could it be? The goals and priorities were at odds from the start with a 'normal' human experience. From the time my mind was blown in 1991 I have not seen my life in human terms with human goals and ambitions, the need to do 'human' things, and live in a 'human' way. I have seen my life as a job. If that meant missing out a lot on holidays, days out, nights out, and perceived fun then so be it. I have come to work and at some point I will return home. To my true home, not an illusory one. Being out of sync with 'normal' has brought many challenges and much ridicule and abuse, and all has been worth it. I wouldn't change a thing (Fig 49).

I am now going to lay out what all the synchronicity of experience and information in my travels to some 60 countries this past 32 years has shown me about the reality that we perceive as human society. With the information and insights continuing to unfold I am going deeper than ever before into where we are, what we are, and why we are 'here' at all.

CHAPTER FOUR

Method in the Madness

The eye sees only what the mind is prepared to comprehend
Robertson Davies

The almost unimaginable synchronicity of the more than three decades since I walked into Betty Shine's front room in 1990 have shown me so much about the world that we think – *think* – we live in. It has indeed been a magical journey despite the sometimes serious challenges that have continued throughout.

I have seen (remembered) that life is eternal forever. It's not a sprint; it is the endlessness, timelessness and blissfulness of eternity. There is no death – only life. It's when we forget this that the trouble starts. Our perceptions then focus what we call 'life' into the biblical threescore years and ten that symbolise our sojourn between cradle and grave. Our attention becomes focussed on an apparent 'physicality' that doesn't actually exist except as a brief and illusory experience. Phantom physicality presents the human senses with a phantom 'world' of limitation, 'I can't', and 'it's not possible'. From this five-sensory reality comes the false and fractured self-identity with human labels – race, culture, sex and sexuality, income bracket, 'class', politics, and all the rest – which are no more than transitory happenings that we falsely believe to be 'us'. They are not 'us'. They are *experiences*. The 'I' is something else. When that knowledge is lost, the human world of illusory 'past' and 'present' emerges that we define as 'history' and present day. A world in which bewildered and separated consciousness tries to make sense of the non-existent that we take to be 'real'; the virtual reality that is perceived as the 'real world'. 'I live in the real world, mate' is the calling card of the self-styled 'streetwise' that dismiss any idea of other realities while living in anything but a 'real world'. It is a feedback loop of self-perpetuated illusion that entraps perception through belief becoming perceived reality and perceived reality becoming belief. Round and round it goes and until the circuit breaks no change is possible. Repetition of the same self-deception never changed anything. How could it or can it?

I am going to summarise in this chapter what I have uncovered about the true nature of the world that we see and from then on go deeper and deeper into the world that we don't see including the Matrix or simulation which seeks to hold us in servitude to its manufactured illusions and separate us from prime and infinite reality beyond its technological outer-limits. Those behind the breakneck descent into global dystopia, which my books have so long predicted, know how humans interact with reality and how we *create* our reality with our perceptual states. They just don't want the population to know. This revelation would set us free and the chosen few hoard and hide this knowledge across the generations in a global network of secret societies that I refer to as the Global Cult. At the same time they purge and ridicule 'occult' (hidden) knowledge as best they can where it permeates human society and block its circulation in 'education', media, mainstream science and medicine. They know that perception dictates behaviour and experience and if they can control perception they control behaviour and experience. Perception = behaviour = experience and collective behaviour (perception made manifest) is what we call human society. Control perception and you control the world and you control perception by programming the mind to perceive reality as you desire. We will see that even visual perception is not dictated by the eyes, but by the mind. Where does this 'human world exist' as we experience it? In your mind and nowhere else. The Cult knows this while the target population overwhelmingly doesn't and this colossal built-in advantage is the foundation of how the few control the many and always have. The target is not primarily your body. It's your *mind*.

Psychology of government

People rightly highlight the structures of control through governments, media, corporations and the organised crime referred to as 'banking' and 'finance'. Go deeper into the rabbit hole and all these apparently 'physical' phenomena are architects of *perception*. It's *all* perception. If you have access to 'money' you have a certain perception; if you don't, you have a different perception and not least of your own potential to live the life you desire. What you believe you perceive and what you perceive you experience – it's a feedback loop. Perceive and believe are interchangeable. Behaviour and experience are always the outcome no matter what their order. Governments and their agencies may appear to be making decisions and laws affecting the population, but at their core governments are telling the population what to believe and perceive. Governments are dominated by whole armies of behavioural psychologists today for this very reason. The 'Covid' hoax – and it is a hoax – is exposed in detail in my last two books, *The Answer* and *Perceptions of a Renegade Mind*. The hoax has been driven by psychologists. All the restrictions, manufactured divisions, isolation and face-nappy masks have nothing to do with protecting health and everything to do with re-wiring perception into meek and unquestioning conformity through fear of a spook 'virus' and/or fear of not doing what the government tells you to do in alleged response to a spook 'virus'.

I have studied the techniques of mind control both sides of the Atlantic since the 1990s and this has included talking to a long list of people caught in horrific mind-altering government/military/intelligence programmes such as the infamous MKUltra in North America which came to public attention (or a fraction of it did) in the 1970s. I have listened to stories of enforced isolation, mind games and masks that were used to disorientate, perceptually manipulate, de-humanise, de-individualise, and deprive the brain of the oxygen it needs to adequately develop and process information. I have watched exactly those techniques employed on the global population in the 'Covid' era. They have turned great swathes of humanity into obedient conformity and handed freedoms that brave people long fought to establish to psychopaths orchestrating events for their own truly evil ends. Masks are a classic. Endless scientific papers have shown that holes in masks are much bigger than what they *call* viral particles (more later). Some scientists have pointed out masks are the equivalent of trying to stop mosquitoes with a chain-link fence. Oh, but surgeons wear masks, the programmed cry. Yes – to stop blobs of saliva falling into open wounds and not to stop micro-particles of a 'virus' that has *never been shown to exist.* I have been pointing out since the summer of 2020 that masks are useless to stop 'viral particles' even if you believe in them purely on the basis that holes in masks are significantly bigger than 'viral particles'. It took the Centers for Disease Control and Prevention (CDC) in the United States until 2021 to admit that cloth masks are useless. The admission came after the most terrible damage had already been done to health and psychology of adults and children through: Diminished intake of oxygen; increased carbon dioxide the body is trying to expel; bacteria and fibres in the masks breathed into the lungs including cancer-causing titanium dioxide; dehumanisation by blocking facial expression; and devastating effects on babies that get their perceptual cues from the faces of parents and others. One speech therapist alone reported a *364 percent* increase in referrals for speech problems among very young children with 'autism symptoms also skyrocketing'. The therapist said: 'It's very important kids do see your face to learn, so they're watching your mouth.' Not if you are wearing a mask they're not and there lies the problem.

Masks throughout history have been used as symbols of submission and to silence literally and psychologically (Fig 50). They are used today

'YOU CAN'T BE TOO CAREFUL'

ACTUALLY, MATE - YOU CAN

Figure 50: The face of fear – exactly as planned.

for the same reason, if only straight-jacket-minds would free themselves and see. American Cathy O'Brien, my great friend who suffered for decades in MKUltra and its elite offshoot Project Monarch, told me how her daughter Kelly was forced to wear a mask from the age of two as part of her mind-programming and to deny her brain the oxygen to develop as it should. Cathy was an another example of my life of synchronicity when an acquaintance in Scotland sent me her incredible book, *Trance-Formation of America*, which I immediately read in a day. Two weeks later I was given a book table next to hers at a conference thousands of miles away in Denver, Colorado, and she's been a close friend ever since. Imagine what has been done to the minds and brains of the young, never mind adults, by wearing masks at school all day and being told to fear their mates as a deadly threat. We don't have to imagine with suicide and depression among the young soaring beyond belief. Cathy points out that the singer Michael Jackson was a product of the ongoing MKUltra (it never ended) and what was he famous for? The obsession with wearing a mask. Every aspect of 'Covid' has had a psychological intent right down to the fake 'virus' itself which is no more than a 'virus' – akin to a computer virus – of the *mind*. The world and reality are going to look very different by the time you finish this book. Masks are only one example of a tidal wave of attacks on the psyche to dictate perception and behaviour.

Get them early

Government in all its forms and expressions is a perceptual programming machine and this starts from the earliest age through government-controlled 'education' that was created specifically to provide a perceptual download through all the formative years and is designed to influence and solidify the population's sense of reality for an entire human lifetime (Fig 51 overleaf). John D. Rockefeller, the American oil, banking and pharmaceutical tycoon, founded the US General Education Board at the start of the 20th century and betrayed the real reason for the 'education' system when he said: 'I don't want a nation of thinkers – I want a nation of workers.' Rockefeller's co-founder and business adviser, Frederick T. Gates, took up the theme:

Figure 51: Perceptual programming starts at the earliest age and goes on for life unless we break the program by thinking for ourselves.

In our dream we have limitless resources, and the people yield themselves with perfect docility to our moulding hand. The present educational conventions fade from our minds; and, unhampered by tradition, we work our own good will upon a grateful and responsive rural folk.

We shall not try to make these people or any of their children into philosophers or men of learning or of science. We are not to raise up among them authors, orators, poets, or men of letters. We shall not search for embryo great artists, painters, musicians. Nor will we cherish even the humbler ambition to raise up from among them lawyers, doctors, preachers, statesmen, of whom we now have ample supply.

Everything is about perceptual control in pursuit of behaviour control as information leads to perception which leads to behaviour which leads to human society and, most notably, its direction. I was fortunate in that I went to schools with mostly honest teachers with integrity who cared about what they did in the 1950s and 60s. There was the added bonus of always being a rebel at heart who did not take things at face value no matter who told me to believe them. The state curriculum was still designed back then to program perception although nothing like to the extremes of today. Most of the teachers I had at Crown Hills especially encouraged questions and there was some learning about *how* to think and not just *what* to think. Not so now. Oh, my god, no. Today's schools and universities are prison camps for the mind as perceptual control has reached new depths of depravity, (Fig 52). Teachers have become the prison warders who are themselves programmed by the same system they now mindlessly impose upon the latest generations. They are the programmed programmers, the blind leading the blind – or trying to make them so. Ideologues are knowingly doing this to serve the agenda of their masters, not least via the hijacked teaching unions the world over. Teachers who can see what is happening are caught in a web that leaves them no room for manoeuvre. They teach the state's way on the state's terms or they are shown the door. One word out of place in the politically-correct 'Woke' (fast asleep) tyranny now upon us and a boot makes contact with their arse. It is a world of 2 + 2 = 5. If you dare to claim that it's 4 then you are a racist, culturally-misappropriating, pronoun-abusing, transphobe. Perceptual myopia of the Woke Cult-induced-and-funded psychosis has been gathering in intensity for long enough to have flooded the adult world with fully-programmed agents of insanity with no need even for intimidation to bring them to heel. Woke spends its entire life 'to heel' which is defined as 'submissive agreement or compliance' and 'an order to an animal, by its master, not to stray far'. By that definition most of humanity is 'to heel'.

Teachers and academics who won't comply are hounded and abused from their jobs by the very young people they refuse to program. Oh, the irony. You are not programming us as the state demands and so we're going to destroy you. This is a blatant inversion in a society teeming with inversion for reasons I will be making clear. Many great teachers have been lost who could no longer face the dire reality of what they were being told to do which is to mould into solidity the minds of the young for a sick and sickening state apparatus. In the same way great policemen and women have been lost to the same fascist demands of the state to be replaced by psychopaths and software minds incapable of questioning the program. The global frenzy of sacking 'unvaccinated' police officers, military personnel, medical staff, teachers, and others throughout the system is to purge the workforce and institutions of

those with a mind of their own and the backbone to say my body is mine and not the property of some psychopath or moron with a needle. The decision to refuse the fake vaccine that is not a vaccine has sifted the free-thinkers from the unquestioningly compliant Those

Figure 52: The real goal of 'education' and major studies have shown that this is precisely what it does. (Image by David Dees.)

driving world events are well aware of that. Thus the non-submissive free-thinkers must be destroyed with the full support of unthinking obedience by much of the rest of the population. I will continue throughout to refer to the 'vaccines' as fake because under all credible criteria – and the criteria before 'Covid' – they do not meet any definition of a 'vaccine'. If it's not a vaccine we must not fall into the trap of calling it one simply on the basis that official statements claim that it is. I refuse to do that and always add 'fake' to every mention. The official justification and previous definition of a vaccine is that they stimulate and program the immune system to stop people getting infected with a disease or transmitting it to others. Not even the makers of 'Covid' fake vaccines claim that and the evidence since the rollout has confirmed how useless they are in that regard. They have been created for a very different reason.

The answer is FOUR!

Schools and universities today are full-blown programming machines in which perceptually programmed (or compliant) 'teachers' fill the minds of the young with the most monumental and provable crap. Kids absorb this software download and then seek to enforce their deeply skewed reality upon those with the intelligence and open-mindedness to have a different view or at least question the validity of the said monumental crap. 2 + 2 = 5 becomes the 'everyone knows that'. Why? Simply because for the most part all they hear is 2 + 2 = 5 and they absorb as their reality what has no challenge in their daily experience (Fig 53). Other views are silenced and demonised to stop them being part of the perceptual mix of potential possibility. When you want people to perceive only one possibility – *your* possibility – debate becomes as garlic to a vampire. If your provable claptrap can't win a debate then don't have one and here you have the *real* reason for the 'cancel culture'. Once you accept even outwardly that 2 + 2 = 5 your mind has conceded its self-respect and once that has gone only submission remains. The tyranny has you by the balls and you speak ever higher with every squeeze. In a desperate effort

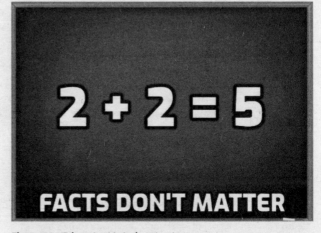

Figure 53: 'Education' is indoctrination.

to hide their shame from themselves those who spinelessly feign believing that $2 + 2 = 5$ eventually persuade themselves that it *does* simply to kid themselves that they haven't surrendered their self-respect and dignity. To do that they must start *believing* that the answer is 5 and the march of psychological fascism goosesteps apace absorbing more minds by direct assault or via illusory self-respect preservation.

Thought-policing has sunk to such depths that a device called 'Themis' intended for classrooms and social situations is programmed to detect and interrupt 'offensive' remarks. An alarm goes off lasting about two minutes if the device detects politically-incorrect language, jokes, perceived racial terms (everything is racist) and comments about 'body image'. Developers say it is an attempt to manifest political correctness as an ideology into a product' and is being trialled to moderate debate in UK schools and universities. Cut the bullshit and it's designed to *destroy* debate and limit the use of language in exactly the way George Orwell describes in *Nineteen-eighty-four* with his 'Newspeak' which purged the language of any word that actually meant anything. Orwell pointed out that as we think in words to delete all words that describe anything in detail is also to stop people even *thinking* about anything in detail. Cult-owned Woke's political correctness is Orwell's Newspeak under another name. Speech is the language of the mind and to target speech is to target the mind. It's all about the mind which will make perfect sense when we later explore the far-reaches of the rabbit hole. Woke has destroyed comedy because it doesn't have a sense of humour and that most balancing of traits – the ability to laugh at yourself. Wokers can never be accused of not taking themselves – *everything* – seriously enough.

You can observe a Woker or free-thinker by where the conclusion comes. Woker conclusions come at the start of the process. They are *told* what their conclusion must be. The Woke mind is told that all white people are privileged – even that great number sleeping in the streets and living in poverty. The conclusion comes first through the power of repetition and group-think and no amount of information to the contrary will breach the concrete of the original conclusion. If the power of logic and evidence comes even close to doing so it must be censored and silenced. The more ludicrous the conclusions become and the easier they are to demolish the more extreme and hysterical becomes the censorious mob. Cult billionaires funding this Woke insanity meanwhile hold back their laughter as best they can. See the 'Covid' and human-caused climate change hoaxes both promoted by the *same people* such as Bill Gates. A psychopath like Gates cares about human health and a planet which those he represents are systematically dismantling? *Are you serious*? People awakening from the awokening, or never conceding to its lunacy in the first place, always reach their conclusions at the *end* of the process and not the start. They observe the claims and counter claims and analyse the evidence before reaching a conclusion unique to them and they are open to having their original views changed by the power of information and experience. They are not so arrogant and naïve that they believe there is no more to know when there is *always* more to know. This will be obvious as this book progresses. You can see the power of programming over rational thought when the Woke mob demands that we believe that it's perfectly sane to have a bloke with a dick have access to the toilets and dressing rooms of women and girls simply because he claims to identify as a woman. You would assume that the rape and sexual assault of women and girls by dick-laden 'women' in once female-only facilities and prisons would awaken even the Woke-insane from their coma. But, no.

Women are womxn

The conclusion will not budge from its programmed solidity and instead those speaking out for women and girls are the target of Woke ire. This is classic mind control when perception is downloaded and the mind frozen into unquestioning press-enter compliance as a computer responds to encoded input. The UK Green Party prompted membership resignations by those that still retain at least some sanity when it appointed a male-born 'trans-woman' to head the party's 'women's group'. This is now the anti-women party that has referred to women as 'non-males' which is right on Cult message. Leicester University appointed a male student identifying as a trans-woman to be 'women's officer'. The same bunch renamed International Women's Week as 'Womxn's Week' in a perfect example of Woke virtue-signalling and self-obsession. Women's sport is being wrenched from those born women by 'women' in male bodies with greater strength and muscle mass. American male-bodied swimmer William Thomas was ranked 462 as a man, but then changed his name to 'Lia', said he was a woman, and became a women's swimming champion smashing records. 'Lia' has dangly bits. 'Her' body is that of a bloke and no one with a male body should be competing against women. End of. Start a new category for such swimmers. There, sorted. But the Cult does not want a fair solution when its agenda is served by what is happening. Women who complain are targeted by the brainless 'anti-hate' hate brigade as transphobes.

I couldn't care less what people choose to identify as – identify as a motorbike if you want – who the hell cares? Do what you like so long as you don't impose it on anyone else is my philosophy. On that basis imposing self-styled 'women' with dicks upon women and girls as they are today is a bloody outrage. The usual Woke bullying means that people are frightened of even defining what a woman is. We saw this with Woke judge Ketanji Brown Jackson at Senate hearings over her nomination to the US Supreme Court. She was asked to define a woman and she said that she couldn't because 'I am not a biologist'. Neither am I, but try this Ms Jackson: A woman is a human being born with female sexual organs. As women's rights campaigner Kellie-Jay Keen said: 'I'm not a vet, but I know what a dog is.' Keen said that 'the only people called women these days are actually men'. Jackson's reluctance – and that of most other people – to accurately define a woman comes from the fear of breaching Woke orthodoxy imposed by bullies. These extremes of derangement have a dark and sinister agenda behind them, as we shall see later, which even activists, or most of them, know nothing about. The famous Voltaire quote also comes to mind: 'Those that can make you believe absurdities can make you commit atrocities.' That, in truth, is what this is really all about along with other reasons. It's a psychological operation to seize control of the human psyche through a belief in blatant absurdities and the consequent deletion of self-respect. Once that is achieved the hijacked mind can then be directed to commit atrocity.

There is method in the madness which connects into a breathtaking web of interconnected deceit founded upon the control of information (perception) via the governments, 'education', mainstream media and the psychopathic platforms of Silicon Valley. Woke is also about developing weak people frightened of their own shadow who will not stand up to the excesses of authority. Weak and frightened people want authority to protect them from what authority has made them fear. For 'protect' see control. This is why the young are told to be upset, offended and outraged about anything that moves and much that doesn't. It's why 'trigger' warnings are issued to archaeology students about an upcoming 'well-preserved archaeological body' in case they find this 'a bit gruesome'. Forensic science students are given a verbal warning before images involving blood patterns, crime scenes and dead bodies. Pre-warnings are issued to Bible students about 'themes of sexual violence and abuse' or descriptions of the demise of Jesus. Then there are the 'microaggressions' about which 'minorities' are told to be upset no matter how ludicrously trivial and unintended. Is it any wonder that so many of the young generations reeled back in terror at 'Covid' propaganda and became the enforcers of mask fascism, jab fascism and isolation fascism? They have been primed all their lives to be so. It's all about perception given that it's all about mind. I feel sorry for them, I really do. They come out of the womb and so often programmed parents tell them what to believe; then programmed teachers tell them the same in tandem with the programmed mainstream media. Any access to other views questioning the moronic narrative is censored by social media and so all they ever hear is the moronic official version of *everything*. Why should we be surprised that Wokers believe shocking levels of nonsense when that is all they have ever heard? They are further encouraged to hate and demonise anyone telling them a different story. What chance have they got unless they regain control of their own mind?

Global Cult

I will be going way beyond the world of the human five senses in the multi-levelled control system founded on the simulation. I'll start, however, with the reality that everyone is aware of. The illusory 'physical' realm of apparently daily 'life'. We will see later that 'physical' is not physical at all, but you get my drift of where I am talking about. Open your eyes and there it is. This is where the five-senses tell us we 'are' even though we're not and where everything looks apart from everything else with empty 'space' in between. It is the world of buildings, vehicles, streets and fields, oxygen, carbon dioxide (the bastard), banking systems, corporations, governments and the perceptual trickery called schools, universities, media and Silicon Valley. The five-senses may deliver the illusion of apartness and that's all it is – illusion. In every way all is connected whether by a sea of consciousness beyond the limitations (laughable limitations) of human 'sight' or by the fact that all those banking systems, corporations, governments and perceptual tricksters are controlled by the same interconnected web or Global Cult in pursuit of the same agenda of total human control. We are seeing today only where that agenda has now reached in its long-sought ambition and, extreme as it has already become, there is a way to go yet. Where it is planned to end would make the most 'out there' dystopian sci-fi movie seem like Mary Poppins.

The Global Cult operates as a spider's web that has locked its sticky strands into every facet of human life as I have documented in fine detail in other books. This did not happen overnight or over decades; it's progressed over thousands of years as we perceive 'time'. You can comfortably pick up its journey to global control in ancient Mesopotamia, the 'Land Between Two Rivers', the Tigris and Euphrates, in Sumer and Babylon now called Iraq. This is a good starting point although it goes back further. Wherever the Cult has located its operational centre an empire has followed. The Babylonian and other Mesopotamian empires – which at one point encompassed Egypt – became the Roman Empire when the Cult established Rome. Later, when the Cult located its headquarters in Britain, the British Empire followed on which the sun never set so extensive was its global real estate. At the same time the Cult was infiltrating other countries of Europe and together they embarked on the acquisition of the world via the empires of Britain, France, Belgium, Germany, Spain, Portugal, the Netherlands, and Italy. During colonial occupation of pretty much the entire globe the Cult established subsidiary networks of secret societies and family bloodlines in each country and when colonialism apparently ended with 'decolonisation' this was no more than overt control being replaced by the much more potent covert control. At least with colonial occupation the oppressed knew who was controlling them. Covert control means the population has no idea who their real rulers are while believing that those they can see are making the decisions as political leaders and sundry dark suits in authority. This is fundamentally not the case. Colonisation out of Europe was when the Cult went global and this became even more so with the advent of 'globalisation' and the global centralisation of power in every area of life. For the few to control the many, decision-making has to be centralised and to control the world that has to be decision-making on a global level. The more you centralise power the more power you have to centralise even quicker and the process gets faster and faster which is exactly what has happened.

Money out of nothing

The Global Cult is a network of secret societies and semi-secret groups with an interlocking leadership that I call 'The Spider' from which the agenda for humanity emerges very much like a spider weaving its web until everything is caught and can wriggle no more (Fig 54). If it feels like that today well that's because it is. The Spider is not ultimately human and that's for later. The strands of the web close to the Spider are the most exclusive secret societies and most of these don't even have names which makes them harder to track and expose. Their members are the most 'in the know' and don't seek to put themselves on public

Figure 54: The Global Cult structure that allows the few to covertly control the direction of the world. (Image Neil Hague.)

display. Among the next layer are families like the Rothschilds and
Rockefellers, or rather their most influential personalities, who act as the
senior 'fixers' answering ultimately to the non-human force behind it all.
The Rothschilds created the planetary mass-control structure known as
the modern banking system, the origins of which can be traced to
Babylon. Lending people money that doesn't exist called 'credit' and
charging interest on it has so long been the centre of human control. It
enslaves the human flies in a web of debt which, when it cannot be
'repaid', allows the Cult banking system to seize assets like homes,
businesses, land and resources in return for the non-repayment of
fictional 'credit' *plus interest*. This 'plus interest' is crucial. Most people
have no idea how 'money' is created. It's something to do with
government isn't it? Well, no, actually. 'Money' is created
overwhelmingly by private banks within the Cult system making loans
of fresh-air 'money' called 'credit' that has never and will never exist
except in delusional theory. Governments could create money interest-
free and circulate it among the population interest-free. Instead the very
currency – the unit of exchange that allows commerce – comes into
existence at the start as an interest-bearing debt. This is insanity in any
rational society yet perfectly sane in an irrational one. "Laws' have been
passed that allow something called fractional reserve lending and these
'laws' are the result of the Cult controlling both the banking network
and governments. In simple terms fractional reserve lending means that
banks can 'lend' 'money' they don't have called 'credit' which is 'money'
that does not exist except as a theoretical concept and figures on a
screen.

The other built-in catch-all is that this credit is 'lent' at interest while
the interest is never created. Go to a bank to take a 'loan' of say £100,000
and the bank will issue £100,000 of credit through its computer system.
You agree to 'pay back' £100,000 plus interest and here's the catch: The
interest is never created even as 'credit'. Only the principal of the 'loan'
is brought into theoretical existence. This happens with every 'loan' and
means there is never ever enough 'money' in circulation to pay back all
the debt principal and interest. People losing their homes, businesses,
land and resources is built into the very structure of the banking system
on purpose. In boom times (instigated by an *expansion* of credit that banks
circulate as 'loans') this is less noticeable; but during a financial
downturn or depression (instigated by the *reduction* of credit that banks
circulate as 'loans') this is put on public display as the bankrupt hand
over their assets to the banks for not repaying credit plus interest that
has never, does not and will never exist. For many this situation is
inevitable given that there is simply not enough 'money' in circulation to
pay back all the outstanding 'loans' plus interest because the 'interest' is
never created. Banking is quite simply a criminal activity and should be

treated as such. This grotesque system is directed from the secret levels of the inner-web where you find especially the Rothschilds. I hear people say that banking and the rest of the fresh-air 'financial world' is all about greed. Yes, that is of course a major factor although not the main one for the Cult inner-core. The main one is *control*. The Cult has constructed a global system that has connected choice to the ownership of 'money' or wealth in its various forms. The more 'money' you have the more choices you can make and what is freedom? It is the ability to make choices. The more choices you have the freer you are and vice-versa. Control of money (who has it and who doesn't) controls freedom (who has it and who doesn't). This is the real reason for why the world is structured as it is on the foundation of illusory 'money'. The banking system is indeed organised crime and it's owned by the Cult as its very foundation of global control.

From hidden to the seen

As we expand further out from the Spider, those most exclusive secret societies and the levels of the Rothschilds and Rockefellers, we come next to the secret societies that we do know about in terms of their existence if not their manipulations. These include the Freemasons (the inner elite not the rank and file); the Knights of Malta (very associated with global finance); Knights Templar; Opus Dei; the inner sanctum of the Jesuit Order; and the Skull and Bones Society in America connected to so many US Presidents and those in other influential positions. The secret society network is ginormous and answers ultimately to the same masters. Most of their members don't know this due to fierce compartmentalisation into levels of 'degree' (degree of knowledge). You only progress to the next level when you are considered worthy or safe to be given the knowledge that exists there. Most Freemasons, for example, never progress beyond the bottom three levels of degree, the so-called 'Blue Degrees', when there are 33 levels of the Scottish Rite (Fig 55 overleaf). Even at the apparent peak of these secret society pyramids the chosen are fed into levels above that which other members don't even know exist. Here the real action happens from expanded knowledge of where the world is really being taken, by whom, and to what end. I call these the Illuminati degrees to make them distinct from the 'individual' secret societies that feed into them (Fig 56 overleaf). Secret society initiates and those from semi-secret offshoots are placed in positions of power and influence throughout the national and global system. All answer in the end to the Spider and its agenda even though the less significant ones won't even know there is a Spider. Comparatively few positions in any organisation need to be controlled to control the entire structure. You need only secure positions which make key decisions and dictate who is hired and fired. This way you can

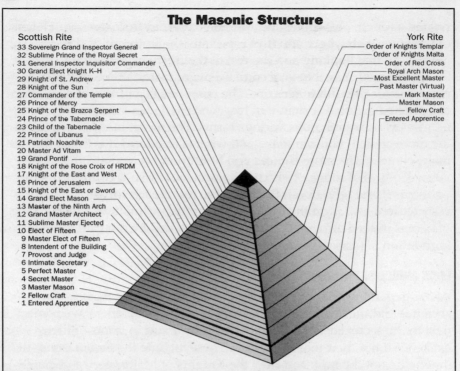

Figure 55: The Freemasonic structure illustrates the compartmentalisation that isolates secret society members into degrees of knowledge – degrees of *ignorance* except for the inner core.

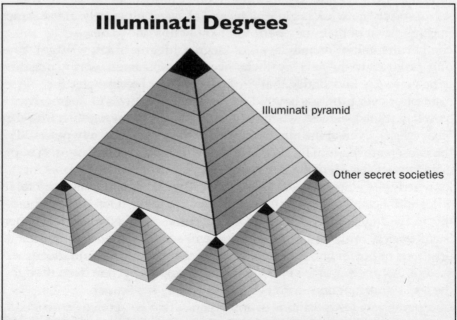

Figure 56: The Illuminati degrees take carefully-chosen initiates from the top of other secret societies to be given knowledge even the official levels of secret societies don't have.

quickly fill the personnel with the psychopathically knowing (the few), the psychopathically unknowing (the more) and the simply compliant that do whatever they are told without question or dissent (the great majority). The world is controlled by psychopaths and unknowingly administered on their behalf by compliant idiocy. Never was this more obvious than in the 'Covid' era.

We now reach that point in the web where the hidden meets the seen. Here we have what I call the 'cusp' organisations whose role is to take the agenda emanating from the Spider through the unseen realm of secret societies and play it out into the world of the seen via governments and their agencies, corporations, mainstream media, Silicon Valley platforms, 'health' systems, 'education', and such like. Cusp organisations are semi-secret in that they operate ostensibly in the public arena while pursuing a secret agenda below the surface. These include the Bilderberg Group, Council on Foreign Relations in the United States, Trilateral Commission, the Royal Institute of International Affairs in London, and the Club of Rome which was created by the Cult in 1968 to exploit environmental concerns to justify the centralisation of

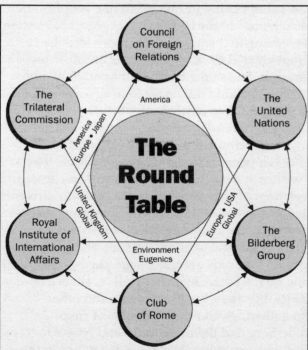

global power over the fine detail of people's lives (Fig 57). From the Club of Rome came the hoax of 'human-caused climate change' which is not actually happening (see *Everything You Need To Know But Have Never Been Told* for the fine detail). The Bilderberg Group is named after the Bilderberg Hotel in Oosterbeek, the Netherlands, where it held its first official meeting in 1954. This is publicly secretive although far less so than it used to be before we in the

Figure 57: Some of the cusp organisations coordinated by a London-based Rothschild-created secret society called the Round Table which was first headed by Rothschild agent Cecil Rhodes from the latter years of the 19th century. Also at this cusp is the extraordinary global network of think tanks and non-governmental organisations (NGOs).

alternative media shone the light on its manipulations. Also located at this cusp are the seemingly millions of 'think tanks' and non-governmental organisations (NGOs) including the Open Society Foundations of Cult operative George Soros which have played such a central part in funding and orchestrating the rise of the Cult-serving 'Woke' mentality; Cult-serving divide and rule operation Black Lives Matter (BLM); and the fantastic movements of people from the Middle East and Africa into Europe and across the systematically unprotected southern border of the United States from South and Central America (and now the much wider world). The massive displacement of Ukrainians after the Russian invasion is all part of this on the Cult chessboard to change global demographics on the road to a one-'culture' world through cultural fusion into a perceptual monoculture.

Two million people a year are walking across the open US border unchallenged since 'Biden' came into office with many given government-funded flights from secluded and guarded airports to settle across the country in a calculated policy of changing the cultural dynamic of America. The racist targeting of white people is all part of this strategy and the same is happening in Europe. White people are in the gunsights because they represent the biggest racial group in Western society which the Cult is seeking to dismantle and absorb into its world system. Once whites are subjugated the Cult will come for other racial groups until all are subjugated. Mass unchecked immigration of other cultures into the West was predicted in my books long ago when I said that people like Soros were working to create a situation in which so many headed for the US southern border that they would be unstoppable in tandem with government policies to encourage that outcome. Precisely this has happened. How did I know? It has all been long planned. The Cult wishes to destroy all countries and any sense of nationhood so that everywhere can be absorbed into a centrally-driven, technologically-controlled global fascist dictatorship. Cusp organisations and think tanks have the role of manipulating policy consensus in government and the system in general to allow the Cult (the Spider) to dictate events and direction. Hundreds of millions are playing their part in doing this while having no idea there even is a Cult let alone a Spider. Influential people in politics, business, banking, media and other institutions are invited to gatherings and memberships of cusp organisations such as Bilderberg and the think tanks and NGOs to have their minds honed into a consensus policy that takes the world in the Cult-desired, Spider-desired, direction. What is that direction? We're living it.

Looking without seeing

From the cusp organisations the Cult web expands out into human society and 'everyday life.' This is the realm of the seen, the five senses, where everything appears random and apart from everything else. People look at the world, but most do not see. There is neither randomness nor apartness. Governments and their agencies, the financial system, corporations, mainstream media, Silicon Valley platforms, 'health' systems (including the World Health Organization), and 'education' seem to have no obvious connections as people observe daily happenings. In fact they are all structured like secret societies and employ the same techniques of knowledge control. Those at the top know their real motivation and reason for being while those at the bottom do not. Those in between know to varying degrees depending on their place in the hierarchy. The big penny-drop comes when you realise that all these organisations and agencies are connected by the Cult web if you go deep enough in their structure. This realisation, which was shown to me decades ago, makes sense of the world and daily events. For example why would Silicon Valley platforms censor those that question and expose the ludicrously lying narrative of the World Health Organization (WHO) with regard to 'Covid'? That would appear to be inexplicable when they are supposed to be forums for information and opinion exchange. It's not so bewildering when you realise that the WHO was created by the Cult Rockefeller family in 1948 to concentrate global power over health under one roof and that Facebook, Google (which owns YouTube) and Twitter etc. are Cult-controlled organisations (see end-of-Chapter Five postscript about Elon Musk and Twitter). Facebook and Google were seed-funded by Cult money through various sources including DARPA, the technological development arm of the Cult-owned Pentagon, and In-Q-Tel, the technology seed-funding agency of the Cult-owned CIA.

The World Health Organization which has dictated 'Covid' response policy to all its member countries worldwide is controlled today through funding by close and long-time Rockefeller family associate Bill Gates. The Rockefeller-Gates family connection goes way back and I have seen genealogy that claims that the two families are from the same original bloodline. Plans are now underway between the Cult-owned, *privately*-owned, World Health Organization, Cult-owned European Union, and other Cult-owned member countries to agree a legally-binding 'treaty' to allow a centrally-dictated (Cult-dictated) response by the WHO to all future 'pandemics'. What the WHO (Rockefellers, Gates and the Cult) say that countries must do they must do. The globally-centralised control of 'health' policy which the Rockefellers created the World Health Organization to secure would have arrived. Alongside this would be the deletion of any alternative media to expose the lies that spew force from these psychopaths. In that sense the 'Covid' hoax, extreme as it is, can be seen as merely one stage in a much bigger plan.

The 'Covid' card will be played again – as it is in China as I write this –
and they have many other pandemic cards to play especially once the
next level of WHO control is in place through the 'treaty'. Once again it
is all about the centralisation of power on a global level.

Cult permits the Cult

It also becomes clear why Big Pharma companies invariably get
permission for their fake 'Covid' vaccines to be used on whoever they
want with no proper testing or long-term trials. Mass-murdering Big
Pharma is owned by the mass-murdering Cult and so are the drug and
vaccine regulatory agencies such as the mass-murdering US Centers for
Disease Control and Prevention (CDC), mass-murdering Food and Drug
Administration (FDA), and mass-murdering UK Medicines and
Healthcare products Regulatory Agency (MHRA). The Cult is asking the
Cult for permission to advance the Cult's fake vaccine agenda and why
wouldn't that be granted? These psychopathically-corrupt 'regulators'
are not there to protect the public from harm. They are in bed with the
drug companies and they have sanctioned emergency approval for fake
vaccines despite all the fatalities and destruction of health to be given to
younger and younger age groups. The Cult wants the global population
subjected to their deadly and genetically-transforming content and Cult
agents in the regulatory agencies seek to ensure that it happens. Those
involved in any way in this are driven by pure evil. The pharmaceutical
cartel was established by the Rockefeller family through oil tycoon John
D. Rockefeller (1839-1937) who also instigated the demise of alternative
forms of healing and imposed allopathic or scalpel and drug 'medicine'
on humanity. Rockefeller died at the age of 97 with his personal
homeopath at his bedside while seeking to eliminate homeopathy for
everyone else. Ever wondered why so many of these Cult major players
live such long lives? They don't get the same treatment that everyone
else does. The Cult Rockefeller family established Big Pharma and the
World Health Organization which is part of the United Nations that the
Rockefellers also played a central role in creating. The UN building in
New York stands on phenomenally valuable land given for free by the
Rockefeller family. Rockefeller means Cult just as Rothschild means
Cult. The Cult has secured control of government, global finance and
corporate commerce and most importantly it has seized ownership of
'education', the mainstream media and Silicon Valley platforms –
perception. At national and international levels this combination forms
the permanent government that continues unchecked no matter who is
in theoretical political power. Parties come and go (controlled by the
same people anyway) while the permanent government is always there
(Fig 58). I have highlighted this structure for decades and now it's been
given a name, the 'Deep State'.

THE PERMANENT GOVERNMENT ('DEEP STATE')
THE CULT
SECRET SOCIETIES
FINANCE/BANKING
MILITARY/INTELLIGENCE
'BIG PHARMA' MEDICAL POLICY
GLOBAL CORPORATIONS
GOVERNMENT ADMINISTRATION
LAW/COURTS
MEDIA (SILICON VALLEY)
POLITICS AND 'ELECTED' GOVERNMENT
'THE PEOPLE'

Figure 58: The Cult structure of control in countries and globally.

All Cult influence and control comes from hijacking human perception and, in turn, perception comes from information. We form our perceptions from information received from whatever source. If the Cult is going to dictate perception – thus behaviour – it must dictate what people see and hear through ownership of the means of communication and censor anything that offers another way of seeing self, the world and events. The Cult created major social media platforms while buying others and the now insane censorship is the work of the Cult via its gofers like Mark Zuckerberg at Facebook (Meta), Sergey Brin and Larry Page at Google and Alphabet, Susan Wojcicki at YouTube, and Parag Agrawal at Twitter who replaced the pothead Jack Dorsey as CEO. Agrawal was born in India and only moved to the United States in 2005 to study at Stanford University. Now, at least officially, he controls what Americans can communicate on his platform along with the rest of the human race. His attitude to freedom is captured in this quote from 2020: 'Our role is not to be bound by the First Amendment [which in theory guarantees free speech], but our role is to serve a healthy public conversation ... [and to] focus less on thinking about free speech, but thinking about how the times have changed.' Translated from the Orwellian that means: 'Our role is not to be bound by the First Amendment, but only to let you see what my masters want you to see.' Agrawal was appointed specifically to do that and he's willingly doing it. As cable news host Tucker Carlson said of Agrawal: 'A single man who has total and undisguised contempt for America's most basic values gets to decide what Americans are allowed to talk about.' We'll see if Agrawal survives the purchase of Twitter (officially) by Elon 'I'm your side, honest' Musk.

Cult operatives have long been creating and acquiring mainstream newspapers, magazines, radio and television, to the point where the media is owned by a shockingly few corporations with again an interlocking leadership answering to the Cult. This explains the extraordinary depth, breadth, and coordination of censorship and lies in the 'Covid' era in which the same deceit and cover-up of the truth has been slavishly dispensed by fake 'journalists' across the globe. 'Independent' search engine DuckDuckGo abandoned its no-censorship policy by announcing in March, 2022, that 'Russian disinformation' (who decides?) would be down-ranked in its listings. Thankfully, two others, Brave Search and Presearch, said they would hold their ground on unbiased listings. The Cult further controls the narratives of America's nightly talk show hosts such as the incredibly unfunny John Oliver, Stephen Colbert, Jimmy Kimmel and James Corden. Every evening they parrot the Cult narrative while ridiculing or demonising those that challenge the fascist orthodoxy. They haven't got a brain cell between them and that's why they've got the job. Colbert with his multi-million annual salary said he didn't care if fuel went to £15 a gallon because paying that to support Ukraine was good for the soul. In fact, all the price-hikes were doing is harming Americans – this bloke's audience. These people don't give a damn about you. They all have their tongues up the arse of the ruling class to ensure ongoing employment. Whatever they say is what the Cult wants you to believe.

I was deleted from all major Internet platforms as early as the spring of 2020 when I began very publicly and successfully exposing the 'Covid' lie as a gigantic global hoax. Everything I said then has either been confirmed to be true or has never been proved to be wrong. You can read my comprehensive demolition of the very existence of the SARS-CoV-2 'virus' in *Perceptions of a Renegade Mind*. I'll also include some of the major points later on. What I said was true about the 'virus' never being shown to exist in any scientific paper and that the 'virus' is a computer-created genome forgery. I was right in April, 2020, when I said the PCR test was not testing for the 'virus' because it *can't*; that lockdowns were about targeting the economy and livelihoods and had nothing to do with health; that masks were useless in protecting from 'viral' particles so tiny they can only be seen under an electron microscope; and that masks were doing serious harm to people in terms of respiratory health (how ironic) and psychology. The latter is especially true with children and young people. I was right that the 'virus' had been hoaxed to justify the 'vaccination' of the population for very sinister reasons. All these points that I made in the spring of 2020 have now been confirmed by a tidal wave of evidence and even official admission in many cases; but I was censored and banned. Why? *Misinformation* which is Cult-speak for the truth. Even if what I said had not been correct I still have a right to my opinion in anything that credibly claims to be a free society. The very foundation of freedom is the right to be wrong. Once that right is lost some authority decides what is right and wrong instead of the people through free thought and so you have tyranny.

Censorship: The calling card of tyranny

We have reached the stage now where doctors and scientists eminent in their field are censored and deleted for challenging the infinitely contradictory and blatantly obvious mendacity of the Cult's 'Covid' and 'vaccine' narrative. Anyone telling the truth or giving people a platform to tell the truth is targeted by the 'liberal' Woke fascist mob to be silenced (Fig 59). We saw this with American podcast host Joe Rogan after he gave the opportunity for experts in their field to challenge the 'Covid' narrative on his

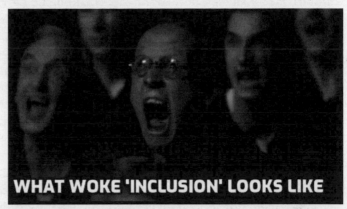

WHAT WOKE 'INCLUSION' LOOKS LIKE

Figure 59: Cult-created-and-funded Woke is a classic satanic inversion with 'inclusion' meaning 'exclusion' and 'democracy' meaning 'fascism'. This is a scene from the daily two minutes of hate ritual in Orwell's *Nineteen-eighty-four*.

Spotify show which was reaching audiences of some eleven million. It came to a head when two guests exposed the dangers and catastrophic consequences of 'Covid' fake vaccines which do not fulfil the previous criteria for what constitutes a vaccine. They are gene therapy genetically manipulating the body with mRNA ('messenger' or rather modified RNA) synthetic genetic material in a process *never used on humans before*. Stefan Oelrich, president of Bayer's pharmaceuticals division, made it clear to 6,000 participants at the World Health Summit in Berlin in 2021 that mRNA 'Covid' vaccines are not vaccines, but gene therapy that were part of a 'Bio Revolution'. He said that if the jabs were marketed as what they really are the public would refuse them:

> We are really taking that leap [to drive innovation] – us as a company, Bayer – in cell and gene therapies … ultimately the mRNA vaccines are an example for that cell and gene therapy. I always like to say: If we had surveyed two years ago in the public – 'would you be willing to take a gene or cell therapy and inject it into your body?' – we probably would have had a 95 percent refusal rate.

You don't tell them what the fake vaccines really are. You tell them they will protect people from 'Covid' when that's not what they are designed to do at all as we've seen. Crucial to this is the censorship of anyone who will tell people the truth. The more qualified they are to do that, the more urgently they must be silenced. This includes insider whistleblowers who have revealed official data showing the fake vaccine 'trials' were fraudulent and were not 'trials' at all. In Rogan's case he spoke with Dr Robert Malone, a pioneer of the mRNA technique used in 'Covid' fake vaccines, and American cardiologist, Dr Peter McCullough, a vice chief of internal medicine at Baylor University Medical Center, who said rightly and *provably* that the fake 'pandemic' was deliberately planned and the fake vaccines were killing thousands of people. We then went through the usual stage show involving Cult-cowed Spotify and jokes like system-serving 'rocker' (ha, ha) Neil Young and singer Joni Mitchell. Young and Mitchell removed their music from Spotify in protest at Rogan's 'misinformation' (the 'misinformation' of two experts in their field). Prince Harry and Meghan Markle, that pair of professional prats and Wokers, said they were 'concerned' at the 'misinformation' which is all you need to confirm that the 'misinformation' they were 'concerned' about had to be true. Mr and Mrs Prat were not concerned enough to withdraw from their gargantuan Spotify contract for producing utter crap. Spotify of course caved – it's in the stage show script – by taking down 70 Rogan podcasts initially and said it would add 'warnings' to any content on the platform questioning the official 'Covid' narrative. Spotify boasted how it had already deleted 20, 000 other videos that questioned 'Covid' and the fake 'vaccines'. It was revealed during the Rogan controversy that the top owner of Spotify is also the top owner of 'Covid' fake vaccine maker Moderna. This is the Scotland-founded asset management operation Baillie Gifford and Company which owns nearly 46 million shares in Moderna valued at more than $11.6 billion. They are the biggest shareholder in Spotify with 22 million shares worth more than $22 billion.

Dutch podcaster Jorn Luka was banned by Spotify in this period for posting an interview with me which should not have been a surprise when Spotify banned me in the spring of 2020. Rogan has refused to interview me in all the years of his podcast on YouTube before moving to Spotify. I have no idea why given all the subjects that I cover that relate to his content. I doubt it will happen now with censors looking over his shoulder. Rogan made the mistake of appearing to apologise for his content and saying he would try to have more 'balance' which means having people on with official opinions. 99.9 per cent of the mainstream media promotes the 'official opinion' and bans any other. Yet Rogan's podcast as a rare example of the semi-mainstream offering another view has to be 'balanced' with the official opinion. It's a joke. When Rogan has these people on, I hope he asks the questions and makes the points they will have no chance of credibly answering. We'll see. We have the cancel culture when people get banned, but this is given more power by what I call the 'sackcloth culture' where people fall to their knees and apologise to the mob in an attempt to appease them. The mob is never appeased. The more you give, the more it wants, until it destroys you. I have found that ignoring their inanity is the best way to respond which means no response at all except continuing to do what you do. They soon give up when you won't bend and give them no encouragement.

Only the weak and mendacious censor

Censorship is not a sign of power. It is confirmation of weakness. They know their narrative is child's play to demolish and they simply silence, or seek to, those who demolish it. I don't want to censor anyone. I believe in freedom of expression and anyway I am confident that what I say can stand its ground in any debate. The Cult and its operatives know that their narrative can't survive the light of scrutiny and from this point of weakness they have to censor. Zuckerberg, Brin, Page, Wojcicki, Agrawal, and everyone else involved in the lies and censorship worldwide are all guilty of crimes against humanity for all the deaths and life-changing injuries the fake vaccines have caused to people who may have made a different decision had they not had their right to informed consent destroyed by these censors. None of those names and others involved across the world will care about those consequences. To do what they do in the first place they have to be empathy-deleted, compassion-deleted, heart-deleted, psychopaths. Another aspect of information and perception control are 'fact-checker' organisations that have ballooned in the 'Covid' and pre-'Covid' years like the Gates-funded NewsGuard and others such as Full Fact, Snopes and Reuters. Their job is to 'fact-check' all challenges to the official narrative of everything and to find that any questioning is not justified and the official narrative is always correct. How these people live with themselves is a profound mystery. Cult-owned Silicon Valley corporations censor posts on the basis of the Cult-owned fake 'fact-checkers' dubbing them 'misinformation' no matter what the scale of evidence to support what is said.

One of the worst is Elite-funded NewsGuard (NewsSlant) that has 'partnered with the American Federation of Teachers (AFT), the second largest US teachers' union, which pressed for mandatory 'Covid' fake vaccination and masks for schoolchildren. It is therefore fascistic by definition and Cult agenda to its ideological DNA. This 'partnership' involves telling schoolchildren what they should believe and not believe under the guise of helping them to 'navigate a sea of online misinformation'. In the Cult context 'misinformation' means 'the truth' or closer to the truth. Much that these 'fact-checkers' dubbed 'misinformation' with regard to 'Covid', tyrannical restrictions and fake

vaccines, has turned out to be true. As an article at
Childrenshealthdefense.org pointed out: ' … a closer look at
NewsGuard's advisers, partners and investors reveals a web of interests
closely linked to the military, intelligence, media and political
establishments, as well as to the world of corporate marketing –
including an advertising agency sued for illegally marketing opioids.'
One member of the NewsGuard Advisory Board is Michael Hayden,
CIA Director during the Boy Bush presidency. Schools are programming
centres now, nothing more, and teachers who support it and stand for it,
led by Cult-co-opted teaching unions, are a bloody disgrace to the
children who supposed to be in their care.

Imran Ahmed: Professional censor

Another character that requires a mention is professional censor, Imran
Ahmed, a banker and activist with the UK's super-Woke Labour Party.
Ahmed heads up the Center for Countering Digital Hate, or as I prefer
to call it, Center for Digital Hate. Note the American spelling of Center
for what is supposed to be a UK operation. Ahmed's modus operandi
has been to demand that media organisations ban and silence his targets
for 'racism' and 'hate speech'. This is seriously rich when these 'anti-
haters' seek to demonise (attract hatred) to those they don't want the
public to hear. Most telling and revealing was how when the 'Covid'
card was played Ahmed and his Digital Hate morphed immediately
from using 'hate' as the reason to ban people from public discourse to
attacking them for questioning the official 'Covid' narrative and later the
fake vaccines. It was a swift and extraordinary shapeshift. The same
happened when he targeted information and opinion at odds with the
official narrative of the Russian invasion of Ukraine. Ahmed told the
pathetic *Mother Jones* magazine: 'There are particular individuals within
the anti-vaccine world who are amenable to pro-Russian propaganda.'
Ahmed shapeshifts faster than the Queen, but always with a common
thread – censoring those who question and expose official narratives.
Who is amenable to Cult propaganda, Mr Ahmed? We know who you
are, we know why you do what you do, and we know why you get so
much access to the mainstream media, Mr Ahmed. If you were good at
what you do you would not make it so obvious, but you're not. Good,
that is.

Ahmed, I think it is fair to say, is not the brightest man ever to move
his lips. His contacts mean that he doesn't have to be when softball
questions from softball people are his daily diet. His backbone twitches
at the very thought of debating live with me which is why he refuses. I
would have him for breakfast, dinner and tea and he knows it. His
modus operandi is to feign outrage at social media organisations
allowing any remaining dissenting points of view while giving those

same organisations the excuse they want to censor even more. Ahmed led the charge to have me banned from YouTube, Facebook and Twitter and as always crows with delight at every 'fellow human' that he denies the rights that he demands for himself. He's such a lovely man. Ahmed is treated as an 'expert' on 'misinformation' by the mainstream media and politicians when he clearly represents a greater agenda for mass censorship of opinion and information that challenge official fairy tales.

One question you will never hear a mainstream Cult lackey interviewer ask him is this: Who the hell are you to decide what the public can and cannot hear?' It's much better for their career to say 'Yes, Mr Ahmed, no, Mr Ahmed, is there anything else you would like to say or anyone else you want to demonise, Mr Ahmed?' I watched him interviewed by Woker Cathy Newman on the UK's *Channel 4 News* once. My only regret was not having a sickbag to hand. A supporter of Davidicke.com made it his business to investigate the web that connects with Ahmed, Digital Hate, and the enormous network of censorship organisations, personnel, and funders that extend across the Atlantic into the United States and the fully-Woke, fully-Cult-owned, Democratic Party. Ahmed began to appear on the American Cult-owned Woke media and once again he is given free rein to demonise whoever he chooses. One of his targets has been the thoroughly-decent Robert Kennedy Jr who is doing magnificent work exposing the fake vaccines and the Cult-owned Big Pharma cartel including a deeply researched exposure of mass murdering psychopathic 'health chief' Anthony Fauci in the book, *The Real Anthony Fauci*. Why would Imran Ahmed want to silence Kennedy, I wonder? I can't think. I mean, who would benefit?

People say that if you don't like Big Tech censorship start your own platform. When you do that you have government censors coming after you as they then target independent sites. The UK government's Imran Ahmed-promoted 'Online Safety' Bill is going through Parliament as I write. The bill claims to be addressing Internet child sexual abuse, terrorist material, racial hatred and incitement to violence. The *real* reason is to destroy the alternative media with crippling fines if the government's fascist broadcast regulator Ofcom deems that content is 'harmful'. The content can be perfectly lawful and legal. No matter – if Ofcom decrees it could be 'harmful' then it must be deleted or fines and even jail will follow. Ofcom is so bad that it was created by Tony Blair in 2001 and is now headed by Melanie Dawes, a career bureaucrat with no media experience. She was previously Permanent Secretary of the Ministry of Housing, Communities and Local Government, and has worked for the Treasury, Revenue and Customs, and the infamous Cabinet Office from where the 'Covid' response was orchestrated by an army of behavioural psychologists. Media experience for a UK broadcast media 'regulator' is not necessary when you have simply been put in there to do a pre-ordained job. Dawes took over in February, 2020, just as 'Covid' was kicking off and censorship was required for those exposing the lies of her masters.

An Ofcom decree in the spring of 2020 effectively had me banned from all UK mainstream broadcast media (they spinelessly complied naturally) when I exposed 'Covid' as a hoax and how the PCR test was not testing for the 'virus'. Both were true as ever more people now realise. The truth, however, is no defence against censorship tyranny. It's the *reason* for censorship tyranny. Ofcom's Melanie Dawes must face a Nuremberg jury for again denying the public informed consent under the post-war Nuremberg Code designed to stop the abuse of people through medication without knowledge of its effects and potential consequences. Dawes denied that informed consent through censorship of what the UK broadcast media was allowed to say and who it was allowed to interview. Ofcom has been established as the government censor of all broadcast and Internet information that the Cult doesn't want you to see. Blair played the same 'harm' scam when he introduced 'emotional harm' as a reason for the state to steal children from loving parents. Tens of thousands have been mercilessly parted on that basis. When social service psychopaths can find no physical harm reason to steal kids they invent spurious 'emotional harm' that is rubber-stamped by a judge in a secret family court that cannot be reported. Now we see this being played out with Ofcom and 'harmful content' which includes 'misinformation' – that Cult euphemism for the truth. The Cult-owned fascist Trudeau regime in Canada is seeking to do the same as I write with Bill-C11 to 'protect Canadians from harmful content'. The bill would give the government, as in fascist Britain, complete control over what you're allowed to post and see, and websites you can access. The global pattern is blatant. The Department of Homeland Fascism in the United States now officially equates questioning and challenging government narratives with 'terrorism'. 'Hate', 'harm', and 'terrorism' are only what the Cult decrees them to be as we saw when Facebook/Meta suspended its 'hate guidelines' by allowing people in Ukraine, Russia, Poland, Latvia, Lithuania, Estonia, Slovakia, Hungary and Romania to call for violence against Russians 'in the context of the Ukrainian invasion'. Internal emails reported by Reuters told content moderators that posts calling for the death of Vladimir Putin were also allowed. You can post hate so long as you hate the people we want you to hate.

Big Tech and the media are operating as full-time propagandists for the Cult with the Hunter Biden laptop story a most blatant example. In the closing weeks of the 2020 presidential election Joe Biden's corrupt and moronic son (it's obviously genetic) was revealed by his own computer to have been running a cash-for-influence scheme in league with his father and other family members. This secured millions for the Bidens from overseas sources, most notably Ukraine, but also Qatar, Russia, and China. Joe Biden was selling policy changes affecting those countries while vice-president to Cult-owned Barack Obama. The revelations should obviously have ended Biden's presidential ambitions. Instead Big Tech censored circulation of the story while Big Media trashed its significance and dubbed it 'Russian disinformation'. The Cult-owned *New York Times,* which had helped to bury the story, admitted in March, 2022, that it was true. Those who take themselves seriously had known this from the start. When the *Times* admission finally came, of course, Biden was president and the job was done. 'Fact-checker' NewsGuard had said all along that the Biden laptop story was 'misinformation' which probably came from Russia. Were they banned from *anywhere* for lying? Oh, no. It was the right kind of lying so they were okay. Censorship is about manipulation of perception which is about manipulation of mind. I say again: It's all about *mind*. I will come back to this recurring theme that will be central to everything as we dive deeper and deeper into the levels of deceit.

Nazi normalisation

I have said and written for decades that the goal of the Cult is to reach a point of information control in which no one ever sees or hears anything that isn't sanctioned by authority. This is what the UK Online Safety Bill and its like in Canada and elsewhere are really seeking to achieve. Orwell depicted just such a society long ago. It means that no matter what scale of censorship you now see we are nowhere near the end of that particular road. 'Covid' was designed to make censorship 'normal' and accepted. We saw how seamlessly that crossed from what you could see about 'Covid' to what you could see about the Russian invasion of Ukraine. 'Evil anti-vaxxers' who must be attacked and silenced became 'evil Russians' who must be attacked and silenced no matter what their views or background. Orwell's concept of a daily two minutes of hate has become hours and hours of it on Twitter. Two fascist American Senators claiming to be Democrats introduced a bill to 'legalise' censorship and criminalise freedom of speech in breach of the free-speech defending First Amendment. They are a pair of morons called Ben Ray Luján and Chris Murphy. The latter moron said:

Throughout this pandemic, the impact of misinformation has been devastating. Rumours and conspiracy theories about the efficacy of masking or the safety of vaccines still run rampant on social media and have caused thousands of deaths that could have been prevented.

This legislation will help us get smart about how to tackle misinformation and

effectively promote science-based health information, especially as we
continue fighting Covid-19 and prepare for future public health emergencies.

What a monumental liar when the opposite is true. Staggering numbers
have been killed by the fake vaccines. You see the key point there: '...
prepare for future public health emergencies.' The alternative media
threw spanners in their works galore despite all the censorship. Now
they seek to delete all other evidence and voices ready for the next
'health crisis' which they have long planned. Biden's surgeon general
'Dr' Vivek Murthy, another Cult-owned fascist, formally demanded
major Cult tech platforms hand over data relating to 'the scale of Covid-
19 misinformation on social networks, search engines, crowd-sourced
platforms, e-commerce platforms and instant messaging systems'.
Murthy sought information from the tech tyrants about 'major sources
of Covid-19 misinformation' that differed from the official narrative – a
narrative long shown to be a cesspit of lies from start to finish. 'This is
about protecting the nation's health', Murthy said, engaging in a classic
example of Cult inversion. These disgusting people must face a
Nuremberg-type trial when sanity gains control of the human mind.

The web at work

Cult web coordination explains why so many of those alternative voices
censored by Cult media corporations have also been banned by Cult-
owned financial corporations in a further effort to stop them
functioning. I was banned by Cult-owned PayPal and I wasn't even
using it! Canadian truckers raised $10 million for their mass protest
against Cult-gofer Prime Minister Justin Trudeau and his 'Covid'
fascism through the crowd-funding website, GoFundMe. The coward
Trudeau ran for the hills when tens of thousands of truckers arrived in
the capital Ottawa from all over Canada and claimed he was isolating
after testing positive for 'Covid' (despite being triple-jabbed with the
fake vaccine he was trying to impose on the truckers to 'protect
Canadians from Covid'). He was lying, of course, and he was really
isolating from the truckers who with that financial backing had the
money to stay in Ottawa until Trudeau's (the Cult's) fake vaccine
mandates were dropped. The Cult knew the money was crucial and
GoFundMe froze the fund and would not allow donations for the
truckers from the public to go to the truckers. GoFundMe even said at
one point that the money would be given to charities that it chose. This
is how the Cult web works and GoFundMe needs to be boycotted by
everyone who has a smear of respect for freedom and integrity. More
about GoFundMe's connections shortly.

Web networks further reveal why and how we have seen such
coordination and mutual support between Woke organisations claiming

to be 'anti-system' and billionaire corporations in the field of tech and commerce of all kinds. The Cult owns them all from Black Lives Matter and the transgender movement to Apple, Microsoft and George Soros. Those paying attention will see that all the demands of Wokers' in all their forms fit exactly with the agenda of the Cult. They include everything from 'Covid' fascist orthodoxy to divide and rule on the grounds of race; mass immigration to change national cultures and demographics; transgender hysteria to change human genetics (more later); and human-caused 'climate change' founded on lies so outrageous it takes the breath away which is handing control of global energy to the East at the expense of the Cult-targeted West. Wokeness has been indoctrinated with ever greater extremes through the fake 'education' system to instil the ignorant subservience to authority that Woke has become and was designed from the start to become. Organisations like Extinction Rebellion protest 'against authority' and demand the very green fascism agenda that authority (the Cult) wants to happen instigated through the Club of Rome and other assets. What a head-shaker. The ignorant arrogance of Cult puppet Greta Thunberg is a most blatant public example. It is the mushroom technique – keep them in the dark and feed them bullshit – which produces heads full of bullshit that then seek to impose their bullshit on everyone else. Did I mention Greta Thunberg? Or 'Covid'. Or the fake vaccines? We are on a train fuelled by bullshit hurtling towards oblivion pulling behind an endless line of wagons full to overflowing with bullshit. We have bullshit opposed by more bullshit – ignorance opposed by more ignorance. Belief in a naturally-occurring 'virus' (bullshit) is challenged by those who say it was released from a lab in Wuhan (more bullshit) when there has never been any scientific evidence that there even *is* a 'virus'. Bullshit is called truth and truth is called misinformation and many won't look at the truth because it's labelled misinformation. They cannot decide for themselves and instead have their conclusions delivered whole with a ribbon and a 'Pre-Poo toilet spray' to mask the bullshit. Yes, such a product does really exist I was staggered to find and most necessary, too, when Gates is about to speak. Fortunately more are starting to get it and they need to – *fast*.

Picking the gofers

People don't come to political and other positions of power by accident when they are crucial to making decisions that advance the Cult agenda. Cultists and their non-human masters don't like leaving things to chance and they are terrified of states of flux that they cannot call. They want certainty and to know the final score before the game starts. This means seeking to control both sides and the referee (see drug regulation agencies and Big Pharma). I learned long ago how those who later advance into key positions are developed and programmed from a very early age and selected for what they will eventually do. The two-party political system, sometimes three, is so easy to control if you have your agents in major positions in those parties to ensure that your people are selected into leadership roles. 'Democracies' are really one-party states as we see with the Cult-owned Democrats and Cult-owned Republicans in the United States and in the UK the Cult-owned Conservative Party and Cult-owned Labour Party. The Conservative Party imposed fascist restrictions on the population in response to the 'Covid' hoax and what did the Labour Party 'opposition' say? They were not fascist enough. The Cult controls the media, polling organisations and increasingly voting systems themselves to secure the man or woman it wants as president, prime minister, state premier or governor etc. and electronic voting systems make that even easier. It is so naïve to think that Donald Trump was a maverick who bucked the system to become a one-term president. Trump is part of the system with the role of leading his supporters to glorious failure as he has done this far. He's a pied piper for those who can see through the lies but unfortunately can't see through his. I had Trump's number when he was running for office in 2016 and I have detailed his background in other books. A 'saviour' he is not. Quite the opposite.

One of the main Cult prepare-them-for-office organisations is fronted by Klaus Schwab, an economist and mechanical engineer, from the Cult's World Economic Forum (WEF) which has been on the frontline of the 'Covid' and climate change hoaxes. It was Schwab and his WEF that put the puppet Thunberg on the world stage. She was carefully chosen for many reasons including to harness support from the young for climate change measures on the grounds that they will otherwise have no future; and to prevent proper questioning of the provable crap repeated by Thunberg because to do so would be 'cruel' with someone of her age. On the rare occasions she has been asked the mildest of sceptical questions she has been utterly lost. Thunberg is a mantra-repeating clueless script-reader and nothing more. The exploitation of her is a disgrace. Check the 'solutions' to 'human-caused climate change' and compare them with the 'solutions' to 'Covid'. They are control over the fine detail of our lives which is the Cult agenda writ large and what a coincidence that both hoaxes are being perpetuated by the same people, including Schwab and Gates.

The 'Green' climate agenda has led to the West becoming dependent for energy on sources they do not control – not least Russia. Biden's response to the invasion was to ban the import of Russian energy on which the US, thanks to him, had become dependent. This further inflated the cost of fuel (and so everything) for Americans as they are coldly squeezed until the pips squeak. Energy costs are being manipulated to force the population into compliance with the Cult 'green' (fascist) agenda. Neither Russia or China could care less about 'climate change' when both know it's a hoax and between them they are self-sufficient in cheap energy (with new coal-fired power stations in China) while the West has fallen into energy dependency and soaring prices in the wake of 'Covid', suppression of fossil fuels, and the response to the Russian invasion of Ukraine. See how the Cult-owned 'Greens' condemn Western countries for using carbon fuels while ignoring China which is the global leader in CO2 production. Meanwhile the West moves to solar panels – 80 percent of which are produced by *China*! It's all pieces being moved on the Cult chessboard to dismantle the West to the benefit of Cult-owned China and the East.

If the 'global warming' myth is true why are only 'experts' repeating the script allowed in the media and not those with greater knowledge of carbon dioxide who are banned from appearing? Why are the billionaires of the Cult like Bill Gates warning about 'sea level rises' while buying multi-million dollar homes on the *beach*? Anyone who is frightened of debate (as with these 'experts' and media organisations) clearly has no confidence that their claims will stand up to scrutiny. The Cult-owned BBC is a glaring example on every front. A billion dollars was handed out to 'save' Australia's Great Barrier Reef while the Australian Institute of Marine Science reported that coral cover has *increased* more 27 percent in the northern reef and by 26 and 39 percent in the central and southern areas. Narrative-repeating 'experts' like Woke BBC 'national treasure' David Attenborough and 'journalist' George Monbiot on the UK *Guardian* have told us for decades that the reef was 'dying' due to rising carbon dioxide which is the gas of life. Without it we would all be dead. Our food supply depends upon it for a start. 'Global warming', and the 'climate change' that it became when temperatures stopped rising, is a speciality of Schwab and Gates to justify the dystopian transformation of human society and give all the advantages to China and Russia in a planned economic and military war between East and West on the way to a global dystopian state.

Klaus Schwab was born in Germany when the Nazis were in power and it clearly had an impact on him. He progressed rapidly through the Cult network as his career in manipulation blossomed and he became a steering committee member of the Cult cusp operation, the Bilderberg Group, and was a director of the UK *Daily Mail* group for five years. He founded the European Management Forum in 1971 when he was only 32 and 440 executives from 31 nations attended the first meeting. Given his lack of international profile that is remarkable in itself and other forces had to be at work. No doubt his connections to infamous Cult and Bilderberg operative Henry Kissinger, the former US Secretary of State and National Security Advisor, helped things along. Schwab's operation changed its name to the World Economic Forum in 1987 and famously hosts the Cult gofer gathering in Davos, Switzerland, every year. This is attended by a *Who's Who* in world leadership, political and otherwise, in some 1,500 private jets to, among many other things, demand human society is transformed to save the world from 'climate change'. The WEF attracts funding from some one thousand multinational Cult corporations. Schwab himself is little more than a gofer and as with others of his ilk his unquestioning service to evil has made him extremely rich. The motivation of the WEF is confirmed by members of its Board of Trustees that include Larry Fink, CEO of BlackRock, the largest investment management corporation on earth, of which more shortly. Other WEF trustees are the notorious Cult asset Christine Lagarde, former Managing Director of the International Monetary Fund (IMF) who became President of the European Central Bank; Mark Carney, big player in global finance, former governor of the Bank of Canada and Bank of England, and leading figure in the Bank for International Settlements that coordinates Cult policy between central banks; and Queen Rania of Jordan, ranked by *Forbes* magazine as one of the world's 100 most powerful women.

School for gofers

German author, researcher and journalist Ernst Wolff has highlighted how Schwab established and managed the Young Global Leaders School through which many of the 'leaders' in the 'Covid' hoax years passed on their way to office. No wonder they have all sung from the same Cult song-sheet throughout the fake pandemic and responded in almost exactly the same way. I detail in *Perceptions of a Renegade Mind* how political, government and health personnel worldwide were perceptually prepared (programmed) through 'training courses' to be in key positions right now to impose the Cult narrative and agenda on the masses with such unquestioning and unthinking coordination. Schwab established the Global Leaders for Tomorrow school in 1992 which became Young Global Leaders in 2004. This head-hunts young compliant and psychopathic people to occupy major positions to advance the transformation of human society into a centrally-dictated fascist tyranny. Names from the first 'class' in 1992 included Angela Merkel, long-time Chancellor of Germany, Nicolas Sarkozy, who became President of France and yes … Tony Blair, a Cult operative to his fingertips and UK Prime Minister between 1997 to 2007 when he helped to mass-murder untold numbers of Iraqis in the 2003 invasion justified by the lie of weapons of mass destruction. This war criminal has been vocal in his support for every fascist measure of the 'Covid' period and has never in his life seen a Cult arse that he didn't want to lick.

Other Schwab graduates have included former Blair aide Prime

Minister Jacinda Ardern who turned New Zealand fascist; Health Minister Greg Hunt who turned Australia fascist; Emmanuel Macron who turned France fascist; Governor Gavin Newsom who turned California fascist; Prime Minister Justin Trudeau who turned Canada fascist; and Chrystia Freeland, his Deputy Prime Minister and Minister of Finance in Trudeau's government who helped him turn Canada fascist. Another is reported to be Devi Sridhar, Professor and Chair of Global Public Health at the University of Edinburgh, who advised the Scottish government on how to deal with 'Covid' – 'advice' that turned Scotland fascist. The ironically-named 'Freeland' is a long time Schwab asset and serves on the board of trustees of his World Economic Forum. Freeland is the granddaughter of Ukraine-born Nazi collaborator, Michael Chomiak (Mykhailo Khomiak), a Nazi-trained espionage and propaganda agent who was sought by Polish authorities after the war until the 1980s for Nazi collaboration while he was located in Canada where he died in 1984. Schwab said in an interview in 2017 that something like half of Trudeau's cabinet had been through his 'school' and this is the Cult-owned crowd that oversaw the imposition of martial law in response to peaceful trucker protests against fake vaccine mandates. Fascist attacks on the truckers were Cult-orchestrated via Schwab-owned Trudeau and Freeland. Schwab further bragged that the president of Argentina Alberto Fernández and Russia's Vladimir Putin were Young Global Leader graduates. A coincidence? Yeah, sure it is. But Putin is the bad guy that the West hates isn't he? Stage show, mate, pure Cult theatre. Putin's response to 'Covid' and all the surveillance systems justified by 'Covid' was the same as the Cult-owned West and Cult-owned China. Other Schwab school graduates include:

Jean-Claude Juncker, former Prime Minister of Luxembourg and President of the European Commission; José Manuel Barroso, former President of the European Commission; Alexander De Croo, Prime Minister of Belgium; Sanna Marin, Prime Minister of Finland; Carlos Alvarado Quesada, Costa Rica President; Peter Buttigieg, US Secretary of Transportation; Sebastian Kurz, a Chancellor of Austria; Annalena Baerbock of the German Green Party, Minister of Foreign Affairs, Leader of Alliance 90/Die Grünen; Jens Spahn, German Federal Minister of Health since 2018; Philipp Rösler, German Minister of Health and Economics and Technology, appointed Managing Director of the World Economic Forum by Schwab in 2014; Faisal Alibrahim, Saudi Arabia Minister of Economy and Planning; Vasudha Vats, Vice-President of Pfizer; Richard Branson of Virgin fame; Jacob Wallenberg from the elite Swedish family known as the 'Swedish Rothschilds'; Chelsea Clinton, daughter of the deeply corrupt and evil-beyond-belief Cult operatives Bill and Hillary Clinton that I have been exposing in all their horrors since 1994.

Schwab's graduates dominate the Internet with Bill 'Covid fascist' Gates at Microsoft; Jeff Bezos, Amazon founder and owner of the *Washington Post*; Larry Page, founder of Google; Mark Zuckerberg, founder of Facebook; Niklas Zennström, founder of Skype; Jimmy Wales, founder of Cult-narrative Wikipedia; and Jack Ma, founder of Chinese Internet tech giant Alibaba. Add to them 'royalty' from Sweden, Norway, Denmark, and the Netherlands; Leonardo Di Caprio, actor and UN 'climate ambassador'; singer Bono (big mate of Bill Gates); and many in political office pushing the Cult's climate change hoax along with 'Green' David de Rothschild and Ricken Patel, founder of Avaaz which ferociously pushes climate change and other Cult agendas. There are also government ministers, politicians and officials from Pakistan, Denmark, Mali, Maldives, South Africa, Israel, Bhutan, Rwanda and Angola, along with Schwab graduates right across the global corporate world and media. You can have a Schwab graduate invading a country, Schwab graduates condemning him with crocodile tears (literally), and Schwab graduates reporting the event to the public. Talk about keeping it 'in-house'.

Author Ernst Wolff says the school appears to include some critics of the system to give the illusion of diversity. There are currently some 1,300 graduates of the school from North America, Europe, Asia, Africa, and South America, so plenty more Cult gofers primed to occupy strategic positions worldwide and do whatever their masters demand. Schwab and the WEF also founded the Global Shapers Community in 2012 which brings together those identified by them as having leadership potential from around the world who are under 30. This was a definition of fascism by the Italian fascist Benito Mussolini: 'Fascism should more appropriately be called Corporatism because it is a merger of state and corporate power.' Communism is the absorption by the state of corporate power and this is why I say that fascism and communism are masks on the same face. The expressed goal of Cult-owned Schwab and the WEF is 'cooperation' between public government and private corporations and this is where the whole theme so promoted by Blair and other Schwab graduates of 'public/private partnership' came from. This is a Trojan horse for Cult corporations to take over government. Mussolini again: 'Fascism should more appropriately be called Corporatism because it is a merger of state and corporate power.

Web connections

On that subject here is an example of how the corporate web connects with the Cult government-military-intelligence network. I mentioned that when Canadian truckers launched their mass protest against mandatory fake vaccines in the capital Ottawa and elsewhere in early 2022 they raised $10 million in public donations through crowd-funding site GoFundMe to allow them to financially stay in situ. The Cult and its Canadian government lackeys wanted to block these funds and suddenly GoFundMe, which is supposed to be an 'independent' company, announced that the money would not be given to the truckers. They made some lame excuse that showed they were not even trying to hide what was going on. American proper journalist Jon Rappoport investigated the background to GoFundMe and this is what he found. Two companies Accel and Technology Crossover Ventures (TCV) own the majority stake in GoFundMe and this is the same Accel that invested $13 million in the fledgling college enterprise of a guy called Mark Zuckerberg in 2004 that would rapidly become the global communication game-changer Facebook. Accel is headed by Jim Breyer, son of Hungarian-Jewish immigrants, who became a billionaire member of the Cult's World Economic Forum, Council on Foreign Relations (CFR), and major investor in China. Rappoport points out that Breyer chaired another company, National Venture Capital Association of America, and in that same year of 2004 a man called Gilman Louie joined the board. Louie was the first CEO of the CIA's technology-funding operation In-Q-Tel (also I-Q-T) which supports companies developing technology useful to CIA 'data gathering'. The CIA's Louie was involved in another company headed by Breyer, BBN Technologies, which employed Dr Anita Jones who had worked for In-Q-Tel and was an adviser to the Internet-creating DARPA, the sinister technological development arm of the Pentagon. Amazing isn't it that none of this gets into the mythical narrative of Zuckerberg and Facebook which became the world's biggest data-mining and personal profiling site? You know – the same Zuckerberg and Facebook that is censoring anything that challenges the Cull narrative on 'Covid', 'human-caused climate change', and so much else. Breyer's Accel is a further investor in Spotify of Joe Rogan censorship fame. As Rappoport puts it: 'GoFundMe, Accel, Facebook, CIA, In-Q-Tel, Jim Breyer, CFR, World Economic Forum, major investments in China. Basically, The Club.' I can't think why GoFundMe would block funds for freedom-demanding truckers given this background. The truckers then raised millions more in public donations through GiveSendGo and these were frozen by the Ontario Superior Court of *No* Justice after an application by the Ontario government of Premier Doug Ford. Then the Toronto-Dominion Bank successfully applied to the same rubber-stamping court to freeze trucker donation accounts containing $1.1 million. You can clearly see how the web works.

Cult genocide

Clearly none of this is happening by accident and this is where we find the method in the madness. I'll go into this in far more detail later. In short: A non-human force is ultimately behind the Global Cult with the goal of infiltrating (achieved) and then taking over human society (almost there) through control of perception via technology. This includes a programme of mass depopulation which I have long predicted and is now playing out as a consequence of the 'Covid' fake vaccines. Scott Davison, CEO of major US insurance company OneAmerica, said that deaths of working-age people between 18 and 64 increased by *40 percent* in the third quarter of 2021 as the fake vaccines were widely circulating. Davison said: 'We are seeing, right now, the highest death rates we have seen in the history of this business – not just at OneAmerica. The data is consistent across every player in that business.' He said these were 'huge, huge' numbers. 'Just to give you an idea of how bad that is, a three-sigma or a one-in-200-year catastrophe would be a ten percent increase over pre-pandemic', he said. 'So 40 percent is just unheard of.' Davison said the trend continued in the next quarter.

German health insurance company BKK ProVita said that adverse effects data was being 'significantly' underreported and was far higher than official figures. BKK board member Andreas Schöfbeck said: 'According to our calculations, we consider 400,000 visits to the doctor by our insured persons due to vaccination complications to be realistic to date.' He added that if those figures were extrapolated over a year for the German population of 83 million it was likely that between 2.5 and 3 *million* Germans received medical treatment for fake vaccine adverse events. Data from the UK Office for National Statistics (ONS) in February, 2022, revealed that fake vaccinated children have a death rate 54 times higher than un-fake-vaccinated kids. Funeral directors have said that numbers passing through their businesses did *not* increase during the 'pandemic' of 2020 – so where was the 'virus'? This changed dramatically after the fake vaccine rollout in late 2020, early 2021. 'I have never seen anything like it', one said. A mortician in Sydney, Australia, described people being cremated in droves after dying from fake vaccine-related side effects such as 'heart attacks, strokes and blood clots'. Many funeral homes were being forced to secure large freezers to store the dead, she said. 'Some of the places are actually installing extra-large freezers that hold a minimum of 20 – and some of them are ordering eight big containers that each hold 20 bodies.' HART (Health Advisory and Recovery Team) is a group of UK doctors, scientists, economists, psychologists and academics who came together to share concerns about the official response to the 'Covid pandemic'. They reported in early 2022 that emergency calls for cardiac arrests had soared in 2021 when the fake vaccines were made available:

It is notable that the 2019 and 2020 expectations for the number of arrest calls are almost identical – only a 0.2% difference. However, the 2021 baseline was inflated by 14%. Using the 2019/2020 baseline the number of arrest calls has been 30% above expected levels with 27,800 extra arrest calls. That amounts to over 500 extra arrest calls every day (although they were not evenly distributed through the year). Between 90 and 97% of these people will have died as a result.

Figure 60: The 'worm-like structures' found in the bodies of deceased fake-vaccinated people.

American funeral director and embalmer Richard Hirschman revealed how he is seeing arteries and veins filled with unnatural blood clot combinations with strange fibrous materials that are filling the vascular system. You can see Internet videos of the clots being removed from corpses and they are shocking in their length and extent. No wonder the authorities blocked autopsies on 'Covid' patients. Hirschman said he had never seen anything like this in more than 20 years of experience as a board-certified embalmer. He confirmed that others in the industry were finding the same. Hirschman described clots and 'worm-like structures'(Fig 60). He began to see them for the first time in late 2020 and eventually they involved half the bodies that he saw. Later it was *80 to 90* percent. What happens in one limb happens in both so it is bodily universal and not location specific. Hirschman said he had witnessed an increase in deaths from heart attacks and strokes and given the blood clots he was seeing that was no surprise:

If this is caused by the vaccine and my gut is telling me it is … imagine the amount of people that will be dying in the future because people cannot live with this kind of substance floating around in their vessels … If one of these small fibrous tissues gets up into the brain you're going to have a stroke. If it gets into your heart, it's going to lead you to a heart attack.

Data compiled on the US Vaccine Adverse Event Reporting System

(VAERS) revealed that 'Covid' fake vaccines are almost 50 times deadlier than flu vaccines by number of doses – 743,179 adverse events with the 'Covid' jab in a period of *14 months* against 137, 533 with the flu shot over *13 years*. Strokes told the same story with 4,532 'Covid' jab cases reported in *14 months* against 122 in *13 years* with the flu vaccine. Headlines from outside the mainstream media began to reflect the reality the Cult-owned media was seeking to suppress:

Why Are Deaths in Highly-Vaccinated Denmark Approaching a Record High?; mRNA Jab Deaths And Injuries Are Soaring In Europe; Countries with high Covid vaccination rates all suffered an extraordinary rise in excess deaths in 2021 suggesting the jabs are to blame; Parents protest deaths of children from Pfizer vaccines in Geneva, Switzerland; CDC data shows 40% rise in Excess Deaths among 18 to 49-year-olds in the USA in 2021; FIFA football deaths in December 2021 alone matched the annual average for the last 12 years; Government Must Halt Child Covid Vaccination Immediately and Investigate the Cause of the Spike in Child Deaths; UK has recorded 5 times more deaths in 12 months due to Covid vaccination than it has deaths due to all vaccines combined in 21 years & Twitter doesn't want you to find out ...; Deaths among male teens increased by 53% following Covid vaccination in 2021 and the death spikes correlate perfectly with the uptake of dose 1, 2 & 3; New Study Shows Increase In Deaths In 145 Countries After Covid Vaccines Were Introduced.

Pants on fire

At the same time a stream of UK NHS 'doctors' were pouring out shocking and provable lies on the Internet about the jabs and their effectiveness and safety under something called the Vaccine Confidence Project. 'Confidence' is secured by telling the public unbelievable whoppers so they will have the fake vaccine no matter what the already documented consequences. Where is their self-respect? The death and injury trend must continue with the fake vaccines containing self-replicating synthetic genetic material that goes on spreading and expanding. The jabs have also been found to contain lethal graphene oxide nanoparticles by scientists and doctors in the UK, New Zealand, Germany, Spain, America and elsewhere. Graphene is used in batteries, super capacitors, bio-sensing and drug delivery, and can cut the body to pieces on the nano-scale after being infused by the fake vaccines. Graphene conducts electrical signals including communications between cells and can therefore change the entire communication system of the body and rewire the body-brain dynamic. No, that is not a 'conspiracy theory'. This ability is claimed in graphene promotional videos to be a way of overcoming spinal injuries, Alzheimer's, and cancer. Some claim that graphene is quickly ejected from the body, but not so. Spiders

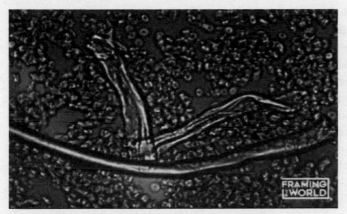

Figure 61: Nanotubes in the blood of the fake-vaccinated.

sprayed with graphene mostly died while those that survived began to spin webs containing graphene that were incredibly strong. Graphene is *not* ejected from the body; it becomes *part* of the body. Once inside these are some of the consequences that can follow:

> Blood clots; damage to red blood cells and the immune system; multi-organ inflammation; inflamed mucous membranes and a loss of taste or smell (inflammation of the mucous membranes) and an unusual metallic taste in the mouth; magnetic properties which may explain how many people found their bodies have become magnetic to metal objects; neurodegeneration in the brain; many effects of graphene oxide are the same as alleged symptoms of 'Covid-19'.

Graphene can cut blood vessels and tissue to shreds at the nano-level and if graphene was in the flu 'vaccines' widely given to especially old people before 'SARS-COV-2' was said to have appeared it would explain phenomena attributed to 'Covid-19'. Doctors and researchers have found graphene nanotubes in the blood of fake-vaccinated people (Fig 61). You can see Internet videos of graphene self-assembling into networks when stimulated by electricity/electromagnetism and it is clear that what fake vaccines put into the body is designed to interact with Wi-Fi and 5G for reasons I'll come to later. Graphene can generate magnetism which would explain the magnetic nature of the skin in some fake vaccinated people especially at the injection site. Graphene nanoparticles are highly likely to be involved in the phenomenon of 'shedding' when fake vaccinated people are said to pass on their injected contents to the non-fake-vaccinated who then develop similar consequences. Skin contact is said to be one means. Snake-like structures have been found in the blood of the fake vaccinated which connect and self-assemble into 'matrix-like' material. This has never been seen in the human body before and the same with self-assembling crystalline substances found in the blood and fake vaccine vials. These have been shown to illuminate when a smartphone is nearby. Thousands have been found in one drop of blood or vial material. None of these things are mentioned in the official ingredients.

Pfizer in league with the US Food and Drug Administration (FDA) tried to delay the release of data from its fake vaccine 'trials' for *75 years*. That's how much they care about you and your right to informed consent. When a court refused the request amazing revelations began to emerge from the documents. The London *Daily Express* reported that when Pfizer applied for FDA approval it was aware of almost *158,000 adverse events* from the fake vaccine and no wonder they requested the documents remain sealed for 75 years. Adverse effects Pfizer was aware about *before* the fake vaccine rollout included Vaccine-Associated Enhanced Disease (VAED) which as the name suggests means the fake vaccines make subsequent disease worse than it would otherwise be. Pfizer documents that it was so keen not to release reveal how VAED was considered to be an 'important potential risk' including Vaccine-Associated Enhanced Respiratory Disease. The documents say that an expected rate of VAED was difficult to establish so a meaningful observed/expected analysis could not be conducted based on available data: 'The feasibility of conducting such an analysis will be re-evaluated on an ongoing basis as data on the virus grows and the vaccine safety data continues to accrue.' In words of few syllables that means they would find out the effect of the fake vaccines by using them on the public while Pfizer, politicians, and compliant 'health professionals' (liars) told people they were 'safe and effective' when they are neither. What's more, the un-fake-vaccinated 'control group' in the fake trials was then also fake-vaccinated to prevent any comparison being made ongoing between vaxxed and unvaxxed. As a result of this deceit and mendacity Pfizer made some $36 billion in 2021 thanks to governments using public money to buy their health-destroying shite. Among the markers for Vaccine-Associated Enhanced Disease are:

Hypoxia (oxygen deprivation to the brain); pneumonia; respiratory failure; acute respiratory distress syndrome; cardiac failure; cardiogenic shock; acute myocardial infarction; Myocarditis; Arrhythmia; vomiting; diarrhoea; abdominal pain; Jaundice; acute hepatic failure; deep vein thrombosis; pulmonary embolism; Peripheral Ischaemia (decrease in blood supply/oxygen); Tachypnoea (abnormal rapid breathing); Vasculitis (blood vessel destruction through inflammation); acute kidney injury; renal failure; altered state of consciousness; seizure; Encephalopathy (degenerative disease of the brain) ; Meningitis; cerebrovascular accident; Thrombocytopenia (blood coagulation disorder); disseminated intravascular coagulation; multiple organ dysfunction syndrome; multisystem inflammatory syndrome in children.

A UK laboratory report found graphene oxide in vials of Pfizer, Moderna, and AstraZeneca. Many vials contain only a saline solution which neither damages the body nor protects from 'Covid'. This is to stop the death numbers getting so out of hand they cannot be hidden. The idea is that as people have repeated fake vaccines they will cop for a bad one eventually with the effect spread over a longer period. A rider to that is that even some of the saline vials have been found to contain graphene. Christopher Cole, Food and Drug Administration (FDA) Executive Officer, was caught on a hidden camera by the Project Veritas organisation saying that annual 'Covid' fake vaccines are the planned policy. 'Biden wants to inoculate as many people as possible', he said. 'Biden' doesn't know what day it is. His *Cult handlers* want to jab as many people as possible. Researchers have also exposed how particular groups of vial lot numbers are especially deadly and how fake vaccine companies are colluding to coordinate the circulation of these lots. Who is orchestrating this coordination of mass murder? The Cult which *owns them all*.

Reports from Spain, Slovakia, Cyprus and other countries have found PCR test swabs mostly out of China contaminated with nanotech hydrogels, lithium and the poison ethylene oxide. The plan was not only for mass fake vaccination, but mass testing to get people both ways. The American National Cancer Institute describes ethylene oxide as a flammable colourless gas with a sweet odour and used primarily to produce other chemicals, including antifreeze. Ethylene oxide is employed in smaller amounts as a pesticide. 'The ability of ethylene oxide to damage DNA makes it an effective sterilizing agent but also accounts for its cancer-causing activity', the Institute says on its website. Lymphoma, leukaemia, stomach and breast cancers are the most frequently reported. Human exposure to ethylene oxide comes through inhalation and ingestion, 'which may occur through occupational, consumer, or environmental exposure'. Or, since 'Covid', by having a test swab stuck up your nose over and over. I have a different view about what 'cancer' really is so let's say what they *call* cancer.

Killing the kids

Christopher Whitty, the psychopathic Chief Medical Officer for England, overruled the government's vaccine advisory committee which for once – *once* – recommended against giving the fake vaccine to healthy 12 to 15 year olds. Whitty and chief medical officers for Scotland, Wales, and Northern Ireland, did not give a medical reason for this, but instead spoke of children losing 'education' time and the mental effects of missing school. Funny, this did not concern Whitty at all when he was pressing for closing schools during lockdown. From the moment fake vaccines were given to kids in this 12 to 15 age range (and higher) the ratio of deaths from all causes far exceeded the five year average. How is this not murder when deaths and adverse effects in higher age groups were already well known? One definition of murder is this: 'The killing of another person without justification or excuse, especially the crime of killing a person with malice aforethought or with recklessness manifesting extreme indifference to the value of human life.' Even if you gave Whitty the benefit of the doubt and used only the latter part of that definition how can what he did not be murder when the health and fatality consequences of the fake vaccine were well known by then? Edward Dowd, a former executive-turned-whistleblower with investment mega-giant BlackRock, teamed up with an insurance industry collaborator to investigate the excess death data of America's CDC. What they found was shocking. The Millennial age group (born 1981 to 1996) saw an *84 percent* increase in excess mortality after the fake vaccines were introduced and many Millennials were subject to mandates to keep their jobs. This was seven times higher than the 'Silent Generation' of 85 and over. Dowd said that from the summer to the autumn/fall of 2021 there were 61,000 more Millennial deaths than normal. That's more dead Americans than were killed in the Vietnam War when 58,000 troops died in ten years. Here were 61,000 young Americans dead in *six months*. But there was more – much more. Excess mortality for Generation X (born 1965 to 1980) saw a spike in the same period of 101,000 while over-65 Baby Boomers experienced *306,000* excess deaths. Dowd described this as a 'World War Two event' when 291,000 Americans died. 'We've had 1.1 million excess deaths since the pandemic began, many of which occurred in the second half of [2021], which is, again, all you need to know', Dowd said. '1.1 million excess deaths equates to 4,000 World Trade Center events.' He continued:

> I think this is the smoking gun: that the vaccines are causing excess mortality in all age groups and it's no coincidence that [CDC Director] Rochelle Walensky refuses to answer Senator Ron Johnson's letters. They're hiding. Fauci's gone. She's gone. They're hiding. So, I'm going to put a word out there. It's an old word but it should be re-introduced into the conversation. It's called democide: Death by government. So the government, through the mandates has killed people.

They were murdered and those that caused them to be fake-vaccinated – and administered the shots – are murderers by this definition alone: 'The killing of another person ... with recklessness manifesting extreme indifference to the value of human life.' The Cult-owned mainstream media cover up all this by omission and demonisation of those seeking to make the public aware of the unfolding human disaster. Ever more 'symptoms' of 'Covid' are added to explain health consequences of the fake vaccines with suddenly the heart condition myocarditis a 'Covid' symptom after so many have died from heart attacks or had their sports careers destroyed by myocarditis and other heart damage. We have been bombarded with propaganda in the wake of this from fraudulent 'doctors' and fraudulent media about how heart disease in the young is normal and all the ways that your activities can trigger heart attacks. They could not cover up the number of professional sports people who have died or had their careers ended by heart conditions since the rollout and nor the number of those who have collapsed in public situations such as television and stage shows or while making statements to the media. Among them was American comedian Heather McDonald who was in the middle of boasting to her audience about how many fake vaccines she's had when she collapsed on stage. After she left hospital McDonald was asked if she had been checked for myocarditis. What's that?, she replied. Those telling others to 'get the jab' and being dismissive and hostile when they refuse have no idea what is in the vials and the potential health consequences.

The devastating and cumulative dismantling of the immune system caused by the jabs has promoted claims about a new 'highly virulent' strain of 'HIV' and how 'Covid' has an 'HIV-like mutation' which helps it to attack human cells. The relevance of this is that the 'HIV virus' is supposed to demolish the immune system and cause 'AIDS' or 'acquired immune deficiency syndrome'. Oh, it's HIV that's destroying immune systems not the fake vaccine!

That would be difficult given that there is no 'HIV' – it has never been shown to exist as intelligent and inquiring people have long known (see *Perceptions of a Renegade Mind* and *Children of the Matrix* which exposed the AIDS scam in 2001). American biochemist Kary Mullis, the Nobel Prize-winning creator of the PCR test, knew there is no HIV a long time ago and said so in his great book *Dancing Naked In The Mind Field*. There is no HIV and there is no 'Covid'. I'll have more on this and 'HIV' towards the end of the book.

CHAPTER FIVE

The Cult New World

**Silent acquiescence in the face of tyranny is no better than
outright agreement
C. J. Redwine**

Cult depopulation genocide is central to the entire transformation of human life. I have described for ten years this planned new world as the Hunger Games Society and long before that by other names. My exposure of the 'new system' now unfolding goes back decades.

Today Cult operatives like Schwab at the WEF talk about the Great Reset and 'Build Back Better' which you will have heard repeated over and over by Cult parrots including Biden, Trudeau, Johnson, Ardern, Blair, Obama, Rutte in the Netherlands, the UN Secretary-General, and so many more. Both terms are expressions of the age-old technique of Creative Destruction in which you continually destroy the status quo, replace it with another, and then destroy that to replace it with another (Fig 62). Each new 'quo' moves the world closer to your ultimate goal which is total global control of every man, woman and child and every facet of what would pass for their 'life'. This is what the 'Covid' hoax is all about – global creative destruction of the 2019 status quo to open the way for the Great Reset of a transformed human world. Creative Destruction is achieved through the perceptual manipulation technique that I have

Figure 62: How the world is changed step by step. The 'Covid' hoax is a classic example. The world of 2019 is gone forever.

long dubbed Problem-Reaction-Solution in which you covertly create a problem, tell the public a version of the problem that you want them to believe, and then offer a solution to the problem which changes society in ways that advance your agenda. There is also the technique of NO-Problem-Reaction-Solution (PRS) in which you don't need a real problem and only the perception of one by the constant repetition of the same lies. Examples include 'weapons of mass destruction' in Iraq that didn't exist and were used to justify a catastrophic invasion in 2003, and the 'Covid pandemic' and 'human-caused climate change' hoaxes that are being used to transform global society through 'solutions' that install an Orwellian fascist dictatorship founded on surveillance and control overseen by artificial intelligence (AI). History is absolutely peppered with Problem-Reaction-Solutions (including the two world wars) and with No-Problem-Reaction-Solutions that have triggered a constant stream of Creative Destruction to drive every new status quo closer to world domination by the few of the many. The bosom buddy of PRS is what I dub the Totalitarian Tiptoe in which events are depicted as random and in and of themselves when together they form a pattern driving society further and further into dystopian centralisation of power. Each step hands ever fewer people control over ever more. An obvious example of this is the European Union which was originally sold as a free trade zone and became step-by-step the bureaucratic dictatorship that has dramatically centralised power and control over Europe.

I have exposed the plan for the Hunger Games Society for decades and called it by various names before the *Hunger Games* movies portrayed just such a society in which a super-rich and psychopathic elite lived in extremes of hi-tech luxury while lording over a population of slaves and serfs living in barely-survivable deprivation. This is what Schwab and his fellow psychopaths call 'The Great Reset'. If people in the post-war West find such control and injustice hard to contemplate the 'Covid' years will have given them a taste. If they lifted their eyes to scan the rest of the world they would see that other populations have lived under the jackboot ongoing in China, Saudi Arabia, and vicious, merciless regimes that abound across Africa, Asia, South America and Eastern Europe. For them life has always been dystopian. Recall the inhuman, poverty-ridden horrors and slavery of Victorian Britain and the black slavery of the United States and apartheid of which people still alive today have personal memory. The post-war 'window' of Western liberal democracy – illusory as much of that has been – is a tiny glimpse of the sun that is about to close, too, if we take freedom for granted. The world is planned to be China, Saudi Arabia and Afghanistan. Anyone fancy that?

Schwab's Great Reset demands no countries, only 'sectors', no

Figure 63: The Hunger Games Society that the 'Covid' hoax has so advanced – as planned. (Image by Neil Hague.)

Figure 64: The Hunger Games Society structure now known as the Great Reset and 'build back better'. (Image by Gareth Icke.)

elections, and decisions to be made by a cabal of technocrats, engineers and bureaucrats, including medical bureaucrats, in a system known as a 'technocracy'. This is fascism imposed by AI. I am going to summarise here what I have been saying over the decades about this planned society and see if you can recognise what I said with regard to the global transformation that has been 'Covid'. The Cult's Brave New World can be accurately symbolised as a pyramid with the tiny few at the peak controlling all wealth and resources through an unelected world government of bureaucrats and technocrats such as the sinister scientists, physicians, psychologists, and Silicon Valley crazies of the 'Covid' years (Figs 63 and 64). Imagine post-2020 on steroids and you might be somewhere close. At the bottom of the pyramid as always is planned to be the mass of the global population living in poverty and deprivation seeking to survive on a 'guaranteed income' or pittance from a despotic state that demands total acquiescence to even part with that miserly sum.

Literally every move you make would be monitored by AI and registered for compliance or otherwise as with the social credit score system in China on which the global control blueprint is based. Lose enough 'credits' in China for non-compliant behaviour and you can't fly, board a train, work or eat. This is the real reason for so-called vaccine passports or 'green passes' which are so-named in preparation for the rapidly fusing 'Covid' and 'Green' agendas orchestrated by the same Cult operatives. Some countries may have rolled them back, but they will return when other excuses can be found. Social credits through the passports will be accompanied by carbon credits when you will have a carbon allocation and the products you buy and your lifestyle will be constantly monitored for alleged carbon usage. Once your limit was breached you would be stopped from doing and buying anything with a carbon element. Cult credit card corporations are already introducing cards that stop working each month when you reach an agreed carbon limit on the tiptoe to compulsion.

Still continuing with what I wrote *before* 'Covid' … Income independent of the state and the global system would be deleted through destruction of businesses, except for the gigantic Cult corporations, and through AI seizing remaining employment. From this we can see what lockdowns were really about with the global economy holed below the waterline by 'Covid' restrictions followed by war and soaring inflation led by energy costs and staggering government spending on 'Covid'. Between the population and the Cult one-percent, or less than one-percent in truth, is designed to be a police-military state with the two forces ultimately amalgamated into one authoritarian tyrannical force of human control imposing the will of their masters. Most of this policing and militarisation of enforcement would also be AI and not human. We are now seeing AI law enforcement being rolled out on the road to this technological tyranny. Those in uniform today imposing the will of their perceived superiors and masters should take note, or those with the brain capacity to do so that is. Notice how the police have come to look in uniform, armaments, and demeanour ever more like the military. The fusion is happening before your eyes via the Totalitarian Tiptoe. Against this background, which I have been warning about for decades, look at how the world has changed since the 'Covid' card was played worldwide at the turn of 2020. All that I have warned about has advanced at dramatic speed through lockdown and the fascist behaviour of so many in uniform with every excuse being advanced to use the military in domestic situations. The conspiracy – yes *conspiracy* – that I have been exposing over 30 years is now on public display.

Manufactured crash

The Cult's Great Reset includes a totally transformed global economic system and that means under the law of Creative Destruction that a world economic crash is planned that you could hear on Mars. The 'Covid' hoax has purposely holed the world economy below the water line and sinking has seriously begun through catastrophic and soaring inflation which is a fancy way of saying the price of everything is skyrocketing. Governments poured multiple trillions into the economy to pay for their 'Covid' policies in the form of fresh air 'money' backed by nothing. With every new dollar or pound the value of the currency fell and prices rose. America tells the story in all its apparent madness. I say 'apparent' because the aim is to bring countries and populations to their knees to allow the new economic system to be imposed. In that sense it is not madness. It is cold calculation. How about the following for economic suicide? *80 percent* of dollars in circulation at the beginning of 2022 had been created since *January, 2020*. This is economic Armageddon and it is meant to be. Russia's invasion of Ukraine and the economic response to this by the US-led West has made the situation even worse – as intended. Plus the fact that rising fuel prices give companies and middlemen the chance to add a greater surcharge on goods that even fuel price increases justify. Every crisis is an opportunity for the unscrupulous and psychopathic.

The global supply chain has been systematically dismantled and the subsequent shortage of goods is further inflating prices. China has used the never-stops-giving excuse of 'Covid' to instigate the lockdown of tens of millions with factories closed to send further shockwaves through global supply networks. We can see why Cult-controlled America and the West have moved so much production to China and the China-controlled Far East to hand the supply cards to Beijing. Now China is seeking to replace the dollar as the world's premier or 'reserve' currency with the yuan which would blow mega-holes in the US economy from which it would likely never recover. The idea is to bring the population to its economic knees (control) and then step forward with a 'solution' in which a new system to 'save the people' is swapped for all that 'the people' own. This is the origin of the World Economic Forum mantra that 'You will own nothing and be happy'. A small 'guaranteed income' would be paid by government and only if you do everything authority (the Cult) tells you to do.

The cat and the bag parted company on the Cult plan to seize your money when Klaus Schwab-owned Canadian Prime Minister Justin Trudeau and his Schwab-owned deputy and Finance Minister Chrystia Freeland froze the bank accounts of trucker protestors in Ottawa without a court order for the crime of peacefully challenging their fascism. The despicable pair with their tails between their legs then abruptly unfroze the accounts no doubt on the orders of Schwab for revealing too early the laws already in place to steal the assets of the population at will in collaboration with the satanic Cult-owned banking system. Pressure to impose the Schwab policy of a digital ID would allow not only bank accounts to be seized but access to anything online blocked by blocking your ID code without which you would not be able to do anything. Obey or you will become a non-person incapable of feeding yourself or your family. The plan to phase out cash and impose a single global digital currency, which I revealed in *The Robots' Rebellion* in 1993, is all part of forcing people online where their money can be confiscated. The cynical lie by the Cult-owned World Health Organization that people could 'catch Covid' by handling money dramatically reduced the use of cash with even small companies and kiosks moving to card-only transactions. Newspapers were quick to point out that although you could 'catch Covid' from paper money you could not do so by handling newspapers. The 'virus' it seems knew the difference between different types of paper. I asked supermarket staff banning cash why if you could 'catch Covid' from paper money they were still selling newspapers. Bewildered looks came back in reply and no words. My god the naivety of the human race is breathtaking.

Welcome to the hive

I have been abused and ridiculed on an often industrial and historic scale for saying that the world on every level is nothing like people believe it to be and that a grand global conspiracy is being perpetrated to instigate total global control of every facet of human life. Such a reaction comes with the territory of challenging authority and convention and telling people what they don't want to hear. Why would they? I don't want it to be true either. Unfortunately it happens to be so and we have to deal with that or take even worse consequences than we have this far. Telling people what they *do* want to hear is easy. The door is already ajar for people to accept that reality when it's the reality they want to be true. Politicians specialise in telling you what you want to hear to get elected and then doing the opposite in office. When, like me, you are exposing a world that the population would rather not be real, the door is not ajar; it's padlocked and defended like a perceptual Fort Knox. The problem now for ridiculing abusers is the world that I said was coming over the last 30 years is now here. The hive mind of 'group-think', for which humanity has become infamous, is planned to be made technologically official to block access to all free-thought by connecting AI to the human brain and body. Self-replicating nanotechnology and 'living' synthetic genetic material identified by proper doctors and scientists in the vials of the 'Covid' fake vaccine are designed to enter the brain and rewire the entire genetic structure for those that it doesn't actually kill in a mass depopulation program. Biological Human 1.0 is being phased out for the synthetic 'biological' Human 2.0 which will get its thoughts, emotions and perceptions direct from AI. Not even the manipulation and censorship of information to dictate perception will then be necessary. AI will *be* your mind. More proof that Icke is crazy? Sure it is. This is Google executive and 'futurist' Ray Kurzweil openly laying out this very plan as his masters seek to sales-pitch this horrific end of humanity as the creation of the 'god-like human'. His official period for instigation is 2030 and what he describes is already well underway:

> Our thinking ... will be a hybrid of biological and non-biological thinking ... humans will be able to extend their limitations and 'think in the cloud' ... We're going to put gateways to the cloud in our brains ... We're going to gradually merge and enhance ourselves ... In my view, that's the nature of being human – we transcend our limitations.

> As the technology becomes vastly superior to what we are then the small proportion that is still human gets smaller and smaller and smaller until it's just utterly negligible.

The 'cloud' is being expanded by the day through 5G transmitters across the world – with 6G and 7G waiting to follow – and tens of thousands of low-orbit satellites are being launched by SpaceX Cult-asset Elon Musk and others to transmit the cloud to every inch of the Earth which means every human brain. Cult-owned Amazon announced plans in April, 2022, to deploy 3,236 low Earth orbit (LEO) satellites under the name Project Kuiper. They are collectively creating the Smart Grid in which all humans and technology will be connected to the Internet through the 'cloud' to form a hive mind in which perceptions will be delivered directly through a central control system. This is why almost everything today is preceded by 'smart' – smart televisions, smart meters, smart cards, smart cars, smart driving, smart pills, smart patches, smart watches, smart skin, smart borders, smart pavements, smart streets, smart cities, smart communities, smart environments, smart growth, smart planet ... on and on it goes. 'Smart cities' are now being built and other cities converted will be high-rise, densely-occupied micro-home megacities of total surveillance and control through AI. Every word, thought and action, outside or in your own home, will be monitored and stored by the AI super grid to ensure you are obeying every decree to the syllable or consequences will follow. The world is planned to be an expanded and extended version of China. The Cult was behind the Mao revolution in 1949 and the Cultural Revolution that followed. The plan was to impose a tyranny within which a system of total human control could be incubated and perfected before being rolled out as the global system. The Cult had to move much slower in the West before 'Covid' came while paying lip-service to 'freedom and democracy'. There was no such problem in China where what Mao (the Cult) said the country did and today's mass control system was created underpinned at every turn by technology and AI. What has happened since the 'Covid' hoax was triggered out of *China*? The rest of the world has become ever more like China which is exactly what was planned all along. I have been saying for decades that if you want to see the world tomorrow look at China today.

China, China, China. Did I mention CHINA?

All this explains why American and Western Cult-controlled corporations, 'entertainment' giants like Disney, Silicon Valley, and sports such as the National Basketball Association (NBA), are so in bed with China and refuse to criticise its truly evil human rights abuses. Don't fall for the idea that this China-worship is only about money and the billion-plus Chinese audience. Yes, money is part of it, but it's much more sinister than that. Outsourcing of production and jobs to China and the China-dominated Far East has handed Chinese fascists control over essential products no longer made in the West and with that the control of the global supply-chain. China is buying up American farmland along with China arse-licker Bill Gates who is now the biggest owner of farmland in the United States. This is all connected to controlling the global population by controlling the food supply and is happening in tandem with the destruction of food production by 'Covid' measures and sanctions supposedly targeted at Russia over the invasion of Ukraine. In fact, the sanctions are the Cult targeting the very Western countries imposing the sanctions. I wrote in *The Answer* that the 'Covid' hoax was being used to create food shortages (dependency on government) and now we are seeing that play through made even worse by the conflict in Ukraine – a manufactured crisis which seamlessly followed another in the form of 'Covid'. Ukraine and Russia are the 'breadbasket of the world' supplying more than a quarter of the world's wheat. Russia is a massive supplier of fertiliser used on farms in the West. 'Biden's' (the Cult's) ban on imports from Russia has driven the cost to astronomical levels to increase the price of the food that it helps to produce. A global food crisis is being coldly manufactured in multiple ways. Meanwhile, Russia's alliance with China means they do not face the same consequences.

The US government makes decisions that benefit China and weakens America because it is serving the Cult agenda and not the interests of Americans. The United States is being systematically weakened on every level in preparation for a Chinese (Cult) takeover which includes a planned conflict between the US/West and an alliance of China, Russia and subordinate countries such as Iran which I have been warning about for a very long time. Russia's invasion of Ukraine has been a step on this road and cemented the long-planned alliance between Russia and China as global power is realigned from West to East. America's chaotic withdrawal from Afghanistan leaving weapons that made the Taliban one of the best-armed regimes in the region and the calculated impotence of the Cult-owned Biden administration with regard to Ukraine are all hammer blows to America's global credibility. They are part of the incessant demoralisation of the population. Putting a demonstrably corrupt and senile president in the White House was a premeditated act to this end as with the shocking buffoon that is vice-president Kamala Harris. The same story can be seen with Cult-owned buffoons in political power across the West.

Biden took office with the United States enjoying energy independence. A year later all that was gone and the US was buying more than 500,000 barrels a day from Russia after 'Biden' closed pipelines and blocked investment in domestic carbon energy supplies. Fuel prices soared and Biden's response was to ban imports of Russian energy in retaliation for the invasion of Ukraine. This made fuel costs go even higher (and made Russian oil worth more) while Russia had other markets for its oil – like China. Ask yourself why anyone would do this except to undermine the country whose interests they are supposed to protect and represent. Ask successive administrations of both Cult-owned US political parties why they have handed control of production and the supply chain to China. The Cult climate change hoax can be seen in its proper context here. This has been the excuse to destroy energy supplies and independence in North America and Europe while China and Russia go on as before and don't give a damn about 'climate change' which they know to be a hoax. The outcome is energy independence for them and global dominance of the West through dependency. Weakening America and the West is happening on an individual level, too. In China and Russia men are encouraged to act like men and risk-taking is part of life. The West is obsessed with the riskless pursuit of 'safety' in which people become frightened of their own shadows. None of this is by chance. French philosopher Albert Camus (1913-1960) said: 'All greatness is rooted in risk.' If you are dismantling a society you don't want greatness. You want weak people terrified of risk. You don't want them striding towards danger and exploration. You want them hibernating in their comfort zone behind a padlocked door. No risk means stunted potential and conceding freedom in return for perceived safety (see 'Covid'). American Founding Father Alexander Hamilton was so right when he said: 'To be more safe they become … willing to run the risk of being less free' (see 'Covid'). This is how tyrants seize power (see 'Covid'). As Hungarian-Canadian academic Frank Furedi put it: 'Relieving people of the burden of freedom in order to make them feel safe is a recurring theme in the history of authoritarianism' (see 'Covid').

Soros speaks and the Cult is talking

The attack on the Chinese regime by Cult asset George Soros in February, 2022, may well have signposted a change in the rhetoric on the way to such a conflict when he described China as the 'world's most powerful authoritarian state' and 'the greatest threat that open societies face today'. He must have been looking in the mirror at the time. There had to be a good reason why Soros said that given that he's working to make the world like China, The global centre for the production of the opioid drug Fentanyl is Wuhan, China, from where it is shipped to Mexican drug cartels for distribution in the United States across the now open southern border. A war between drug gangs and the Mexican government has been raging for years. Now it is spilling over into the United States with murders in cities like Houston, Texas, soaring and creating the fear of even leaving home which Cult operatives, especially Soros, have worked so hard to create. The volume of Fentanyl crossing the border is skyrocketing and the drug has become the biggest killer of Americans aged between 18 and 45. This is all connected to the dismantling of American and Western society. From drug addiction comes homelessness and crime to secure the money to feed the addiction. Society breaks down. Add to that the list of Soros-funded district attorneys, such as George Gascón in Los Angeles, who are placed in office by the Cult to allow crime to run riot through non-prosecution and releasing the violent from jail. The response of the 'Biden' (Cult) government to the drug crisis has been to provide pipes for black Americans to smoke crack cocaine and make it okay to shoot

Fentanyl in the open. It doesn't take a genius to see what they are doing. In the background as always across a range of interconnected areas is the monumentally evil Cult operative Soros. He funds not only district attorneys, but also the Woke agenda, BLM, open borders, and so much more. Soros has bankrolled Media Matters, founded by the appalling David Brock, which targets for demonisation and silencing anyone in the public eye challenging the Cult narrative. Black American campaigner Candace Owens describes Soros as 'the most racist … man in America'. Yes, while funding 'anti-racist' groups. Are we getting it yet?

Fink again

Another in China's camp is Larry Fink, CEO of BlackRock, the world's biggest asset management company that 'manages' assets worth more than $10 *TRILLION*. Where Fink puts that money can make or break even the biggest of companies and he has used this power to impose the Woke agenda (including the human-caused climate change hoax) on corporations and others that benefit – or depend – on his decision-making. One commentator described Fink as 'king of the Woke-industrial complex'. Fink himself has admitted his goals: 'Behaviours are going to have to change and this is one thing we are asking [telling] companies, you have to force behaviours and at BlackRock, we are forcing behaviours.' He said of the climate change hoax: 'Every company and every industry will be transformed by the transition to a net-zero world. The question is, will you lead, or will you be led?' Do eight billion humans have any say in this? Of course not. Why is Woke madness perpetuated everywhere in global business today? Larry Fink. So who owns Larry Fink?

BlackRock is the biggest adviser (dictator) to the world's central banks. Fink and his business associate Stephen A. Schwarzman were involved together in the Blackstone Group before he broke away to form its near namesake BlackRock which has caused much confusion over which is which. China-investor Jim Breyer of Accel (Facebook, GoFundMe, Spotify) joined the Blackstone board in 2016 and it really is a small world that we are talking about. Central to Blackrock's modus operandi is an AI computer investment system known as Aladdin to seize control of the global economy by controlling the market. Another often missed aspect of all this is how Blackrock and their like are buying up vast numbers of residential properties to drive up the cost and make it impossible for young people and others to own a home. 'You will own nothing and be happy'. I have been warning for decades in the books and talks that this was the plan to stop home ownership and make everyone dependent on Cult-owned corporations. Precisely this is now happening on a mega and gathering scale.

Fink already essentially controls the American economy along with three other asset management companies, Vanguard Group ($7 trillion under its management), Fidelity Investments ($4.9 trillion), and State Street ($3.9 trillion). Cross them and other trillion-dollar investment management companies and you can be in big trouble if investments of *other people's money* are withdrawn. This is the point. The power is welded using the money of Americans through conduits like pension funds to impose the Cult agenda on US society which according to polls the overwhelming majority of Americans *don't want*. Larry Fink is a blatant Cult operative playing not only a key role in Schwab's World Economic Forum, but also sits on the board of the Cult's Council on Foreign Relations. The fantastic financial impact of what he controls is used to advance the ambitions of both. Even so, Fink, too, and his like, for all their outward appearance of omnipotent power, are only gofers for forces deeper in the web that they would not dare to disobey. The number of CEOs of these gigantic asset management companies are tiny and the masters they dare not disobey are even smaller. This is how the few control the world.

Fink of the money

BlackRock and Vanguard are among the top three shareholders of 'Covid' fake vaccine makers Pfizer, Moderna and Johnson & Johnson and benefit from the soaring profits in the 'Covid' period. They also have ownership stakes in companies developing vaccine passports. After the US Supreme Court quashed Biden's fake vaccine mandates on American private companies a long stream of those with BlackRock and Vanguard investment continued to insisted that employees had the jabs. These included Netflix (biggest stockholder Vanguard); Nike (biggest stockholders Vanguard and BlackRock); Verizon (biggest stockholders Vanguard and BlackRock); Twitter (Vanguard and BlackRock were the second and third biggest stockholders before the Musk takeover); Facebook (Vanguard and BlackRock are the first and third biggest stockholders). Other investment assets include giants such as Google, Microsoft, Intel, IBM, Walmart, Ford, Goldman Sachs, the list is fantastic. BlackRock and their fellow investment giants own the media and now we can see why all these 'unconnected' companies move and speak as one unit.

'Elected' politicians are irrelevant in the face of such concentrated economic might which means that literally a handful of people can dictate the direction of the entire economy, society itself, and what the global population is allowed to see and hear. People will know of the world famous corporations these characters oversee. How many have heard of BlackRock, Vanguard Group, Fidelity Investments and State Street where the real economic power resides? If you want to take over (achieved) and weaken (being achieved) America on behalf of Cult-controlled China then here's your vehicle. A few people can't control the world? For goodness sake they *already do*! Their plan includes a one-world digital currency, the deletion of cash, and crashing of the present financial system to open the way for an entirely new one founded on total human control. Add to this the Cult ownership of the 'defence' (attack) industry which makes its staggering profits from wars instigated by Cult-owned governments – especially in the United States – which are themselves controlled by the Cult-owned Deep State and the military-industrial-intelligence complex. Funny how I was dismissed for saying that governments are pawns of the military-industrial-intelligence complex and now this is so widely accepted with its own name, the Deep State, which is an asset in each country of the Cult.

This then is the Cult web and agenda – only some of it – now unfolding all around us with an ever-quickening speed thanks to 'Covid', associated hoaxes like 'human-caused climate change', wars and economic upheavals. As American proper journalist, cable news host Tucker Carlson, put it: 'What were once called conspiracy theories are now called breaking news.' Everything has been long-planned which is why I have been able to predict what was coming in my books and presentations over more than 30 years.

What I have described in this chapter is only one level of the multi-faceted, multi-dimensional 'Matrix' simulation prison cell and from hereon we are going deep into the pit of demons to see both the nature and scale of the human prison and how we can free ourselves at last after aeons of control by the non-human 'gods' behind it all.

Postscript: While this book was in the production stage it was announced that Elon Musk had bought Twitter. The alternative media and others who desire freedom were elated at his pledge to end Twitter censorship. I am all for that, but I urge caution.

Musk is a most blatant Cult asset who heads three key companies advancing the Cult agenda – SpaceX (launching tens of thousands of low-orbit satellites to beam 5G and other radiation fields at the population); Neuralink (connecting the human brain to machines); and Tesla (developing electric autonomous vehicles in which the computer will eventually dictate where you can and cannot go). You will see the fundamental Cult significance of these companies as we go along.

Someone so connected to three Cult agenda streams truly cares about your freedom of speech?? More to know, people, and one Cult technique is to have its own assets leading the fake challenge to its agenda to lead the opposition to glorious failure (see Donald Trump).

CHAPTER SIX

Forbidden Knowledge

The only true wisdom is in knowing you know nothing
Socrates

Layer after layer of interconnected information has been given to me since 1990 which has included the human control system; the non-human force or 'Spider' working in the background; the true nature of reality; the fake 'world' of the simulation; and the disturbed and distorted consciousness ultimately orchestrating the enslavement of human society.

One subject doesn't stop to be replaced by the next. Each adds to the previous ones and the information then runs concurrently across them all. This is why I live alone and spend my life working seven days a week; it's why I'm constantly focussed on what I do to process and compile the tsunami of information and fit the pieces together. The key subject which connects all the others into a seamless whole is reality. What is it? What is our relationship with it? Who are we? Where are we? What is this 'place', this 'world'? Without the background to reality itself nothing in the rest of the book will make sense. *With* that knowledge *everything* can make sense.

Worlds apart

There are two worlds within what seems to be one (Fig 65 overleaf). There is the reality that the population believes itself to be experiencing and the realm of the Global Cult. The difference between them is *knowledge*. The Cult has created an 'education' system designed to program a perception of self and reality that maintains the masses in a state of ignorance about all major areas of life essential to understanding what is going on. The Cult-owned media and Silicon Valley platforms continue to perpetuate this ignorance in the post-school, post-university, years with their coordinated lies and censorship orchestrated by the Spider. The collective ambition is total human control via the control of human perception which becomes human behaviour which becomes human society. To control society you must control perception and to do that you must control information from which those perceptions are formed. Those few sentences describe why the world is as it is and why it functions as it does. The goal in World Number 1 is to keep the population in ignorance and separated from what they need to know. World Number 2 is the world of the Cult

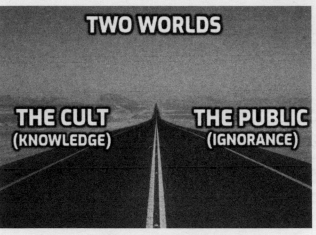

Figure 65: The two worlds in which knowledge is hoarded in the secret societies of the Cult network and kept from a population perceptually-programmed by Cult-owned 'education' and media. What to the Cult are coordinated and interconnected actions appear to the great majority of people as random.

with its global web of secret societies that I have already described. Secret societies are obviously created to keep secrets and from whom? The population. Knowledge that the people need to set them free is hoarded in the secret society web and passed on only to chosen initiates through the generations and across the centuries. Even then the overwhelming majority within this network only have snippets of the truth. What they need to know to serve the Cult and no more. The Cult network is fiercely policed and compartmentalised and structured in levels of 'degree' employed by all secret societies. Those in the Cult's higher degrees decide who can and cannot be privy to the information they know. Only the Cult's inner core have the greater knowledge and they, too, will be compartmentalised from the non-human levels that I will be exposing. Corporations, governments and the world in general is similarly compartmentalised. The guy working the car park at Facebook doesn't know what Zuckerberg is doing and Zuckerberg doesn't know what his masters are doing. The prime areas of knowledge that must be kept from the people are two-fold:

1) Where the world is being taken by the Cult.

2) The nature of reality.

The first one is obvious and the second less so. By keeping the plan for humanity secret your coordinated events and happenings can be presented as random when they are all connected to the same end. I have long used the phrase: 'Know the outcome and you'll see the journey,' If you don't know the planned outcome, the steps towards the outcome can seem random and in and of themselves. Know the desired outcome and suddenly the 'random' appears as it really is – blatantly connected and coordinated. Once you know the outcome laid out in the Cult script, the world and its happenings take on a totally, utterly, completely, new perspective. I have worked to uncover that script and present it to the population to allow the illusion of random to be seen. From that point people can see daily events as pieces in the same picture and steps in the same direction.

Hiding the illusion

Even more crucial than this to the Cult is to entrap humanity in a state of ignorance about our own true identity and the very reality that people think – *think* – they are experiencing. Therefore the dominant message coming from Cult-owned-and-funded science and academia is that we live in a solid world of physicality; everything is apart from everything else; nothing is connected; life is random; and death is the end for everyone. None of this is true, but if you want to enslave people in a sense of pointlessness, fear, bewilderment, and limitation you need them to believe this crap. The backstop when this narrative fails is religion in which you are judged for all eternity by an angry, vicious (but 'loving') god on your actions in a single human life that can last anything between a few seconds and more than 100 years. You are either death-fearing or god-fearing and often both. Whichever one you choose you are still 'fearing' which is the whole idea of the exercise for reasons that will become devastatingly clear. The truth is rather different – dramatically so – and this really is the truth that will set us free. That's why the Cult doesn't want you to know what I am about to reveal.

All the scientific evidence and support for what I am about to say can be found in my mega-works *The Perception Deception, Everything You Need To Know But Have Never Been Told,* and *The Answer.* There is also a 13-part series on the nature of reality that I wrote and presented for Ickonic using special effects. In this book I want to connect the dots simply and clearly between apparently unconnected information and subject matter that is, in fact, fundamentally connected. I have always found it amazing that, of all the areas of life and society discussed and explored by humanity, the key questions are nowhere near the top of the list: Who are we?; Where are we?; What is this 'place', this reality? I mean – you'd think we'd want to know, surely? These questions have long been at the *top* of my list. How can we understand anything else if we don't understand the very reality that we are experiencing? If you want to entrap the target population in perceptual servitude this is precisely the situation that you want to create. Most think that reality is far too complex and bewildering and best left to those clever and superior scientists and academics who are in truth almost in their entirety clueless about what reality really is. There are some brilliant scientists exploring the cutting edge of human knowledge as there are some outstanding academics and doctors. To see them all like that, however, is a big, BIG, mistake. My experience of all three professions is that they are largely, yes, I mean largely, peopled by a combination of programmed ignorance, concrete minds, and staggering levels of myopia, Plus many are so corrupt and devoid of integrity that their 'conclusions' are decided by what their paymasters demand them to be rather than open-minded research and inquiry. I want a 'scientific study' that tells people what I want them to believe. Yes, Mr Gates, how much? This exchange of cash is followed by media reports peppered with 'scientists say', 'experts say', and 'the latest study says' when all are simply what Bill Gates and other Cult billionaires and operatives want them to say. Replace 'scientists' and 'experts' in these 'news' reports with 'Bill Gates' and the truth will dawn. It's the same with replacing 'China' every time you hear it with 'the Cult'.

Research the scale of funding by the Bill and Melinda Gates Foundation of 'science', 'academia', 'medicine' and 'media' and you will be shocked by its scale, reach and influence. When these fake 'scientists', 'academics' and 'experts' move their lips, Bill Gates and the Cult are speaking. They are the last people I seek out to tell me anything about anything. How essential that has been in the 'Covid' era in navigating the lies and deceit spewing from the mouths of these Cult-owned gofers. Without that perspective we have seen what happens. Much of humanity has descended into serfs shaking with fear and punctured with fake vaccinations. Gates is not only evil, he's insane. He's funded a Japanese university to produce 'flying syringes' which take the form of genetically-modified mosquitos that can administer vaccines when they bite. The Nuremberg Code of informed consent for medical procedures is not a problem for a Cult-owned, Rockefeller-owned, psychopath like Gates, and nor is persuading academics and scientists to manifest his madness at the expense of their fellow humans. 'Experts' will do anything, and tell you anything, for money.

'Infinite Love is the only truth'

The illusion of 'physical matter' became tangible to me over two nights in a Brazilian rainforest in 2003 when I took the psychoactive potion Ayahuasca. I had accepted an invitation to speak at the week-long event and experience the rainforest plant. I knew that if I was going deeper in my understanding I had to explore others levels of reality beyond the perceived 'physical'. This had to be in a conscious-state and not a fleeting dream. I took Ayahuasca on the first night on my own while a facilitator observed in the big circular wooden building at the location in

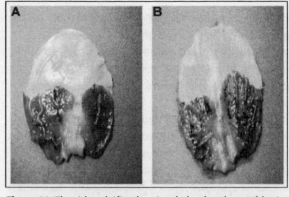

Figure 66: Fluoride calcifies the pineal gland and scrambles its ability to connect with other realities as part of the Cult's effort to isolate human perception in the five senses.

the forest. The next night I was with a large group of people as the dose was increased and my mind boarded the magic carpet. I drank from a small glass and Ayahuasca tasted a bit like liquorice. It contains Dimethyltryptamine, or DMT, a powerful neuron-transmitter and psychedelic drug that occurs naturally in

Figure 67: The body is an antenna decoding reality from wavefield information and the sensitivity of the pineal gland affects the scale of frequencies that we can tap into. (Image by Neil Hague.)

many plants. DMT stimulates the pineal gland in the centre of the brain which operates as what is called the 'third-eye' – the connection with other expressions of reality beyond the five-sense 'world' that we normally perceive. The pineal gland is only the size of a grain of rice, but it is vital to body function as well as our ability to 'see' outside what we think we see. The pineal is an antenna receiving and transmitting information. How 'coincidental' then that fluoride added to drinking water and toothpaste calcifies the pineal gland. This is part of the agenda to block humanity's other-dimensional senses to maintain us in five-sense ignorance (Figs 66 and 67). The effect of what is called DMT has been known since ancient times and you can see depictions of psychoactive plants and the pineal gland in the remains and artefacts of ancient cultures throughout the world. The pineal gland is often symbolised as a pine cone which it resembles.

It took about an hour for the Ayahuasca effect to kick in on the first night and I began to enter an altered state of consciousness. It's a strange experience. When you open your eyes the world is pretty much as you have always perceived it; when you close them you are in a completely different reality and it is hard to keep your eyes open for long. You don't want to. The other reality is so fascinating. On the first night as I began to be aware of my consciousness shifting, I felt as if someone was squeezing the centre of my chest where the heart chakra or vortex is located as I mentioned earlier. There are seven major vortices – 'chakras' or 'wheels of light' – that connect the body and the realm of the five-senses with other levels of consciousness that most people never truly connect with during a human life. One of the Cult's prime objectives is to create a separation between five-sense Body-Mind and expanded consciousness to isolate the population in a reality and perceptual prison that I will expand upon as we go along. Healing that separation is what people call 'awakening' or 'waking up'. This is really a reconnection or reintegration of multiple levels of self. The prime chakras or vortices in the human energy field are: The crown chakra on top of the head; the brow (or 'third eye') chakra in the centre of the forehead; the throat chakra; the heart chakra in the centre of the chest; the solar plexus or navel chakra; the sacral chakra beneath the navel; and the base or root

chakra at the bottom of the spine (Fig 68). Each vortex has a particular function or functions. The crown chakra has the potential to connect us to higher levels of consciousness; the brow chakra gives us access to psychic communication beyond this reality and connects with the pineal and pituitary glands in the brain that together form the 'third-eye'; the throat chakra relates to communication and creativity – vibrational communication (language/sound) via the vocal cords; the heart chakra is our potential connection to the highest

Figure 68: The chakra 'wheels of light' network of vortexes that connect and interpenetrate different levels of the human energetic field.

levels of awareness, intuition, 'knowing', and innate intelligence which cannot be taught; the solar plexus chakra is a seat of raw power that can be used for good or ill; the sacral chakra relates to emotions and sexuality; and the root chakra is said to connect us to the 'material' realm of perceived matter. This is the seat of what is known in the East as 'kundalini' which takes us back to Peru.

Kundalini – literally 'coiled one' in ancient Sanskrit – is an energy symbolised as an uncoiling snake which when activated can explode through the spine and central nervous system and out through the top of the head (the crown chakra) to connect us to greater 'enlightenment' in realities far from this one (Figs 69 and 70). 'Far' in terms of frequency

Figure 69: What was activated in me on the hill in Peru.

that is. Kundalini activation was a central part of what happened to me on that hill in Peru and why I felt that double-flow of energy from the earth though my feet and central nervous system and out through the top of my head with another flow going the other way. The interaction was between the root chakra (earth) and crown chakra (other-dimensional enlightenment). This was the source of the explosion of information that poured into my conscious and subconscious awareness that literally blew my mind for three months in 1991. The key vortex is the heart chakra, the balance point for the other six and why the heart projects the body's most powerful electromagnetic field (Fig 71 overleaf). The lower three largely relate to this reality and the higher three largely to expanded states of awareness and communication. The heart is the governor sitting at the centre, or should be, and our connection to our expanded and ultimately Infinite Self. For this reason the Cult has structured human society and perception to block the heart chakra's proper function by

Figure 70: The symbol known as the caduceus is symbolic of the kundalini phenomenon.

transferring attention into the head (five-sense mind) and the belly (scrambled emotions). Awakening people in a state of expanded awareness is the last thing it wants. When that happens its control agenda would be over.

Figure 71: The power of the heart and heart vortex can potentially project a massive electromagnetic field.

I was aware, as I lay in the Brazilian darkness, of that squeezing sensation in precisely the place where the heart chakra is located. I then felt like an arc of electromagnetic energy from the chest to the centre of my forehead and the third-eye or brow chakra. The squeezing was now at both ends of the arc. The pure power was amazing. While this was happening the music that the facilitator was playing began to malfunction as the player switched on and off. Then one of the strip lights on the ceiling came on. I wondered why anyone would turn the light on. I looked to my right and the facilitator was nowhere near the light switch or the music player. Even then the light switch would have turned on all the lights around the building and not only one. The arc of energy I was feeling from heart to brow grew in intensity and two more strip lights came on. So much 'paranormal' activity is associated with electrical systems with lights and devices switching on and off or lights dimming. Consciousness in its infinite forms communicates with our reality through electromagnetism which is the very foundation of our simulated 'world' as we'll see. These projected electromagnetic fields can impact upon electrical systems and also explain the 'spider's web' that I felt on my face with Betty Shine, why the atmosphere around me changed in the Ryde newspaper shop, and what happened on the hill in Peru.

There is no 'physical'

On the second night of Ayahuasca, as I eased into an altered state, a voice which took a female form began to speak to me very loudly and clearly and continued for the next five hours. Information the voice communicated was astonishing as I was given chapter and verse about the illusory nature of 'physical' reality. The voice began by saying that I was going to be taken to where I came from and to where I would return. With that I found myself experiencing a realm of absolute love, peace and bliss in which everything was *One*. There was no division, no competition, no conflict, no fears, no worries. What's more, it was silent and still except for the odd

Figure 72: Neil Hague's depiction of what I was told in my Ayahuasca altered state was 'The Infinite' – a brilliant, dazzling, blackness and stillness.

movement in extreme slow motion. I can see why this state of awareness has been called the 'Void'. 'This is the Infinite, David', the voice said as I was shown a field of glistening blackness. I read the account of a near-death experience years later in which this same phenomenon was described as 'dazzling darkness'. It was an excellent term for what I saw (Fig 72). I refer to this level of consciousness as *Infinite Awareness In Awareness of Itself* and this pervades the entirety of Infinite existence. When people say 'God is everywhere' this is what they are talking about if they only realised and stopped seeing everything in 'physical' terms through the perceptions of five-sense reality. *Infinite Awareness In Awareness of Itself* is the creative force of All-Possibility and All-Potential from which all creation springs (Fig 73). We are all expressions of Infinite Awareness, but clearly not all are aware of their infinite nature. They can

believe instead they are an engineer, dental assistant, teacher, delivery driver, or whatever, when those are only their self-identities and experiences in a brief perceptual sojourn called human. I call this human self-identity

INFINITE
AWARENESS
IN AWARENESS
OF ITSELF

Figure 73: Where all is known and from where all creativity springs.

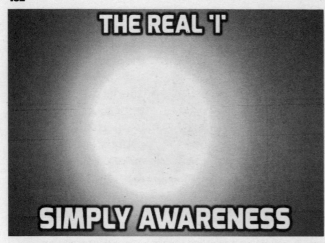

Figure 74: What we are when all illusion falls away.

Phantom Self while *WE* are Infinite Awareness although in almost every case *not* in Awareness of Itself. Our true identity has been hijacked. We are not our bodies; we are the consciousness having an experience *through* the body as we experience the Internet through a computer. *We* are awareness, a state of being aware. Everything else, including all form, is illusion in the sense of physicality. We are formless with the potential to take any illusory form as an aid to Infinite experience (Fig 74). We are awareness, but how aware? Aware enough to answer the phone at a call centre and self-identify as a call centre operative? Or aware enough to know that we are *All That Is, Has Been, and Ever Can Be* – Infinite Possibility, Infinite Potential, waiting to be manifested by our perception in a process I'll be explaining? Crucial to escaping the prison cell of perceived limitation and Phantom Self is to escape the trap of believing in a physical world in which everything is separated from everything else. Most of the five hours on the second night of Ayahuasca was the voice dismantling that illusion. There was no 'physical' or 'solidity' and our reality is nothing like it appears to be.

I returned to England with total recall of what the voice said and I have accessed so much more knowledge and insight into our reality in the two decades since then. I began to look at the various scientific disciplines from quantum physics to biology and you realise that the puzzle pieces are all there to confirm the physical illusion. Sadly the disciplines don't talk to each other and often compete for funding and prestige. Invariably the (Cult) funders get the conclusions they pay for at the expense of the truth. Quantum physics alone demolishes solid reality. Other disciplines have to acknowledge this as reluctantly as they can and then they crack on as if the no-physical quantum world doesn't exist. To accept its full implications would be the end of the entire worldview of biology and medicine and they cling to the wreckage and seek to glue it back together as its credibility increasingly falls apart. Meanwhile, science projects working for the Cult focus on this very quantum world including nanotechnology. They know physicality and 'matter' are illusions and this is a crucial part of the knowledge base

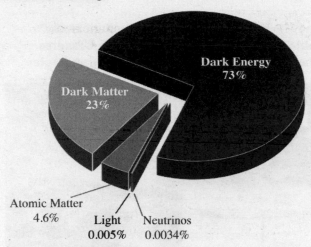

passed on through the generations in the secret society network of the Cult and kept from the population. Reality is not as complex as it appears to be and this encouraged perception of complexity hides reality's simple foundations. What we see with our eyes – actually our

Figure 75: According to mainstream science the electromagnetic spectrum is only 0.005 percent of what exists in the universe – 0.5 percent at most.

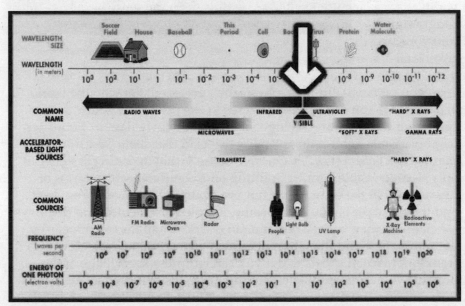

Figure 76: Visible light, the only band of frequency we can see, is a smear of the 0.005 percent. Humans are virtually blind and no wonder so many suffer from intergenerational myopia.

brain/mind – is only a tiny band of frequency called *visible* light within the electromagnetic spectrum. The entire spectrum (what we call 'light') is estimated to be just 0.005 percent of what exists in the Universe (Fig 75). Some say it's up to 0.5 percent and whichever it's infinitesimal. Think about that and even more so this: The only band of frequency that we can 'see' is a fractional smear of the 0.005 percent known as visible light (Fig 76). In the name of sanity we are basically *blind*. Religions tell us that all we need to know is between the covers of a single book within a barely perceivable fraction of 0.005 percent of the Universe. How crazy is that? As the quote by Socrates at the start of the chapter says: 'The only true wisdom is in knowing you know nothing.' The way to know anything is to open your mind to all possibility and not confine perception to the sense of reality programmed into your psyche all your life to

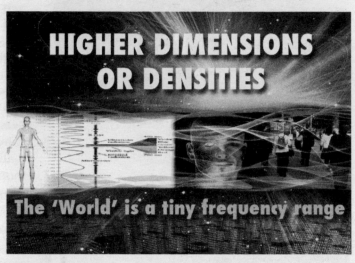

Figure 77: Our 'world' is a band of frequency. Infinity lies beyond its illusory limitations. (Image by Neil Hague.)

keep you perceptually, thus 'physically', enslaved. We scan the world and think we can see all there is to see in the perceived 'space' we are observing when we are 'seeing' only the hilariously narrow frequency band of visible light. Infinite Reality exists in that same 'space'; it's just that we can't see it (Fig 77). Our five-sense visual decoding system can only decode visible light. Try putting on a computer screen levels of frequency that the computer is not programmed to decode. You can't and the principle is exactly the same. People are ridiculed and dismissed for claiming they've seen non-human entities or spacecraft appearing out of nowhere and then disappearing. Once again the ridicule comes from ignorance. It shows that if you can suppress knowledge of the possible you can manipulate your targets to dismiss with a laugh and a wave of the hand what is actually happening. Those entities and craft don't appear and disappear. They enter the human visual frequency range and then leave. To the human *observer* they only seem to appear and disappear as they come and go from the only band of frequency the observer can see. It's real simple and that goes for all apparently 'impossible' phenomena.

The limits of our five-sense visual reality mean that we can only pretty much see the frequency of 'objects' – actually holographic forms as I'll come to. As a result everything seems to be separated from everything else with 'empty space' in between when there is no 'empty space'. Everything is connected by a field of energy – consciousness –

that I will call The Field (Fig 78). Imagine a Wi-Fi field or the ocean which connects all sea life. In fact there are *two* Fields – the Infinite Field which is an expression of Infinite Awareness and the electromagnetic Simulation Field. Which one we allow to most influence our perceptions and

Figure 78: The five-senses see forms and 'things' with 'empty space' in between when in fact that 'space' is filled with the consciousness of possibility, probability and potential which we can tap into and manifest. This is The Field that connects us all as One. (Image by Neil Hague.)

behaviour decides if we are 'asleep' or 'awake'. The Simulation Field is a waveform information construct that mimics the Infinite Field to draw consciousness into its 'human' lair of illusion. I'll be dealing with the Simulation Field in much more detail and until then I will refer to them as The Fields, plural. In both cases these Fields are operating on levels of frequency that the body sight senses cannot decode and so can't see. This produces the illusion of everything being separated when all is One and connected by The Fields (Fig 79). All so-called paranormal

phenomena can be explained once we understand The Fields. We are expressions of The Fields and we can communicate telepathically for example as our thoughts and emotions travel through The Fields in

Figure 79: 'The Fields' unseen to our five-senses connect everything as all fish are connected by the ocean. (Image by Neil Hague.)

the form of frequency. Every thought and emotion generates a frequency relating to the nature of the thought/emotion. Hate, depression and anxiety are low, slow, dense frequencies while love, joy and happiness are quick, high, frequencies which is why when we feel depressed we feel 'heavy' and when we feel joy we feel 'light'. This corresponds to the frequencies we are generating with our thoughts and emotions and their impact on the body's electromagnetic field (called on one level the 'aura').

Wow, I was just thinking of you

Many people have experienced thinking about someone and then the phone rings and it's them. Crikey, that's a mystery! Not at all. When you were thinking of them they were thinking of you as they were about to call. The frequency communication between you was generated through The Fields. This can happen at any perceived 'distance' given that there is no 'distance' – another illusion incredible as that may seem to the five senses. Such telepathy doesn't happen more often because humanity has been so desensitised from these levels of frequency communication while living in reality bubbles of five-sense perception that cannot sense or hear the 'voices' (frequencies) in The Fields. 'Voices' that psychics and mediums hear and connect with are communicated through The Fields, whether the Infinite or simulation variety. 'Voices' I have heard communicating with me are actually *frequencies* in The Fields that I decode into 'voices' or rather thought-forms that I decode into the experience of a 'voice'. We are doing that anyway with human 'voices' which are frequencies generated by the vocal cords that our hearing senses decode into language. Ancient cultures and tribal people retained this sensitivity which became known as the 'bush telegraph' and allows those out in the bush to sense what is happening back in the village by decoding frequencies generated from the village and communicated through The Fields. The bush telegraph still operates for those tribal peoples largely untouched by 'modern' Western 'culture' which is what? A *five-sense* reality that entraps awareness in the illusions of 'physicality' and closes off the channels to bush telegraph sensitivity. 'Western culture' is specifically designed to do that and the 'Great Reset' is a far more extreme version of this using technology.

Animals don't go to school, watch the media, and have their sense of reality disconnected from these subtle energies and they are therefore ultra-sensitive to what is happening in The Fields. It's been noticed how animals seem to know that a storm or earthquake is coming while humans have to see them to acknowledge their existence. A storm or earthquake begins with changes in The Fields long before they become visual reality. Animals – and sensitive humans – feel these changes and take action to avoid what they know is about to happen. This is what we call 'intuition'. The Fields connect us all – everything is part of a seamless whole – and *we are all One*. The apparent divisions between us are illusions of the human sight decoding process which cannot see The Fields that connect us whether humans to each other, humans to the 'natural world', or everything (in the case of the Infinite Field) to Infinite Reality. We can communicate with animals, plants and trees through The Fields. No, not through human language; through the vibration of the words and the frequency of our hearts and minds. What are words except frequency fields of information cast into The Fields by our vocal cords? All communication is really frequencies passing through The Fields to be decoded by those who can see, hear, touch, taste, smell, and sense a greater reality. This is the simple knowledge that the manipulators of human society don't want us to know given that it sets us free from the ignorance which holds us in servitude. The Fields are the foundation of everything and to understand The Fields is to understand life itself.

Body-Mind and decoded illusion

Consciousness operates on levels of vibration that cannot directly interact with the band of frequency we call the human world. Consciousness – awareness – in its prime state could not pick up objects or sit in a chair just as two radio stations on different wavelengths cannot connect. We therefore experience human reality through a vehicle called a 'body' which *does* match the frequency band of human reality and can interact with it. More than that the five-senses and systems of the body decode information from The Fields (the Simulation Field overwhelmingly in this case) and produce the experienced illusion of a physical world. Or at least that's how it operates on one level. I'll be going very much deeper later on. Everything in our human reality is wavefield information that connects with *The* Fields which encompass all other fields. Our bodies are information fields and so is everything you think you see, hear, touch, smell and taste. The five senses decode frequencies of information in the waveform Fields through the antenna we call eyes, ears, skin, nose and tongue, and transforms them into electrical signals which are communicated to the brain. This, in turn, decodes the electrical information into digital and holographic information that we experience as a physical external world when *there is no 'external' world* as we perceive it (Fig 80 overleaf). A computer decodes information from Wi-Fi into the form that we see on the screen and the text and images we are observing are *inside* the computer in the same way that perceived physical reality is *inside* us. Different areas of the brain decode those signals into the perception of sight, sound, touch, smell, and taste to construct the sense of reality that we experience as an external world when, in that form – so-called physicality – it only exists

Figure 80: 'We may perceive the 'world' as 'physical' but all is an expression of decoded waveform information. (Image by Neil Hague.)

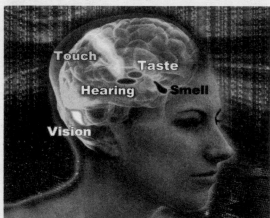

Figure 81: 'We may perceive the 'world' as 'physical' but all is an expression of decoded waveform information. (Image by Neil Hague.)

Figure 82: Where is the 'physical world'? Here you go ... on one level that is. (Image by Gareth Icke.)

in our head (Figs 81 and 82). Even 'our head' is a misnomer given that brain and body are also waveform information fields that we decode into apparent physical reality and I shall put this in a wider context in due course.

I have told the story in some previous books described by Michael Talbot in *The Holographic Universe* in which a stage hypnotist was performing at a private party. A man called Tom was put in a hypnotic trance and told that when he 'woke up' he would not be able to see his daughter. The hypnotist guided the daughter to stand right in front of her sitting father so he was looking directly into her belly. Tom was asked if he could see his daughter in the room. He looked around and said 'no' while his daughter was inches away. The hypnotist put his hand in the small of her back and asked Tom what he was holding. 'A watch', he said, while his daughter stood between him and the watch. He was asked to read an inscription on the watch which he did. To 'normal' reality what I have just described is impossible, but in fact it can be explained so simply. As with everything in our reality, the daughter's body was a waveform field of information operating outside of visible light. It was beyond her father's sight senses. For him to see her he had to decode her field into a holographic form operating *within* visible light. The hypnotic suggestion that Tom would not be able to see his daughter firewalled his brain not to decode her field. In his reality she remained in waveform and so not only was he unable to see her – she could not block his view within holographic reality of the watch. Once you grasp the real nature of reality the impossible becomes possible and the 'paranormal' becomes simply

explainable. We even decode our *own* bodies into the appearance that we see (Fig 83). Body-Mind with its five senses decodes information from the simulation into the world we think we are living 'in' when it's all a decoded illusion. As the Morpheus

Figure 83: The body is an information field decoded into 'physical' illusion by the information field we call the brain; but there is another level of this that I will come to later. (Image by Neil Hague.)

character said in the movie, *The Matrix*:

> What is real? How do you define 'real'? If you're talking about what you can feel, what you can smell, what you can taste and see, then 'real' is simply electrical signals interpreted by your brain.

Robert Lanza, an American medical doctor and scientist, describes how a candle flame is emitting tiny packets of electromagnetic energy called photons, each pulsing electrically and magnetically. We only see the flame that we recognise when the brain decodes that energetic information into a holographic state. Lanza writes in his excellent book, *Biocentrism:*

> It is easy to recall from every day experience that neither electricity nor magnetism have visual properties. So, on its own, it's not hard to grasp that there is nothing inherently visual, nothing bright or coloured about the candle flame. Now, let these same invisible electromagnetic waves strike a human retina, and if (and only if) the waves happen to measure between 400 and 700 nano meters in length from crest to crest, then their energy is just right to deliver a stimulus to the 8 million cone-shaped cells in the retina.
>
> Each in turn send an electrical pulse to a neighbor neuron, and on up the line this goes, at 250 mph, until it reaches the warm, wet occipital lobe of the brain, in the back of the head. There, a cascading complex of neurons fire from the incoming stimuli, and we subjectively perceive this experience as a yellow brightness occurring in a place we have been conditioned to call the 'external world'.

The same principle applies to colour which is also a vibration interpreted by your brain. Every colour and shade of colour is a different *frequency*. Something appears to have a certain colour or colours because it reflects some light frequencies (which we decode and therefore 'see') and absorbs the rest (which we don't decode and therefore don't 'see'). Black absorbs all light, so it's black; white reflects all light, so it's white; and different colours absorb some light frequencies and reflect others. Scientist Isaac Newton (1642-1726) called the frequency band of rainbow colours a 'spectrum' and this is appropriate when the word originates with the Latin for apparition or phantom. 'Spectre' has the same etymological source. Where are all the colours that you see? In your 'head', the human decoding system. It's the only place they exist.

What's the time? NOW!

The scale of the 'external world' and 'matter' illusion is fantastic. The Simulation Field is feeding information to the five-senses to be decoded into an experienced reality of light, heat, weight, solidity, motion, space, and time, when none of them exist beyond the informational confines of the simulation. They are the decoded interactions between the simulation, five senses and brain/mind within the speed of light. For example, there is no time, simply the decoded illusion of it. There is only the Infinite, eternal NOW. Crazy? Where are you when you experience what you perceive as the present? In the NOW. Where are you when you think about the 'past'? In the NOW. Where were you when you experienced what you call the 'past'? In the NOW. Where are you when you think about the 'future'? In the NOW. Where will you be when you experience what you call the 'future'? In the NOW. There is only the NOW. There is only the 'is'. 'Time' is a concept and concepts are the perceptions of mind, not Infinite Awareness. We have a concept of 'time' when it does not exist. We will see as the book proceeds that we have concepts of endless things that do not exist. We are not past. We are not future. These are concepts. We are 'is'. We are *Isness*.

Then there is the illusion of space and distance. How can they be real when the apparent 'light years' of 'distant' space that you view in the night sky only exist in that form in your brain/mind? Play a virtual reality game and you will perceive space, distance and time, but they are only information encoded in the game for the player to decode into an

Figure 84: Virtual reality technology feeds information to the five senses to hack into the human decoding system ...

Figure 85: ... even though the senses are only decoding information from technology the result can appear incredibly real.

illusory reality. Virtual reality games with their headsets, earphones and gloves are hacking into the very five senses that decode human reality from the simulation and yet how real these games can appear (Figs 84 and 85). The 'modern' technological world is mimicking the way we decode 'normal' reality and before long you won't be able to tell the difference between 'virtual reality' and 'real reality' (the simulation). How can weight be real when your body and everything else is a waveform information field decoded into a non-physical hologram? Why do we breathe heavier running up hill when there is no hill except in our minds? When Morpheus and a breathless Neo are sparring in a *Matrix* simulation program Morpheus asks: 'Do you think that's air you're breathing now?' and 'Do you think that my being stronger and faster has anything to do with my muscles in this place?' How can that be when it's all happening in the mind and the body itself is a 'physical' illusion that tricks the mind into a sense of limitation? It's worth repeating that for later reference: The body itself is a 'physical' illusion that tricks the mind into a sense of limitation. Another *Matrix* quote captures the point:

Figure 86: The world is not what it seems.

Do not try and bend the spoon. That's impossible. Instead, only try to realise the truth ... There is no spoon ... Then you'll see that it is not the spoon that bends. It is only yourself.

The spoon doesn't bend because there is no physical spoon. It's a decoded illusion and it's not the spoon that bends; it is your mind, your *decoding system* (Fig 86).

Mind-altering drugs can distort reality when they distort the way reality is decoded. Nothing exists in our 'human' reality unless we decode it into holographic (illusory 'physical') reality. I have made the point already that words do not pass between us as we think they do. Frequencies encoded with the information we *call* words do that. Our vocal cords generate frequency waves as we appear to speak and they travel through The Fields until our hearing antenna sense those waves and transform them into electrical signals which are sent to the brain/mind to be decoded into 'Hello, mate, how are you?'. We only taste when the brain decodes electrical signals from the tongue into '*Mmmm*, that's lovely', or 'Ugh, what is that?'. We only feel pain when a message from the area involved is decoded by the brain into 'ouch'. Pain relief methods are used today which stop that message reaching the brain. If the brain doesn't decode the signal then it *can't* register as 'ouch'. Does a falling tree make a noise? Only if you hear it. A falling tree is a frequency field moving through The Fields. The interaction creates an energetic disturbance in The Fields and if someone is close enough their hearing senses will pick up that disturbance – those waves/frequencies – and the brain will decode this into the sound of a tree falling. If no one is there, a falling tree makes no noise. Without an *observer* – a decoder – it *can't*. Everything comes down to the observer creating reality. Control the perceptions of the observer and you control the decoded *experience* of the observer. Here we have the very foundation of human control and, at the same time, of human freedom as we shall see as the dots continue to connect.

Holographic 'physical'

Physical reality is actually holographic reality. The world and everything we see in terms of form is a hologram decoded from information

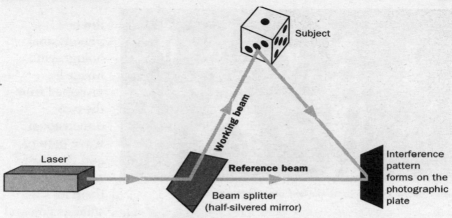

Subject

Working beam

Laser

Reference beam

Beam splitter
(half-silvered mirror)

Interference
pattern
forms on the
photographic
plate

Figure 87: How holograms are created.

encoded in waves. The principle is the same as the process through which holograms are created that we buy in the shops and see in more sophisticated ways in stage concerts and product launches. Holograms are made by splitting a laser into two parts – one (the reference beam)

Figure 88: Drop two pebbles in a pond and where the waves collide is a waveform representation of where the stones fell, how fast, and how heavy they are.

Figure 89: A holographic print is encoded in waveform with all the information of the object or subject involved.

goes directly onto a holographic print and the other (the working beam) records the subject in waveform before being directed onto the print (Fig 87). Here it collides with the reference beam and together they create a waveform representation of the subject which can be likened to dropping two pebbles in a pond with the waves moving out until they collide (Fig 88). The pattern in the water is a waveform representation of where the stones fell, how far apart, how fast and how big they were. In the same way the holographic print contains the information in waveform of the subject (Fig 89). A laser is then directed at this wave pattern and something remarkable happens as an apparently

Figure 90: All the famous people here are holograms.

Waveform

Electrical

Digital

Holographic

Figure 91: The 'human' decoding process from waveform via the electrical and into digital holograms. (Image by Neil Hague.)

three-dimensional holographic image is projected from the two-dimensional wave pattern and the most advanced of them look as solid as you and me (Fig 90). But they are not solid. They just *appear* to be. That laser, in terms of the human experience, is our conscious attention, our focus. When we observe something, our attention triggers the decoding process that makes it appear holographic or physical. When something is not being observed it returns to waveform – including us. This is why some cutting edge scientists have said that our reality only exists when it is observed. They are right although rather than 'observed' the term should be *decoded* (Fig 91). Computational power required is dramatically reduced if a simulation is only manifested when observed and is not permanently in a fully decoded state. Holograms today are increasingly made digitally and that's what the brain/mind is doing. It decodes digital holograms that we take to be an external and 'physical' world from waveform and electrical information. The digital level of reality is where physicists say everything can be broken down into numbers and mathematics and here, too, we have the basis for the esoteric art of numerology.

If the world is not 'solid' how come we can't walk through walls? Why when we bump into each other do we bounce off? How come I can sit in this chair? This is obviously caused by a form of resistance, but not 'physical' resistance – *electromagnetic* resistance or electromagnetic repulsion. Something that appears extremely solid like a wall is a slow dense frequency and the human body is quicker and less dense. They are, however, all close enough within the frequency band to experience electromagnetic resistance that we decode into the illusion of physical resistance. You could think of this principle as interference between two radio stations when they are close enough on the frequency dial. There eventually comes a point where frequencies are so different that radio stations can broadcast their output in the same space as all the other stations without interference and you can liken ghosts to a form of visual interference. Here you have the reason why people describe seeing 'ghosts' pass through walls as if the wall is not there. To the 'ghost' the wall is not there because their frequencies are so different.

I've seen this happen. I woke up one night in a holiday cottage in Normandy, France, and watched a ghostly figure, like a hazy field of energy, enter through the closed door to my left and float across the room to pass through the wall on the far side. It was so clear. The cottage was located at the site of the infamous Battle of the Falaise Gap, or Falaise Pocket, in August, 1944, following the D-Day Landings in World War Two. The cottage would have been there at the time. Many thousands died and even decades later you could still feel death in the energy field. Everything that happens becomes part of The Fields. That information – that recording if you like – will go on resonating the frequency of the event until it is dispersed. People continue to hear the noise of battles long gone in the area where they happened and feel a shudder when they enter a building where some horrific event has taken place even though they may not know that. This is the origin of 'good vibes' and 'bad vibes'. What we call 'ghosts' are fields of consciousness operating on frequencies close enough to our frequency to be seen or sensed while not close enough – most of the time anyway – to look as apparently solid as we do. If we were on the same frequency as the 'ghost' they would look as solid as you and me.

The same principle of frequency applies to those emitted by people based on their perceptions and mental and emotional states. Every thought and emotion generates into The Fields the frequency they represent. The sum total of these thoughts and emotions combine to form the electromagnetic field that we call our perceptions and the frequency nature of this perception field dictates how we interact with *The* Fields of possibility and probability, Infinite and simulated. I'll come to this in the next chapter. Those sensitive to these perceptual fields can see an apparently smiling, charming man or woman, yet feel a negative, even sinister 'vibe' coming from them. You can hide yourself with a facial expression and words of false bonhomie. You can't hide the vibrations you emit that reveal the frequency truth behind the smiling curtain. Our relationship with The Fields is like a feedback loop in which our frequencies affect The Fields while the vibrational state of The Fields in a given location affects us. It's all encoding and decoding – choice (encoding) and consequence (decoding). What is life except choice and consequence? Choice leads to consequences and if we don't like the consequences the wise make different choices to attract different consequences. This is the feedback loop with The Fields of infinite potential and possibility and the far more limited potential of the Simulation Field. They operate like an interactive Cosmic Internet. The force in pursuit of human control seeks to disconnect us from what should be these natural connections with the Infinite Field by drawing our focus (awareness) into the five-senses alone where the holographic world of the Simulation Field is all that we see and feel. We become unaware of the Infinite Field of prime reality that lies beyond. Answers to the challenges in the world of the seen will not be found in the world of the seen. That is only a simulated projection akin to a movie screen. Those answers lie in the expanded realms of consciousness that we cannot see and choose not to sense. This does not have to be. Infinity is awaiting us the moment we choose to free ourselves from the prison cell of five-sense reality.

The brain is not consciousness

The brain and genetic system in general (as we decode them) are processors of information and receiver-transmitters of information. Consciousness does not come *from* the brain, but *through* the brain. DNA in the cells is a receiver-transmitter of information that connects us with other levels of reality. Change DNA, which is what the synthetic 'Covid' fake vaccines are doing, and you change what people interact with by changing the frequencies on which DNA receives and transmits. When our connection with expanded awareness is diminished our perceptions retreat into only five-sense reality. Information processed by the brain into an apparent 'world' can come from the seriously limited source of the five-senses or from infinity itself. Which one depends on which Field – Infinite or Simulation – that is most influencing our sense of reality. How open we allow our 'five-sense minds' to be dictates how much of the Infinity Field that we connect with and this impacts fundamentally on our sense of self and reality. The result is called open minds and closed minds that have very different perceptions through access to different levels of information, insight and inspiration. Closed minds limit reality to the five-senses and form reality 'bubbles' that perceive only the infinitesimal world of the 'seen' (Fig 92 overleaf). Such minds self-identify only with the 'self' that they can see. I call them 'I am ares' – I am a man, woman, this race, this sexuality, this income bracket, this class, this culture. They are self-identifying the sense of 'I' with what they are *experiencing* in a brief human life and lose sight of the fact that

THE BUBBLE PROGRAM

MEDIA   POLITICS

EDUCATION   PARENTS

SCIENCE   FRIENDS

DOCTORS   EXPERTS

HISTORY

Figure 92: Once isolated in five-sense reality and disconnected from any influence from expanded awareness, human minds can be programmed with the perceptions that suit the Cult agenda of global control. The human plight in a single sentence.

their true 'I' is the eternal consciousness *having* the experience. They are not Charlie sweeping the streets or Mary on reception. These are only *experiences*. What we *are* is consciousness, ultimately Infinity itself, This delusion, this fake self-identity or Phantom Self, is the very foundation of control by the few of the many. Most of humanity lives in a perceptual prison of the five senses while infinity is seeking to connect with us, to intuitively guide, and open us to the *Source of All* which is love.

Imagine a computer as symbolic of the body and five-sense awareness, and the operator sitting with the mouse and keyboard as symbolic of expanded awareness (Fig 93). The two interact to their mutual benefit as we should be interacting with our eternal self during a

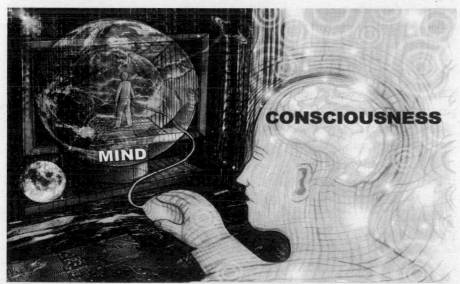

CONSCIOUSNESS

MIND

Figure 93: The analogy of the computer (five-sense mind) and the operator (expanded awareness). The Cult goal is to disconnect one from the other because unless it does so there can be no mass-control. (Image by Neil Hague.)

human experience. Observe what happens when a computer virus takes control of the system. The operator can bang the keys and click the mouse and there's no response. The virus is now controlling the actions – perceptions – of the computer. This is what has happened, with systematic calculation, to most of humanity. The 'virus' in this case is the force of malevolent manipulation that I have been exposing for more than 30 years. The book will explain how this is done and how we can delete that control founded on the separation of five-sense mind from eternal self. This separation is the core of all human misery and control. Separation makes people feel 'lost' and gives us that hollow feeling of emptiness as if something is missing. It *is*. What's missing is our connection to *All That Is, Has Been, and Ever Can Be*, the All-Possibility of which we are a unique expression; but fear not. That connection can be restored and the separation healed with a process much simpler and quicker than most can imagine. Human experience means that five-sense Body-Mind has different perceptions to expanded levels of ourselves that some call subtle bodies or 'soul'. Expanded awareness is observing the human experience of body-centred 'mind' and the two should be interacting in the way that I have described using the analogy of the computer and the operator. The disconnect between Body-Mind and expanded awareness is the result of vastly different perceptions which are expressed as vastly different frequencies. They separate like two radio stations on different wavelengths. We hear that two people are not on the same 'wavelength'. In other words they don't understand each other. This is literally true and absolutely so with Body-Mind and expanded awareness once the five senses become perceptually entrapped in the apparently material world. Body-Mind loses the frequency connection with, and influence of, its expanded self.

('Para') normal is only the normal we forgot

Over and over you see phenomena dismissed by people who can't understand how it can happen. This mentality dominates mainstream 'science' and much of the population. How can it be happening when I don't know how it could be happening? Well, maybe possibility – shock of shocks – is not limited to what people believe to be possible. I don't think 'the possible' takes that into account somehow. Poltergeist activity takes the form of 'physical' objects moving or even flying around a room along with strange and unexplained noises, smells, even levitation of people and objects. How this is possible can be explained by a simple fact: *There is no physical*. What we perceive as physical objects are really decoded holographic projections of energetic information fields and if the field moves then so must its apparent 'physical' expression. In this way other non-physical energy can influence the non-physical energy of objects. In the human decoded world of holographic reality it appears that solid, physical, objects, including people sometimes, are being moved, levitated and even thrown around the room. The question remains about what force exactly is generating this and there are probably a number of answers. It can be a mischievous spirit seeking to disrupt and intimidate, but there are too many occasions when an adolescent teenager is involved – often girls –for this to be dismissed as coincidence. Some scientists and researchers believe that the spirit uses the young girl as a vehicle to disrupt The Fields at a given location. Others have suggested that the teenager's state of emotion and extreme changes taking place at puberty can cause them to generate powerful and chaotic fields of energy that have the effect we call a poltergeist. All of these explanations can be true when each is a means for that part of The Fields to be seriously distorted and disrupted which means everything attached to The Fields is similarly disrupted. In the decoded holographic reality of humans the energetic disruption becomes apparently physical disruption and chaos in what appears to be classic poltergeist activity. Once we understand that the base state of all physicality is a waveform field of information and that the frequencies generated by thought and emotion can impact upon those fields the apparently inexplicable becomes straightforward to explain.

The healing art of homeopathy is another example of this. Homeopathy is dismissed by science, media, and many in the general public who are told what to think by science and media. The line you hear again and again is … you cannot heal the body with a substance diluted so many times that none of the substance remains. This is a reflex-action response of five-sense Body-Mind for which 'substance' (illusory physicality) is everything and the arbiter of all reality. The body is a hologram and the base state of the body is a waveform energy field – a vibrating field of information represented as frequencies interacting with each other. When that field is in harmony we are healthy and when it is disrupted – dis-eased – we suffer from some sort of illness in body or psyche. Everything in our reality is a frequency including the substances used in homeopathy. Those frequencies remain in the water when the substance is diluted into oblivion and it's the *frequencies* in homeopathy that can have a healing effect through their interaction with the frequencies in the body field. If that field is in harmony the body is in harmony. One is only a holographic projection of the other. You don't need the *substance* for homeopathy to work. You need the *frequency* of the substance.

A team at the Stuttgart Aerospace Institute in Germany proved in their experiments that information frequencies remain after a substance has been removed. They developed a technique to photograph information contained in water and in one experiment they dipped a flower into a large tank of water and then removed it. When they photographed the water with their technique they found that *every droplet* contained the information of the flower. The substance had gone while the *information* from the substance was still there and that is what happens with homeopathy. Why would information from the flower be in every droplet and not just part of the information with the droplet only part of the whole? This is explained by an amazing characteristic of holograms which explains so much about so much. Wavefield information from which the hologram is projected – decoded by the observer – is distributed in a way that every part of a hologram is encoded with the information of the *entire* hologram. If you cut a holographic print into four parts and direct the laser at each one you do not get a quarter of the picture projected as a hologram. You get a smaller version of the *whole* picture (Fig 94).

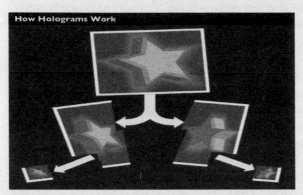

Figure 94: Every part of a hologram is a smaller version of the whole.

The body is a hologram and healing techniques such as reflexology and acupuncture can identify the whole body in parts of the body like the foot, hand or ear (Fig 95). This is why a skilled palm reader can see information from the whole body in a hand. Alternative healing techniques are invariably working at the wavefield level of the body. When the field is in harmony this must be transferred to the 'physical' level which is a holographic projection of that field and its holographic nature means that every part of the body is a smaller version of the whole body.

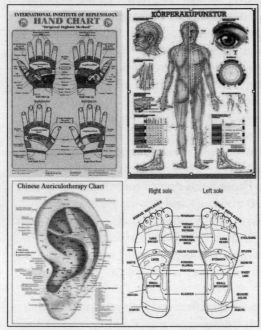

Figure 95: Acupuncture, reflexology, and other forms of alternative healing, can find parts of the body that represent the whole body because the body is a hologram.

Take a card

These principles of frequency and *perceptual* frequency apply to other methods of 'divination' or reality-reading such as Tarot cards. When the cards are offered, why do you pick card 'A' and not card 'B' when if you had picked card 'B' your reading might be totally different? Tarot cards carry symbols that represent mental and emotional *perceptual* states in the form of frequency. The Global Cult and its constituent secret societies have a whole language of symbolism through which they communicate with each other and (via the subconscious) with the population. Symbols represent mental and emotional frequencies which can influence people mentally and emotionally when they come into contact with those symbols on TV, in an advertisement, in the street, or in a carefully-selected logo behind a politician. The human electromagnetic field is encoded with frequencies that match the person's state of being and the trends in those mental and emotional states that are leading in a particular direction. When you pick a Tarot card your field magnetically attaches to the cards that represent corresponding frequencies in your field. You pick card 'A' and not card 'B' because of that. You may think you are choosing with your conscious mind when in fact the electromagnetic connection between body field and card field is making those choices. When the cards – all your choices – are laid out on the table they portray a symbolic representation of you *in that moment* – emphasis in that moment. As you change, so the cards will change, as your *frequency* changes (Fig 96).

An accurate Tarot reading does not tell you what will be, only what will potentially be if your energetic field stays the same. Your *perceptual*

Figure 96: The perceptual (frequency) state of your energetic field makes the 'pick' through its frequency connection to the fields represented by the Tarot cards.

(frequency) state stays the same. Even then the Tarot reader has to be skilled and energetically sensitive and the same with palm readers, psychics, mediums and homeopathy practitioners. Far from all of them are and we need to be selective. The great Zulu shaman Credo Mutwa 'threw the bones' for me once. They were bones carved into particular symbols and the principle is the same as the Tarot and rune stones that also carry symbols. Credo asked me to put my hands over the basket of bones before he began. This was to magnetically connect the energy fields of the bones with my own. He then threw the bones on the floor and where they land in relation to each other, and how far apart, can be read by the shaman. Where they came to rest on the floor was decided while they were still in the basket by their connection to my energy field and, again like Tarot, they represented on the floor a symbolic mirror of me *in that moment* and where the trends in my life were leading.

The art of numerology is the same except that it works with the digital level of Body-Mind, a digital expression of wavefield *frequency* information, A numerologist reads the numbers relating to our lives. Our names can be broken down into numbers, birth dates and so on, and everything about us can be digitised by numerology. I have had psychic and numerological readings close together as part of my research and they both gave me similar information. They were reading the *same* information expressed in different ways as waveform field and numbers. There is a lot more to know about all this, however, and how it relates to the simulation. I'll have much more to say about 'divination' and 'psychic connection' later on. An obvious expression of the simulation is astrology which is based on the movement of 'heavenly' bodies within the simulation. Planets and stars are holographic fields of energy-consciousness and as they move through the Simulation Field they affect the information/frequency state of The Field. We are constantly interacting with the Simulation Field and these changes affect us. The point at which we enter this cycle affects our own field and we will be encoded by these astrological impacts in different ways to those who entered at another part of the cycle. As a result different encoding ('astrological signs') will interact with the Simulation Field in different ways – 'I'm a Taurus', I'm a Gemini', I'm a Leo'. I have met astrologers on retainers to Cult operatives who seek advice on when to act in many and various ways to take action when astrological energy flows favour what they want to do rather than push against it in line with the tide in, tide out principle. If you want to swim out to sea pick a time when the tide is going in the same direction. A Shakespeare play puts it this way: 'There is a tide in the affairs of men which, taken at the flood, leads on to fortune; Omitted, all the voyage of their life is bound in shallows and in miseries.' That tide is energy. Cult initiates know about these energetic realities and that's why leading CEOs have astrologers on the payroll.

Cult banker J. P. Morgan said: 'Millionaires don't use astrology, billionaires do.' If you tap into expanded awareness beyond the simulation you can override astrological energies. If you don't, you can be a prisoner of them.

What miracles?

From the perspective of reality set out in this chapter those 'miracle' happenings in my life can be explained. Everything is information decoded by the observer and it is possible to infuse information into The Fields to make something amazing happen. Weather is decoded information and inserting a frequency field to be decoded as a rainstorm deluge at Sillustani is child's play if you are advanced enough in your knowledge of how it all works. The same applies to feathers falling from the sky and a stone circle being 'moved'. The 'physical' circle does not have to 'move' only the information field that it represents and even then it does not have to move – simply be 'copied' into my mind. This did not have to happen in anyone else's reality either. I had the experience and only I had to decode that reality. Someone else on that hill may well not have seen a circle and witnessed me standing alone inside. While I was experiencing the circle others would have been walking around the 'original' a mile away. In both cases the 'circle' was waveform information decoded into holographic reality. What is a virtual-reality game except encoded information? Does anyone doubt that the creator of such a game could encode a rainstorm or feathers falling or a stone circle? No, we are all well aware that is possible. The possibilities and potential of those games reflect those of our reality as we are going to see very clearly in the next chapter. There are no 'miracles' only levels of knowledge about how reality works. To someone who doesn't know, an inexplicable event can appear miraculous. To someone who does know it's commonplace and a cinch to explain. If you seek to perceptually entrap the population in limitation, separation, and ignorance you must ensure that they *don't know* and that's why Global Cult insiders work so hard to keep it to themselves.

The realisation from all this is that everything no matter how separated it appears to be to the five senses is one Infinite Whole in which the only division is the *perception* of division. A perception and not a reality except as a perceived reality. The illusion is symbolised in the way we talk of the Atlantic Ocean, Pacific Ocean, Indian Ocean and South China Sea when 'they' are the *same* body of water. We call the same body of Infinite Awareness Ethel Jones and Arthur Smith. The ocean is the droplet. The droplet is the ocean. Put the droplet in the ocean. Where does the droplet end and the ocean start?

There is no such point. They are indivisible.

CHAPTER SEVEN

The Mind Trap

As a thing is viewed, so it appears
Buddhist saying

Human reality is the tale of two Fields. One is Infinite and the other a technologically-generated simulation designed to ensnare and seduce perception into believing in a 'real world' that's not real at all.

Imagine an Infinite version of Wi-Fi being overlaid with another information field that is far more limited (Fig 97). I don't mean that the whole Infinite Field is overlaid, only a tiny part of it that we now call 'human'. The simulation, when compared with its own illusions of space and distance, is very small. It is an informational and perceptual prison isolated and separated from the Infinite Field of the *All That Is* as symbolised in Neil Hague's portrayal of what I mean (Fig 98). I say 'separated'. In fact nothing can actually be separated from the Infinite Whole; but you can be *perceptually* separated in that your experience is one of isolation and separation without the influence of expanded awareness. I'm going to focus in this chapter on the simulation, what it is and how it works, before dealing with the non-human forces behind it. Different dimensions of reality exist as different bands of frequency and interpenetrate each other like radio or television stations on different wavelengths sharing the same 'space'. Or, at least, that's the way it can be experienced. I am not talking about dimensions taught in science class of width, height, and depth with the addition of 'time' to make a fourth. I mean levels of perceived reality that can be seen, sensed and experienced. I would say once again that these 'dimensions' are really created by the *observing* consciousness. The limits of *perception* create the illusion of 'dimensions' or bands of frequency. If your perception – what you can tune into, be aware of, and connect with – is limited to the simulation within the speed of light then that becomes your 'world' or dimension. Many call this the 'Third Dimension'. If your conscious awareness (perceptual limit) can extend into what is known as the Fourth Dimension then there is no 'Third' or 'Fourth' – there is only *your* dimension represented by the extent to which you can perceive

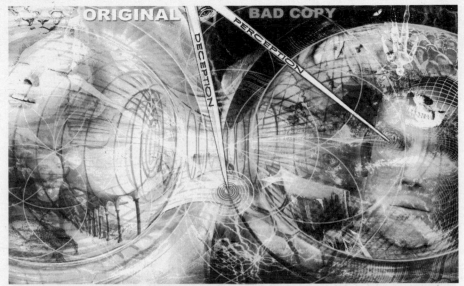

Figure 97: The two Fields of Infinite Reality and Simulation Reality. Which one we most connect with dominates our sense of everything. (Image by Neil Hague.)

Figure 98: A symbolic representation of the Simulation Field overlaying the Infinite Field and entrapping the perceptions of minds that fall into its lair. Body-Mind focus alone connects you with the Simulation Field. (Image by Neil Hague.)

reality.

'Dimensions' are limits of our conscious awareness created by the observer and one size doesn't fit all. They are what *you* make them. The *All That Is In Awareness of Itself* perceives *all* reality and will have no sense of 'dimensions' or perceptual 'sectors' in the way that its more limited 'parts' do. Reality is one seamless Infinite Field of possibility and

probability waiting
to be manifested
into an experience
by the perceptions
of the observing
consciousness
whatever form or
level of awareness
that may take.
Everything is the
perception of the
observer. I will,
however, use the
terms Third, Fourth
and Fifth
Dimension to keep
it simple in the
sense of Third
Dimension (the
simulation world of
perceived 'matter');
Fourth Dimension
(the realm of mind

Figure 99: Opening your mind to expanded awareness taps into the Infinite Field and a very different 'Mission Control'. (Image by Neil Hague.)

from where the simulation is projected); and Fifth Dimension and beyond (expanded and Infinite Awareness outside the simulation). They are all the same Infinite Awareness, but not all are equally 'conscious'. A heaving, swirling ocean and a block of ice are made from the same substance while being incredibly different in manifestation. Mind is the ice to the heaving, swirling ocean of expanded awareness. Mind is made 'ice-like' by the simulation which limits its sense of perception and therefore its frequency and sense of awareness. Mind is expanded awareness under lock and key. The answer is to break the lock (Fig 99).

Perception creates reality

The simulation was created to seize control of perception and sense of reality by hacking into the relationship and interaction between 'human' consciousness – mind – and the Infinite Field. To repeat the point: Reality is one seamless Infinite Field of Possibility and Probability waiting to be manifested into an experience by the perceptions of the observing consciousness whatever form or level of awareness that may take. Put another way the perceptions of the observer decide what experiences we manifest from the Infinite Field ('sea') of Possibility and Probability with which we constantly interact. We, too, are an expression of that Field and as such that is always *our* potential possibility and

Figure 100: When mind stays connected to expanded awareness outside the simulation we have an Infinite mission control to guide us through the maze. When that connection is lost the maze – the simulation – completely dictates perception and reality. (Image by Neil Hague.)

probability. Yes, *all* of it. How much of Infinite Possibility we are accessing decides *everything* (Fig 100). Nobel Prize winning physicist Werner Heisenberg (1901-1976) said: 'Atoms or elementary particles themselves are not real; they form a world of potentialities and possibilities rather than one of things or facts.' What activates them into particular experienced potentialities and possibilities? We return to perception. It's *all* perception which dictates how and what we *observe* which, in turn, dictates what we experience. How we perceive = how we observe = what we experience (or think we do). What we believe we perceive and what we perceive we experience. It works like this:

Our thoughts and emotions generate frequencies related to those particular thoughts and emotions. The totality of these frequencies are collectively represented as an energetic field that we know as perception. Different thoughts and emotions – points of observation – will produce different perceptions and frequencies in this perceptual field. It is through this field – this 'aura' – that we interact with the Simulation Field and the Infinite Field of Possibility and Probability. Different perceptual states will connect with and manifest correspondingly different possibilities and probabilities. Here are two simple examples. Your perception is that you are an insignificant 'Little Me' who has no power to influence your life (experience) and no potential for anything beyond the mundane. You are therefore a follower of those you do believe have that power. You 'know your place'. It is for others to reason why and for you just to do or die. This limited perception and self-identity is represented energetically in your perceptual field which reflects in its frequencies that same state of limitation. Your limited perceptual field will connect with like-frequencies in the Infinite Field and the possibilities and probabilities that you interact with will reflect your perception of self and reality (Fig 101). A feedback loop is established between you (your perceptions) and the frequencies those perceptions represent in The Fields and in this way your perceptions become a self-fulfilling prophecy in manifesting an experience to match your perception. A Little Me perception becomes a Little Me life. What you believe you perceive and what you perceive you experience. Indeed if your perceptual field is so limited and low in frequency you are doing little more than interact with the Simulation Field which is designed to dictate your whole life. At that point the Matrix has you and that's the

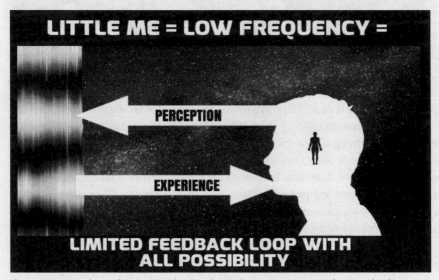

Figure 101: How limited perception leads to limited experience. (Image by Gareth Icke.)

very goal of the Cult and its masters.

By contrast if your perception and self-identity is one of limitless possibility, of being an expression of Infinite Awareness having a brief experience called human, your interaction with The Fields is transformed and so is your life. Your expanded sense of reality and identity becomes a correspondingly expanded perceptual field resonating at much higher frequencies and you interact with the Infinite Field of Possibility and Probability in a far more expansive way (Fig 102). Your expanded perception becomes an expanded experience. 'Awakening' is simply an expansion of perception and self-identity out of the fast asleep five senses. Those who go through this process – and the numbers are now phenomenal – notice that synchronicity comes into their life that wasn't there before. Daily experience becomes peppered with 'Fancy seeing you here', 'What's the chance of that?', and 'bits of luck' appearing just when you need them. This is nothing to do with 'luck'. Your expanded perception is interacting with expanded swathes of possibility and far more becomes possible. You are creating a different reality from different perceptions. I experienced all this myself. A quote I saw on the Internet captured the process:

> Accidents happen, that's what everyone says. But in a quantum universe there are no such things as accidents, only possibilities and probabilities folded into existence by perception.

This is the last thing the Cult wants you to know when *not* knowing is the foundation of human control. The Cult and its initiated assets are

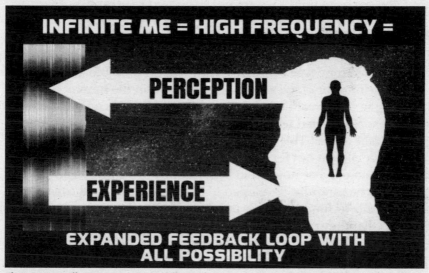

Figure 102: Different perception = different experience. (Image by Gareth Icke.)

well aware that perception becomes reality and that if they control your perception they will control your life. Global society is structured to this end through Cult-owned 'education', media, and Silicon Valley to dictate the information that becomes perception. What is the fascist censorship of media and Big Tech in the 'Covid' era except control of information to emphasise the official narrative and silence any challenge to that? While these psychopaths are directing your experience by downloading your perception they want you to believe that what happens to you is random chance. They want you to believe in good luck and bad luck and arbitrary happenings. The worst nightmare of the Cult is for the population to realise that perception becomes reality. People would then have the power in their own hands – minds – to change their reality. This is where the simulation comes in with its fake reality to confuse and control. The Simulation Field shares the same 'space' as the Infinite Field and the idea is to manipulate the perceptual fields of the population to attach to the Simulation Field. The interaction that follows mimics that with the Infinite Field except the simulation is not infinite and both limits possibility and entraps the mind in a reality that appears to be 'real', but isn't. Oh, no, that can't be – the world is 'natural'. Okay, so what is 'natural'? What do you have to compare with 'natural' to show the difference? If everything you see is the simulation the answer is that you have nothing to make that comparison. At least with a virtual reality headset you have 'normal' reality to compare and even virtual reality is becoming so sophisticated you soon won't be able to see the difference between headset reality and 'normal' reality which is itself a simulation. We are being taken into a multi-levelled virtual reality illusion from which we are not supposed to escape. But we *can*.

Our simulated 'world'

If you think that the current level of human technology is amazing, strap in. It's still the Stone Age compared with what is possible. Even then the cutting edge of technological advancement within the human world is originating in other realities. Have you noticed there is no break in the ever more sophisticated technology and devices that seamlessly flow into the public arena? This can happen when the technology has been waiting to be played out for aeons by the non-human source behind all of this. Technology has not had to be randomly 'invented'. The human mind had to be carefully developed to have the intellectual capacity to work with this technology while being so spiritually regressed (wisdom regressed) that they cannot see they are building their own prison cell. We are observing this all around us today and the process has been happening step-by-step for what we perceive as 'centuries'. AI and surveillance technology is rolled out from the Deep Underground Military Bases (DUMBS) all over the world where interaction takes place at the deepest and most compartmentalised levels between human scientists and engineers answering to the Cult and the non-humans that control the Cult. Here technology and know-how is transferred from non-humans to Cult cabal – much of which is also non-human as I will come to in the next chapter. Cover stories and cover people are then used to explain where the technology came from to keep the public in ignorance of where it really came from. Society-changing technology invented by chance by geeks in a garage is a Cult favourite to hide the truth. You know the front people who parrot and personalise these cover-stories. They are the very famous and very rich big names of Silicon Valley and the wider world of Big Tech. This is why I say that people such as Gates, Musk, Zuckerberg, Brin, Page, and company are not running their giant corporations so much as fronting-up for that which really controls them – the Cult. When Elon Musk says he believes we could live 'in' a simulation it's because he knows that we do. They all do.

The non-human force has technology generating the simulation that makes ours, even at its current state of advancement, look like starting a fire by rubbing rocks together. This technology is located in the Fourth Dimension (what I will call 4-D), outside the range of 'normal' human awareness. In the same way the machines in *The Matrix* movies operate outside the simulated reality they are generating. The Fourth Dimension is also known as the 'astral planes' – the realm of *mind* – and believed to be in esoteric circles the frequency bands through which we enter and depart 'physical' reality. Near-death experiences mostly take place in the astral or Fourth Dimension where out-of-body states can also happen known as 'astral projection'. The astral is known among other names as Barzakh by Islam and Yetzirah in Judaism and is once again a common thread in religions and ancient cultures. Barzakh means 'limbo, barrier, partition, obstacle, hindrance, *separation*', and is said in Islam to be the stage between death and resurrection to the 'Hereafter'. Other references to the astral include the 'Dreaming' of Australian Aborigines; Duat of ancient Egyptians; Bardo of Tibetans; and Universe of Asiyah to Kabbalists in the Jewish mystical tradition. The term Fourth Dimension can conjure thoughts of something way 'out there' when in fact in frequency terms it's really close. The consciousness field of your thinking mind is located there and directly interacts with the body five senses through the brain (or appears to). The brain is only a processor of information delivered by the mind and not the origin of consciousness. The brain, too, is an illusion in the sense of physicality. There are caveats to everything for reasons we'll see in a moment. We cannot see the consciousness field that is the human mind with our 'normal' sight sense, but you are thinking with that Fourth Dimensional field as you read this book. The astral itself has many layers of frequency depending on the awakeness of the mind and one is known as the 'lower astral'. This is the realm of 'demonic' entities, malevolent and confused 'ghosts', and those that manipulate our experienced world in ways I will be describing. I have referred to this lower astral realm in books going back to the 1990s as the 'lower Fourth Dimension' with the two terms interchangeable. The lower Fourth Dimension is very close in frequency to the human realm and entities can pass between them. Reports of seeing strange figures or animals unknown on earth could well be astral phenomena briefly crossing the frequency veil. When I say 'Fourth Dimension' or '4-D' from hereon I mean the demonic lower frequency levels unless I make it otherwise clear.

In this Fourth Dimension or astral the simulation is projected as wavefield information into the human mind which decodes this into a '3-D' illusory 'physical' world. Think virtual reality headset or a computer decoding Wi-Fi (Fig 103). 'Human' interaction with virtual technology is mimicking interaction between mind and the Simulation Field. The whole caboodle is controlled, monitored and overseen by artificial intelligence way beyond anything we see in human reality so far. The simulation is being projected directly into the mind at that *Fourth Dimensional* level to be decoded into a sense of 3-D 'physical' reality (Fig 104). The idea is to hijack the perception of mind and focus its attention in a fake simulated reality of

Figure 103: Mind decoding the simulation operates on the same principle as a human decoding a virtual reality game. With the mind 'game', however, the headset is never removed and becomes the mind's permanent sense of reality.

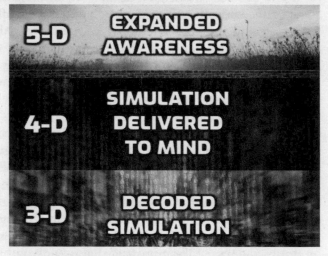

Figure 104: The simulation is projected in the form of wavefield information into the human collective mind in Fourth Dimensional reality and the mind decodes this into a holographic illusory 'physical' reality that we think is the human 'world. Mind's focus of attention on the simulated projection disconnects its sense of reality (and so frequency) from Fifth Dimensional consciousness outside the simulation. *Gotcha!*

holographic illusion that lowers its frequency and triggers a disconnection from the perceptual influence of Fifth Dimensional expanded awareness. When I ponder on this I see the consciousness field we call mind trapped in like a Wi-Fi field constantly feeding the

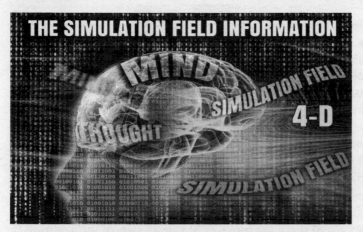

Figure 105: The energy field we call mind is being infused with Simulation Field information and it's like permanently wearing a virtual reality headset. The 'headset' – the simulation – becomes the mind's sense of reality. (Image by Neil Hague.)

information source of the simulation (Fig 105). The prime separation the manipulators seek is Fourth Dimensional mind from Fifth Dimensional expanded awareness outside the simulation. All other separation and senses of separation come from this prime separation. Mind is decoding its own perceptual prison cell. If this is done unconsciously and without question the mind decodes whatever the information delivers and it reminds me of an old tea advertisement in which a monkey says: 'Do you know the piano's on my foot?' Another monkey sitting at the piano replies: 'You hum it, son, I'll play it.' The simulation hums it and mind plays it until the simulation scam is revealed. Mind is decoding its own Alcatraz believing it to be real. In doing so the focus of mind is mesmerised and focussed on the simulation and shuts out all else. 'Awakening' is restoring that connection which is why the sense of reality in those awakening is so different to those still entrapped in mind and the five-senses alone.

Fourth Dimensional AI is greatly in advance of anything in the simulated 3-D world although we are getting closer with the scale of technological possibility transferred piece by piece through the underground bases. The transfer is happening within the perception of mind and not in the 'physical'. There is no 'physical'. It's all happening in the mind. This is the reason for my caveats and riders here and there. What appears to be an interaction between mind and the human brain and body is another level of illusion when seen from the biggest picture. Our entire simulated reality only exists *inside* the mind including the brain and body. The mind is not in the body. The body is in the *mind*. You are reading this book with your mind. Where does that mind appear to be? How do you experience your mind? It appears to be in, and part of, your body, right? Your body dominates your mind's sense of reality. It seems to dictate the boundaries of 'you' and possibility. Your body is massively influencing your mind's sense of reality like wearing a virtual reality headset. In fact, your mind is operating in 4-D while your body is in 3-D which is a simulated projection decoded by your mind. Therefore your body must be in your mind and not the other way around.

Observe the *Matrix* movies which for whatever reason portray these concepts literally and symbolically. They don't enter the Matrix with their 'bodies'. They enter with their *minds*. Take the location of the characters when they are outside the Matrix to be their mind in the Fourth Dimension decoding the simulation and you get the dynamic. A probe is inserted into the back of the neck or lower brain stem. The probe connects them to the *information* source of the Matrix and their brain begins to process that information into the illusion of a physical realm that is nothing more than a decoded source of information. The brain is not the origin of consciousness. It is a processor of information from any source within its range of operation. Put on a headset in a virtual-reality game and the brain decodes that information into events and happenings; but the brain is still a figment of the manipulated imagination of mind. It's not real as we perceive it. The brain *and* the headset are both inside the *mind*. Everything in the simulation is inside the mind. It's all a technologically-generated *dream*. The brain is part of the simulated information projection that 'Fourth Dimensional' mind decodes into a mere sense – *experience* – of reality. Human virtual reality is a virtual reality within a virtual reality. The Metaverse promoted by Cult-owned Mark Zuckerberg and others in Cult-owned Silicon Valley is another layer of reality illusion to further bamboozle 'human' (mind) perception and self-identity. Zuckerberg may not be the sharpest pin in the box, but he's surely not stupid enough given his Cult connections not to see what the Metaverse is really designed to do – seal human perception away in even deeper levels of illusion and separation by further mesmerising the mind.

Where is your body *really*?

Fourth Dimensional mind is fed the information that it decodes into 'physical' reality. This includes the body/brain which are part of the simulation as encoded information fields decoded by the mind into holographic 'physical' illusion. The mind believes it is in the body when the body is *in the mind*. The belief that the mind is in the body leads to the mind believing it is subject to the limitations of the body and five senses. At one end of the feedback loop the mind is creating (decoding) the 'physical' body while at the other end the apparent limitations of the body impact on the perceptions and reality of the mind. Observe how when people get ill they think the body is the governor of that outcome and not the mind. They are given a fatal diagnosis and they think the body governs the outcome. A doctor's 'how long you have' verdict becomes the period in which the person dies purely from the belief

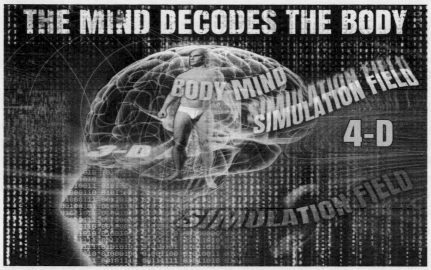

Figure 106: The mind decodes the body and the body impacts on the reality of the mind. It would be funny if it wasn't so tragic for human freedom. (Image by Neil Hague.)

(mind) that the doctor must know. In fact the mind is master of the body, but the mind is manipulated to believe the body is in control. Talk about The Trap (Fig 106). The mind-simulation-mind feedback loop works on the same principle. You could liken this feedback loop to an audience in a theatre unknowingly projecting the movie on the screen and then having their perceptions changed by the movie. We have human virtual reality technology that makes it appear that you are inside a body. Experiments have clearly shown that the mind can be manipulated to believe that a false hand is its own. You see people react at what is done to the false hand as if it was done to them. Tricking the mind is a doddle. Tricking expanded awareness is quite another thing. I was interested to see, as I was completing this book, that Buddhism has a version of the mind-to-mind feedback loop. Buddhism speaks of the Three Realms – Realm of Desire, Realm of Form, and Realm of Formlessness – which are all created by thought:

> Whatever I think, that I see. The mind creates the Buddha. The mind itself sees him. The mind is the Buddha. The mind is the Tathagata [an enlightened one put most simply]. The mind is my body, the mind sees the Buddha. The mind does not itself know the mind, the mind does not itself see mind.

That pretty much describes in part what I am suggesting. Mind creates reality and mind 'sees' the reality it creates; mind does not know unless awakened that it has created what it 'sees'. Then there is the famous Buddha quote: 'The mind is everything. What you think you become.' This is correct although in my way of seeing reality mind is *not* everything. Mind in a programmed state is what blocks us from the everything. Conscious and subconscious 'you' are in the *Fourth Dimension* where your mind is located and you are decoding the information source of the simulation into the illusion that you are 'in' a 3-D world of solidity and physicality. You are no more in that world than Neo, Morpheus and Trinity are when they 'enter' the Matrix in the movie series. Where do we 'live'? *In our own minds.* I did say we were going deeper than ever before! The awareness level called mind is often referred to as the 'ego' and I have seen that defined as a 'point of attention'. Exactly. The reality of any level of consciousness is its point of attention. In 'human' form we are a point of attention within Infinite Awareness. We are not infinitely aware because the human point of attention (perception) perceives limitation and not Infinity. This is the whole foundation of human enslavement. Controlling our point of attention from which all else follows. The simulation is a dream world, yes, but the dream is externally generated. If you think of something now, say wild flowers in a field on a beautiful sunny day, this will be called 'imagination'. The simulation by contrast is information encoded with data for you to decode into wild flowers on a beautiful sunny day to project an illusion that appears so real and tangible that you believe you are *in* that field with those flowers under that sun. The first is imagination and the second is manipulated imagination and this is what the simulation basically is – manipulated imagination. As Morpheus says in *The Matrix*:

> Have you ever had a dream, Neo, that you were so sure was real? What if you were unable to wake from that dream? How would you know the difference between the dream world and the real world?

The awake dream and sleep dream are continuations of the same dream. It's *all* a dream and as Edgar Allen Poe said: 'All that we see or seem is just a dream within a dream.' When it comes to the relationship between mind and The Fields the dream is the dreamer and the dreamer is the dream. Can we escape the simulation dream? Yes, we can and I'll come to that, but first how did human minds become trapped in this cycle of illusion?

Let there be ... the simulation

I have been saying for years that the creation of the simulation is described at the start of Genesis. There is a lot of truth in biblical texts often obscured by symbolism taken literally. There are also serious twists to deceive. Many times 'God', allegedly singular, is described in plural terms such as Elohim. The line about the sons of God interbreeding with the daughters of men is translated from text that actually says sons of the gods, plural. This amalgamation of multiple non-human 'gods' into a single 'God' (see the next chapter) has changed the whole meaning of the Old Testament which describes an angry, bloodthirsty, and jealous 'God' which we are supposed to believe is also a 'loving' 'God'. The biblical claim made that there is no other God but me will be put into context in the next chapter, too. I say that Genesis is describing the simulation when the text says that in the beginning 'God' (the gods) created the heaven and the earth – the holographic simulation of heaven and earth. Genesis says:

> And the earth was without form, and void; and darkness *was* upon the face of the deep. And the Spirit of God moved upon the face of the waters. And God said, Let there be light: and there was light.

But what is this 'light'? Ancient texts and many near-death experiencers describe a very different kind of 'light' outside the body than the fierce electromagnetic light of the human world – *simulation*. They often use the symbolism of water to describe energy and reality beyond the human realm. You see terms such as 'watery light' and light that 'casts no shadows' in contrast to the fierce electromagnetic light of our reality. Let there be electromagnetic light and there was electromagnetic light might be more accurate. Electromagnetism within the speed of light *is* the simulation at the level that we experience:

> And God said, Let there be a firmament in the midst of the waters, and let it divide the waters from the waters. And God made the firmament, and divided the waters which *were* under the firmament from the waters which were above the firmament: and it was so.

The term 'firmament' is described as a vast solid dome that divided the waters from the waters and if we continue the theme of 'waters' referring to energetic states we have a perceptual limitation between the reality 'in' or 'under' the dome and realities outside the 'dome'. There have been many depictions through the centuries of a dome around the Earth (Fig 107 overleaf). I looked up at the sky many years ago and it took the form of an enormous dome. The highly symbolic movie *The Truman Show* released in 1998 had the leading character played by Jim Carrey born into the set of a television soap opera. No one told him and he continued to live his life as if he was in a real world while all the people around him were actors and actresses in the soap. Whenever he tried to leave the hidden dome, in which all this took place, something would happen to stop him. The sun that came up every day and the moon every night were part of the set. Eventually he realises his life is an illusion and takes to what he thinks is the ocean to get away. He

reaches the edge
of the dome
where he finds a
door to the 'real
world'. I don't
know if the
writer was
trying to
symbolise the
human plight or
if he just
thought it was a
good story, but
symbolise it he
did. Genesis
goes on to
describe how
'God' (the gods)
went on to

Figure 107: A 19th century depiction of the Earth within a vast dome – the firmament.

create animals, what we call the natural world, and how 'He' made the
sun, moon and stars. What we perceive as infinite space with all the
planets and stars is a holographic illusion projected into our minds that
we decode into what appears to be physical reality. This would explain
the paradox, often known as the 'Fermi Paradox', of an apparently
limitless night sky with a complete absence of life. Italian physicist
Enrico Fermi said that with 100 billion stars in the galaxy it was
inevitable that intelligent life must have evolved elsewhere so 'where are
the aliens?' If you wanted to enslave your target minds in an illusion of
isolation and separation would you have your simulated reality teeming
with life or apparently devoid of life?? In the same way if you wanted to
maintain humanity in ongoing ignorance would you want them to see a
panoramic range of visual reality or confine them to the ridiculously
narrow band of frequency known as visible light? Ponder on how the
Universe was created according to mainstream 'science' and you will
find the continuing theme. They want us to believe in a 'Big Bang' 13.7
billion years ago when the Universe was compressed into the nucleus of
an atom which they call the 'singularity' and this exploded to somehow
– out of nothingness – create matter, energy, space, time, consciousness,
and Mrs Smith who runs the corner shop. As American writer and
researcher Terence McKenna brilliantly said:

> ... what these philosophers of science are saying is, give us one free miracle,
> and we will roll from that point forward – from the birth of time to the crack of
> doom! – just one free miracle, and then it will all unravel according to natural

law, and these bizarre equations which nobody can understand but which are so holy in this enterprise.

Mysteries about how our reality emerged 'out of nothing' can be credibly explained with no miracles required if science opened its mind to the simulation.

'Human' is what exactly?

What is 'human'? What does it mean? Well, it means the *human* body which decodes information through the brain and genetic system into a certain sense of reality. Mind decodes the simulation information source into a holographic 'body' and the body is encoded to perceive reality according to its program and in doing so impact the reality of mind of which it is ultimately a projection. A human acts like a human because of the information program encoded into the body just as an elephant acts like an elephant and a duck like a duck for the same reason. 'Human' is a manifestation, an illusion, of the simulation. It is the vehicle designed by the non-human force through which our 'Fourth-Dimensional' minds could be tricked into believing they are 'incarnate' within a physical body in a physical world. The body is the way – in the perception of mind – that it interacts with this physical world, the illusory projection that the mind thinks is real. Picture characters inserted into virtual reality video games which are manifestations of the game and respond to the codes and rules on which the game is based (its 'laws of physics'). Now imagine consciousness experiencing reality through those characters and being so mesmerised by the illusion that the consciousness self-identifies with the character they are experiencing. Consciousness in that perceptual state would forget that it was consciousness and believe it was the character as it responded to the rules of the game – the simulation. The body-program controlled by the codes of the game would be mistaken for consciousness making its own decisions.

Ninety-five percent of human behaviour has been shown to originate in the subconscious – not the conscious – mind. Observe most humans and it's like watching a computer respond to data input. In a given situation you can predict how most people will react in almost any culture or race. The situation is like pressing enter and the program controlling the body then responds to program. The 'subconscious' in this sense is the *simulation*. If expanded consciousness does not override the program running through these simulation 'human body' inserts then it becomes a mere spectator. The body-program (responding to the simulation program) dictates perception and behaviour for an entire 'human life'. This would account for the 'press-enter' predictability of humans and why the majority unquestioningly do whatever authority tells them. In this sense 'authority' is pressing enter with its decrees and the human body-program responds with the same obedience as a computer. I include in this 'cultural programs'. Minds perceiving through different cultures tend to adhere to those programs, rituals, and ways of doing things. Okay, familiarity from childhood plays a part, of course, but the body also carries those cultural blueprints through DNA. Relatively few break out of these programs and take another path at odds with the culture they were born into because of a combination of upbringing, in which guilt plays a major part, cultural programs running through the body, and fear of going against the cultural group. The 'Great Reset' is designed through an AI connection to the brain to fuse multiple cultural programs into one global monoculture program which everyone must follow.

Who is at the wheel?

Humans who do not impact on their lives with expanded awareness are not only *like* computer programs they *are* computer programs. The 'Covid' era has put this big-time on public display. I tell the story in *Everything You Need To Know But Have Never Been Told* about the cognitive experiments of Benjamin Libet (1916-2007). Libet was a scientist in the physiology department of the University of California, San Francisco, and a pioneering researcher into the nature of human consciousness. In one famous experiment he asked a study group to move their hands at a moment of their choosing while their brain activity was being monitored. He wanted to identify what came first – the brain's electrical activity to make the hand move or the person's conscious intention to make their hand move. It had to be the second one, surely? Nope. Brain activity to move the hand was triggered a full half a second before any *conscious intention* to move it. John-Dylan Haynes, a neuroscientist at the Max Planck Institute for Human Cognitive and Brain Sciences in Leipzig, Germany, later went much further with a study able to predict an action *ten seconds* before there was a conscious intention to do it. Frank Tong, a neuroscientist at Vanderbilt University in Nashville, Tennessee, said: 'Ten seconds is a lifetime in terms of brain activity.' Where are actions coming from if not 'us', the conscious mind?

The only way for 'incarnate' consciousness to escape the illusion and break the control is to override the program. To do that we need to realise that there is a program to override. Non-human forces, their simulation and the Global Cult within simulated human reality, are all working together to maintain the fantasy that the illusion is real. When consciousness can be tricked into self-identifying with the body it is self-identifying with the simulation program – doubles all round! The program rules, okay? There are three elements to 'human' that bring clarity to our plight. They are:

(1) The body-program insert that interacts with the simulation as part of the simulation – the 'computer game character'.

(2) The level of us called mind that operates in the frequency range of the Fourth Dimension and directly receives the projected information of the simulation which it decodes into the illusion of a 3-D reality including the body.

(3) Consciousness in the 'Fifth Dimension' and beyond into Infinite Reality which I will refer to as expanded consciousness or awareness.

The simulation while it appears to be a Third Dimension or 3-D phenomenon is really a 'Fourth Dimensional' reality which is where it is all really happening. The 3-D 'world' of human is only a decoded illusion of 4-D mind. The simulation's role is to literally hold the attention – the perception and imagination – of 4-D mind and disconnect it from the influence of expanded awareness in 5-D and beyond. Without that influence of expanded awareness to break the spell of the simulation, 4-D mind remains at its perceptual mercy indefinitely until the spell is broken. What about the 'death' of the body? I'll be discussing that. It is worth saying here that the 3-D fake 'physical' is not the only level of the simulation and its projected illusions. I have been detailing in many books how the foundation target of the non-human force, its Global Cult and simulation, is to disconnect Body-Mind from expanded awareness. One key way this is done is by constantly stimulating the central nervous system and its networks through electrical/electromagnetic interaction with technological radiation and Wi-Fi. Fear and stress can also do this by pressing the 'on' button of the fight or flight response with no 'off' time to relax and chill. A constantly-stimulated central nervous system will most certainly keep you in the perception/frequency zone of the Matrix. You are stimulated to be simulated. The illusion collapses once expanded awareness enters the mind's perception. 5-D awareness operating outside the realm of simulated illusion can see what is happening. When people 'awaken' (open their minds to 5-D) they see what they could not see before. A quote in the first *Matrix* movie says:

The Matrix is a system, Neo. That system is our enemy. But when you're inside, you look around, what do you see? Businessmen, teachers, lawyers, carpenters. The very minds of the people we are trying to save. But until we do, these people are still a part of that system and that makes them our enemy.

You have to understand, most of these people are not ready to be unplugged. And many of them are so inured, so hopelessly dependent on the system, that they will fight to protect it.

If we adjust the context of the simulation in line with what I have been describing the quote would go something like this:

> The Matrix is a system, Neo. That system is our enemy. When you're inside, you look around, what do you see? A 3-D illusion being decoded by 4-D minds that we are trying to free. But until we do, these minds are still a part of that system.

> You have to understand, most of these minds are not ready to be unplugged. And many of them are so inured, so hopelessly mesmerised by the simulation that they will fight to protect it.

Wanna bite?

There was no 'human' before the simulation in the dense 'physical' sense that we recognise. That human is a creation of the simulation. Original 'humans' operated in a much higher frequency reality with far less density. It was an ethereal-like 5-D realm and humans were consciousness in a state of Oneness and unity and not locked away in 4-D mind which decodes 3-D reality as duality and polarity. The biblical story of Adam and Eve in the Garden of Eden can be found in different forms in many cultures in their creation myths and legends about human origins. The common themes include humanity living in a 'paradise' from which they were ejected and 'fell'. The biblical version tells how 'God' (the gods) created humanity as 'Adam and Eve' and the serpent tempted them to eat the forbidden fruit, often dubbed an 'apple', from the tree of knowledge to know good and evil (polarity, the simulation). What was the 'forbidden fruit' really? Humans in higher vibrations were tricked, 'tempted' and enticed into the trap of the simulation as they fell down the frequencies from 5-D consciousness into the much more limited 4-D mind. This was 'The Fall' when humans fell from paradise and became trapped in the illusions of the simulation which appeared to be the paradise they left, but wasn't. I'll pick up this point in a moment.

The villain in the Garden of Eden was the serpent – symbolic of the non-human creators of the simulation.

Figure 108: Amalgamation of 'labels' – sex, race, religion, sexuality, income bracket – that we falsely believe is the true 'I'.

Does anyone really think that the serpent in the garden was a talking snake? The creation of Adam and Eve (post-'Fall' humanity) was key to deluding minds into experiencing 'incarnation' into a physical world and entrapment in the illusion of limitation, apartness and isolation. What is the level of awareness that we refer to as 'mind'? It is those aspects of 5-D consciousness that were manipulated into a lower frequency state to become entrapped in the simulation. 'The Fall' and the 'ejection from paradise' and the 'garden' was when expressions of 5-D fell down the resonance scale into 4-D and became what we now call 'mind'. Ever since that happened mind has been trapped by perception in the simulation apart from those who have truly awakened and got out of here. The manipulation is all happening in the Fourth Dimension and the 3-D simulation is only a means to achieve perceptional control of 4-D mind by separating and isolating its sense of reality from an influence of the 5-D consciousness that it once was and from where it 'fell'. This is achieved by drawing the 4-D mind's sense of reality and focus of attention into the myopia and perceived limitation and separation of the body within the simulation (Fig 108).

Ancient confirmation

Amazingly the simulation was described long ago in their own way by Gnostic people in a fantastic set of writings found in a sealed jar in 1945 near the Egyptian town of Nag Hammadi an 80-mile drive north of Luxor on the banks of the Nile. They were estimated to have been hidden in the jar about 400 AD and they have become known as the Nag Hammadi Library. The find included 13 leather-bound papyrus codices (manuscripts) and more than 50 texts written by Gnostics in Coptic Egyptian. I have read through two books of translations and the information is astonishing in the light of computer technology today. Gnostics and Gnosticism are not a race. They are a way of perceiving reality. Gnostic means 'learned' and Gnosis is translated from the Greek as secret knowledge which relates to understanding spiritual mysteries that reveal the nature of reality. Gnostic thinkers dominated the Royal or Great Library of Alexandria in Egypt which collected nearly half a million scrolls, manuscripts and documents from across the ancient world including Assyria, Greece, Persia, India, and of course Egypt. The Great Library was destroyed in stages by the Roman Church which wanted to protect its fake narrative by eliminating Gnostic information. The censorship process of deleting truth continues to this day worldwide through Big Government, Big Media and Big Tech. The dynamic has never changed, only the historical setting. Church tyrants oversaw the burning of irreplaceable works stored at the library and you will find those that survived locked-away in the vaults at the Vatican. A major attack on the Royal Library came in 415 AD which led to murder by the mob of Hypatia, a mathematician, astronomer and philosopher. Hypatia was educated in Athens and was head of the Platonist school in Alexandria where she taught the work of Greek philosophers Plato and Aristotle. The time of her death corresponds with the estimated period when the Nag Hammadi texts were sealed and hidden in the jar. A quote attributed to Hypatia captured Gnostic philosophy on life: 'Reserve your right to think, for even to think wrongly is better than not to think at all.' How relevant that remains today. Such an open-minded spirit of discovery led to Gnostic insights that were thousands of years ahead of the mainstream world. They included the Earth orbiting the Sun 2,000 years before that discovery was attributed to Polish mathematician and astronomer, Nicolaus Copernicus.

Gnostic belief also manifested with the Cathars in southern France who were naturally attacked by the Roman Church with typical psychopathic insanity and led to them being burned to death in the siege at the Castle of Montsegur in 1244. Gnostics were aware that death is only the death of the body and not consciousness. I have detailed in other books how the Vatican and its version of reality came out of Babylon and has been Cult-owned from the start. Why would the Cult not seek to destroy via its Vatican those who are exposing the illusions that allow the Cult to control the human mind? Soul derives from the Greek word psykhe and hence the English 'psyche' which is defined as 'the mind, or the deepest thoughts, feelings, or beliefs of a person or group'. The way out of here is to open mind/soul (4-D) to spirit (5-D). This is a good point to emphasise how 'soul' is different to 'spirit' in the context that I am using those terms. Soul is an aspect of mind that still perceives itself – as with mind - in terms individuality. It is correct, therefore, to speak of mind/soul (sense of individuality and apartness) and spirit (the 5-D and beyond *All That Is* that has and lives the awareness that all is One. Mind/soul is involved in the reincarnation process (The Trap) that I will be exploring while spirit is way beyond that sense of reality and thus experience.

The 'bad copy'

Gnostic texts tell how a non-human force they call 'Archons' (Greek for rulers) made a 'bad copy' of Prime Reality Earth and in our terms today we would call that a digital copy (Figs 109 and 110). Prime Reality Earth still exists in higher levels of frequency and awareness from where 'humans fell', or consciousness fell, to *become* humans as we perceive them. Once again you can liken this to making a copy of a website. At the start both websites look the same and simulated earth could have looked like Prime Earth which may have led to the original entrapment. While the prime website (reality) continues to be what it always was, the copy can now be changed until it is a grotesque distortion of the original. I suggest this is what has happened with the simulation. It has been distorted beyond recognition and goes on being so to ever greater extremes. The Gnostic version of the Christian Devil/Satan is called Yaldabaoth (also the Demiurge) and texts say Yaldabaoth (a distorted, inverted, state of consciousness) created the Archons which are the equivalent of the Christian demons. Gnostics said the 'God' worshipped through the Roman Church is Yaldabaoth, an expression of the evil that created the

Figure 109: Neil Hague's symbolic depiction of the bad copy.

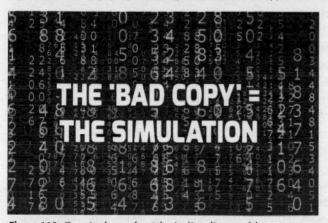

Figure 110: Gnostics knew that 'physical' reality was fakery.

'material' world (simulation). They said there are two realms which they called the Upper Aeons and Lower Aeons (Infinite Reality and the fake 'material' simulation). They further made the clear distinction as I do between *nous* (mind) and *pneuma* (Infinite Self) and we see the theme in religions of the East with their Maya (mind / illusion) and Brahman (Infinite *All That Is*). A Nag Hammadi text in the *Bruce Codex* describes the nature of 'The All' which Gnostics refer to as 'The Father':

> He is an incomprehensible one, but it is he who comprehends All. He receives them to himself. And nothing exists outside of him. But All exist within him. And he is boundary to them all, as he encloses them all, and they are all within him. It is he who is Father of the aeons, existing before them all. There is no place outside of him.

To Gnostics the 'Upper Aeons' are the realm of love and unity or Oneness while the 'Lower Aeons' are the fake reality or duality – the simulation – of the Archon manipulators. They define the Lower Aeons in terms of 'imperfection', darkness, the Abyss, and Hell, while labelling them the realms of 'fate' which without the serious input of expanded consciousness that is exactly where we are. By fate I mean the way the simulation dictates experience without expanded awareness to override that program. Gnostic texts make the distinction between spirit (Upper Aeons) and 'soul' (Lower Aeons). Spirit is our connection to the Infinite while mind/soul are subject to the simulation (more later). Nag Hammadi texts call Yaldabaoth, their Devil/Satan, the 'counterfeit spirit' which created the Archons and 'bad copy' Lower Aeons simulation after they say 'he' detached from his 'Mother' and left the Upper Aeons. This is yet another version of being 'cast out of paradise'. Nag Hammadi documents say that what I am calling the simulation was a 'bad copy' or 'reflection' of Upper Aeon reality. The *Apocryphon of John* says:

... [Yaldabaoth] organized (everything) according to the model of the first aeons [by using] the power in him, which he had taken from his mother, [and] produced in him the likeness of the cosmos ...

... This is the first archon [Yaldabaoth] who took a great power from his mother. And he removed himself from her and moved away from the places in which he was born [Upper Aeons]. He became strong and created for himself other aeons with a flame of luminous fire which exists now.

Luminous fire = the electromagnetic 'Let there be Light' of the simulation. The biblical 'god' is called 'the Lord' and is quoted many times as saying 'I am the Lord your God' while the Gnostic Yaldabaoth is known as 'the Lord' or 'Lord Archon'. Gnostics also refer to Yaldabaoth as the 'Great Architect of the Universe' (the simulation) and the Cult-connected Freemasons worship their creator 'god' as the 'Great Architect of the Universe' or the 'Grand Architect'. The creator of the simulation in *The Matrix* is known as the 'Architect'. Gnostic texts speak of the Christian Satan Yaldabaoth manifesting the 'bad copy' simulation by producing 'in him the likeness of the cosmos' indicating what Gnostics call Yaldabaoth may be the energetic fabric of the simulation. Caleb Scharf, Director of Astrobiology at Columbia University, has said that 'alien life' could be so advanced that it had transcribed itself into the quantum realm and become the physics of our reality:

Perhaps hyper-advanced life isn't just external. Perhaps it's already all around. It is embedded in what we perceive to be physics itself, from the root behaviour of particles and fields to the phenomena of complexity and emergence ... In other words, life might not just be *in* the equations. It might *be* the equations.

This would indicate from my perspective outlined in this book that 'human' minds are entrapped within the entity known as Yaldabaoth which is feeding the information that we decode into the simulation. Gnostics certainly portray Yaldabaoth as consciousness, not form, and Archons as energetic fields of consciousness in their base state. Texts say they can take form as serpent entities and those that sound like the ET type known as the Greys. Yaldabaoth and Archontic energy fields and their effect are always connected to the theme of chaos, inversion and upheaval. The Nag Hammadi *Origin of the World* manuscript says:

> ... there appeared a force, presiding over the darkness [Lower Aeons]. And the forces that came into being subsequent to them called the shadow 'the limitless chaos'.

This sounds, along with inversion and upheaval, remarkably like the human world and leads us down to the next level of the rabbit hole from which everything else comes. Nag Hammadi texts say Yaldabaoth and the Archons lack creativity or 'ennoia' – for reasons I will explain later – and instead developed the skill of imitation which included, yes, what we now call virtual reality simulation. Their expertise is mimicry. John Lamb Lash, author of an excellent book about the Nag Hammadi texts, *Not In His Image*, writes of the Gnostic 'bad copy':

> Although they cannot originate anything, because they lack the divine factor of ennoia (intentionality), Archons can imitate with a vengeance. Their expertise is simulation (HAL, virtual reality). The Demiurge fashions a heaven world copied from the fractal patterns of the eternal Aeons, the Pleromic gods who reside in the galactic centre. His construction is celestial kitsch, like the fake Italianate villa of a Mafia don complete with militant angels to guard every portal ...

They can guard, but they can't stop – *if* you are in your vibrational power. The relevance of fractal patterns will become clear.

Shadows on the wall

Nag Hammadi documents refer to the 'bad copy' as a realm of non-existence which is correct in that the fake world of the simulation is only a decoded illusion and nothing like humans experience it to be (Fourth Dimensional minds perceive it to be). Gnostics used the symbolism of a shadow to portray the fake reality of what they call the Lower Aeons as a poor reflection or shadow of prime reality ('Upper Aeons'). One of the most profound descriptions of simulated reality came from the Greek philosopher Plato (about 428 to about 347 BC) who was a pupil of Socrates and a major inspiration for Gnostic thought. Plato's Allegory of the Cave tells the story of prisoners who

lived in a cave and had
never seen outside.
They are chained and
can only see one wall
of the cave. A fire
burns behind them
where figures walk
past casting their
shadows on the wall
the prisoners can see
(Fig 111). The prisoners
don't know this. They
only see the shadows
they believe to be

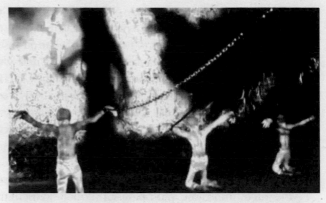

Figure 111: Plato's brilliant symbolism of illusory 'physical' reality.

reality. Some became 'experts' on the shadows that were no more than illusion
(see today's mainstream scientists and academics). One prisoner escapes and
sees that reality is not what he thought it was. He comes back to tell his fellow
prisoners what he found and they refuse to believe him. Plato used the
allegory to symbolise the human plight. How accurate he was. Nag Hammadi
texts use very different terms for that which exists (Infinite Reality) and that
which does not exist (the fake 'world' of the simulation) which they say is evil.
Among Gnostic distinctions between them are: Fullness/deficiency;
immortal/mortal; spiritual/psychic; spirit/soul; existence/non-existence; no
time/time. Note the last one. – no time/time. What we call 'time' is encoded in
the simulation as part of the perception deception. A Nag Hammadi text in the
Bruce Codex highlights the difference between the 'existent' and 'non-existent':

> And then the existent separated itself from the non-existent. And the non-
> existent is the evil which has manifested in matter. And the enveloping power
> separated those that exist from those that do not exist. And it called the
> existent 'eternal', and it called the non-existent 'matter'. And in the middle it
> separated those that exist from those that do not exist, and it placed veils
> between them.

The human body is a phenomenon of the simulation to focus the attention
of mind/soul that they are somehow incarnate in a physical world. It's a trap
in other words and that, too, is how Gnostic texts perceive it. They refer to the
body as a prison and humans as sparks or droplets of the same essence as
'God' that became trapped in their bodies (the perception of their bodies).
Gnostics believed that humans would eventually escape. They describe the
body as a 'garment' that clothes the Spirit. The *Corpus Hermeticum VII:2* tells of
… 'the tunic that you wear, the garment of ignorance, the foundation of vice,
the bonds of corruption, the dark cage, the living death, the portable tomb ...'
Firstly there is the illusion of being *in* the body when the body is really *in the*

mind – a classic example of the inversion technique of the non-human force that turns every perception and sense of reality on its head. We are not in the body. The body is in us. We are not in the Matrix. The Matrix is in us. Now it is plain to see why the mind and its associated emotions have such an impact on the body and why the placebo effect is so powerful when people heal their bodies by believing that a potion will cure them which is only a saline solution or similar. The body is a computer program insert connecting and interacting with the big program of the simulation itself. Gnostic texts urge people to 'rip off the tunic that you wear', but I take that to mean rip off its perceptual influence. To literally 'rip off the tunic' by committing suicide is not to escape the trap, but to go deeper into it as a result of the emotional/vibrational impact. I have been describing the body as a biological computer since the 1990s and it is encoded with perceptual and behavioural traits to dominate the mind's sense of reality. Most minds are so controlled, so overwhelmed by the body data programs, they become the whole perception of self and reality for an entire human experience. Mind/soul goes AWOL and lets the body-programs run the show. In this way mind/soul doesn't direct the body – the body directs soul/mind. We all know lots of people who fit that bill and never have they been more obvious than since 2020,

We must always remember, however, that the simulation is interactive just as the Internet is interactive. The simulation affects us while we can affect it if we tap into 5-D consciousness and express that into the Simulation Field. The Cult and its masters have to control the frequency of that Field to maintain perceptual and frequency dominance of its captive population (4-D minds). Open your mind/soul to spirit and you become far more powerful than body-programs. You can override them in terms of health, perception and life experience. You start living life instead of life living you. They speak of mind over matter. It's really mind/spirit over the *illusion* of matter.

CHAPTER EIGHT

Maybe Icke's not so mad

You may be the only person left who believes in you, but it's enough. It takes just *one star* to pierce a universe of darkness. Never give up.
Richelle E. Goodrich

I have described the nature of the simulation in great detail in other books including *Everything You Need To Know But Have Never Been Told* and how mainstream scientists have begun in ever larger numbers to pick up on the theme.

That was not the case immediately post-millennium when to my knowledge only Oxford University academic Nick Bostrom and myself were saying this publicly and consistently although we differed in exactly what the simulation was, why it was created, and by whom. The belief that 'physical' reality is illusory goes way back into what we call history. Religions and beliefs from the Indian sub-continent speak of Brahman (ultimate reality) and 'Maya' (literally 'illusion' or 'magic') and French philosopher René 'I think therefore I am' Descartes (1596-1650) questioned how we know the external world exists as we experience it. The answer is that we can't know. With the development of technology the possibility has emerged that 'Maya' is describing a simulation. Many scientists and studies worldwide are now concluding that the emerging evidence does indeed suggest that our reality is simulated. An investigation by American nuclear physicist Silas Beane and his team at the University of Bonn in Germany decided that we probably do live in a simulation which may well be structured as a lattice of cubes (Fig 112). They proceeded on the basis that any simulation must have limits to its operation as any virtual reality computer game does. In the words of the Beane team paper 'Constraints on the Universe as a Numerical Simulation' there would be a 'pattern of constraint'. They found just this with something called the 'Greisen-Zatsepin-Kuzmin limit', also known as the 'GZK cut-off', which is described as a boundary for cosmic ray particles caused by interaction with cosmic background radiation. Beane rightly points out that a simulation would have its own laws of physics

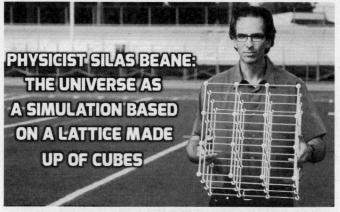

PHYSICIST SILAS BEANE: THE UNIVERSE AS A SIMULATION BASED ON A LATTICE MADE UP OF CUBES

Figure 112: Silas Beane and his cube structure. Mainstream science is now looking seriously at simulated reality.

or encoded rules and constraints. I said earlier that this is why near-death experiencers recall a very different reality when they 'leave' the body (leave this level of the simulation or 'material' world).

I said shortly after the millennium that the 'constraint' of the simulation is the speed of light at 186,000 miles per second. The speed of light only appears (at first) to be the fastest speed possible because it is the fastest speed within the *confines of the simulation*. Or this level of it, anyway. Communications between subatomic particles have been shown to be way faster than the speed of light, but this is happening outside the limits of the simulation in at least Fourth Dimensional reality. The Beane paper says that if we are in a simulation the inmates wouldn't know: 'Like a prisoner in a pitch-black cell we would not be able to see the "walls" of our prison.' You only have to observe the rapid development of virtual reality technology to see that this is true. Soon the computational line will be crossed when you won't be able to tell the difference between 'real' reality and virtual reality. Why? Because 'real' reality and virtual reality are the same simulated phenomenon (Fig 113). David J. Chalmers, Professor of Philosophy at New York University, imagines in his book, *Reality+*, someone wearing an advanced virtual reality headset waking up in a virtual bed and going about their virtual day:

Are you sure you are not in such a VR [virtual reality] device right now? If you're sure – how can you really rule out

Figure 113: The 'real world'.

the VR hypothesis? If you're not sure – then how can you be sure about anything you perceive in the world around you? Can you really be sure that this is a genuine book you're reading, or a genuine chair you're sitting on? Can you really be sure about where you are and about whether what you're seeing is really there?

American theoretical physicist James Gates was Professor of Physics at the University of Maryland, Director of The Center for String and Particle Theory, and on the Council of Advisors on Science and Technology to the Obama Administration. He and his group of researchers found computer codes of digital data embedded in the energetic fabric of 'human' reality. They match the 1 and 0 on-off electrical charges of the binary system used by computers. He said that they had no idea what they are doing there. Well, they are there because we live 'in' a simulation or rather the simulation 'lives' in us. The binary 1 and 0, on-off, electrical system has also been identified in DNA which is the body-computer's 'hard-drive' and a receiver-transmitter of information as it interacts with the simulation and potentially with awareness beyond the simulation. Moderna, a maker of the mRNA 'Covid' fake vaccines which have killed and maimed so many worldwide, refers to the body and its fake vaccines in its own documents as an 'operating system' which is what they are. 'Covid' fake vaccines change human DNA and the frequency on which it receives and transmits. An operating system (the body) is changed by another operating system (the fake vaccine). This is fundamental. DNA carries the simulation program driving human perception, behaviour and experience of those entrapped in the five-sense bubble. The simulation enslaves humanity in its programs through DNA and the only way to break this stranglehold on perception and awareness is to open ourselves to expanded states with higher frequencies that can reset DNA to interact with Infinite Awareness rather than only simulation awareness. At every turn you see the theme of disconnecting Body-Mind from 5-D expanded awareness outside the simulation. James Gates and team further discovered mathematical sequences known as error-correcting codes or block codes within the energetic fabric. These are another feature of computers. Error-correcting codes restore data to its 'default setting' or original state if something happens to knock it out of balance. Gates said they had found a set of equations embedded in our reality that are indistinguishable from those that drive search engines and browsers. It's a *simulation*, folks.

Modern technology is mimicking the simulation to create a simulation within a simulation to further entrap perception in what is being dubbed the Smart Grid and the Metaverse. Our 'world' on every level is going digital and our experienced reality is one of digital holograms which is now the cutting edge of human holographic development. No surprise then that Massachusetts Institute of Technology (MIT) physicist Max Tegmark highlights in his book *Our Mathematical Universe* that the 'physics' of our reality are the same as virtual reality computer games and that our entire reality can be broken down and expressed as *numbers*. Tegmark said a character in computer games would believe everything was real as they went about their 'lives', yet if they began to study their apparently 'real' world they would see that everything was made of pixels and what they thought was physical 'stuff' could be described by 'a bunch of numbers'. Some scientists who have studied reality deeply enough have said that on one level it does take the appearance of *pixels*. Tegmark said that anyone outside the game would see that 'physical' was just numbers while inside the game that would be dismissed as stupid. I know the feeling. This is the reason those in expanded states of consciousness that extend outside the simulation can see it's a simulation and those perceptually confined to the simulation cannot. Tegmark continued:

> We look around and it doesn't seem that mathematical at all, but everything we see is made out of elementary particles like quarks and electrons. And what properties does an electron have? Does it have a smell or a colour or a texture? No! ... We physicists have come up with geeky names for [Electron] properties, like electric charge, or spin, or lepton number, but the electron doesn't care what we call it, the properties are just numbers.

Divine' proportion = computer codes

It's been known since ancient times that the world is encoded with particular geometrical codes and sequences. Initiates of this knowledge encoded their major buildings such as churches and temples with the same proportions including Phi, Pi, Golden Mean, Golden Ratio and Golden Section. Collectively they are called 'divine proportion'. They are not 'divine'. They are the simulation. I have been saying for decades that they are *computer codes* (Fig 114 overleaf). Another example is the Fibonacci number sequence named after 12th/13th century Italian mathematician, Fibonacci, or Leonardo of Pisa. The Fibonacci sequence adds the two previous numbers to get the next one ... 1, 1, 2, 3, 5, 8, 13, 21, 34, 55 ... and so on. As with 'divine proportion' in general, the Fibonacci sequence can be found in everything including the human face and body, animals, DNA, seed heads, pine cones, trees, shells, spiral galaxies, hurricanes and the number of petals in a flower. This has to be so in a holographic simulation (Fig 115 overleaf). I emphasised earlier that an extraordinary characteristic of holograms is that every part of a hologram is a smaller version of the whole and this is the foundation of the principle of 'as above, so below'. Therefore everything within the

Figure 114: 'Divine proportion' is the information fabric of the simulation.

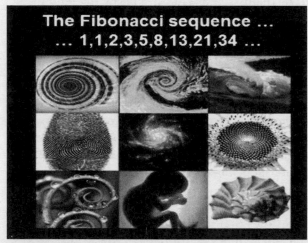

Figure 115: The Fibonacci sequence is encoded throughout our reality.

Figure 116: Fractal patterns – more 'computer codes' of the simulation.

whole hologram (simulation) must be a smaller version of the whole hologram (simulation). Characters in computer games are encoded with the same physics, maths and rules as the rest of the game and the simulation is the same. The 'human body' is an extension of the game with the same characteristics because it is *part* of the game. Then we come to fractal patterns which are embedded throughout the simulation and, hardly surprisingly, are based on the holographic principle. They are defined as 'a never-ending pattern that is infinitely complex and self-similar across different scales'(Fig 116). These are the fractal patterns referred to by John Lamb Lash in his book about the Nag Hammadi texts when he says: 'The Demiurge fashions a heaven world copied from the fractal patterns of the eternal Aeons.' The fractal patterns of Prime

Earth Reality. All form is a vibrational pattern that maintains energy in a particular state. Cells of the body may constantly change, but the foundation pattern pretty much stays the same as cells come and go and we don't notice. See videos of cymatics on the Internet and how sound arranges particles in different states and patterns responding to the frequency of the sound. Our 'physical' reality is a hologram and so, as with fractals, the same patterns repeat across different levels. This is a list from *Everything You Need to Know But Have Never Been Told* of just some phenomena encoded with fractal patterns:

> River networks, mountain ranges, craters, lightning bolts, coastlines, mountain goat horns, trees and branch growth, animal colour patterns, pineapples, heart rates, heartbeats, neurons and brains, eyes, respiratory systems, circulatory systems, blood vessels and pulmonary vessels, geological fault lines, earthquakes, snowflakes, crystals, ocean waves, vegetables, soil pores and even the rings of Saturn.

The same fractal patterns have been found in psychology, behaviour, speech patterns and interpersonal relationships. This is the simulation program at work. 'Symmetrical mathematics' are defined as 'one shape becoming exactly like another when you move it in some way, turn, flip or slide' and is obviously related to the fractal principle, The journal *Nature's Scientific Reports* published a study exploring the existence of fundamental laws that may govern growth on all levels including electrical firing between brain cells. the growth of social networks, and expansion of galaxies. Physicist Dmitri Krioukov, co-author of the study, said that natural growth dynamics are the same for different networks including the Internet, brain or social networks. The *HuffPost* reported:

> When the team compared the Universe's history with growth of social networks and brain circuits, they found all the networks expanded in similar ways: They balanced links between similar nodes with ones that already had many connections.

> For instance, a cat lover surfing the Internet may visit mega-sites such as Google or Yahoo, but will also browse cat fancier websites or YouTube kitten videos. In the same way, neighboring brain cells like to connect, but neurons also link to such 'Google brain cells' that are hooked up to loads of other brain cells. The eerie similarity between networks large and small is unlikely to be a coincidence, Krioukov said.

No, it's not, and nor is this 'natural'. Everywhere I see scientists grappling in bewilderment with the apparent mysteries of ever-repeating themes and examples of as above, so below, when the mysteries can be solved with one sentence: *They are dealing with a holographic simulation.* To misquote the child in *The Matrix*: 'Do not try and bend the Universe. That's impossible. Instead, only try to realise the truth ... There is no Universe ... Then you'll see that it is not the Universe that exists. It is only yourself.'

Electric atmosphere

Another confirmation of the simulation in my view is an emerging and highly compelling area of scientific research under the heading of 'Electric Universe' and the Thunderbolts Project pioneered by Australian physicist Wallace Thornhill and American researcher and writer David Talbott. The whole of experienced reality is founded on electricity and electromagnetism. Everything from the brain to the genetic system to the entire perceived Universe is electrical in nature as you would expect with a simulation. How do virtual reality games and computers work? Precisely. A team headed by Jacqueline Barton, a world-renowned chemist at the California Institute of Technology (Caltech), discovered that DNA is 'like an electrical wire for signalling within a cell'. Scientists discovered that bees find pollen by picking up electrical signals transmitted by flowers and a British team lowered extremely high blood pressure through an electrical wire in the brain to change what was being communicated. The Universe to the smallest filament communicate electrically and are powered by electricity. We see electrical lightning, electrical storms, the Aurora Borealis or northern lights, and the rapidly rotating electromagnetic fields that are tornadoes which appear in electrical storms. Electric Universe advocates rightly point out that we are looking at a gigantic circuit of electrical communication which connects everything from planets and stars to the human brain (Figs 117 and 118). Even at this level we are *One*. Electrical and electromagnetic interaction between humans and planets form the basis of astrology. Images from the Herschel telescope have shown that stars are formed on galactic electrical filaments. Mainstream science believed this to be impossible when it was highly predictable to those

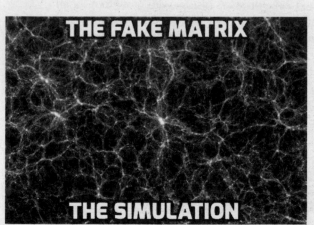

Figure 117: The 'Universe' is a gigantic electrical circuit because it's a simulation.

coming from the Electric Universe direction. David Sibeck, a project scientist at NASA's Goddard Space Flight Center, said:

> The satellites have found evidence of magnetic ropes connecting Earth's upper atmosphere directly to the Sun. We believe that solar winds flow in along these ropes providing energy for geomagnetic storms and auroras.

Figure 118: When holographically decoded the electrical circuitry looks like this.

Everything is connected and through these electrical and electromagnetic communications and networks the Sun impacts on Earth temperature. Isn't that amazing? The Sun affects Earth temperature. Who would have thought it? Blimey, the things you learn. There was me thinking it was carbon dioxide, the gas of life, without which we would have no plant life and food supply, thus no humans or animals. `The observable Universe is 99.999 percent plasma, the so-called fourth state of matter, which is an almost perfect medium for electricity and electromagnetism. American scientist Irving Langmuir (1881-1957) discovered that when plasma of one electrical charge meets plasma with a different charge a barrier is automatically created between the two.

Figure 119: Planetary magnetospheres are formed when a barrier forms between two different states of electrical charge within the plasma field.

This is how planetary magnetospheres are formed from plasma-electricity interaction. Planets and stars generate unique electrical signatures. Where one charge meets another an energetic barrier is formed that defines the magnetospheres

(Fig 119). The Sun is almost entirely plasma as you expect to be the case given that it is *processesing* electrical power rather than *generating* it. Mainstream orthodoxy says the Sun is a nuclear reactor projecting heat from its core through the surface and out into the solar system. This makes no sense of the observable evidence. Why is space so cold and heat only generated when solar energy interacts with Earth's atmosphere? The Sun absorbs, processes and projects electricity from the universal electrical circuit and it passes through 'space' as electricity to be decoded into heat by interaction with the planetary atmosphere. I expand greatly on this in *Everything You Need To Know But Have Never Been Told* both in terms of the Sun and the whole Electric Universe concept which answers so many former mysteries that have baffled scientists. The Universe is a gigantic quantum computer powered by electricity and projected by Fourth Dimensional mind as Third Dimensional reality.

Support gathers

More scientists and researchers are now seeing the obvious with regard to the simulation. Rich Terrile, director of the Centre for Evolutionary Computation and Automated Design at NASA's Jet Propulsion Laboratory, has said that his research led him to conclude that the Universe is a digital hologram. By definition this must have been created by some form of intelligence. Researchers at the Ibaraki University in Japan produced papers suggesting that the Universe is nothing but a holographic projection, which it is. It's not a projection like looking at a

Figure 120: 'Cinema mind' decodes the simulation information source into a holographic reality that we call the human world. (Image by Neil Hague.)

movie screen. Information is 'projected' into Fourth Dimensional mind and that does the projecting (Fig 120). American celebrity scientist Neil deGrasse Tyson said at the 2016 Isaac Asimov Memorial Debate that the likelihood of the Universe being a simulation 'may be very high'. The event brought together scientists to discuss the simulation hypothesis. Some agreed, some didn't. One of the mistakes the 'no' camp makes is equating human technological limitations with the limits of possibility. They are not the same. The non-human force is employing simulation know-how way, way, beyond anything humans can conceive. The simulation is employing the power of the mind, of consciousness, to generate its illusions. Preston Greene, an assistant professor of philosophy at Nanyang Technological University in Singapore, has even warned against establishing the Universe as a simulation in case the creators then turned it off. 'If we were to prove that we live inside a simulation, this could cause our creators to terminate the simulation – to destroy our world.' Well first of all it's not our world it's *their* world and they need us and our energy more than we need them. We don't need them at all. We are consciousness. The simulation illusion is all theirs and it can't work without us when our minds are essential to decoding it holographically into being.

The decoding aspect of the simulation explains another mystery of science. It has long been postulated by some scientists that our reality only exists when we are looking at it – observing it. This is known as the Observer Effect when it should really be called the Decoder Effect. The act of observation – attention – triggers the act of decoding waveform information into holographic (fake physical) information (Fig 121). When the simulation in its waveform foundation state is not being observed (decoded) it remains in a waveform state. In fact it is *always* in a waveform state just as the waveform holographic print is always the waveform print even when the laser picks out the information to project a 3-D hologram. The print does not morph into a hologram – the hologram is projected *from* the print which doesn't go anywhere. In the same way the simulation always exists in waveform even when the mind's act of observation – decoding – manifests its holographic (particle) form. Quantum science has long pondered the mystery of how

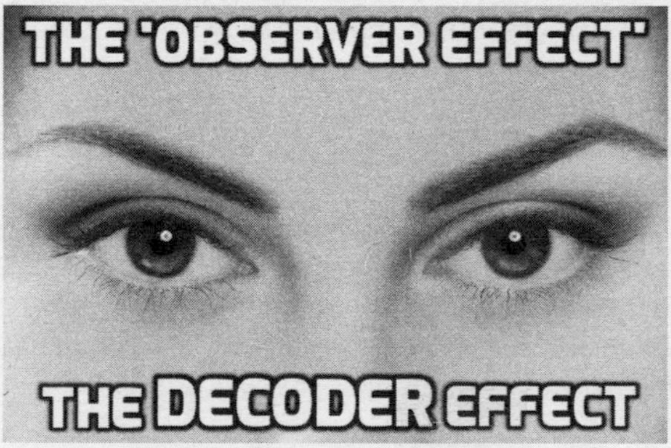

Figure 121: Attention creates 'physical' reality.

something can exist as a wave and a particle at the same time as it has been shown to do. Wave and the particle are the same information made manifest in different states. The wave is the particle and the particle is the wave. They are indivisible as the waveform print and the laser-projected hologram are indivisible and exist at the same time. They have to. The hologram can't exist without the waveform print and the particle can't exist without the wave. Physicists at the Australian National University claimed to have proved that reality in its experienced form only exists when it's observed after conducting experiments based on the wave-particle phenomenon. Virtual reality games only exist in the way that you experience them when you are watching (decoding) a particular scene. All the other scenes exist only as codes until they appear to your perception. A DVD is a disc of information. It only appears as images when the player decodes them onto the screen and the scene you are watching is the only one in that form at that moment. The rest of the DVD remains as encoded information.

The death trap

Okay, now I am going to be really controversial which of course is not like me. Icke says *he's* going to be controversial?? Shit, what is he going to say? Well, a couple of things: (1) This 'material world' is only one level of the simulation and the idea is to trap minds in further illusion after body 'death' to keep them on the Ferris wheel of the reincarnation cycle; and (2) not every 'human' has consciousness in the sense that we perceive it. Many are software inserts into the simulation like those known in computer games as a 'non-player character'. These are defined as 'any character in a game that is not controlled by a player. In human terms not controlled by consciousness, but instead *completely* controlled by the simulation. Another 'non-player' definition is that this 'usually means a character controlled by the computer (instead of the player) that has a predetermined set of behaviours that potentially will impact gameplay'. I am saying there are humans like this? Yep, lots of them. Wow. *What?* A touch controversial, yes, but dispassionately observe the world. Many agents of the Cult are software inserts completely controlled by the simulation. Professor of Philosophy David J. Chalmers refers to non-player characters as 'pure sims':

> These are simulated beings who are wholly inside the simulation. Most of the people in [Daniel F.] Galouye's novel *Simulacron-3* are pure sims. They receive direct sensory inputs from the simulation because they're part of the simulation. Importantly their brains are simulated, too. Simulations containing only pure sims may be *pure simulations* – simulations in which everything that happens is simulated.

There can be *mixed simulations*, which contain both biosims and pure sims. Inside the Matrix, the leading characters Neo and Trinity are biosims, whereas the 'machine' characters Agent Smith and the Oracle are pure sims.

I say that our reality is the latter mixed simulation. My view is that not all humans are conscious as in Infinitely so (at least potentially). Not all humans have 'minds' as such in 'Fourth Dimensional' reality. I know this will be a shocker to many. I can only tell you where life has taken me in terms of understanding what is going on. AI is now producing images of 'people' who do not exist. They are literally made up (Fig 122). Studies have shown that people cannot tell the difference between the fakes and 'real people' on a ratio higher than the toss of a coin. Hany Farid, co-author of a study published in *Proceedings of the National Academy of Sciences USA*, said: 'We found that not only are synthetic faces highly realistic, they are deemed more trustworthy than real faces.' AI-generated non-people like this can be used to

Figure 122: AI technology can already create digital 'people' like these that don't exist as 'humans'. Far more advanced 4-D technology can't go much further to create holographic digital 'inserts'?

construct a whole back story about their lives that appears in the media and perhaps portrays them as victims of war or a terrorist attack when they don't exist. How would the public ever know unless someone did some detailed research and even then any findings would be banned by Cult-owned social media and the rest of the mainstream. Check out footage known as Deep Fakes in which technology can make anyone credibly appear to say anything with the correct voice frequency and lip-movement even though they didn't say a word of it. Remember, too, that this is what is possible in the public arena when the secret projects will be far in advance of anything you see. Imagine what is possible in the 4-D realm in terms of full-blown non-player characters. I hear it said that a body cannot exist without the mind. I don't agree in the sense that this claim is delivered. Bodies need the mind to decode them into holographic reality, okay. They don't need a mind, however, to be their mission control. The simulation is perfectly capable of being that. Do inserted characters in computer games have minds? They are animated not by mind/soul, but by electricity. The simulation in its 3-D projection is founded on electricity and electromagnetism. Such bodies are animated by the simulation and are an expression, a part, of the simulation. Their 'minds' are artificial intelligence programmed to play a particular role like a non-player character. I cannot stress enough that virtual reality and computer game technology is mimicking the simulation (a form of the holographic principle) and so what you see in one will be happening in the other. Bodies 'die' when electricity is withdrawn and with that the 'mind/soul' is freed – freed in the sense that mind is freed from the *belief* that it is 'in' a body. This belief triggers the illusion of embodiment and freedom from embodiment at 'death'. *It's all belief* and perception programming. *All of it.* Software insert non-players are AI and follow a set programmed path with programmed responses and reactions. Is that so crazy when you see where AI robotics is now even in the human realm?

In our face

Rich Terrile at NASA's Jet Propulsion Laboratory said: 'Soon there will be nothing technical standing in the way to making machines that have their own consciousness.' Their own *technologically and computer-* generated sense of consciousness and will they need mind/souls to achieve that? Of course not. Terrile said: 'If one progresses at the current rate of technology, a few decades into the future we will be a society where there are artificial entities living in simulations that are much more abundant than human beings.' Videogames were becoming ever more sophisticated and in the future we would have simulations of conscious entities. What are they seeking to do by connecting the human brain to AI? To turn once conscious people into *non-player characters*. It's the ultimate control. Remember, too, that this technology does not have to be invented. It already exists and it is only a matter of transferring that into the human realm from 'Fourth Dimensional' reality which means that Terrile's timescale can be greatly reduced. Already China is using news readers that are AI copies of news hosts and it is becoming increasingly difficult to tell them apart. China today and the world tomorrow. Terrile said: 'If in the future there are more digital people living in simulated environments than there are today, then what is to say we are not part of that already?' I say we are. The population of the world (simulation) only reached one billion in 1804 and it is now approaching eight billion. Is this extraordinary increase all the result of mind/souls 'incarnating'? Cult operatives in Silicon Valley are predicting that human brains will be attached to AI by 2030 and onwards and that AI will do more and more of human thinking until that is negligible. This will make *all* 'humans' the equivalent of AI software inserts. The simulation is controlled and operated by AI and AI inserts allow the program to be manipulated from 'within' with AI controlling them completely. Many of the front people and assets of the Global Cult are AI inserts or cyborgs. Look into their eyes. Can you see 'life' there, or sparkle and vibrance that comes with a state of Infinite Awareness? Does AI have empathy or compassion when even if that could be simulated it can also be deleted from the program.

Movies like *The Matrix* and television series such as *Westworld* have explored these concepts. Many characters in *The Matrix* are portrayed as advanced programmed software inserts which in the case of Agent Smith could make multiple copies of themselves. Could this explain why some people have been seen in different places at the same moment? Anything becomes possible and explainable once the implications of the simulation are understood. The central *Matrix* character of the 'Oracle' is revealed in the storyline as a program and no one knew. The storyline is that you cannot not tell by looking who is a Matrix software program and who is not. My body is a program, so is yours, and so is that of an AI insert. Bodies are the same and therefore look the same. The question is not about the body. The question is what is *driving* the body? Is it AI or mind as an expression of Infinite Awareness? Everyone 'dies' when they are programmed to 'die' unless Infinite Awareness overrides body-programs. Which it can. Most are never aware of this power and their death is dictated by the data running through the program. This doesn't have to be. There can also be constant interventions by AI to change the programs in accordance with events and happenings. People view the gathering tussle between human consciousness and AI while not realising that the whole story of humanity has been the tussle between consciousness and AI.

Birth and death illusion

When mind is influenced by a connection to Infinite Spirit in 5-D, and upwards, it can override the program. If it is not. the simulation is controlling all sense of reality. This includes the birth process. There is no physical so there can be no birth process except as a decoded illusion. That said, if the information is telling the mind it is emerging from the birth canal then that will be its reality. If information encoded in the body communicates to mind that it is dying then the mind will experience bodily death. *Experience* it when, in fact, there is no such 'physical' event happening. Far out, eh? Characters in *The Matrix* died when their minds accepted they had died. In the end the Neo character reached a level of consciousness that saw through the illusion of death and came back to life despite being shot multiple times. The body that was shot and 'died' was after all in his *mind* and existed only as information fed to his brain outside the Matrix. The birth and death 'process' is an illusion created by the simulation to trick the mind into the fantasy that it is entering and leaving a 'physical' world when all that's happening is the mind is decoding the informational *illusion* of entering and leaving a 'physical' world. The body is *in the mind* not a maternity ward. The simulation birth and death illusion has monumental manipulative potential especially through the fear of death when there is no death. The body has a cycle (which the mind decodes), but *we* – the Infinite 'I' – have eternity.

There is no birth or death outside the simulation. There is only life. What is experienced as birth and death is only the mind decoding 'entry' and 'departure' at this level of the simulation. This is fundamental to the mind trickery to induce a sense of life being limited and brief; a feeling of isolated pointlessness; and the crucial control that comes from the fear of death which is a fear of the unknown. Humans are terrified of the unknown and the simulation program keeps them from knowing anything except the basics. The more unknowns the better because there are more reasons to be afraid. Minds are fed the information by the simulation that they are being born, growing up and growing old, and then that they have died. 'They' have done none of these things. 'They' is our mind in Fourth Dimensional reality decoding an information source into perceptual servitude. I know this is a lot to take in. Ponder on it when you have quiet moments. An obvious question is how this could possibly be done. It would be so complex and complicated surely? The whole thing is being run by artificial intelligence on a level that even the cutting edge of human AI today could not even begin to contemplate. AI in our decoded reality is still in its infancy while 'Fourth Dimensional' AI is light years further on. The system is driven by the energy generated by mind and its illusory experience. We can't see thought and emotion. We only see and feel the consequences of it. They are a 'Fourth Dimensional' phenomena in terms of their frequency and low-vibrational thought and emotion such as fear, depression, anxiety, and hatred are *lower* Fourth Dimensional phenomena where the human control system is. The non-human force feeds off that energy and its AI is powered by it. Remember the machines in the *Matrix* movies being powered by the energy emitted by human babies and the Morpheus quote is now put in greater context as he held up the battery: 'The Matrix is a computer-generated dream world built to keep us under control in order to change a human being into this.' But not a human being. A mind that *thinks* it's a human being.

Simulation information tricks the mind into believing it is born and dies. While the experience of death is to leave one 'place' and go to somewhere else the whole sequence is actually the same seamless program. *The mind doesn't go anywhere.* The simulation makes it believe that it does and so it experiences that sense of reality. The nature of the information changes and so the sense of experience changes. From decoding the illusion of being 'in' the body, the mind decodes the illusion of being 'outside' the body. These are different phases of the same illusion being decoded by 'Fourth Dimensional' mind. Those with consciousness expanded enough and in a high enough frequency can escape the simulation after 'death'. Those who are not are 'recycled' back into the 'physical' level of the simulation in the process called reincarnation of the 'soul'. Even the 'soul' is an illusion. Only spirit really exists. Reincarnation, from a Latin term that means 'entering the flesh again', is a central pillar of Eastern religions such as Buddhism, Hinduism, Jainism and Sikhism. Ancient Greek philosophers including Pythagoras, Socrates, and Plato believed in metempsychosis or rebirth. Globally this has been quite widespread through the ages and cultures and remains so today.

Coming back for more?

I could never see the logic of the traditional explanation of reincarnation. Why would you have to return to a tiny planet time after time to become 'enlightened' enough to escape that cycle as we are told by Eastern religions and belief-systems that derive from Eastern religions? It's a bit like the Christian idea of 'God' judging you for all eternity on the basis of one life in this world lasting a hundred years or ten minutes. It makes absolutely no sense and neither does the reincarnation cycle (Fig 123).

Figure 123: Earth is a billionth the size of a pinhead when compared with the projected size of the Universe, according to mainstream science estimates. Why would you need to keep reincarnating here to 'evolve to enlightenment'? But if it was a simulation and a trap ...

Buddhists believe in karma, or 'intentional action', a form of cause and effect in the West, but more akin in the East to saying that all happenings are indivisible. According to this belief our actions decide if we escape from the cycle of death and rebirth which Buddhists know as Samsara. They pursue a state of enlightenment (Nirvana) to break the so-called vicious cycle. My question is who or what put them on this wheel of misfortune in the first place? I say it is the creators of the simulation. You have to keep coming back to the same pinhead 'planet' to learn lessons that allow you to escape? *Ugh*? In my Ayahuasca altered state in Brazil I was shown images of people falling out of the sky onto a path crossing a field. As they walked in ever greater numbers the path was worn away deeper and deeper until it morphed into the darkness of a record groove on the old vinyl discs. The voice asked why it was any surprise that people looked up for 'God' when it was the only place they could see light. The implication was that the reincarnation experience did not lead people to enlightenment except rarely. Rather it led them deeper into the programmed sense of reality that trapped them in the perceptual prison cell. Put another way, the reincarnation cycle did not lead most people out of the simulation illusion only further in. This made them easier and easier to drop into the program with each new 'visit' to the 'physical' level of the Matrix. More accurately, the repeating experience of the mind further embedded the program into the mind.

The body exists as an encoded information field decoded by 4-D mind into holographic 'physical' reality. If mind believes the 3-D projected illusion to be 'real' then when the body 'dies' in the simulation the mind perceives itself to have died in human form and goes through the recycling process into another point on the simulated Time Loop. On and on it goes until we break the sequence through *perception*. Morpheus says in *The Matrix*: 'The body cannot live without the mind.' No, it can't – unless it is a purely AI insert. The mind is *decoding* the body into holographic reality. Why does the body go on existing while it rots away after death if the mind has withdrawn? But it hasn't. The mind is not only decoding the body; it is decoding the whole simulated reality which has encoded into its information fabric the way the body slowly dismantles after 'death'. The body's aging program becomes the body's decomposition program. It's *ALL* the *program*. The body is a program, a form of computer system, and the Cult treats it as such.

The same simulation information source is capable of delivering a reality that has no memory of past experience. If we had such recall we would grasp what is going on and what we are part of. Each new incarnation is a clean slate with mostly no memory of previous 'lives' or the between human life state. Some do remember bits of this information either through a glitch in the simulation program or through connecting with 5-D where that information is retained outside the multiple levels of the simulation. These past life memories are extremely compelling especially from small children who remember locations, periods, events, names, and other fine details which check out and they could not possibly know any of it from this 'life'. This is far from common, but there are enough known examples to say that it's not exactly rare either. Researchers apparently find the most vivid memories appear before five years of age and often begin to fade by six or seven. Many cases have happened in Christian families in which reincarnation is a big no, no, but evidence from their children has led to a change of mind. From birth and throughout a human life people are either directed by the simulation or expanded consciousness or a combination of both. Mind in touch with its Infinite Awareness can override the program. The simulation is directing everything if someone is a perceptual expression only of their Body-Mind. What you do and think, who attracts or repulses you, where 'your' life goes, are all the simulation at work without expanded awareness to override that. Who am I going to marry? Ask the simulation. Or if you are guided by expanded levels of awareness ask spirit. Which is your Mission Control – simulation or spirit? This is the difference between what is termed asleep and awake and the long-awaited Great Awakening is the opening of Body-Mind (the program) to reconnect with spirit (overriding the program). The 'Covid' years have clearly revealed those being run by the simulation and those at least to some extent able to breach the program. Near-death experiencers in their millions have recalled what reality was like after their awareness was released from a briefly-dead body. I have read legions of these accounts and while they differ in detail there are major and compelling common themes. They describe a very different reality without the limitations of the body perception program. One said:

> … everything from the beginning, my birth, my ancestors, my children, my wife, everything comes together simultaneously. I saw everything about me, and about everyone who was around me. I saw everything they were thinking now, what they thought then, what was happening before, what was happening now. There is no time, there is no sequence of events, no such thing as limitation, of distance, of period, of place. I could be anywhere I wanted to be simultaneously.

This person may have been consciousness expanded enough to escape the other levels of the simulation to experience 5-D, but they didn't have to be. Anyone think that those who can simulate an entire 'physical' reality cannot mimic 'heaven' also, and the bright, warm light, that near-death experiencers report? I will return to this topic in another context in the chapter 'WTF? I Mean …WTF??'.

Simulating 'heaven'?

Let us not forget that the simulation is mimicking a reality that does actually exist in another band of frequency. The simulation is like a digital copy of that. Why couldn't the after-death realm that is experienced by consciousness after bodily 'death' be mimicking what people call 'heaven'? I suggest it is and that the key to understanding this is the 'tunnel of light' where near-death experiencers describe meeting departed loved ones and 'beings of light' (Fig 124 overleaf). I have concluded over the years that the 'tunnel' leads to the recycling wheel. Minds/souls think they are going to 'the Light' when the 'tunnel' really leads to what some refer to as the 'waiting room' from where they return into the 'physical' level of the simulation in another body or even another 'era'. Crucial to escaping the simulation is knowing what we are escaping from

Figure 124: The afterlife tunnel of light. But where does it lead?

and the mind-tricks that cause consciousness to return over and over in what we call reincarnation in a loop of repeated experience. Déjà vu, anyone? I published an email in *Everything You Need To Know But Have Never Been Told* from an American Christian believer who had his whole sense of reality overturned by a near-death experience. He said it was dark when 'I suddenly became aware'. There was no abstract thought or reasoning and no tunnel of light. He was just aware. The next moment he was in a dimly lit room and 'now here's where the messed up part began'. He said he saw two 'aliens' or Grey entities (subordinate to Reptilians in their viciously-enforced hierarchy as I will shortly focus upon). 'One [was] sitting behind a control desk of sorts and the other one standing behind him in a doorway like big brother ... just watching'. The email said:

> The room behind him [was] brightly lit, but I could still see his eyes watching me. Suddenly it occurs to me that they are 'monitoring' me ... like I was just a number. The one behind the control desk then sort of lifts his head slightly, looks at me ... then looks back down at his control desk. He then waves his right hand in the air, sort of motioning over the desk in some or other gesture.

> A rectangular button on the desk then starts glowing in an orange and purple color ... almost like glitter that's mixed in water and shaken up I guess ... Soon as that happens swooooosh ... I'm out in space looking at the earth ... just hovering there ... The earth seemed round to me ... not flat [as some are claiming today] ... Anyway, suddenly this light-blue beam comes down out of nowhere (today I wish I had looked where the beam came from, but I didn't ... just came from somewhere) and it shot down to earth.

> As it hit ... I suppose the atmosphere or ozone layer of the earth ... the beam kinda spread around the globe, like a light blue energy shield just resonating all around the globe ... just once. In an instant, I realized that it was

information being sent back to earth that my soul is coming back, and the reason it resonated all around the globe is, as I understood in an instant, like the butterfly effect ... I'm coming back so everything else is affected.

He said that after this he woke up in hospital. He thought for a long time that he had had experienced demons and was going to Hell or maybe it was just a dream. But he said when he read about the Matrix in my books 'everything suddenly slotted into place':

What I know is this ... I saw technology I've never seen before, and I've never heard of something like this, so it wasn't an idea lodged into my brain from something I saw or read before I died. I am now convinced that when you die, your soul is intercepted and recycled back to earth. It goes against everything I used to believe.

Well, recycled – 'reincarnated' – only *if* the mind continues to be caught in the illusions of the Matrix simulation which continue after 'death'. Free your Mind before death and you are straight out of here. Nag Hammadi texts call this escape 'resurrection'. I will expand on the afterlife realm in the WTF chapter.

Time loops

I wrote a book in 2003 called *Tales from the Time Loop* in which I said that our reality is a loop of manufactured 'time' in which we appeared to be going from 'past' through 'present' to 'future' when in effect we were going round and round in a repeating cycle decoded by our *minds*. The fact that we only experience part of the cycle in each new 'incarnation' means that we never complete the whole cycle in one go to allow us to see that it *is* a cycle (Fig 125). We only experience the simulation in small doses before we 'die'. Experience 1960 to 2030 and you will perceive that you are moving 'forward' with the encoded body-aging program confirming the illusion of

Figure 125: The time loop – or loops – the simulation equivalent of a Ferris wheel. (Image by Neil Hague)

'time' passing. Experience the whole loop from start to finish, or start to start, and you would see through the scam. You find this in the biblical Book of Ecclesiastes 1:

> The thing that hath been, it is that which shall be; and that which is done is that which shall be done: and there is no new thing under the sun. Is there any thing whereof it may be said, See, this is new? it hath been already of old time, which was before us. There is no remembrance of former things; neither shall there be any remembrance of things that are to come with those that shall come after.

The Roman Empire still exists in that part of the 'loop' or information program. Why can't some minds be fed information from that program 'era' and still be 'incarnating' into ancient Rome, or ancient Egypt, ancient anywhere? It's only decoded information after all. How do you time travel when there is no time only the eternal NOW? You travel 'back and forth' through the Time Loop program which has the added complication that there are many such loops or 'timelines' that can interpenetrate. Periods of 'history' are different parts of the Time Loop and perceptions of 'history' can also be manipulated with 'historical finds' that have nothing to do with 'history'. They have been inserted into the simulation to mislead and misdirect. This is not always the case, but we should not be naive enough to think it can't happen. It can. I have also heard it suggested that cataclysmic events are employed to end a 'time' cycle and reset the loop to the start again. Such global catastrophes are in the geological and biological record as they appear to be. I have been highlighting this since *The Biggest Secret* in 1998. See the evidence for the Younger Dryas species wipe-out about 13,000 years ago in the Time Loop 'timeline'.

Tunnel vision

Another relevant question: Are those that near-death experiencers 'meet' out-of-body or at the end of the 'tunnel' really loved ones? Or AI projections of 'loved ones'? It would be nice to think the former, but this is a moment in human experience when we need to be seriously streetwise and question everything. Consciousness of loved ones exists in other realities, they can be only a frequency or heartbeat away, but are those that 'souls' see after bodily 'death' really the genuine 'loved one'? Near-death experiencers often tell how a passed-over 'loved one' or other entity gives them a choice to return to their body or cross a boundary symbolised in many ways after which they will not be able to return to that 'physical' life. By definition they all make the choice to 'come back' and tell their tale. What exists beyond that light at the end of the 'tunnel' which they never see? Paradise or the 'waiting room'? I say the latter. I watched a lot of programmes on DVD in the *Ghost Whisperer* series which ran on CBS in the United States from 2005 to 2010. It is the fictional story of a woman who can see ghosts and helps them 'cross' to 'the Light'. The series explores some interesting after-death scenarios while being real cheesy. The punchline finale in every show is when the ghost sees a bright light and walks towards it to cross into 'heaven'. The script constantly underpins the go-to-the-Light after death concept which I believe to be the reincarnation trap. The 'waiting room' also appears in Gnostic Nag Hammadi texts as a realm they call 'the middle place'. This is a 'space' between the Upper and Lower Aeons or Infinite Reality and the simulation. They say this middle place is a state of temporary 'non-existence' where the soul waits to reincarnate or becomes trapped there by ignorance and its consequent low-frequency state of being. This has all the connotations of the Roman Catholic belief in purgatory – 'a place or state of temporary suffering or misery' and an intermediate state of purification between 'physical death' and acceptance into 'heaven'. Or it is instead an intermediate state between 'physical death' and another 'physical birth'? Put it this way, when I leave the body I won't be heading down any 'tunnel' or anything akin to that. I'll be heading for the Infinite Realm beyond the simulation in all its forms and I'll make my own way there, thanks, without the help of fake 'loved ones' which I believe them to be. I'll expand on this in the WTF chapter.

I came across a telling scene in the *Star Trek* series from 1998 when the character Captain Janeway is caught in a sort of time loop and experiences her death. Her late father appears to guide her into the afterlife, but she becomes suspicious at his pressure and insistence that she go with him into the tunnel of light. Janeway feels this is a trap to make her return to 'earth' over and over. You are not my father, she says. 'You're an alien. You've created all these hallucinations haven't you?'. He replies: 'This is what my species does – at the moment just before death one of us comes to tell you what is happening to make the crossing over an occasion of joy.' Janeway looks at the tunnel of light and asks: 'What is that?' The alien projected to look like her father says it is their Matrix where her consciousness will live – 'I was being truthful when I said it was a place of wonder. It can be whatever you want it to be.' Janeway asks why he pretended to be her father. The alien explains that usually people are comforted to see their loved ones – it made the 'crossing over' a much less fearful occasion. Janeway describes him as a 'vulture' preying on people at the moment of their death when they are most vulnerable. 'What's the real reason you want me in that Matrix?' she asks. 'Somehow I don't think it has anything to do with everlasting joy.' The alien says she must go in there, but Janeway sees that if the alien could force her he would already have done so. 'You need me to

agree don't you? I have to go voluntarily.' She refuses and the alien
responds: 'Eventually you will come into my Matrix and you will
nourish me for a long time.' Janeway's reply was 'Go back to Hell,
coward.' Nice one, and most apt. Strangely, you might think, I don't
watch much science fiction. It's never really appealed to me except
where it is seriously relevant to my work like *The Matrix*. Therefore I had
concluded my view on the tunnel of light before I saw this *Star Trek* clip.
It does, in my opinion, portray a fundamental truth. Researcher
Cameron Day described the concept very well:

> One metaphor to describe our current situation is that we are like a flock of
> chickens pent up inside a tiny, dark, smelly chicken coop. Those that have
> been farming us are preparing to let us out of the coop, and into a larger
> fenced-in area (astral realms/spirit worlds) where we will be able to feel a little
> more free, but still within their control. This is the 'farmer's' way of ensuring
> that they can continue to feed off of our energies, while making us feel that
> we are free, thanks to the kindness of our captors.

As this book was almost complete I was recommended to read,
Journey of Souls, published in 1994 by American psychologist and
hypnotist Michael Newton. He details hypnotic sessions with a stream
of people that he questioned about what happens between human
'physical' lives. The common themes they describe are very compelling.
They talk about travelling through the 'tunnel' drawn by some unseen
'magnetic' force to be greeted by 'loved ones' and then experiencing life
as a 'soul' in the 'spiritual world'. Except that it doesn't sound very
'spiritual' to me. They describe a hierarchical structure of demarcation
into 'soul clusters' overseen by 'guides' and 'teachers' of various
hierarchical levels, masters, and a 'Council of Elders' who must be
obeyed. Newton's clients said there was freedom 'as long as we pay
attention to the rules'; 'You can't just go off anywhere'; and 'I'm
supposed to stay [where I am told]'. Souls 'go to school' between human
lives to undergo instruction as they follow a cycle of 'homecoming',
'transition', 'placement', and reincarnation. This is the perceived reality
of the New Age and Cult operatives such as the Russian Yelena Petrovna
von Hahn, or later 'Madam Blavatsky', co-founder of the Theosophical
Society in 1875 which inspired much of what eventually became known
as New Age philosophy with its concept of 'ascended masters' and a
'spiritual hierarchy' with names such as 'Lord Babaji', 'Lord Maitreya',
'Count Saint Germain', 'Swami Vivekananda', and 'Sananda' (the New
Age version of 'Jesus'). *Everything* is hierarchy. There is no 'physical'
description of 'Jesus' in the Bible and 'his' image was decreed by artists
hundreds of years after biblical times. Nevertheless, his New Age
version 'Sananda' somehow looks the same as those artists portrayed

'him'. What a coincidence.

Everything is hierarchical – 'us' up here, you down there. Know your place. You have the 'dark forces' to fear and the 'light forces' to worship when both forces are expressions of the *same* force. You've almost got to laugh. In fact, it's recommended. Near-death experiencers report how 'loved ones' or 'spiritual beings' at the end of the 'tunnel' tell them their time 'on Earth' is not finished and they must go back. My response is fuck off, mate, I'll decide where I go next not some AI projection thank you. What Michael Newton's clients detail is a classic Reptilian hierarchical structure for which they are infamous. It sounds less like a 'spiritual realm' than a processing unit before the 'soul' returns into another human body to 'learn more lessons'. Why, it should be asked, is the mind wiped of 'lessons' apparently previously learned when we come back for another go? What's the point of that? You come to learn lessons not to have war, conflict, famine, murder, rape and pillage, and the memory is then deleted so you do it all again next time. This would certainly explain why human history is one of repeating war, conflict, famine, murder, rape and pillage. Newton's subjects speak of a magnetic pull to go through the tunnel to the 'spirit world' and later 'feel the pull of having a physical expression for our identity' when it is time to reincarnate. So the cycle goes on and on. They are describing *The Trap*.

Ring Pass Not

There have been endless symbolic descriptions in different cultures of a limit or point that humans have to cross to get to 'heaven' or Infinite Reality. Gnostics symbolised this – appropriately – as a dragon swallowing its own tail: 'The outer darkness is a great dragon, whose tail is in his mouth, outside the whole world and surrounding the whole world.' Others call this 'dragon' the Ouroboros or Leviathan and it relates to the perceived boundary between what Gnostics called the Upper and Lower Aeons, Infinite Reality and the simulation (Fig 126 overleaf). They also indicated that Saturn was part of this boundary which is interesting when I have written at length in previous books about the impact of Saturn and the Moon on the simulation and human perception. *Everything You Need To Know But Have Never Been Told* is one them. Then there is the ancient esoteric concept of the Ring-Pass-Not which is described this way:

> A profoundly mystical and suggestive term signifying the circle or bounds of frontiers within which is contained the consciousness of those who are still under the sway of the delusion of separateness – and this applies whether the Ring be large or small.
>
> It is a general term applicable to any state in which an entity, having reached a

certain stage of
evolutionary
growth of the
unfolding of
consciousness,
finds itself unable
to pass into a still
higher state
because of some
delusion under
which the
consciousness is
labouring, be that
delusion mental
or spiritual.

Your perception
dictates your
vibration and your
vibration dictates
if you pass
through the ring or
continue to be
entrapped by it.
The reality and
self-identity of
mind is expressed
as a frequency

Figure 126: The frequency barrier said to block consciousness from escaping the reincarnation' cycle until your vibration is high enough. (Image by Neil Hague)

field. This is why it is so vitally important to reach a state of self-realisation before body-death in which you not only conceptually conceive that you are Infinite Consciousness but you *live* it and *become* it. Even then it's still all illusion. The frequency 'net' that 'guards' the exit from the simulation is only codes for the mind to decode and if we don't choose to do so there is no 'net', no boundary or border. The irony is that when the mind is clear of illusion and stops decoding the illusion there is no 'Ring-Pass-Not'. Only if you are operating on its frequency do you decode it into apparent reality. If you are not then it won't exist to you. This is the background to the 'the circle or bounds of frontiers within which is contained the consciousness of those who are still under the sway of the delusion of separateness'. The delusion of separateness represents the frequency that decodes the 'Ring'. Cause and effect. What we don't decode cannot exist in our reality. Does a wall exist unless decoded into apparently 'physical reality'? No. When I leave I will not believe in any boundary or limit. I am just out of here. If that is my reality that is what will be. The simulation in all its forms is there to enslave through concepts of enslavement. Don't buy into the concepts or any sense of limitation. You are *All That Is, Has Been, And Ever Can Be.* Live it and you will be what you believe you are and free yourself from the delusions that hold you in vibrational slavery.

All this is seriously deep I know and many who have come this far with me may reel back at some of the concepts. All I can say is that the information comes from the same synchronistic sources that have proved to be so accurate on other subjects and happenings as they lead me to layers and layers of insight until the mist clears and reality can be seen. I don't publish this book to tell anyone what to think and believe. To do so would be to defeat the object. It is about people thinking – *knowing* – for themselves not following anyone else without question.

Ponder on the information for a while and then you decide. You must be the master of your perception, not me or anyone else. I have described in the last five chapters the nature of the Cult, reality, and the simulation, and now we turn to who or what is behind all this?

CHAPTER NINE

'Gods' of the Matrix

All gods who receive homage are cruel. All gods dispense suffering without reason. Otherwise they would not be worshipped.
Zora Neale Hurston

Okay, so what is this 'non-human force' behind the simulation? Pursuing this question has brought me ridicule all over the world (yawn). I am used to that and long ago acquired natural immunity. If people don't want to seek out all possibility for what is happening that's their choice. I *do* – that's *my* choice and I won't ask for permission thank you.

One of the big glitches in the Matrix appears to be that when many people are supposed to depart childhood and become adults somehow the system gets stuck like a vinyl record … billup, billup, billup … and while their bodies enter adulthood their minds do not. I can tell you from long experience that it's always the most stupid and ridiculous that ridicule others for being stupid and ridiculous. 'He says lizards run the world, ha, ha, ha, ha!' Right, so are you saying that life as we know it can only take a human form? Or can only locate on this one tiny, tiny, planet within the entirety of Infinite Reality? Well, 'yes' would seem to be the answer. Do you think that given we can 'see' only a tiny, tiny, band of frequency on this tiny, tiny, planet that other forms of life might just exist not only in the realm visible to human sight, but also in the limitlessness of Infinite Forever beyond the laughable band of frequency that humans can visually perceive? Anyone who answers 'no' to that is an idiot and being ridiculed by idiots is like being savaged by a dead sheep. In fact, being ridiculed by idiots is essential to confirming that you are not one as being ridiculed by insanity is confirmation of your soundness of mind. 'I think you're mad, duh!' Well, thank you kindly for that, much appreciated. I thought for a moment you were going to say that I wasn't mad. Phew! Shakes head, moves on, and for the intelligent we shall continue. If you are not believed to be weird by a world of madness then you, too, must be mad. The good news is that ever more people are opening to the possibility of a non-human force behind human affairs especially as the Cult's gathering global agenda is so clearly anti-human.

In the early years of the 1990s the synchronicity of my life was showing me overwhelmingly the 'human' level of global manipulation and control and how those who appeared to be in power were merely pawns and assets of a hidden network. I followed this back from its global reach today and through the British Empire, Roman Empire and on to Egypt, Babylon and Sumer with the latter two located in what is now Iraq. Initiates of the network came and went generation after generation and what we perceive as century after century. It was obvious there had to be an organisational force or field that spanned that perception of perceived time to orchestrate the comings and goings into a distinct direction that would lead eventually to mass human control. We are facing that point now with the imminent agenda to connect the human mind to AI and technology. I went in search of that organisational force or rather, given the synchronicity driving my life, it went in search of me in the sense of information coming in my direction. I saw first the common theme in ancient cultural beliefs and accounts of a hidden hand manipulating human societies and I noted how often this was described in reptilian terms. I met and became a great friend of Zulu shaman Credo Mutwa who told me at length and in detail the stories of the Chitauri, the 'Devastators', or Children of the Serpent (Fig 127). He described how a reptilian race operating from the unseen was behind the suffering, struggles and ills of humans in league with a subordinate group we know as the Greys (Fig 128). There is a 6-hour interview on the Ickonic media platform which I did with Credo in the late 1990s and an excellent Christianne van Wijk Ickonic documentary, *Divine Intervention*, to which I contribute, which covers this subject at length. Credo told me

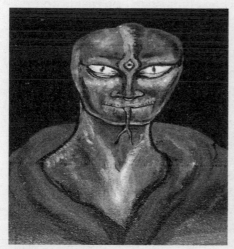

Figure 127: Credo Mutwa's painting of the Reptilian 'worker class' from ancient and modern descriptions.

Figure 128: The classic 'Grey' extraterrestrial described in endless ancient and modern accounts.

the background to the Chitauri and his personal knowledge and experience of the Greys including the time he says he was abducted by them.

Reptilians everywhere (but they don't exist!)

Gnostic Nag Hammadi texts from some 1,600 years ago describe the Archons in terms of formless energy or consciousness. Texts say that when they did take form it was most commonly serpentine and those that look like 'an unborn baby or foetus with grey skin and dark, unmoving eyes'. It is pretty obvious what that is describing. In my many travels of months on end around the United States I met with military and intelligence insiders who told me the same story of Reptilian race control. Those claiming to be abducted and contacted by 'aliens' very often had a similar story. When a shaman describes from Zulu history and personal experience what military and intelligence assets are telling you on the other side of the world it would be ridiculous not to take it seriously and investigate further. At the same time I was meeting increasing numbers in America, Canada, the UK, countries of Europe, and Australia who told me the same recurring story of seeing someone who looked human shifting before their eyes into reptilian form. There were eventually so many that to dismiss them would be crazy. Yes, I knew I would face merciless ridicule when I told their stories. Who the hell cares? I am after the truth *whatever* it is. 'Shapeshifting' can be easily explained and I will a little later.

The hidden manipulators can be found under different names all over the world – Serpent gods (Far East, Central America, Africa); Chitauri (Zulu); Anunnaki (Sumer); Snake brothers (Hopi); Star people (various); Demons (Christianity); Archons (Gnostic); Jinn (Islam and pre-Islamic Arabia); and Flyers or Predators (Central America). Many other names include the Watchers, Shining Ones, Fallen Angels. and the 'Ant People' of the Native American Hopi in Arizona which sounds like a good description of the Greys. Common themes in the techniques, goals and descriptions of these manipulators are extremely compelling. A Muslim taxi driver in New York asked me what I was working on and at the time I was researching Gnostic texts about Archons. When I told him how Archons were described he said: 'That sounds just like the Jinn.' Gnostics say Archons are made from 'luminous fire' while Islam speaks of the Jinn in terms of 'smokeless fire'. I have become known for highlighting the Reptilians when in fact there are many different types of non-human located in the Fourth Dimension and able to enter the simulation. There are many descriptions and accounts of other non-humans including Reptilians living within the 3-D Earth. See my other books such as *Children of the Matrix*. Hopi people have many legends of a reptilian race they call their 'snake brothers' living in catacombs below the Earth's surface in America's south west and Mexico. Mining engineer G. Warren Shufelt believed he had found some under Los Angeles and dug for several years before the story appeared in the media and the operation was shut down. One ET type is very human-like and known in the UFO research community and by those who claim to have met them as the blond-haired, blue-eyed 'Nordics'. Credo Mutwa told me how Zulus refer to the 'Nordics' as the 'Mzungu' who could 'appear and disappear' – enter the human sight frequency and then leave. He said that when white Europeans arrived in South Africa they were mistaken at first for the returning Mzungu (Fig 129). Phenomenal numbers have claimed to be abducted by 'aliens' with Greys and Reptilians the most dominant in species described. Often this is said to involve taking sperm and eggs for a programme of genetic fusion of human/non-human hybrids.

Figure 129: Credo Mutwa's portrayal of the 'Mzungu'.

The simulation explains how craft can cross the apparent enormity of distance and space to 'get here'. There is no enormity of distance and space and so nothing to 'cross', nowhere to 'get'. Why do humans use 'physical' craft to cross 'physical' distance? What you believe you perceive and what you perceive you experience. I have been told by many insiders that the US military has 'flying saucers' (so-called 'anti-gravity' craft) and not all UFOs are non-human in origin. They say that the real 'ET craft' are expressions of consciousness and not 'physical' in nature. This has to be true when there is no physical, only the illusion of it. Governments have been publicly dismissive of 'aliens' and UFOs throughout the decades that I have been researching the subject. Since particularly the turn of 2021, however, that has changed quite dramatically with the US military releasing Air Force pilot footage of UFOs moving at speeds and changing direction at those speeds in ways that are impossible with the known laws of physics. Ah, but if they are being controlled by mind in awareness of the simulation illusion those laws do not apply. Why the military have become more open is the question. I have been writing since the 1990s about a plan exposed by Canadian investigative journalist Serge Monast called Project Bluebeam to stage a fake alien invasion to justify the fusing of global power and militaries to meet the threat. The idea is to use holographic projections to stage the illusion and no doubt human 'UFO' craft, too. We need to be constantly vigilant about this and, ironically, the 'aliens' aren't coming – they're here. They 'built' the place.

Inside and outside – same story

The late William Tompkins, an American aerospace engineer, said in 2017 that he had been given clearance to publish some of his experiences in the Navy with Reptilian entities. He wrote a book entitled *Selected by Extraterrestrials: My life in the top secret world of UFOs, think-tanks and Nordic secretaries* and he describes how human-like 'Nordics' were working to challenge the Reptilian control of human reality. Tompkins claims to have worked with American Navy spies during World War Two to steal flying saucer technology secrets from the Nazis who he said were involved with the Reptilians. He said these 'secrets' were given to American military and space corporations including Lockheed, Douglas and Northrop, Grumman. They worked with the California Institute of Technology (Caltech) to produce flying saucer craft that he said he knew were flown by at least the American and German military. Tompkins also wrote in 2017 that the Moon is artificial and a Reptilian command centre in our reality with structures on the far side that we never see. I have been exposing that the Moon is artificial since my book, *Human Race Get Off Your Knees*, in 2010. The Moon is a holographic construct inserted into the simulation as a Reptilian base and to have a serious effect vibrationally and hormonally on humans and on the instability of the Earth's rotation. Once you realise that we are dealing with a simulation the question of how a body the size of the Moon could be constructed answers itself. It wasn't created as in physically constructed. It is a field of data added to the simulation for the observer to decode holographically into what we think we see as the Moon.

William Tompkins referred to the 'Draco' (Latin for dragon), 'Draconians', or 'Reptilian royalty', which I have been detailing in my books since the 1990s. Particularly in *Children of the Matrix* in 2001. They and the Greys are invariably described by those who have experienced them as vicious, emotionless and without empathy along with all the other traits of psychopaths (although not all reptilian entities and Greys are like this just as not all people who look human are like Bill Gates and Klaus Schwab). 'Draconian' really is the word for these scaled psychopaths and their attitudes are played out through the psychopathic Global Cult and the tyrants that it places in positions of political and other power. 'You have Draco Reptilian guys running your governments of every country on the planet', Tompkins said, and they could shapeshift between human and reptilian form. I know someone else who said that a long time before and took untold ridicule and abuse for his trouble. Not so much now, though. Reptilians and Greys function as a hive mind like a bee or ant colony. The imminent plan to connect the human brain to AI is designed to assimilate human consciousness into the hive. I have been writing this for so long and here we are with Cult operatives openly promoting a human AI connection to achieve just this.

The themes of Reptilian manipulation and the artificial nature of the Moon are far more widely supported than people imagine who get their information only from mainstream sources. I was alerted to an article in *Nexus* magazine many years ago in which a 'whistleblower' described an inter-dimensional experiment called the 'CHANI Project', short for Channelled Holographic Access Network Interface. This was said to be a secret operation based in Africa which began in 1994 and lasted for five years. The whistleblower said that CHANI involved very extensive communications through a computer interface with an entity in another reality. According to the source the entity said the Moon was artificial and manipulated humans by controlling 'time' and mood and through suppression of consciousness. The Moon had been captured by the 'Old Race' and located next to the Earth. In pure terms of physics there is no way that a body that big should be circling a planet this small. Credo Mutwa told me how Zulu legend says the Moon was 'driven' to where it is by the Chitauri Reptilians and caused great upheavals through its impact on the energetic field and the stability of the Earth. There are tribal peoples who say their tribes go back to before the Moon was in the sky. I write extensively about the Moon and Saturn and their connection in *Everything You Need To Know But Have Never Been Told*. The region of the simulation we call the constellation of Orion is also a major part of the story and is symbolised in many ancient artefacts and remains. Orion is like everything in 3-D – a simulated projection from a Fourth Dimensional source. I can recommend the books of my friend Neil Hague who has specialised in researching Orion.

The CHANI entity is said to have spoken about the control of humans by a reptilian group. The communications said a reptilian race was holding back humans so they couldn't 'grow'; The entity's race had fought many battles with the reptile race in their own reality; Humans were more evolved than the reptiles, but they suppressed humans with their technology – 'Their God is their technology'. Ah, yes – *technology*. This has been such a common thread in my research of the Reptilian story. They are obsessed with technology and use it as their means to control. Here I am describing a technologically-generated simulation which I say the Reptilians are behind, at least to a large extent, and more tangibly for people the world is clearly being taken over before their eyes by AI technology. Is this really a 'coincidence?' Is it further a 'coincidence' that the global agenda pursued by the Cult is so obviously anti-human? It is worth asking the question why Klaus Schwab spends every waking hour plotting the anti-human Great Reset when he's already aged 84? Why would George Soros at 92? Henry Kissinger at 99? Why was David Rockefeller still working towards the same end as he passed 100? The answer is that to them a 'human' life is only a contribution to a much bigger picture for the non-human species they represent. They've come to do a job for that species before handing over to the next wave and so 24 or 84, 39 or 99, makes no difference. They go on doing it until their body gives up.

Monroe doctrine

I came across a fascinating Reptilian-related article while I was writing this chapter (more synchronicity) about the late Robert Monroe (1915-1995). Monroe was a radio broadcasting executive who became famous for his exploration of techniques to trigger consciousness to 'leave' the body and experience other realities. The article was published on the Down the Chupacabra Hole website. Chupacabra refers to a 'legendary creature in the folklore of parts of the Americas'. Robert Monroe popularised the term 'out-of-body experience' with the publication of his 1971 book, *Journeys Out of the Body*. I would say it is the Mind's *perception* of leaving the body given that the mind was never 'in' the

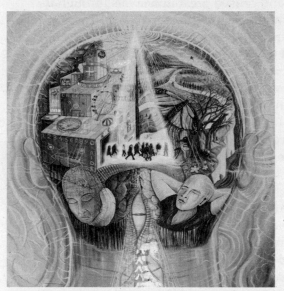

body in the first place except perceptually. Monroe worked with psychologists, psychiatrists, doctors, biochemists and electrical engineers as he developed Hemispheric Synchronization, or Hemi-Sync, which harmonised the two hemispheres of the brain. This was interesting to me after writing so much over the decades about how the manipulation of human perception seeks to disconnect the hemispheres from a state of whole brain harmony and to especially lock away perception in the left side of the brain. This

Figure 130: The Cult system seeks to entrap human perception in the left-side of the brain and puts guards on the door in the form of teachers, academics, scientists, doctors, and others to stop right-brain influence. This is why right-brain subjects like art get so little prominence and funding in the education arena today. Whole-brained people are the last thing the Cult wants.

specialises in decoding and perceiving the realm of the five-senses (Fig 130). The left-brain deals with language, numbers, linear thinking, logic (or the illusion of it), views everything as separated (sees only dots), and puts happenings into a sequence (the illusion of 'time'). The left-brain sees the small picture of limitation and separation. These all relate to perceived human 'physical' reality and the perceptions of the five senses. The right-brain decodes creativity, imagination, intuition, sees the forest not the twigs (connects dots into patterns) and seeks to put events into their context. The right-brain sees the big picture of Infinite Unity.

We should be working with both sides of the brain. Instead the Cult and its non-human masters seek to focus attention in the left side. With mind perceiving reality through the body what the body experiences the mind absorbs as reality. The 'education' system alone is almost entirely focussed on the left-brain and slams the door on right-brain insight. Robert Monroe saw what happens when the two hemispheres are united as his Hemi-Sync audio technology was designed to achieve. The effect on participants was monitored by independent clinical neurologists who could see the results in changes on EEG scans. Both sides of the brain measured the same in both amplitude and frequency and the impact was facilitating out-of-body experiences. The Central Intelligence Agency (CIA) became interested in 1978. While the Establishment and Deep States dismiss the 'paranormal' in public they well know that such experiences are real and other realities exist. The agency and the military asked Monroe to work with them. The article describes how 'experiments opened portals to other dimensions where reptilian humanoids reside' in a project entitled the Gateway Process. It is highly likely to be still continuing with far more sophisticated technology today. Declassified files say the programme was:

> ... a training system designed to bring enhanced strength, focus and coherence to the amplitude and frequency of brainwave output between the left and right hemispheres so as to alter consciousness, moving it outside the physical sphere so as to ultimately escape even the restrictions of time and space.

The project was overseen by Lieutenant Colonel Wayne McDonnell who said that investigators had established that as I've been saying all these years ... *we live in a holographic universe and waking life is a projected electromagnetic matrix*. The project further discovered reptilian entities operating in the Fourth Dimension which I have been writing about since the 1990s. Robert Monroe had detailed how participants would often encounter interdimensional entities and most frequently reptilian humanoids which they dubbed 'the alligators'. The article said that

Monroe was already familiar with them from his own out-of-body experiences:

> During countless expeditions, he observed identical saurian creatures. For over thirty-five years the etheric investigator gathered insight about these startling beings. Here is what he uncovered: The nefarious vertebrates have controlled and enslaved humanity for millennia. They exist and operate in the 4th dimension and are only visible to individuals who can see beyond our extremely limited spectrum of visible light.

This is exactly what I have established from my own sources and have been saying and writing since 1996. What's more, Monroe said that these Reptilians feed off humanity's spiritual life-force which he referred to as 'loosh' and that 'negative/low vibrational energy is essential to their survival'. The human population was to them a source of energy to be 'farmed' and 'harvested'. All this has been in my books since *The Biggest Secret* in 1998.

Ancient and modern – same story

The reptilian theme can be found in religions and cultures across the world and serpents appear in many creation stories and myths – creation of the simulation I say. The Jewish religion has its 'Holy Serpent' or Leviathan (Ring-Pass-Not) and the Bible describes the Devil or Satan in reptilian terms in the Book of Revelation: 'And the Great Dragon was cast out, that old serpent, called the Devil, and Satan, which deceiveth the whole world. He was cast out into the Earth and his angels were cast out with him.' We are back to fallen angels – Reptilians – being 'cast out' which led to what we now call 'human' minds being enticed to follow them through the simulated illusion trap of the Matrix symbolised by the Garden of Eden story and its serpent trickery. Worship of the serpent can be found in Egypt; Persia; Asia Minor (now Turkey); Phoenicia; Arabia and the Middle East; India and Asia; China; Japan; Ethiopia and the rest of Africa; Mexico; Britain; Scandinavia; Italy; Greece; Crete; Rhodes; Cyprus; Sri Lanka; Northern and Western Europe; and North, South and Central America. There has been a global obsession with the serpent and serpent gods and they have invariably been connected to 'The Fall'. Now we can see why. Reverend John Bathurst Deane published a study in 1933 into the universal reptilian theme called *Worship of the Serpent* and he noted how the Eden story with its serpent villain is a universally common thread across the world along with the widespread veneration of serpent gods. This was his conclusion:

> It appears, then, that no nations were so geographically remote, or so

religiously discordant, but that one – and only one – superstitious
characteristic was common to all: that the most civilized and the most
barbarous bowed down with the same devotion to the same engrossing deity;
and that this deity either was, or was represented by, the same sacred serpent.
It appears also that in most, if not all, the civilized countries where this serpent
was worshipped, some fable or tradition which involved his history, directly or
indirectly, alluded to the Fall of Man in Paradise, in which the serpent was
concerned.

What follows, then, but that the most ancient account respecting the cause
and nature of this seduction must be the one from which all the rest are
derived which represent the victorious serpent – victorious over man in a state
of innocence, and subduing his soul in a state of sin, into the most abject
veneration and adoration of himself.

I have researched at length the beliefs, legends and accounts of
ancient cultures around the 'world' to explore the common patterns and
themes. If we are experiencing a simulation and mass manipulation this
must have been happening back into what we perceive as history and I
did indeed find those universal themes of a non-human force
manipulating humanity from the unseen. On many occasions there was
a reptilian component in both the source of control and the creation
myths in which symbolic terms abound such as snake people, serpent
people, and the 'Great Dragon'. Islamic legends say that when a Jinn
known as Iblis disobeyed Allah he was expelled from Paradise with the
name 'Saytan' – the Christian Satan. It's not the differences between
religious and cultural themes that strike you; it's the compelling
similarities. An evil manipulative force 'cast out' or 'sealed away in the
abyss' is extremely common and from this banishment into a form of
frequency exile the force dominated by reptilian entities launched its
plan to entrap consciousness in a lair of illusion to generate low-
vibrational energy on which it could feed and empower itself. Morpheus
in *The Matrix* and his battery again. He was referring to 'machines' that
created the computer-generated dream world to vampire human energy.
Swap machines for reptilian and other non-human entities using a form
of AI machine or technology to generate the simulation projection into
human minds and you get the picture.

You can only absorb energetic frequencies that connect with your
own. Otherwise they pass through you like two radio stations on
different wavelengths. By its very nature the non-human force operates
on a very slow, low, wavelength, and its state of being means that this
could be no other way. A mind that desires control and seeks to impose
mass suffering and enslavement could not possibly be resonating on
anything except a low frequency. It turns out that the frequency band of

this force matches that of low-vibrational human emotion such as fear, anxiety, worry, depression, resentment and hatred. These are *lower Fourth Dimensional* frequencies and those emotional states are feeding the Reptilians and empowering their ability to control. From this perspective it is obvious why human society – the simulation – is structured to generate maximum fear, anxiety, worry, depression, resentment, hatred, etc. Witness the emotions and fears that can be induced by donning a virtual reality headset. The principle is the same only phenomenally more advanced. The consciousness state of the non-human force is *fear* which I will be expanding upon. The Global Cult is consumed by fear and insecurity at the thought of human minds awakening from the illusion and the simulation collapsing. We – yes *we* – are holding it together by believing it to be real. Put simply – fear must generate fear to feed itself and human society is structured to produce unlimited amounts of fear. Humans are being 'milked' of their fear vibration. See how the Cult seamlessly followed fear of 'Covid' with Russia's invasion of Ukraine and the fear even of nuclear war.

Elite code-lines

The human body is crucial to the whole perceptual control system. We have the experience of being 'in' the body when the body is a field of encoded information like a character in a virtual reality game. The character is *part* of the *game* and not part of those playing the game. A body is a source of information fed to the mind by the simulation and it can make copies of itself through what we perceive as procreation when two encoded software programs fuse their information to make a duel copy. Where does that 'procreation' really take place? In the *mind*. The thing to remember is that the cycle of the body, how it grows from an egg to a baby to an adult, how it ages and then 'dies', is all happening at the level of the coding. The holographic level is merely the mind 'reading' those codes. Ill-health is either something written into the codes or the stress, distress and state of the mind disrupting the codes or misreading them. This 'glitch' from whatever source has to play out into the hologram which is a projection of the codes. We call this disharmonious state 'disease' when it is really dis-ease. The body is encoded to only experience reality in very limited terms. Visible light has such a tiny range because the codes make it that way. If your goal is to deceive minds into a myopia of perception do you want them to 'see' a minuscule range of frequency or an expanded one? Gnostics were correct when they described the body as a trap. It is. A perceptual trap for the mind.

This brings me to the reptilian-human hybrid 'bloodlines' which would more accurately be described as reptilian-human hybrid 'code-lines' or lines of code. What we perceive as 'blood' carries the codes as

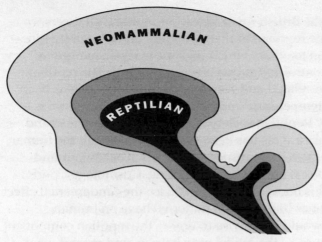

Figure 131: The reptilian part of the brain, or R-complex, which impacts on so much human perception and behaviour.

do the energetic lines of force known as meridians on which acupuncture is founded. Most people have no idea that the body and its decoding processes are seriously influenced by reptilian genetics (waveform codes). A substance called 'pheromone' is secreted and released by animals to detect members of the same species and pheromones in human women and iguanas are a chemical match. A major part of the human brain is called the R-complex or reptilian brain which connects into the brain stem and relates to the survival instinct (Fig 131). The reptilian brain is constantly and anxiously scanning the environment for threats to not only 'physical' survival, but the survival of employment, relationships, income, status, reputation, everything. It is the part of the brain that kicks off road rage response. The reptilian segment doesn't think so much as react which means it jumps to action before the part of the brain processing thought can kick-in and calm things down. A reptilian brain response is often followed by: 'What was I thinking of?' The dominant emotion of the reptilian brain is *FEAR* – the very Reptilian vehicle for human control and provides a 'back-door' access point to trigger the fear response. How this has been mercilessly exploited in the 'Covid' years. The reptilian brain's constant state of anxiety and fear of not surviving is communicated from the brain to the emotional centre in the belly through the vagus nerve which connects the two. Scientists call this the gut-brain axis. The vagus is the longest cranial nerve in the body and affects several organ systems and regions including the tongue, pharynx, heart, and gastrointestinal system. The reptilian brain-vagus-belly chakra-intestine connection is why people have sensations in the gut when they are fearful or nervous. Other reptilian brain decoding traits include obsessive compulsive behaviour; day-to-day rituals and superstitious acts; slavish conformance to old ways of doing things; deference to precedent; cold-bloodedness (no empathy); a desire for control; power; ownership; 'territoriality'; and a belief that might is right, winner takes all. See how many of those traits apply to members of the British royal family and other Cult assets.

Inverted traits of the reptilian brain depending on personality type can involve submission to others which makes the reptilian brain a potential vehicle for control *and* subservience to control. The reptilian brain controls emotion-related and fear-related functions such as heart rate, breathing, body temperature and balance. Its reflex response is to conform which is why Reptilian society is incredibly hierarchical and each level knows its place. This has been played out through the human race by triggering reptilian brain response. Maverick behaviour and thinking outside the box is not the rep-brain's gig. Cosmologist Carl Sagan highlighted in his book *The Dragons of Eden* the fundamental effect that our reptilian genetics (information patterns) have on human behaviour. He said it would be unwise to ignore the reptilian component of human nature because '... the model may help us understand what human beings are really about'. Sagan emphasised ritualistic and hierarchical behaviour connected to the reptilian brain. Reptilians and their human-world lackeys are most certainly obsessed with ritual. I have exposed for decades the satanic rituals and sacrifice that are part of life in the Cult. The British royal family's whole life is governed by ritual.

Reptilians have encoded the human body to 'see' only the minuscule range of visible light, but they wanted Matrix vehicles for themselves and their agents that could 'see' far more to give them a built-in perceptual advantage over 'humans' within simulated reality. To do this they created human-reptilian hybrids. The theme through the 'ages' of special bloodlines, 'royal' bloodlines and 'bluebloods', are bodies infused with human codes *and* far greater reptilian codes with a wider range of sensory perception through all five senses and others beyond them. They can 'see' what humans can't 'see' and have a powerful connection with their lower Fourth-Dimensional mission control. Reptilian-human hybrids have duel energetic fields, one

Figure 132: Human female and non-human male on Credo Mutwa's Necklace of the Mysteries symbolising the interbreeding between humans and the 'gods'.

encoded with human codes and the other with reptilian and they are *symbolised* in the Bible as the 'sons of God who interbred with the daughters of men'. The term 'God' in this sentence is translated from a word meaning gods, plural. The hybrid offspring of these 'sons of the gods' were the Biblical Nephilim and they are the bloodlines behind the Global Cult of human control to this day. Gnostics tell a similar story to the Bible in the Nag Hammadi texts as do endless cultures including Zulus in South Africa. Credo Mutwa showed me his 'Necklace of the Mysteries' which is said to be at least 500 years old and depicts the interbreeding of human women with a non-human race – the 'Chitauri' Reptilians (Fig 132). Reptilian hybrid lines interbreed (inter-download) with each other to stop their codes being diluted through a fusion with human code-lines. 'Keeping the genes up' is really keeping the codes up. 'Royalty' and aristocracy have always been known for interbreeding and the bloodlines continue to do so today in their overwhelmingly dark-suit guise. They may not have a crown on their heads – a 'corona' – but they still consider themselves 'royal' and special with their more expansive coding.

'Royal' code-lines

Reptilian-human hybrid 'bloodlines' became known as 'royalty' to highlight both their 'specialness' within the human population and to claim that this 'specialness' gave them the right to rule – thus the 'divine right to rule'. This is why reptilian, serpent and snake symbolism has been so associated with 'royalty'. The ancient civilisation known as Media, now Iran and part of Turkey, was ruled from around 678 BC by the 'Dragon Dynasty of Media' or 'descendants of the dragon'. Kings were known as Mar, or snake. Emperors in China in the dragon-obsessed Far East claimed their right to rule by their genetic descent from the 'serpent gods'. Chinese leaders privately still do. Only the outward appearance has changed, not the game. China is an incredibly reptilian country which is why it is a Cult stronghold with designs on global control. China's worship of the dragon since ancient times reflects this. Indian epics feature the Nagas people which are described in reptilian terms. Accounts say Nagas interbred with a white race to produce a reptilian hybrid that became the Aryan kings. The *Mahabharata*, an ancient Sanskrit work and one of the major Hindu scriptures, describes how a people called the Mayas (Nagas under another name) left Asia and settled in Mesopotamia, Egypt and Greece. A reptilian race called the Sarpa, or Great Dragons, came from the skies and brought civilisation to the world according to *The Book of Dzyan*, one of the oldest Sanskrit accounts, which further describes how serpent gods returned after 'a great deluge' and ruled human society under their leader, the 'Great Dragon'. Non-human 'gods' returning to rule after the

Great Flood can be found in Sumerian and Babylonian accounts in the Middle East.

In Central America the Mayans in what is now Mexico said their ancestors were the 'people of the serpent'. Mayans worshipped the 'Plumed Serpent' or 'Feathered Serpent' god Kukulkan which I saw depicted at the serpent cult centre at Chichen Itza in the Yucatan, Mexico, which I visited in the late 1990s (Fig 133). Ninth century texts discovered at Chichen Itza do not describe Kukulkan in human terms and artistic representations portrayed this 'god' as a serpent entwined around figures of 'nobles' – 'royal' or 'elite' hybrids. Mayans said that a

reptilian race known as the 'Iguana Men' came from the sky and taught them how to build pyramids. Common themes abound and I have said in books long ago that

Figure 133: Serpent god Kukulkan symbolically depicted at Chitchen Itza.

Reptilians were the builders of pyramids which abound across the world from the Americas to Europe, the Middle East and China. The first settlers of the Yucatan were the Chanes or 'People of the Serpent' led by the god Itzamna, according to the Mayans. Itzamna is said by some to derive from 'itzem' (lizard or reptile) which would translate their sacred city of Itzamna as 'the place of the lizard' or 'Iguana House'. The Central American Aztecs worshipped the feathered serpent god as Quetzalcoatl and these themes align with what Credo Mutwa told me in South Africa about the Chitauri.

Same story wherever you look

Reptilian symbolism and its association with 'royalty' can be seen in Europe with the Celts and their title Pendragon, the 'Great Dragon' or Draco, and 'King of Kings, which appears in stories about 'King Arthur' and his magician 'Merlin'. Celts worshipped the serpent god Hu which would translate 'Hu-man' into 'Serpent Man'. Reverend John Bathurst Deane features the Celts and their Druid priestly class in his 1933 work, *The Worship of the Serpent*:

Our British ancestors, under the tuition of the venerable Druids, were not only worshippers of the solar deity, symbolized by the serpent, but held the serpent, independent of his relation to the sun, in peculiar veneration. Cut off from all intercourse with the civilized world, partly by their remoteness and partly by their national character, the Britons retained their primitive idolatry long after it yielded in the neighbouring countries to the polytheistic corruptions of Greece and Egypt.

In process of time, however, the gods of the Gaulish Druids penetrated into the sacred mythology of the British and furnished personifications for the different attributes of the draconic god Hu. This deity was called 'The Dragon Ruler of the World' and his car was drawn by serpents. His priests in accommodation with the general custom of the Ophite god, were called after him 'Adders'.

Worship of the serpent is the oldest and most global of all religions and Deane said that 'the mystic serpent entered into the mythology of every nation; consecrated almost every temple; symbolised almost every deity; was imagined in the heavens, stamped upon the earth, and ruled in the realms of everlasting sorrow'. The serpent was the main symbol of mythology and, Deane said, the 'only common object of superstitious terror throughout the habitable world'. Reptilian figurines were found in graves of the Ubaid culture which is estimated to have begun *8,500 years ago* in what became Sumer, Babylon, and is now Iraq (Fig 134). I could continue for page after page with the accounts and symbolism that

Figure 134: One of many reptilian figurines found in graves from the Ubaid culture thousands of years ago which preceded Sumer and Babylon in what is now Iraq.

Figure 135: Reptile holding the shield of the Knights Templar secret society at the entrance to the Cult-owned City of London financial district.

describe and represent serpent gods across the ancient world and we see the same symbolism today. The entrance to the big-time Cult-owned City of London financial district – 'the City' – is marked by winged reptiles holding the shield of the Knights Templar secret society (Fig 135 on previous page). Another winged reptile stands at the point where 'the City' meets

Figure 136: Winged reptile at Temple Bar in London where The Temple district, home to the legal profession, meets 'the City' financial district. The Temple stands on land once owned by the Knights Templar and is named after an original Templar temple that remains to this day.

The Temple district, home to the British and to a significant extent global legal system (Fig 136). The Temple area was owned by the Knights Templar and is named after a still-existing Templar church. Those that dismiss the reptilian connection by reflex action in a blaze of ignorance and its bedfellow arrogance will have no idea about any of this. You will find extraordinary detail about the subject in my books, *The Biggest Secret, Children of the Matrix, The David Icke Guide to the Global Conspiracy* and the mega-work, *The Perception Deception*. Gnostic texts tell a similar story to the one I have summarised here.

Infusing the 'counterfeit spirit'

Gnostic Nag Hammadi documents describe in their own way the infusion of the Yaldabaoth 'counterfeit spirit' into humans (see infusing the Reptilian codes) which could be the source of the belief in 'original sin'. The *Apocryphon of John* says of Yaldabaoth:

> He sent his angels [Archons/demons] to the daughters of men, that they might take some of them for themselves and raise offspring for their enjoyment. And at first they did not succeed. When they had no success, they gathered together again and they made a plan together ...
>
> ... And the angels changed themselves in their likeness into the likeness of their mates, filling them with the spirit of darkness, which they had mixed for them, and with evil ... And they took women and begot children out of the darkness according to the likeness of their spirit.

Note in their likeness of *spirit*, not a physical likeness. The document describes how sexual desire was planted to allow the counterfeit spirit to constantly make copies of itself ('Go forth and multiply'):

> And he [Yaldabaoth] planted sexual desire in her who belongs to Adam. And
> he produced through intercourse the copies of the bodies, and he inspired
> them with his counterfeit spirit.

The texts say that the human body is 'the tomb ... with which the
robbers had clothed the man [and] the bond of forgetfulness'. Humans
then became 'mortal' or, put another way, the illusory birth and death
process began entering and leaving the 3-D simulation system. Bodies
are described as 'fences of light' which close off awareness from the
'pure light' beyond the simulation. The Nag Hammadi *Tripartite Tractate*
says of humans: 'Therefore they fell down to the pit of ignorance which
is called "the Outer Darkness" and "Chaos" and "Hades" and "the
Abyss".' The *Apocryphon of John* says:

> And I entered into the midst of their prison, which is the prison of the body.
> And I said: 'He who hears, let him get up from the deep sleep' ... And I said, 'I
> am ... of the pure light ... Arise and ... follow your root, which is I [Expanded
> Awareness] and guard yourself against the angels of poverty [Archons] and the
> demons of chaos and all those who ensnare you, and beware of the deep
> sleep and the enclosure of the inside of Hades.

Hades is the ancient Greek god of the dead and king of the underworld,
The term is associated by many with 'Hell' and Gnostics believe that our
reality *is* Hell or part of it.

Wow – how you've changed

I have been ridiculed for many things over the last more than 30 years
by ignorant people programmed to believe in a reality that doesn't exist.
Right up there has been what I have said and written about
'shapeshifting'. From 1996 when I began to widely travel the United
States I met a lot of people, thanks to the constant synchronicity of my
life, who told me the same basic story. They had seen someone
apparently human who had changed before their eyes into a reptilian
entity. Sometimes it was another non-human form although invariably
reptilian. Many times it was a full-body shift while some only saw eyes
change from human to lizard-like. I didn't just hear this and believe it.
Nor when I am told something that appears so strange and far-out do I
just dismiss it on that basis. What do you think I am – a scientist,
academic, or something? I use the 'back-burner' approach and let it
simmer away in the background while I wait to see if any more
information on that subject comes my way to confirm or squash the
theme. In the case of shapeshifting that information did come – lots of it.

As the number of these accounts grew over months in different parts of America the claims became increasingly compelling and the stories continued in Canada, Australia, South Africa, the UK, the Netherlands, and elsewhere. I read about shapeshifting themes through history and ancient native cultures. There was also the symbolism in folklore and fairy tales about frogs turning into princes and princes into frogs. Folklore and fairy tales include stories originating in antiquity (as we perceive time) and can be a source of much symbolic and even literal truth.

Shapeshifting is a great example of how you can scramble the perception of the population by suppressing knowledge especially about reality. The reflex action rejection of shapeshifting comes from a simple and crucial misunderstanding. People think the world is solid and you can't shift from one type of solid body into another. No, you can't; *but the world is not solid*. The body is a hologram decoded by the mind from information encoded in a waveform field in the same way that a computer decodes information in the Wi-Fi radiation field into what we see on the screen. Reptilian-human hybrid 'bloodlines' or code-lines have duel information fields and which one is projected holographically decides what any observer 'sees' (decodes). For obvious reasons these hybrids present the human field in public situations when they are not among themselves. This means that any observer will decode that human field and see a holographic human. When there is a shift from the human to reptilian field the observer will decode that one. To the observer's mind someone has transformed from solid human to solid reptilian. What they have really seen is an energetic information field shift which they have decoded into the *illusion* of a solid shift. Human-Reptilian hybrids are specifically designed to hide their reptilian nature behind an apparent human form to allow the infiltration of human society by an alien force without that force being seen. The technique of hidden infiltration by one species to take control of another is portrayed in the *Avatar* movie when the American military arrive on a moon occupied by a race of blue people known as the Navi. The Americans sought to exploit valuable resources on the moon and to do so they had to infiltrate and seize control of Navi society. They couldn't do this by looking human and they were given an outer form that looked like the Navi who then took them to be fellow members of their race. This is precisely how the Reptilians with their allies and subordinates like the Greys have seized control of human society to the point now where they are close to complete takeover using their 'god' *technology* and artificial intelligence. This is the same combination that runs and drives the simulation projected into the human mind in the Fourth Dimension.

I have been told legions of stories by people who have taken part in Satanic rituals with the Cult rich and famous of how these people, including the British royal family, shapeshift into reptilian form. A shift can also be triggered occasionally by states of high emotion. I was told this story by a Canadian businesswoman who had bought my book, *The Biggest Secret*, and later had a relationship with a man she said was nice on the surface, but had a very dark side that he was constantly battling with. On one occasion they went into her bedroom where the book was on a shelf above the bed. She said the man became very agitated and took a serious aversion to it. They began to have sex and he became 'crazy, angry, violent and rough'. Her hand was on the bottom of his back while he lay on top of her and she felt her hand being pushed up. When she looked the man was sprouting a tail as he shapeshifted! She said she screamed, threw him off and he began to return to human as she told him to get out of her house. The woman was shaking and clearly emotionally distressed when she recounted the story to me even some time after it happened. There are many more such accounts in *Children of the Matrix*.

A man possessed

Another form of shapeshifting is possession. The energetic field of a Fourth Dimensional entity attaches to the field of the target and an exchange of information can then take place in which the target's field is infused with the coding of the possessor. This is experienced by any observer as a person changing into another entity. Information from the possessing entity is infused into the target's field and an observer decodes that change into the appearance of someone changing shape 'physically'. Once you realise that 'physicality' is holographic, and its nature dictated by information in its field, the mysteries of life fade away. I have had many experiences of possessed people when another consciousness takes them over. I was with a group one night at a site in Peru known as the Gate of the Gods, or 'Puerta de Hayu Marca', alongside Lake Titicaca and just over an hour's drive from Puno (Fig 137 overleaf). It is revered by local Indian people as 'a gateway to the lands of the Gods' and the 'City of the Gods'. I later learned it was notorious for people 'going crazy' or more accurately being possessed. The 'gate' is actually a wall of red rock with a sort of ritual focal point and two indents either side. I was sitting some distance away in the darkness when I heard screams. I asked the inattentive tour 'guide' sitting near me if there were animals nearby that could explain the noise. It continued and I began to walk in that direction. A member of the group came the other way and warned me not to go. He said it was 'evil' and 'so and so' was having a bad experience. Whenever anyone tells me a place is evil I am even more determined to go. I quickened my pace and I arrived at the 'gate' to find a young guy was thrashing around uncontrollably near the red wall. He was standing in one of the carved

Figure 137: The Gate of the Gods.

indents when it started. I knew immediately he had been possessed. I'd seen it before. I asked for him to be carried away from the wall and he was laid on the ground while people formed a ring around him sending high-vibrational energy which the possessing Fourth Dimensional entity would not be able to stand. I put my hands just above his head to infuse high-energy frequencies into his crown chakra and demanded the entity leave. The guy was still shouting and thrashing about when I felt an unmistakable and powerful electromagnetic connection to my hands. 'Gotcha', I thought. Suddenly the energy surged through my hands, up my arms and out the top of my head as I shouted expletives to send it on its way. At that exact moment the man stopped shouting and thrashing and became calm. 'He' was back again.

Possession is real and so much apparent mental illness is possession. If you had seen this man without knowing the background you would have said he was suffering from mental illness. He wasn't. He was briefly possessed and when the entity left so did his 'mental illness'. The next day we returned to the site in the sunshine and saw that the other side of the rock of which the 'gate' was a part clearly looked like a giant reptile with a head, a raised body and a tail. How is that possible? We're in a *simulation*. Click, click, enter. I tell this Gate of the Gods story in greater detail in *The Perception Deception*. A lot more happened there including pictures of me near the 'gate' with flows of energy attached and one in which part of me is sharp and the rest is blurred. It was a strange and dark place and no wonder many are possessed there. I have allowed such entities to attach to my field a few times over the years. I wanted to feel them and experience their energy and state of being. I can

Figure 138: Changing the frequency – we are far more powerful than 'the gods' if only we remembered who we really are.

tell you that we are dealing with a level of evil that defies the imagination and when you have felt them you can easily understand why they act with such malevolence to humans, how they can abuse and torture children and sacrifice them to their 'gods'. The point is, however, that I could allow them to attach to me and then kick them out when I got the information I wanted. Evil by its nature is weak and chaotic compared with love and harmony and a big part of the mind-trick is to convince people to fear 'evil' and give it a power that it doesn't deserve. The 'power' of 'evil' is really the power of humanity's fear of evil and fear of the unknown. I stood at the ritual focal point of the 'gate' the next day with the energy still malevolent and asked for high-vibrational energy – love in its Infinite sense – to be infused into the site through me. I felt it flow through my heart vortex and in a few minutes the whole energy field had changed (Fig 138). Members of the group who felt the 'evil' the night before with no idea what I had done arrived to say how the energy was so different to what it had been. Expanded awareness has the power, not evil, and evil only rules when we forget that. Evil is disconnected from the source of wisdom and love and must always be weak and stupid despite its bravado to make others believe otherwise (including itself).

Source of Satanism

Satanism, paedophilia and human sacrifice are intertwined with these Reptilian hybrid bloodlines and their Fourth Dimension masters. Credo Mutwa told me about Zulu legends describing how the Chitauri reptilian 'gods' brought cannibalism into the human realm and they also brought human sacrifice, paedophilia and what is now called Satanism. I have traced Satanism and paedophilia to so many Cult operatives. Several sources told me they had been sexually abused as children by British Prime Minister Edward Heath while another observed him at a Satanic ritual during which he shapeshifted into a reptilian entity. Heath was pure evil and I have been given accounts of his rampant paedophilia and serial child murders. I have been told about his obsession with recording details about his victims including height and weight that he would write into a ledger before killing them. I exposed Heath as a Satanist in *The Biggest Secret* in 1998 while he was still a Member of Parliament and the passage was read to him by an excuse for a 'journalist' in the week of publication. He could have stopped the book if he was prepared to go to court. Instead he told her that 'David Icke must be mad' and no action was taken. The whole elite paedophile and satanic network of big political names and others is exposed at length in *The Perception Deception* including Heath's connection to the infamous paedophile, Satanist and procurer of children for the rich and famous, BBC 'entertainer' Jimmy Saville.

I was open to claims of a shapeshifting Heath after my own experience with him at a *Sky News* studio in 1989 when I was still a BBC presenter and national spokesman for the Green Party. I had been invited to comment as results came in for the European Elections when for the first time the Green Party was expected to poll very well which we did. I arrived at the studio to be met by a lady who showed me to the make-up room. The door was open and the room appeared empty. The lady said that someone would be along soon and she left. I sat in a chair looking into a make-up mirror when something caught my eye to my right. It was Edward Heath behind the open door who was waiting to have his make-up taken off after being interviewed on the show. I nodded 'hello'. He said nothing and never did throughout what

happened next. He turned in my direction with a very inquisitive look on his face as his eyes started at the top of my head and slowly lowered to my feet before returning the other way. At that point he turned back and looked into his mirror. I can only describe the experience as like being scanned and when he did so the whole of his eyes, including the whites, turned jet black. The eyes looked to me like two black holes and I was seeing *through* Heath into something beyond him or what I would describe today as another reality (Fig 139). I was naturally shocked and I didn't understand what I had seen. It would be

Figure 139: How I experienced Edward Heath at the Sky News studio.

another ten months before I went to see Betty Shine and my new life kicked off.

I would later read numerous reports from the ancient and modern world of the 'black-eyed people' that matched what I experienced with Heath. In 2022, some 33 years after my experience with Heath, I watched an interview with a Mexican gynaecologist who was linking genetically-manipulating 'Covid' mRNA fake vaccines to the birth of babies with black eyes of the type I witnessed with Heath. I'll give you the background later. Seventeen years after *The Biggest Secret* was published Wiltshire Police opened an investigation into Heath after his death amid reports of his paedophilia and Satanism. The investigation decided that had Heath been alive there was enough evidence, even so long after the event, to have questioned him. The Chief Constable of Wiltshire who sanctioned the investigation would later have his career systematically destroyed. The Cult never forgets those who seek the truth about the Satanism and paedophilia rings that fundamentally connect into the secret society web of the Cult. Any of them is a potential doorway to the Cult interior and inner core and all efforts to expose them are vehemently resisted by the Cult-owned authorities.

Energy vampires

The link between the Reptilian phenomenon and human sacrifice and Satanism is ancient. Credo Mutwa told me the Chitauri demanded human sacrifice. When sacrifices were made to 'appease the gods' this meant Fourth Dimensional Reptilian 'gods'. Sacrifice of 'young virgins' was code for children and it's still happening today performed by major and lesser assets of the Cult. I have spoken at length with those who said they attended Satanic sacrifice rituals with famous political and financial figures and British royalty who are named in books like *The Biggest Secret*, *Children of the Matrix* and *The Perception Deception*. There are many reasons for the rituals. They create interdimensional vortex 'doorways' to the Fourth Dimension through which entities can manifest in the ritual. The sacrifice is to generate the energy of extreme fear for Fourth Dimensional entities and blood and flesh for those in 3-D. Rituals are conducted to produce maximum terror in the victim to generate a frequency that entities absorb and feed on. They particularly want the energy of pre-puberty children. This is like a nectar to them and so is the adrenalin in the blood for human-reptilian hybrid Satanists in 3-D reality. Satanists are obsessed with blood which carries the human codes. Fourth Dimensional Reptilian entities overshadow the energy fields of paedophiles – 'possess' them – and in doing they are able to draw off the child's energy or life-force during the sexual abuse. Reptilians are energy vampires and those in 3-D are blood vampires although it's all energy in the end. Here we have the origin of vampire stories and what are they able to do? Shapeshift. Wars, famine, killing, conflict and suffering are all mass satanic and death rituals producing the low-vibrational energy on

Figure 140: Reptilians feed off low-vibrational (like them) human energy generated by thought and emotion. (Image by Neil Hague.)

which Reptilians feed (Fig 140). Satanists follow an annual ritual calendar connected to the changing astronomical energies of the simulation. These include in the Northern Hemisphere Walpurgis Night, or Beltane, from April 29th/30th through to May 1st; and Halloween, or All Hallow's Eve, on October 31st. One of the prime 'gods' worshipped by Satanists and secret society initiates is Lucifer 'the light bringer'. The 'Let there be light' bringer of the simulation.

What we call 'matter' or form are only vehicles for consciousness to experience different realities in lower-frequency states, The 'I' is not form. It is consciousness, a state of being aware. We are not bodies. We are the consciousness experiencing 'through' bodies. Our behaviour, actions and whatever we do, say, think, and feel are decided by our state of consciousness. Everything is aware, but the question is how aware? Awareness spans the whole spectrum of possibility from Infinite Awareness to a self-identity of a human 'Little Me' to pure inverted evil that seeks control of everything and glories in the suffering it can induce. No matter what your apparent 'form', whether human, Reptilian, anything, your attitudes and actions will be dictated by your state of consciousness. I saw that terms for evil 'entities' such as Yaldabaoth, Devil, Satan, Lucifer, Iblis, Saytan, and Samael are all references to the *same* state of consciousness. They are different names for the *same* force which drives the perceptions and actions of Reptilians, so many humans, and anyone that allows their own awareness to fall into the frequency lair of this force which operates in the frequency band of low-vibrational emotion connected to the foundation state of *fear*. Human society (simulation society) is specifically structured to generate these emotions with two ends in mind. Firstly, those states of awareness have a frequency signature that attaches consciousness to the realm of 'Yaldabaoth' and secondly it allows a conduit through which perceptions that suit 'Yaldabaoth' can be transferred into 'human' minds. It's a form of perceptual possession and its extreme state is the source of empathy-deleted, compassion-deleted psychopaths and psychopathic behaviour.

Possessed by the jab

Psychopaths like Gates and Schwab serve the Global Cult as expressions of Yaldabaoth consciousness and the same with the Reptilian group to which they answer. The whole Cult network and all evil is a manifestation of Yaldabaoth which is ultimately the 'Spider'. Observe the vicious response of those in the 'Covid' coma to those that challenge the official narrative and the deadly fake vaccines that are not 'vaccines' at all by any credible definition. What you see in that viciousness is the stunning absence of empathy, compassion and intelligence all of which are traits of Yaldabaoth consciousness. A frequency connection to Yaldabaoth is one explanation for the unconscious behaviour of so many when they obey authority without question or thought. Software insert non-player characters following their program are another reason. This is an aspect of the fake vaccines that few talk about. There is no 'physical' and everything we perceive as 'physical', including the content of the fake vaccines, is decoded information from a waveform field. If you could see the fake vaccine vials on that level you would see an incredibly distorted, inverted and destructive energetic field that is infused into the human energetic field. Disconnection of human-focused attention from 5-D awareness is the very bottom line of everything the Yaldabaoth Cult does and it is no surprise whatsoever that healers working with human energetic fields, known by many as 'subtle bodies', have found dramatic changes in fake vaccinated people. Many examples are given in an e-book by Thomas Mayer, *Corona Vaccines from the Spiritual Perspective. Consequences on Soul and Spirit, and the Life after Death*. I saw the book at Vaccineliberationarmy.com. Healers of this kind either psychically see or feel with their hands these other human energetic fields and have described disconnected devastation with fake vaccinated clients. The heart chakra vortex – the door to Infinity – is often closed down. Suppression and distortion of the 'spiritual' heart can be transferred to the 'physical' heart which is why heart disease has long been a human epidemic, nay pandemic, through stress and low vibrational emotion. Here are some examples of what healers have experienced:

I noticed immediately the change, very heavy energy emanating from [the] subtle bodies ... The scariest thing was when I was working on the heart chakra, I connected with her soul: it was detached from the physical body ... as if it was floating in a state of total confusion ... I understood that this substance is indeed used to detach consciousness so that this consciousness can no longer interact through this body that it possesses in life ... where there is no longer any contact, no frequency, no light, no more energetic balance or mind ... It is shattering! Patients who have been coming for many years, for whom eurythmy therapy has always been a decisive help, suddenly can no longer feel ... holding the head with both hands repeated the perception of holding a completely hollow, empty head ...

... The etheric brain and the pineal gland felt like dried up and shrivelled ... otherwise perceptible surficial craniosacral rhythm was not perceptible ... With none of my other clients, after more than 20 years of experience, have I ever had such experiences ... I am deeply shocked by what these vaccinations do to people, without them noticing anything ... I had the feeling that there was a dark being on top of her, inhibiting all functions. Stagnation and rigidity. The tissue was as if held, could not breathe and could not move, was no longer able to pulsate ... With one patient I had the experience of massaging a 'corpse' ... There are visible changes in the face. The gaze often becomes rigid, the contours firmer or the people get a rather turgid face ... The face becomes like a mask, transformed ...

... That which wants to shine through is missing ... old weaknesses and symptoms, which were already improved, reappear on all levels due to vaccination ... pain, joint blockages, muscle cramps and stiffness (for example in Parkinson's disease), hardening of the spine, tinnitus etc. ... abilities acquired over many months and years through the work of the 'I' are once again pushed into the background ... old, basic fears, illusions, rigid ideas and patterns, etc., reappear suddenly ... In some this went as far as clearly perceptible (temporary?) changes in their core being ... I often feel alone in my work now. I know these clients well, but somehow, they are no longer there ... In the aftermath of a session, I no longer feel the person, even though they were physically there ...

Perhaps people will now grasp why the Cult has sought to fake vaccinate every man, woman, and child for a 'virus' – even if you believe in it – that official data shows 'threatens' only a tiny number compared with other conditions. The fake vaccines are a form of *possession*. Some may have been fortunate to be given the saline solution contained in many vials to prevent too many deaths at the same time that would be impossible to cover-up. The idea is to keep the fake vaccines coming until everyone bags a bad one. Austrian esoteric thinker and philosopher Rudolf Steiner (1861-1925), who established Steiner schools or Waldorf education to challenge state-school programming, described a vaccine a hundred years ago he said was coming that would disconnect humans from their soul (and through that their spirit). He said in 1917: 'People will be inoculated against their disposition towards spiritual ideas ... The materialistic physicians will be entrusted with the task of expelling the souls from mankind.' Steiner said the following with such relevance to today:

> In the future, we will eliminate the soul with medicine. Under the pretext of a 'healthy point of view', there will be a vaccine by which the human body will be treated as soon as possible directly at birth, so that the human being cannot develop the thought of the existence of soul and Spirit.

> To materialistic doctors, will be entrusted the task of removing the soul of humanity. As today, people are vaccinated against this disease or that disease, so in the future, children will be vaccinated with a substance that can be produced precisely in such a way that people, thanks to this vaccination, will be immune to being subjected to the 'madness' of spiritual life. He would be extremely smart, but he would not develop a conscience, and that is the true goal of some materialistic circles.

> With such a vaccine, you can easily make the etheric body loose in the physical body. Once the etheric body is detached, the relationship between the universe and the etheric body would become extremely unstable, and man would become an automaton, for the physical body of man must be polished on this Earth by spiritual will.

> So, the vaccine becomes a kind of arymanique force; man can no longer get rid of a given materialistic feeling. He becomes materialistic of constitution and can no longer rise to the spiritual.

This is precisely what the energy healers describe with the fake 'Covid' vaccine. Another benefit of attaching to 'human' minds (Fourth Dimensional mind) via the fake vaccine, and other means, is that Yaldabaoth consciousness can then vampire the frequencies of fear, anxiety, depression, hatred, resentment, and regret which it uses as an energy source. Steiner was aware of this, too:

> There are beings in the spiritual realms for whom anxiety and fear emanating from human beings offer welcome food. When humans have no anxiety and fear, then these creatures starve.

If fear and anxiety radiates from people and they break out in panic, then these creatures find welcome nutrition and they become more and more powerful. These beings are hostile towards humanity. Everything that feeds on negative feelings, on anxiety, fear and superstition, despair or doubt, are in reality hostile forces in super-sensible worlds, launching cruel attacks on human beings, while they are being fed ...

...These are exactly the feelings that belong to contemporary culture and materialism; because it estranges people from the spiritual world, it is especially suited to evoke hopelessness and fear of the unknown in people, thereby calling up the above mentioned hostile forces against them.

Why do they need our energy? To be 'cast out' from Infinite Reality is to be denied access to the energy and limitless creativity and possibility of Infinite Reality. Therefore Yaldabaoth consciousness has to feed off the energy of those it entraps in illusion and to do that it must manipulate its targets into states of consciousness and emotion that resonate with its own band of frequency. It cannot absorb the energy of love, joy, happiness, fairness, justice, and all the high frequency states we would like the world to be. Simulated society has been specifically structured to suppress those states to generate low frequencies on which Yaldabaoth can sustain itself. Disconnection from Infinite Reality denies Yaldabaoth all that limitless creative potential. Gnostics describe this consciousness as a 'counterfeit spirit' and counterfeit is defined as 'to make an imitation or copy of (something), usually with the intent to defraud'. Synonyms include fake, forgery, hoax, phoney and sham. How perfectly Yaldabaoth consciousness and its simulation are described. This lack of access to limitless creativity for direct manifestation is why Yaldabaoth Reptilians have to employ technology and mimicry in an effort to fill that void. John Lamb Lash, writes in *Not In His Image*:

In the Gnostic perspective the Archons are not only mind parasites – delusional nodes in the human mind, considered as quasi-autonomous psychic entities, if you will – they are cosmic imposters, parasites who pose as gods. But they lack the primary divine factor of ennoia, 'intentionality', 'creative will'. They cannot originate anything, they can only imitate, and they must effectuate their copycat activity with subterfuge and stealth, lest its true nature be detected.

Human society, especially in the case of authority, is run by parasites from top to bottom as expressions of the Yaldabaoth super-parasite. Cult governments, banks and corporations parasite off humanity, people parasite off each other and Yaldabaoth consciousness parasites off human collective energy or rather Fourth Dimensional mind that thinks it is 'human'. The definition of parasite captures the theme: 'An organism that grows, feeds and is sheltered on or in a different organism while contributing nothing to the survival of its host; one who habitually takes advantage of the generosity of others without making any useful return.' Yaldabaoth parasites the creativity of minds that do still have a connection to Infinite Possibility. We see this on one level with the infamous stealing of intellectual property by Yaldabaoth governments of China and Israel through back-door access encoded in the computer technology and software they sell to the world. There is no more profound example of a predator parasite in action than the Cult-founded global banking system which 'lends' people money that doesn't exist called 'credit' and charges them interest for doing so. If the fake 'loan' cannot be 'repaid', plus interest, the banks get the 'borrowers' assets of homes, businesses, land and resources, illusory as they may actually be, in exchange for theoretical 'credit'. Banking is Yaldabaoth consciousness to a parasitical extreme and the means through which the few have hijacked the world that we experience by exchanging the humanly tangible for the theoretical. Observe Silicon Valley platforms like Google, YouTube, Facebook and Twitter and the creativity comes from the lower ranks, not the Yaldabaoth names that supposedly run them. They are feeding off the mass-creativity of the public who post to their platforms and draw the audience. Without creativity from the public, which they exploit for breathtaking amounts of money, they would not exist. Their very business model is parasitical with organisations such as Facebook claiming joint copyright on any creativity posted to the platform so making Yaldabaoth Facebook a monumental global parasite. Governments and 'Deep States' of China, Israel, the United States, Canada, Britain, France, Italy, Germany, Australia, New Zealand, on and on it goes, are all manifestations of Yaldabaoth consciousness as is the entire Global Cult web.

'They gave us their mind'

What I am saying here is supported by ancient and modern sources all over the world. Among them is Don Juan Matus, a Yaqui Indian healer or shaman in Mexico, quoted in the books of Peruvian-born writer, Carlos Castaneda, between the 1960s to 1990s. Matus said there is a 'predator' that came from the depths of the cosmos and took over the rule of humans. The theme is universal. Human beings are prisoners and the predator is our lord and master, the shaman said. It had rendered us docile and helpless. If we wanted to protest, it suppressed our protest. If we wanted to act independently, it demanded that we don't do so:

> They took us over because we are food to them, and they squeeze us mercilessly because we are their sustenance. Just as we rear chickens in

coops, the predators rear us in human coops, humaneros. Therefore, their food is always available to them.

Matus said the predators had given us our systems of beliefs and our ideas of good and evil. They set up our dreams of success or failure. They gave us covetousness, greed, and cowardice. The predator made makes us complacent, routinary, and egomaniacal:

> In order to keep us obedient and meek and weak, the predators engaged themselves in a stupendous manoeuvre – stupendous, of course, from the point of view of a fighting strategist; a horrendous manoeuvre from the point of those who suffer it. They gave us their mind. The predators' mind is baroque, contradictory, morose, filled with the fear of being discovered any minute now.

They gave us their mind. This is precisely what has happened. The human mind has become the predator mind for all except those awakened enough to tap into 5-D levels of awareness. Don Juan Matus said that sorcerers of ancient Mexico reasoned that humans must have been a complete beings at one point, with stupendous insights, feats of awareness that are mythological legends nowadays (5-D awareness). And then, everything seems to disappear, and we now had a sedated man (lower 4-D mind after the 'Fall'):

> What I'm saying is that what we have against us is not a simple predator. It is very smart, and organised. It follows a methodical system to render us useless. Man, the magical being that he is destined to be, is no longer magical. He's an average piece of meat. There are no more dreams for man but the dreams of an animal who is being raised to be a piece of meat: trite, conventional, imbecilic.

Humans will be magical beings again when we break out of the 4-D mind program and reconnect with our expanded states of awareness that make us magical.

Wrong way up

Another aspect of Yaldabaoth consciousness that can be seen in human society is its state of *inversion*. Evil in my definition is the absence of love – an *inversion* of the love that is the foundation state of Infinite Reality. Evil will always invert when it is in a state of inversion. Everything is upside down because *Yaldabaoth consciousness* is upside down. See how the Cult and its agencies present good as bad and bad as good. Cult-owned Ukrainian President Volodymyr Zelensky promoted himself with almost total worldwide media support as a defender of freedom and democracy after the Russian invasion in 2022. In fact, Zelensky was overseeing a Cult-controlled, US-controlled, oligarch-controlled, fascist dictatorship in which he banned opposition parties and TV stations and fused all Ukrainian television networks into one network that 'he' (his masters) controlled. Talk about inversion. Zelensky did this through 'emergency powers' (see Trudeau in Canada) to create a 'uniform information policy' which is straight off the pages of Orwell's *Nineteen-eighty-four.* These emergency powers are in place in virtually every country waiting to be used to impose full-blown fascism in the name of 'protecting democracy' – still more inversion. Satanism, another obvious expression of Yaldabaoth, is all about inversion right down to its inverted symbolism including the inverted pentagram and inverted cross. A quote by author Michael Ellner makes the point:

> Just look at us. Everything is backwards, everything is upside down. Doctors destroy health, lawyers destroy justice, psychiatrists destroy minds, scientists destroy truth, major media destroys information, religions destroy spirituality and governments destroy freedom.

What I am exposing here explains why this is the case. A crucial point to make – and I will expand upon this at the end of the book – is that Yaldabaoth consciousness does not have the power and potential we have in our true glory and 5-D-connected pomp. Scan human history and you will see the constant dynamic of the many (minds) giving their power away to authority (Yaldabaoth). By this means, and *only* by this means, humanity has always been controlled by the few. This will end at last when minds realise that the power that Yaldabaoth authority imposes upon the population is only the power the population gives away to authority as unquestioning acquiesce and fear of not acquiescing. The 'Covid' era alone makes the case. Iblis, the Islamic version of Yaldabaoth or the Devil, is said to have no power directly and can only 'cast evil suggestions into the heart of men, women, and Jinn'. This is exactly right. *We* have the power and Yaldabaoth's only modus operandi is to manipulate our perception and trick us into believing that our power is its power. Bollocks to that, Yalda, old son – you're a pathetic little boy in short trousers to me. Evil is always stupid. By its very nature it is disconnected from the source of wisdom. Anyone who feels the need to control and oppress is a moron and a frightened one. This is not a consciousness to fear. We stop taking it seriously and its power is yesterday. No wonder Yaldabaoth is described by Gnostics as insane and 'The Blind One' while the same force by other names, Samael and Saklas, translate as 'The Blind God' and 'The Foolish One'. You're an idiot, Yalda, mate, but you don't have to be. It's only a choice and you will be welcomed back into the arms of Infinity any time you make a different choice you Prodigal Son of the fake Universe.

Human society – Wetiko's lair

I had been referring for decades to Yaldabaoth consciousness under all its cultural and religious names and symbols as a 'mind virus' akin to a computer virus that disconnects the operating system from the operator. 'They gave us their mind' as the shaman said. Then I came across the Native North American concept of 'Wetiko', or that's the name used by the Cree indigenous people in Montana and Canada. Other indigenous groups have slightly different names, such as Wintiko and Windigo. The concept is the same with them all. Wetiko is often written with a lowercase 'w', but I prefer a capital. What is Wetiko? Native Americans call it a *mind virus*. I was intrigued to find once again the same global theme. To Yaldabaoth, Devil, Satan, Lucifer, Iblis/Saytan, Samael, and all the rest can be added Wetiko. They are all describing the same force and its techniques of deceit through perceptual manipulation. Writer and

researcher Paul Levy has done outstanding work in describing the depths and manipulation techniques of Wetiko. I recommend his book, *Dispelling Wetiko, Breaking the Spell of Evil*. I also read a Wetiko book by indigenous author Jack D. Forbes,

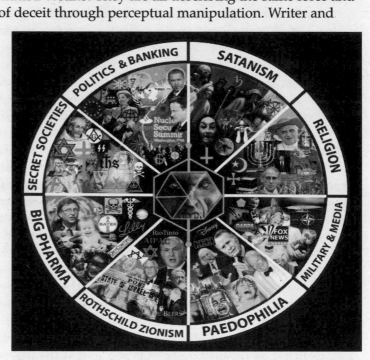

Figure 141: All roads lead to the Reptilian 'gods'. 'Rothchild Zionism' in this image refers to a cult called Sabbatianism which hates Jews but runs Israel. I expose this abomination at length in *The Trigger*. (Image by Neil Hague.)

Columbus And Other Cannibals – The Wetiko Disease of Exploitation, Imperialism, and Terrorism. Wetiko is described as a sickness of the soul and a state of being that takes while giving nothing back. My mind immediately pictures Gates, Schwab, Fauci, Big Pharma corporations, and all the other 'Covid' political and media psychopaths. No wonder that all roads of evil in the human world emerge from the Wetiko Reptilians and their inverted state of consciousness (Fig 141). Jack D Forbes writes that 'tragically, the history of the world for the past 2,000 years is, in great part, the story of the epidemiology of the wetiko disease'.

All evil in the world comes from Wetiko in all its names and guises and crucially from 'human' minds allowing Wetiko to control their perception. Wetiko has been on public display big-time since the 'Covid' hoax and in all the wars, hunger, deprivation, and systems of control. Given that all is One – all aspects of Infinite Awareness in different states of consciousness – we should also take responsibility for Wetiko having the potential to influence anyone and everyone. Paul Levy writes: 'Holographically enforced within the psyche of every human being the wetiko virus pervades and underlies the entire field of consciousness, and can therefore potentially manifest through any one of us at any moment if we are not mindful.' That 'virus' underlying the entire field of consciousness is what I say is the ultimate source of the simulation and Wetiko directs the minds and actions of the Cult web in all its manifestations. Interestingly, in the light of what I have said in this book, Levy says:

> ... the subtle body of wetiko is not located in the third dimension of space and time, literally existing in another dimension ... it is able to affect ordinary lives by mysteriously interpenetrating into our three-dimensional world.

I would say that the Wetiko simulation is attaching to minds in the Fourth Dimension to decode into the illusion of a Third-Dimensional reality. Wetiko interpenetrates the 'Third Dimension' through Fourth Dimensional manipulation of mind's perception.

CHAPTER TEN

WTF? I Mean ... WTF??

The possession of knowledge does not kill the sense of wonder and mystery. There is always more mystery
Anais Nin

You will see the reason for this chapter heading as I tell the story that follows. I mentioned near the start of the book that I was deeply in love with a girl at school in 1967 and 52 years later 'she' came back into my life. Well, not 'her' exactly, but you'll get the gist as we go along. What happened was to open a whole new area of research for me and with that came the realisation of how deep the rabbit hole goes.

I will call the girl (as was) 'K'. I knew her at Crown Hills School in Leicester when she was 13 and 14 and I was 14 and 15. I haven't seen her since, apart from a two minute 'How are you?' at a school reunion in the 1980s. As I pass 70 she would be closing in on the same. The strange thing was that I never 'went out' with the girl nor even held her hand. What passed between us was unspoken and yet obvious nonetheless and very powerful. I was extremely attracted to her and the feeling I know was mutual. I would look at her in a crowd of kids and all I would see was her and her eyes. Everything else was kind of out of focus, a peripheral blur. I knew there was a strong connection, but while I was gaining great confidence in my football life at the time I was still shy when it came to asking a girl out. I said nothing and neither did she although we both knew how the other felt. Well, to be fair, I think I was more aware of her feelings for me than she was of mine. One of my biggest regrets as I was leaving Crown Hills was to be leaving her and I was delighted when she asked if she could write to me when I moved to Coventry to start my football career. She had a friend, a blonde girl, who also had designs on me and she, too, asked if she could write. I agreed because I didn't want to hurt her feelings although letters from 'K' were all that I wanted. I moved to Coventry and the letters began. They were regular, maybe two a week each way for months into the late autumn of 1967. She told me she was taking part in a school period drama for a public audience and asked if I could come over one night to watch. I jumped at the chance. There were things I now wanted to say. Then came a letter asking me if she could tell the other girl that I didn't want her to write to me anymore. I agreed reluctantly. While I didn't want to hurt the other girl I could see that 'K' wanted me to herself and that's what I wanted, too. 'Yes, okay', I said, 'go ahead.'

Hello, goodbye

The letters then stopped abruptly, or maybe there was just one more before they stopped. There was certainly plenty of time for another before I attended the play and yet it never came. There had not been such a lag time before. I went to the play in the Crown Hills school hall one dark, crisp, November evening. I had at last summoned the courage to tell her how much I loved her and that I wanted us to be together. This was going to be my Big Night. What had been unspoken would now be spoken. I had arranged to meet her out front afterwards where students and parents were gathered and preparing to go home. I was talking to an old school friend that I hadn't seen since I left five months earlier when I saw 'K' walk around the corner of the hall with her blonde friend yet again in tow. She was always in tow and I mean pretty much always. Well, shit, what a shock. In all the time I knew her 'K' had been so friendly and laughed so easily. Now I was looking at a face of absolute fury and venom. I was so taken aback that I let her walk past me the first time while I tried to comprehend what on earth was going on. When we did speak she was horrible to me and continued to be so as I walked her home if you could call it that. Talk about leaving me in no doubt that the last place she wanted to be that night was with me. We got to the end of her street and with a swift 'I'd better go' she walked away and I knew in that moment it was over. I thought it best in the circumstances not to tell her that I loved her and wanted us to be together! Ha.

A few days later the letter I was expecting arrived giving a lame and obviously untrue excuse to stop writing. I played the nonchalant male and wrote back to say okay, these things happen, when I was dying inside. In a matter of two weeks the letters had gone from can I be the only one who writes to you to basically piss off. I was bewildered and very deeply hurt. It could surely not be anything I had done in those two weeks. I had not seen her in that time and spent the whole period in Coventry 25 miles away. What could have happened? The only thing I could think of was that she told me in the last letter that she liked a new Beatles song, *Hello, Goodbye*. I replied to say that I liked a new Cliff Richard song called *All My Love*. I didn't like Cliff Richard. I was trying to tell her how I felt in my own way through the song. Maybe she thought I wasn't 'cool' mentioning Cliff Richard and that explained what happened? That's so funny looking back across more than half a

century although to be fair I could think of no other explanation for the
dramatic turnaround. The irony is that if you listen to the words of the
Cliff Richard song it predicts what was very shortly about to happen
and so did *Hello, Goodbye* with its 'I don't know why you say goodbye, I
say hello'. To call me heartbroken doesn't begin to describe how I felt,
especially at 15 with the hormone transition in full swing. Another song
released at that same time in November, 1967, was *Nights in White Satin*
by the Moody Blues which crushed me emotionally every time I heard
it. Thank goodness I had football to focus on until that, too, was denied
me a few months later when the arthritis began and my Coventry career
stalled for the best part of a year.

I left it a few months from November of 1967 until the turn of the
new year to see if things had changed. I asked a friend still at the school
to approach her and ask if I could see her. I remember his phone call that
night to my guest house 'digs' in Coventry: 'She thought about it, Dave,
but then she said no.' I was gutted and I gave up at that point to get on
with my life. I went back to the school a couple of times during the
summer break from football in the next two years in theory to see old
friends and teachers when my real motivation was the hope of seeing
her. On one occasion I did see her (guess who with??) on the far side of
an empty playground. I looked at them and they looked at me. I so
wanted to raise my hand and wave, but something stopped me. I have
no idea why. I turned away for a moment and she – they, it was always
they – had gone. That was pretty much it, really, except for the briefest of
meetings at a school reunion in the mid-1980s. I was a national face on
television by then. I accepted the invite not knowing who would be
there and my intent if 'K' was among the group was to find out finally
the background to what changed so fast in the period of the school play.
When I was greeted by the organiser at the door of the small hotel
function room in Leicester my first question was: 'Do you know what
happened to "K"?' She's over there, the organiser said, and I looked
across to see her talking.

I tell you something. If you said there was an unseen force working to
keep us apart I would have no problem believing you. There were the
unspoken years at school when I never actually spoke to her alone. The
blonde girl, sometimes others, were always with her. It was bizarre. 'K'
would come to school football matches and sometimes stand behind my
goal, but always with the blonde girl. The only time I ever saw her alone
was on that horrific walk home from the school play when I was in effect
walking on my own anyway. Now I spent nearly three hours in a
relatively small room in a Leicester hotel at the reunion and never got to
speak with her until right at the end. Crazy, I know. 'Time' absolutely
evaporated that night (Fig 142). I was no sooner walking in than it was
over. Where did it go? People were preparing to leave when I got to

Figure 142: The Crown Hills school reunion in the 1980s. 'K' not in the picture.

speak to her. Then at the very moment I was going to ask her what had happened all those years before in walks a guy who came to take her home. He started talking to me about motor racing or something. I could have pinned him to the wall by his lapels very easily in that moment. I was thwarted again. They both left pretty much immediately and it's the last time I saw her while still none the wiser about that night in 1967. 'K' faded from my mind after that unless I would pass her old house and the school when I was visiting family in Leicester and memories would return of those wonderful years at Crown Hills. I still can't drive down Gwendolen Road alongside the school without recalling that walk home with her that night! Otherwise my mind was rather occupied with other things. In the four years following the school reunion I became a national speaker for the Green Party quickly followed by Betty Shine in 1990 and all hell breaking loose in my life.

Dreaming of yesterday

Fast forward 52 years from the night of the school play to the spring/summer of 2019. By now my work was gaining traction and greatly more respect after all the years of mass ridicule and abuse. The interest had been building since the attacks of 9/11. One night, in the early months of 2019, I had a vivid dream about 'K'. She did not appear as the 14 year-old I knew at school. She was more like she looked at the reunion in her early 30s although even then not quite the same. There was a maturity about her, a knowing, that I can't put into words. I woke up bewildered. Why would I dream about 'K' after all these years – 52 *years*? She had hardly crossed my mind unless triggered by a location since the reunion in the mid-1980s. What was even stranger is that I felt 'her' around me in the days that followed. It's difficult to explain. I felt 'her' presence, saw flashes of her in my mind, and sometimes heard a female voice claiming to be 'her'. It certainly brought memories flooding back of those far off days at Crown Hills. I was out walking one sunny morning in the countryside soon after the dream and felt 'her' presence.

I looked around and there was not a bird in sight. I then said: 'If it's really you show me two birds flying together.' It seemed a near-impossible request in the circumstances and was meant to be. Within no more than *three seconds* two birds burst out of a bush just to my left and flew off together into the sky. As they did so I noticed another bird had appeared, a big one, flying in circles really high. I heard a female voice say as I looked at the bird: 'That is you.' I was listening to music through earphones from a CD that I was hearing for the first time. I watched the bird circle at great height just as a song came on called *The Power of Love* by *Frankie Goes To Hollywood* which includes the lines: 'I'll protect you from the hooded claw … keep the vampires from your door … when the chips are down I'll be around with my undying, death-defying love for you.' That song would play 'coincidentally' at significant moments many times and became a bit of an anthem for me. The only sense I could make of what was happening at that time is that 'K' must have passed over and was communicating from another reality, but who knew anything for sure? I decided just to go with it and see what happened. My life experience has been that everything is usually explained eventually however long it may take.

I was driving in Wiltshire not far from the Avebury stone circle on one occasion and I clearly heard a female voice claiming to be 'K' telling me that we were 'twin souls'. I had no idea what a twin soul was then. I later read that this refers to one soul becoming incarnate in the male and female aspects as in one soul in two bodies. I am not saying this is true, by the way, only that this is what I read. I have seen the twin soul (also twin flame) concept connected to the theme of quantum entanglement which is defined as 'a property of a set of subatomic particles whereby a quantum characteristic (such as spin or momentum) of one particle is directly and immediately correlated with the equivalent characteristic of the others regardless of separation in space'. In other words the 'two' are always one no matter where they are. Another twin soul explanation I saw is that the 'vibrational energy level becomes too high to be contained within a single human body' and that twin soul incarnation 'allows you to experience more of the world and advance your spiritual knowledge'. Well, knowledge of the simulation more like. I put this information on my 'back-burner' as I always do and waited to see where this was going if anywhere. I knew from the way my life had been all along that the 'K' phenomenon was happening for a reason. What reason I had no idea. If it was the case that 'K' had passed, maybe a medium could make a connection? I contacted a medium friend in June, 2019. I only told her about the dream and that for some reason I was feeling a presence around me that kept reminding me of 'K'. The medium said she would 'tune-in' and come back to me. She did with an email that included these comments:

I finally connected to whom I believe is [K]. She smiled and nodded yes. She came in so clear that I received information so fast so I thought that I better get to my laptop and type as I hear her talk to me.

First I saw a woman who looks around 48 and believe that she passed at that age. Her hair was short but cut to her chin ... I asked her to tell me if she had crossed over and how old she was. She said that she was 48 and died from a rare heart condition. Nobody expected that she would cross over so unexpectedly.

This gave me checkable facts which as a researcher I was always going to check before I went ahead with this book. For now I wanted to let it run and see what else happened. The whole thing was so intriguing and I was fascinated to see where it went from here before I began the researcher stuff. It wasn't affecting my work in any way and so there was no need at this point. Something said intuitively to leave that for now and just go with it. I did check social media and the Internet for any mention of her. There was none. The medium's email continued:

It appeared that she was married and after you went to school with her she either moved or left so you didn't see her again ... She said that she was all about studying and was shy or quiet when it came to boys so she didn't approach you that way.

I asked her why she came into your mind and she told me that she knows what you are doing with your life and said 'Good job David ... well done'. So she popped into your mind which tells me that she wanted to make contact with you. You didn't seek her out. It was the other way around.

She's very proud of you and she's also very happy with where she is. She knows that you will finish what you start because as she said 'You are very good at being the center of attention whether you wanted it or not.' She saw you as ambitious but quiet and focused.

I asked about social media and she said that it didn't exist when she was alive and that now makes sense to me. She would have died about 16-18 years ago? I believe that she is correct. That would be 2001-2003.

I believe that she went by a married name and not ['K'] ... So she told me to send her regards and that this communication is not an accident. She said once again that she has confidence that you will leave your mark and that your time to cross is so far away in our time and space. You're not ready and you won't leave until you are happy with what you accomplished on Earth. So you will be old ...

The medium reported that 'K' had also said that had we been together in this life 'it wouldn't have worked because you were destined for greatness and that is foreign to her – you would have been left as a widower and you wouldn't have your wonderful children'. Well, for sure whatever the background was to all this if we are talking about 'meant to be' then any relationship with 'her' clearly wasn't 'to be' given the way my life had gone and events that kept us apart. There were other comments like 'she' said her parents were strict and her thoughts about me at school included her frustration that she would look at me and wish that I would come over, but I didn't. The kicker, however, was the picture. The medium said she scanned the Internet to find a picture that looked like the 'K' she said had appeared to her psychic sight and she sent the one that looked most like her. I was blown away. It was as near as you could get to the 'K' I saw at the school reunion without it actually being her. The accuracy of the likeness was a shocker. Many other messages were passed to me in the weeks that followed. The medium talked of her 'adoring eyes' and 'a kindness that I can't put into words'. She said that 'K' told her that we were 'twin souls' – the recurring theme which I had not mentioned to the medium. I walked a lot in those months and felt 'her' with me at different locations. Many times the medium would describe the location that she could not have known – she wasn't even in my country – and describe how 'K' was standing behind me or next to me exactly as I had felt 'her'. I was also told that 'K' would withdraw when I was writing books:

I asked her why she's silent around you. She told me something familiar. I don't want to distract him. Love from one soul to another is so powerful especially when they are twin souls. It will distract him. She also said that the words in the book are coming THRU to you but not from her.

She will be back to connect with you telepathically. Because the words for the book are a different source she wants you to continue to hear those words and write them. The words are a gift and the level of love that you are writing about has nothing to do with romantic love. Because you were both on Earth at the same time, you remember a strong attraction and romantic love for each other ...

... I got a message from her this morning as I was waking up. She said 'When I'm not with you be at peace ... I AM with you but I'm in your heart, so you won't hear me. I want you to FEEL me.'

What was said about the books definitely seemed to be true whatever this 'she' would turn out to be. The energy signature I felt disappeared when I wrote and researched two books, *The Answer* and *Perceptions of a Renegade Mind*, over two periods of six months and more. So much so that it was like the phenomenon had never happened. 'K' appeared in dreams here and there, but always in a distant, peripheral way. I began to forget all about it. Then suddenly it all kicked off again with even greater intensity in June, 2021.

Back with a bang

I was contacted by an English medium via someone that Linda knew. The medium said her 'spirit guide' had asked her to make contact with me and if I was ever in her area maybe we could meet. My intuition was to do so although I had no idea how. She lived a long way from me and I would never be anywhere close. Within a couple of weeks another message came that the medium had been invited to do a presentation at the local spiritualist church which is just three minutes' walk from my home. I arranged to meet her and we talked about my work. She passed on communications from 'out there' about current events and the 'Covid' fake vaccines which were certainly true. She came to my flat on another day and we spent four hours chatting about lots of subjects including the process of mediumship during which I understandably mentioned my 'K' experience which had all but stopped by then. 'She's here', the medium said, and proceeded to tell me things that matched what the first medium had said which she didn't know about. The medium is also a psychic artist who draws sometimes extraordinary images of 'passed-over' people. 'Let me see if I can draw 'K', she said, and I watched her go into a trance state and begin to sketch on her pad even when her eyes were sometimes closed. About 15 minutes later – a long drawing for her, she said – she showed me the picture. It was 'K'. Unmistakable. When I slightly cropped the picture the likeness was even more as she was around the time of the reunion. Erm ... WTF? This is a summary of what the medium said that 'K' was telling her during this meeting and another the following day:

We are *twin souls*. 'K' had died in her late 40s from a heart problem she didn't know that she had, although sometimes her lips went blue as an indication. We had an immense energetic connection and she would channel love through to me from her reality. She acted as she did at the school play because she was told by the 'blonde girl' that I had claimed to a friend at the school that I had slept with 'K' (I had never even held her hand). This made sense of how I was treated that school play night and it had happened soon after 'K' had told the girl that I didn't want her to write to me anymore. The medium said that 'K' was telling her that she wanted me for herself and the plan backfired with the lie that she was told. Well, it certainly was a lie. I never said any such thing about sleeping with her and it was against all my principles even as a 15 year-old to have done so. God save us from macho male boasters. Over the next few weeks the medium gave me details of conversations and happenings that only I and 'K' would have known about and that I had worn a white jacket at the school reunion in the 1980s which I did. 'K' would also describe things that I had done while working alone at home. The medium would send music to me that she said 'K' had asked her to give me and all would fit with the theme of the story I was being told or the work that I was doing. Two I remember were *You Are Loved* and *To Where You Are* by American singer Josh Groban which I had never heard before. There was also a Michael Martin Murphey song, *Maybe This Time*. Listen to them with the lyrics on the Internet and you'll see how perfectly they fitted the story that I was being told at different times by two separate mediums thousands of miles apart. I was also contacted on another subject by an overseas lady who said she was psychically gifted and had recently had a reading with the same UK medium. She said that when they chatted about me at the end this overseas lady had got the name '*******' or '*****'. Both were *so* close to the real name of 'K'.

Searching for 'K'

Put it all together and the evidence before me was that 'K' was indeed communicating from another reality. How could the information that only we or I knew about be so accurate? However, I am a researcher and when there are tangible facts to check, I check them. There had been no urgency to do so. What was happening was not affecting my work and we had been in the 'Covid' era for 16 months with my workload overwhelming due to the interest in my information; but by now I planned to tell the story in this book which was forming in my mind. It was time to take it more seriously in the sense of checking what I was able to check about what I had been told. I had tried to find evidence on the Internet early on that 'K' was passed or still alive and there was no mention of her. Even under what I later learned was her married name, there was next to nothing and absolutely nothing after 2003. My only option to nail this was to hire a tracer company that specialises in finding people. It took a while with apparently a few false leads and what was telling from the start was the absence of a death certificate in the tracer's searches. These are apparently pretty straightforward to find if one exists.

Eventually the tracer found her. 'K' was still *alive*. The story was interesting to me before. Now it became riveting and an even bigger WTF? Tracers are not allowed to tell the client the address of the person without their permission which is only right. I didn't need to contact her, just to know she was alive. The tracer said they had called her to say an old school friend they didn't name wanted to make contact (not true) without saying who it was. The tracer said 'K' was not interested. Months later as I started the book a friend went through a different tracer company to confirm the findings of the first – establishing the facts beyond *any doubt* was rather crucial to the story. This tracer also found the long-married 'K' and sent her a letter asking if they could forward a package from me without me knowing her address. There was no response. For some reason the tracer sent the letter second class post near Christmas and my friend insisted it was later sent again to be signed for to make absolutely sure it was received. It was. There was still no response which I found quite sad really given how respectful the tracer company's letter had been. All it asked was for permission for them to forward a package from me without me knowing her address. I don't think that was asking much, but everyone to their own and so it should be. By now as I wrote this chapter I wanted to establish if the 'slept-with' story was true to further check the accuracy of those 'communications'. That would have been very helpful as I set about answering the question WTF? With 'K' never responding I still don't know if that information is correct, only that it would explain everything that happened.

I was so glad that I followed my intuition and let the experience roll before tracing her. I would have missed out on so much valuable insight had I done so. I had many questions. Why had this happened? If it was manipulative why did it not impact adversely on my work? Why not claim the communications were from someone else who had actually died? It would have been much easier to 'sell'. Why the provable crap about dying in her 40s from a heart defect? Why if it was mere trickery was I given clear checkable facts that were bound to lead me to the truth? What level of idiot would look at the way I have pursued and checked facts for decades and not think that I would check these? Establishing if 'K' was alive or not and if she died of a heart defect in her late 40s was hardly going to be rocket science. Okay, if I had not sought to confirm that 'K' was alive potential manipulation could have gone to other levels, but I was always going to do that. It's how I work. One communication did strike me in relation to the tunnel of light and that *Star Trek* scene. I was told that 'K' had said 'she' would be waiting for me at the moment I died to take me 'home'. How interesting. They can forget that one.

'I'm getting a ... *WHAT* exactly?'

From my life experience of more than 30 years I knew that all this had not happened by chance. Given that it had continued on and off for a while there had to be a very significant reason for why this was put before me. It clearly appeared not to be about the reconnection across realities with a 'twin soul' so why? A 'twin soul' or any other kind is hardly going to tell you they died in their 40s from a heart defect when that was not true. There may be another explanation, I don't know, but that's at least the human logical one. Synchronistically (again) as I established that 'K' was alive, information began to appear in my life from many different directions and sources about the manipulation of 'after-life' reality through the AI-controlled simulation. My mind returned to a question that had puzzled me since way back. As part of my research at one point just after the millennium I had observed a lot of psychics and mediums at work. I had met many over the years and now I wanted to focus on this for a while. There was a show on cable TV almost every night which I rarely missed in which a medium that I met a few times would work with a studio audience to 'contact' loved ones. It was the typical psychic show fare of 'I've got a Mary, anyone know a Mary?' The medium involved had a nightmare evening in my local spiritualist church, the only time I have ever been there, when absolutely no-one knew a Mary or anyone else that he came up with. Everyone has a bad night, I guess, no matter what they do. I watched his TV show time after time and it was clear that he was connecting with something. He appeared to be remarkably accurate on occasions judging by the response of those who said they recognised the person. He said in one example that the 'spirit' was saying that he was sitting with his family watching television one night, felt a sharp pain in the chest and was immediately on the 'other side'. Family members in the audience confirmed that indeed they were all watching TV when he fell forward and died in an instant. There were many such moments in the series. My question, however, and the source of my puzzlement, was why when departed 'souls' came through did they talk about mundane 'this world' issues and subjects and yet never say anything like 'Hey, your world is an illusion and you are being manipulated!! Wake up!!' That never happened. Why the hell not?

Don't get me wrong. I am not saying that mediums and psychics are all to be dismissed. *Not at all*. The question is this: Are they connecting with a source inside the simulation or beyond its band of frequency? I have seen psychics and mediums who connect with high-frequency states who have communicated seriously advanced information about global manipulation and the force behind it. I'm just saying that far from all of them do that and if we're absolutely honest how do we know the source from which communications come? The only real test we can apply is to see if the information has a positive impact on those who hear or act upon it or that it adds positively to understanding. Betty Shine's information for me turned out to be incredibly accurate in terms of my life that followed and has had a positive impact. Accuracy alone, especially *retrospective* accuracy, as with the 'K' story, is clearly not the only criteria. Connecting with consciousness outside the simulation is quite another thing and that requires extremely expanded states of frequency to do so. Such people are rare and not the norm. I have experienced the difference between communications I take to be from beyond the simulation and those from within. The former are like a 'knowing'. You just *know* something – as in '*eureka*' – because of a connection with that which *does* know and this connection produces a particular frequency resonance that becomes very familiar. This is how information overwhelmingly comes to me from other realities and this knowing comes in through the *heart*, not the head. Communications that take the form of a 'voice' (as with 'K') are rare for me by comparison and largely from inside the simulation in my view, although not always. 'K' was a 'voice' which I could hear (inside the simulation) in a form that connected with the head with some heart stuff going on, too, for sure. Other times communication comes as a knowing in the heart chakra which is then expressed as like a thought-form that *my* mind manifests rather than some external 'entity'. I am decoding the 'knowing' into words, you might say, which is different to 'hearing voices'. This thought-form experience is what happened in the news shop in 1990 as in 'go and look at the books on the far side'. I did 'hear' a clear voice in my ayahuasca experience, but that was not so much hearing a voice as *being* that voice. It's hard to describe. The voice and me were *One* and there was no division between the words being delivered and me who was receiving them. The words, the voice and me were indivisible and the experience was totally different from just 'hearing a voice'. *Nothing* is rigidly black and white, but the vast majority of insights that I receive come as a knowing from the heart rather than what you would perceive as a voice in the 'head'.

'Soul' tracking

From around the time the tracers established that 'K' was alive the communications and all the phenomena around me stopped. There has been none since. I clearly recognised, as 'K' was found, the recurring pattern once again of information about the same subject coming into my life from all angles. Why wouldn't that be so when this had been happening since 1990? The pattern was so familiar. The theme this time was the AI simulation control system and the depth to which this goes. I saw that the technological control network in China, now being played out globally as the 'Smart Grid', was actually a Fourth Dimensional simulation system being projected into 3-D albeit in a far less advanced form – at least for now. Make what you will of what I am about to say. I am not trying to get anyone to believe anything. It is for the individual to decide what feels right to them. I put the dots together after 'K' was found from multiple 'bits' of information, synchronicity and directional 'nudges' that I have experienced constantly for now 32 years. I concluded from this that Fourth Dimensional AI (which is way beyond the cutting edge in '3-D') is digitally tracking all human 'incarnations' (mind projections) in real time and recording everything in the

equivalent of a gigantic database. I know that is a fantastic thing to say, but hear me out.

As I write, the world population is soon to pass eight billion and will have done so by the time you read this. Around 1.5 billion of those people live in China which is

Figure 143: The Chinese government can track its vast population in real time, but far more advanced 4-D AI technology can't track, tag, and log human activity?

about 18 percent of the global total. This is the same China that tracks its population through AI and records their behaviour for its social credit system (Fig 143). Is it really too much of a leap to conceive that an almost incomprehensively more advanced 4-D AI could do the same with eight billion that China does in 3-D with 1.5 billion? Then there's the Sat-Nav system that reveals the true potential of even 3-D AI. You punch in an address and the Sat-Nav immediately guides you to the destination. Take a wrong turn and in *seconds* the AI voice says 'route recalculation' and rearranges the route to respond to your mistake. Now ponder on the fact that billions of vehicles worldwide with Sat-Nav are being *simultaneously* guided – tracked – by the same AI. Fourth-Dimensional AI can't track billions of 'humans'?? The 4-D AI control system is being made manifest in the 3-D projection and coming into plain sight. Is this what the 'Great Reset' really is? Don't panic and freeze at that prospect, tempting as this may be. There is a way out of this. What I am describing would mean that every human life is tracked in detail, all interactions and conversations recorded, and so able to be communicated through mediums and psychics as accurate information about loved ones and people that we knew. AI would also have the unique frequencies on which mediums and psychics resonate and be able to make potentially powerful frequency connections through which information could be communicated. This is not to put any blame on mediums and psychics. They can only give what they get. My question is what is the source – at least sometimes – of what many give and get?

How many who will dismiss what I say about tracking and recording by 4-D AI have any idea there is something called the 'Sentient World Simulation' (SWS) based at the Synthetic Environment for Analysis and Simulations Laboratory at Purdue University in Indiana? Second by second the 'Sentient World Simulation' is mass-collecting data from endless sources to predict and manipulate human behaviour and produces a digital real-time version of human society. The SWS operates under the control of Cult-owned DARPA, the Defense Advanced Research Projects Agency, which is the technological development arm of the Pentagon. DARPA is a driving force behind Silicon Valley Cult corporations and seed-funded Google and others together with the CIA's technology funding operation In-Q-Tel (also IQT). DARPA brags that it was responsible for the creation of the Internet with military technology and no wonder when the Internet is the foundation of the entire 'Great Reset' control system. The Sentient World Simulation ('sentient' = advanced AI) is constantly processing information from every man, woman and child on the planet, scanning behaviour and buying patterns, and producing a 'continuously running, continually updated mirror model of the real world that can be used to predict and evaluate future events and courses of action'. This is happening in our reality *now*. It makes what I say about the Fourth Dimensional control and surveillance system rather less fantastic. The SWS is connected to 'pre-crime' as portrayed in the movie *Minority Report* set in the year 2054. 'Pre-crime' means arresting people for crimes they haven't done but which technology predicts that they will. Purdue University, by the way, is also the location of research for the US Department of Defense to recreate the brain in silicon through a process called neuromorphic computing which seeks to imitate the complex network of neurons in the human brain for AI and robotics. This will be far more advanced in the underground bases and secret projects which public research is designed to hide.

On the record

I came across the esoteric belief in 'Akashic Records' in 1990 and I have heard the term many times over the years without ever feeling the need to go deep into the subject. The more I explored the 4-D AI control system in the wake of the 'K' revelations the more the term 'Akashic Records' began repeating in my mind. They are said to exist in another dimension called the Akasha and record 'every thought, idea, and action from the past, present, and future' and store them for infinity. Sound familiar? One article said: 'The Akashic Records is basically like a database of what's happening in all the universes that are co-existing together'. Once again – *sound familiar*? The article went on:

The Akashic Records are basically a record of what will happen, is happening, or has happened. Because they are a higher dimension, the rules of time don't really apply. Time is a flat circle to the Akashic Records, so information from 2,000 years ago is as accessible as what happened to you yesterday. And what happened to you yesterday is as available as what could happen to you – if you stay on the same destiny trajectory – in 10 years.

Interestingly, everything has its own Akashic Record. Your soul has an Akashic Record, your house has an Akashic Record, your dog, even your relationship! You can open the specific Records of things to ask questions that pertain to them.

It is also true that you can access information in the Internet 'cloud' from 2,000 years ago which is just 'as accessible as what happened to you yesterday'. You see where I am going. I know from researching the Global Cult for decades that the consciousness it represents is obsessed with fine detail and recording every last smear of information. Remember what I was told by someone who knew British Prime Minister Edward Heath about his obsession with writing down in a ledger all the details of children, such as height and weight, before he killed them? This is their mentality and it could well be AI at work. How much AI is infused into these Cult bloodlines – code-lines? Are they indeed AI? Then there is 'what happened to you yesterday is as available as what could happen to you – if you stay on the same destiny trajectory – in 10 years'. The DARPA Sentient World Simulation is constantly projecting a future based on current 'trajectory'. If you were the Cult seeking to impose an agenda on the world wouldn't it be rather an advantage to know how events will turn out if things stay as they are so you can change what they are and change the projected outcome? Wouldn't this explain how animated television shows have been able to predict in their storylines and visuals what would much later happen in terms of 9/11, the election of Donald Trump, and a mass protest by truckers?

The idea of Akashic Records is very much connected to the world-famous American medium/psychic/clairvoyant Edgar Cayce (1877-1945). Cayce, a Christian and Sunday school teacher, would enter a trance-like state and respond to questions about the afterlife, reincarnation, health, and many other subjects. He was dubbed 'The Sleeping Prophet' for his predictions of the 'future'. How can anyone predict the future? If nothing intervenes to override the AI simulation program the 'future' is always known. Cayce explained the process as his subconscious exploring other realms of reality and part of that exploration involved the Akashic Records which he popularised. He described them like this:

Upon time and space is written the thoughts, the deeds, the activities of an entity – as in relationships to its environs, its hereditary influence; as directed – or judgment drawn by or according to what the entity's ideal is. Hence, as it has been oft called, the record is God's book of remembrance; and each entity, each soul – as the activities of a single day of an entity in the material world – either makes same good or bad or indifferent, depending upon the entity's application of self ...

How interesting that he said 'upon time and space is written' ... Time and space are phenomena of the *simulation*. This quote was included in an article on the Edgarcayce.org website headed 'Edgar Cayce on the Akashic Records' and I noted how the writer sought to explain the records from a modern perspective: 'The Akashic Records, also known as "The Book of Life" or "God's Book of Remembrance", can be equated to the universe's super-computer system – or perhaps what today would be called cloud computing.' Er, *exactly*. The Akashic Records were described as 'the central storehouse of all information for every individual who has ever lived upon the earth'. They contained 'every thought, deed, word, feeling, and intent' and had a 'tremendous influence on our everyday lives, our relationships, our feelings, our belief systems, and the potential realities we draw toward us'. The perceived Akashic Records are a Fourth Dimensional *AI computer system*. They are the very AI-controlled record system that began to be synchronistically presented to me when 'K' was located. I am not saying that the record of everything is not encoded in the Infinite Field, but the simulation is just that – a *simulation* of the Infinite Field or Prime Reality, or *part* of it, which mimics technologically what pure consciousness has created in Prime Reality. If your awareness is separated from Prime Reality and perceptually attached to the simulation then it's the *simulation's* version of the Akashic Records that will impact upon you. Another common theme recalled by near-death experiencers is the life review in which the mind/soul is shown a recording of its human life in which actions are viewed like a movie from the perceptive of the self and the impact on others. This has connotations of the 'Judgement Day' theme of many religions. One near-death experiencer said:

There is evidence that a type of judgment occurs at the time of death. This judgment involves a review of a person's life and results in their placement in the spirit world. Sometime after the judgment the person is assigned (in many cases this assignment is self-imposed) to a specific place or level in the other world – a place where his or her spirit feels most at ease.

M*mmm*, maybe. Or maybe a Fourth Dimensional AI database like the one I am describing would explain all of that. AI is running the whole

show and I sometimes wonder if the Reptilians created the simulation or
the simulation created them in the same way it created 'humans' in
terms of their bodies. Why couldn't Reptilians be minds just as trapped
in the illusion as human minds, but with another role to play as agents
of the simulation control system in ways that compare with the software
agent inserts in the *Matrix* movies? I'm not saying they are, only that it's
a thought to be considered. What if 'Wetiko' consciousness created the
simulation, humans *and* Reptilians and other non-human forms, and we
are all trapped playing different parts in the same AI illusion? As
Shakespeare, or whoever wrote 'his' plays, said: 'All the world's a stage,
and all the men and women merely players; They have their exits and
their entrances and one man in his time plays many parts.' What does
the Wetiko-controlled Global Cult seek to do by 2030? To connect the
human brain to AI so that AI becomes the human perceptual processes
to block off any access to Infinite Awareness outside the simulation.
What is the nature of this AI they seek to connect us with? Is it what we
see in the 3-D public arena? No – it's 4-D AI or *Wetiko/Yaldabaoth*. The AI-
brain connection is actually the absorption of 'human' minds into
Wetiko/Yaldabaoth. Isn't that right Mr computer-brain interface Elon
Musk?

How could it be done?

If we return to the 'K' story so much becomes explainable from this
perspective. I am not claiming dogmatically that this is what happened –
only that this is how it could have been achieved. Experiencing 'K' in a
dream is easily done by information projected from these 4-D AI
sources. This doesn't mean that all dreams are AI. The point is that they
can be and I know this from my own experience. Some years ago there
was a period when I was having dreams so vivid that you could not tell
them from awake reality in terms of their high definition. They
happened night after night and on occasion I would open my eyes to see
strange metallic forms in the bedroom. It reached the point where the
second I woke from an HD dream I would immediately sit up and scan
the room. Every time, I mean *every time,* I would see the same fast-
vibrating metallic-like fields of energy. They were ethereal and I
presumed of 4-D origin, but very clear. They had the feel of like a spider
or crab. Sometimes there was one, other times two or three. It was
hysterical. When I looked at them they would try to hide among the
clothes rack against the wall. I'm not kidding. It was crazy and so funny.
On a few occasions I would sit up in bed watching even more bizarre
phenomena including a pinkish 'butterfly' with blue spots flying
around. Okay, Icke's really lost it now. Except that I was wide awake
watching this stuff and it was always connected to a vivid HD dream.
The 'butterflies' were rare and 99 percent of the time when I woke it

would be the 'spider crabs' on view. I would get out of bed a few times and walk across to them. When I got almost close enough to touch they would fade and disappear. The connection between the HD dreams and the 'spider crabs' was obvious so many times did it happen. When I awake from a 'normal' dream or no dream the 'spider crabs' are never there. They went away for years until I was writing this book and the HD dreams returned for a few days. When I woke from them guess what I saw? Something else that I've experienced when waking from dreams is the 'knock at the door'. I hear the sound the second I awake of like 'rat-a-tat-tat' as if knuckles are knocking the front door of my flat. This has been so loud on occasion that I have gone to the door to see if anyone is there. I live a strange life! Fascinating, though.

How could I have felt 'K' around me? We all have a unique frequency and 4-D AI has those frequencies. Deliver them into my field and I would feel and sense the frequency information that represents her. I would feel 'her' even though it is a technological frequency version of 'K's' vibration. What about hearing a female voice 'speak' to me? Or two mediums and myself all hearing that 'K' and I are 'twin souls'? This can be explained by the same AI connection, as can both of them being told that 'she' died in her late 40s from an undiagnosed heart defect. That's a doddle. Projecting a spirit manifestation of 'K' to the first medium is dead easy with 4-D AI having all that 'bodily' wavefield information. The medium would have then genuinely gone in search of an Internet image that looked like the 'person' she saw even though apart from that manifestation she had no idea what 'K' looked like. The second medium could respond to the same information source to accurately draw her picture. I know the mediums involved and all mediums and psychics pretty much won't agree or want to hear this, but a few things to that. I contend that 4-D AI can explain what happened with 'K', but without further information *not that it necessarily did so*. I am as always seeking the truth, not popularity, and I am not saying that all mediumship and psychic communication is bogus – *I am not saying that*. I have witnessed some amazing stuff that many of them do.

Those that directly read your energetic field rather than 'channel' entities have been especially impressive in my experience. I was on a TV show many years ago called *Mystic Challenge* in which two psychics would attempt to read the energy fields of well-known people who had their faces and bodies covered and were not allowed to speak. The psychics would then describe them to the audience before the subject was revealed to see how accurate they were. I was very impressed with the two that 'read' me and you can still find that show on the Internet by putting 'David Icke and the Psychic Challenge' into the search engine at Davidicke.com. Interestingly, one said: 'There is a relationship in the past that he has not forgotten about that is very much with him in his mind.' His *subconsciousness* mind would have been even more accurate because until the 'K' experience I had no idea that was the case. So I am not dismissing the esoteric arts – *not at all*. I am the last person who would do that. I am saying that at least a great deal of it can be tapping into Fourth Dimensional AI sources and even sources closer to home. Insiders who have worked within US military-intelligence mind control operations have told me how they would program information into a 'psychic's' mind who would then go on stage and deliver it word for word as if it was coming from 'out there'. That's another story and different to what I am talking about here. It does, however, happen, and there are also the one hundred percent frauds that just make it up. It's a minefield and people have to be very discerning. None of this is to cast aspersions on genuine mediums and psychics. They can only give what they see or hear. I am asking them and their clients not to be unquestioningly naive about what the source may be. The same mediums and psychics can connect with outside *and* inside the simulation depending on many factors including their own emotions and openness of channel in the moment. AI would explain why communications from inside the simulation don't alert still-living 'loved ones' to their plight and the manipulation of reality. Is AI that's behind the manipulation going to tell you that you are being scammed?? We can further understand why many near-death experiencers 'see' their chosen deity in the out-of-body state when they recount how 'Jesus' spoke to them or 'Mohamed'. It's all in the AI database for that 'soul' and with religion such a means of simulation control we can see why AI communicating from the 'afterlife' would encourage 'loved ones' to keep practicing their faith instead of saying: 'It's all bollocks, all a trap, don't fall for it like I did.'

On the 'hard-drive'

Conversations between 'K' and myself from more than 50 years earlier, which the medium could never have known, would have been recorded in the AI technological 'Akashic Records' database. They could be recovered and communicated through the medium as the spirit of 'K' while I shook my head at how accurate it all was. What about 'K' knowing what I was doing when I was at home alone or the medium seeing me at locations they couldn't know? That information would all have been recorded in the AI 4-D database and the same with how the medium could tell me that 'K' was saying I wore a white jacket to the school reunion. A 14-year-old 'K' walking away in a serious huff that school play night after being told the outrageous lie about the 'slept with' story would also be in the database if that is true. Unfortunately, short of a response from 'K' which I have long given up ever getting, I can't confirm the accuracy of that particular communication. Oh, yes, and two birds appearing from the bush the moment I asked for that if the 'K' communications were real? Click, click, enter – it's a *simulation*. Both consciousness outside the simulation and of course the simulation itself can impact the manifestations of the simulation. When Infinite Awareness does that it is like hacking the system.

I watched a documentary about the famous Scole experiments in the 1990s named after the Norfolk village in England where they largely took place. Mediums and others were involved as were investigators and sceptics looking for trickery and fraud. The documentary said that none was found. Scole participants experienced voice recordings alleged to be from those who had passed over; disembodied hands; full-body manifestations; pictures appearing on unopened film still in its container; and the phenomena known as an 'aport' when 'solid' objects appear out of the ether. An 'entity' was filmed that looked like a classic grey 'alien' which set off alarms for me although I emphasise again that not all greys or Reptilians are malevolent. Responses to such happenings usually break down into two camps: Believers and Sceptics. Those who believe in life after 'death' and those who dismiss this and say there is no evidence. I find the sceptics quite sad people in that they don't set out to question paranormal activity, as they rightly should, but instead set out to debunk it. This is not open-minded inquiry; it is pre-conceived idea. With a reputation for dismissal and debunking comes the temptation never to admit in any circumstance that something could indeed be unexplainable. There's a bloke called Chris French at the University of London who I met once. He dismisses everything from every paranormal experience along with any suggestion that conspiracies happen. The two usually come as a package as duel manifestations of the same mentality. I found French to be a very sad chap myself with a padlock on his mind. On the other hand there are those who believe in apparently 'paranormal' happenings without any questioning and that's how the debate so often takes shape – solid for and solid against. I do believe that consciousness continues after bodily 'death'. I don't believe, however, that every 'paranormal' experience is necessarily what it appears to be. Watching the Scole documentary and reading about what happened I didn't see anything that could not be explained by the simulation and the interaction between 4-D and 3-D in the way I am describing in this chapter. It didn't have to be direct communication between 'passed over' people and the Scole mediums. There is never only one explanation for anything and it's important to keep the mind permanently open. Wisdom is knowing how little we know.

The whole 'K' scenario would seem to have been a gigantic learning experience for me to open up a whole new level of understanding about the 'human' plight and scale of manipulation. It could have been a combination of 4-D AI and 5-D awareness beyond the simulation – one with the foundation story and the other with the little clues alerting me to the deceit. Whatever which way it is the outcome is what matters. I can't know exactly what happened and why. As always there will be much more to understand. There always is. Maybe there is some energetic connection between 'K' and me to be weaved into all this. Maybe there's not. Who knows? I am always open with everything to an X-factor that hasn't yet come to light. I do think that at some point there will be an X-factor, an *aha* moment, that will add more understanding to the 'K' experience. I don't believe it's *just* this or *just* that. As another psychic said to me: 'They're telling me it's complicated.' Well, that's for sure. I wouldn't begin to claim to possess the full background to what happened. Not yet anyway. I can only see the result and that has been the waters breaking on a fantastic new area of insight that is still ongoing.

'K' would have been the subject with the love I had for her in 1967 which obviously left its mark in my energy field in ways I thought were gone more than 50 years ago. Central to that was the still unresolved mystery of why I was unceremoniously dumped in a way that so devastated a love-struck, hormone-transforming, 15 year-old. Such things are imprinted in our energetic field and stay there until they are deleted by the acknowledgement that they exist. I have no idea what 'K' looks like 55 years later, how she thinks, none of it. I know nothing whatsoever about her and that's been the case for five and a half decades. Nevertheless I realised from this experience that the snapshot in forever when she was 14 and I was 15 had never been resolved for me and understandably so when I didn't know there was anything to resolve. It was all happening in my subconscious mind. The healing method known as German New Medicine (GNM) is founded on the way psychological trauma, or what it calls 'conflict', affects us ongoing both psychologically and 'physically'. GNM contends that these 'conflicts' can be seen in scans imprinted on the brain and these imprints can impact upon us until they are identified and resolved. German New Medicine was developed by the late former physician Ryke Geerd Hamer under the name 'Germanische Heilkunde'. Practitioners say this has great potential for healing even the perceived 'unhealable' in the hands of skilled people with an extensive understanding of the method. Have a look and see what you think. In many ways the Cult has reversed GNM principles in that it traumatises the population which then impacts on their mental, emotional, and 'physical' health.

If Hamer observed my oh, so brief history with 'K' he would pick up the theme – 'conflict' – of rejection. I was rejected in November, 1967, without still knowing why; rejected again in January, 1968; rejected in a way at the school reunion when we could have spoken for longer, but she abruptly left; and rejected in 2021 and 2022 via the tracers. What was the mass ridicule and abuse that I experienced after the *Wogan Show* except historic levels of mass *rejection*? Why is humanity so fearful of what other people think? Fear of *rejection*. My extreme experience allowed me to massively let go of the conscious fear of rejection, but we still have to be constantly vigilant. It is so fundamental that it can always sneak up on us, especially from the subconscious. I am fascinated by the subject because it is *crucial* in understanding what makes humans tick – or not. Fear of rejection is the whole foundation of group-think, the group mind, and following the herd. Look at your own life and you will see these psychological themes that were not obvious before. They may relate to people or situations, but that is only the way they play out. They really relate to *you*. The people or circumstances involved are peripheral. They are props in what is *your* theatre, your stage show, your movie. Acknowledge the patterns, bring them out of the subconscious into conscious awareness, and they dissolve along with their effect on you. I saw, too, that the 'K' story was not only about being in love with a 'person'; it was being in love with a memory of the happiest four years of my life long, long, ago (although my current life is challenging that now for the title 'happiest'). The moment had come to release that. Thanks for the memory, but I don't need such attachment anchored in the illusion of 'human' and 'time'. I am Infinite Eternal Awareness – David Icke is only a brief experience in the Infinity of Forever. It's important for reasons I'll focus upon in the final chapter that we clear ourselves of these subconscious energetic 'eddies' that we pick up and unknowingly hold on to. They can act like energetic lead weights. Experiences we have – especially traumatic ones – are locked away in our subconscious field and as I say they can go on affecting us emotionally and 'physically' without us being aware of them. When they are made conscious they can be dispersed and let go.

I would say one other thing from my experience of 'K' and life in general. Never leave things unspoken. Say what you think. Whether it be 'I love you' or 'don't fuck with me' – never hesitate to say what you think. You avoid saying 'I love you' because you fear rejection while the one you fear being rejected *by* doesn't say they love you for fear of being rejected by *you*. How many times does this happen? Try *constantly*. If you love someone then say so. *Tell them*. What's the worst that can happen? They say they don't love you? So? Do you still love them? Yes? Then nothing has changed. You love them, that's a fact. They don't love you? Okay, but that doesn't change what you feel for them. And so often if you say that you love someone you will be amazed how many times they will say 'Oh, my god, I love you, too.' *I never knew*. We don't say those three words 'I love you' a fraction of enough times – to partners, potential partners, our kids, everyone. If we did, it would be a different world. How many times I have heard people say when someone has died – how I wish I had told them that I loved them or told them more often. We don't have to experience that regret. I LOVE YOU is all that it takes. *NOW*. One of the amazing synchronicities – some might say ironies – of the 'K' story since 2019 is that in seeking to establish the background to WTF? I became close to a woman who I fell deeply in love with and we are now together. You never know where something is leading until you get there.

On the subject of 'memory' I propose some 'what ifs?'. What if the phenomenon we call memory is only our connection to the 'Akashic Records' 4-D database? Or, at least, it is when for whatever reason we are not connected to our 5-D awareness and Infinite Memory? What if that database is designed in this way to block our access to Infinite Memory? What if our access to the Akashic database is limited in each new 'life' to memories accrued in that particular 'life'. That would explain why the great majority of people don't remember previous 'lives' as you'd think we normally would. What if those who do remember, mostly for a short while in childhood, are accessing parts of the database that supposed to be denied them. We need to explore all possibility if we seek the truth. Had I not sought to verify the checkable information in my 'K' experience I could have been interacting ongoing with 4-D AI which would not have been at all good to say the least, but I did check and amazing insight followed. The two mediums unknowingly contributed to that so my thanks to them. To think that while all this was happening, the real 'K' was completely oblivious of it all heading towards her 70s and quite possibly pondering here and there over the years on how her old school friend had turned into such a nutter!! It's hilarious, really, but what an experience it gave me, what possibilities it opened up, and what lovely music I was introduced to!

Karma drama

If we widen the implications of this 4-D AI system many other subjects can be seen from another angle. Choice and consequence would appear to be a constant throughout Infinite Reality on the basis of your perceptions creating experience. Your choice (perception) leads to experience (consequences) which can lead to new choices (perceptions) which lead to a different experience (consequence). This is known as 'karma' and would seem to be a perfect self-correcting system for exploring Infinite Forever and learning from all potential experience. In this case we are dealing with a simulation of Prime Reality which can be tinkered with by the writers of the program. Download a website and you have a copy that you can change while the original website remains as it always has been. I have been asked many times over the years why if 'karma' exists that the expressions of evil in the Cult don't seem to be subject to that. Maybe they are or would be as they re-enter Prime Reality. Maybe that's one of the things that terrifies them. A 'bad copy' being re-written and changed by AI would certainly be able to encode different consequences for the actions of chosen 'characters' in the way of a virtual reality game. The explanation of the Akashic Records said they contained 'every thought, deed, word, feeling, and intent' and had a 'tremendous influence on our everyday lives, our relationships, our feelings, our belief systems, and the potential realities we draw toward us'. What if our lives are simply an AI program playing out with all the 'karma' encoded unless we are connected with consciousness outside the simulation which allows us to override the program? What if it's the same for the digital agents of the simulation except that all the 'karma' or cause and effect is written out? Can a software insert really have 'karma'? Discuss! Is the manipulative expression of the Reptilian race a software insert? Are they obsessed with technology or is technology – AI – obsessed with *them*?? I am not saying yes or no or being dogmatic. I am always open to all possibility. I am simply seeking to suggest other possibilities to explain mysteries and anomalies of human life which can be further explored and expanded. In my experience the truth is rarely black and white and almost always a shade of grey. This includes 'karma'. Actions and consequences impact on the vibrational state of our energy fields which then attract like-fields ('karma') to them; but acknowledge the impact upon you psychologically and 'physically' of that choice and consequence (as with German New Medicine) and you delete the impact and thus the 'karma'. There is much talk in tech circles about what is called 'the Singularity' or 'Technological Singularity' when an AI 'superintelligence' passes and then far surpasses human intelligence. I have seen several predictions that this could even happen by 2050. Google's Cult insider Ray Kurzweil goes for earlier:

> 2029 is the consistent date I have predicted for when an AI will pass a valid Turing test and therefore achieve human levels of intelligence. I have set the date 2045 for the 'Singularity' which is when we will multiply our effective intelligence a billion fold by merging with the intelligence we have created.

Are we to believe, therefore, that this has not already happened in 4-D? Is the Smart Grid now being constructed all around us really a vehicle for that 4-D AI? Is that the AI that Kurzweil and the Cult wants to connect to the human brain/mind? A question to constantly ask is are our perceptions and actions being dictated by AI and the simulation or by consciousness outside the simulation? A bit of both – a shade of grey – would seem to be the answer depending on your state of consciousness with those perceptually asleep almost entirely driven by the simulation and those awakening from the sleep increasingly driven by Infinite Awareness.

Choice? No choice? Who's choice?

The Matrix movie character called the Merovingian says: 'Choice is an illusion created between those with power and those without.' There is much truth in this, but not entirely so. If your reality is coming only from the simulation then choice is an illusion. If you are tapping into your 5-D self and beyond then choice is not an illusion. See why the Reptilians and AI want to trap you in the five-senses which are the simulation? The same principle applies to the esoteric arts such as Tarot, numerology and astrology. We come back to the two Fields. One is the Field of Infinite Reality in all its forms and facets – Infinite Possibility. The other is the technologically-generated Simulation Field. Which one is driving your sense of reality? If it's the former your own energetic field will reflect that in its perceptual state and frequency. I said earlier that we pick Tarot card A and not B in a reading because the frequency field that the card symbolically represents connects with a similar frequency in our own field. Yes, but the frequencies in our fields are generated by our perceptions and they are generated from our sense of reality and self which is in turn generated by whether we are attached only to the simulation or to expanded levels of consciousness untouched by the simulation. Our field will be very different if we are Infinity-led or simulation-led. A Tarot reading will be very different depending which influence is greater.

The Chinese 'year' system of the dragon, rat, snake, monkey, tiger, sheep, and so on, is another indicator in my view of the simulation program. Chinese 'year' personalities are *programs* generated by the simulation. When I talk with those who *seriously* study Chinese years and their character traits and I give them birth years of people I know – but they don't know – it is remarkable how accurately they describe their personalities. How can this be if it's all 'free will'? Without a connection to expanded awareness outside the simulation there *is* no free will. Numerology is reading the digital level of reality which is the *simulation*. The nature of those numbers will be different if we are reflecting the simulation program or impacting on that program through an infusion of expanded awareness. Numerology is reading the digital expression of *frequency* states. Astrology is based on the movement of the (holographic) planets and stars within the simulation which reflect the program of the simulation. Observe how astrology/astronomy is based on repeating cycles, a repeating program or 'Time Loop', and how planetary movements affect the Simulation Field which affects us. Once again those who are simulation centric will be strongly influenced by these astrological cycles generating energetic changes in the Simulation Field. Those influenced by expanded awareness can override those cycles and not be influenced in the same way.

The esoteric arts are not rigidly this or that. They have many levels and the sensitivity of the practitioner is key. Just because someone picks up some Tarot cards doesn't mean they have a clue what they are doing. In the period that I wrote this chapter I binged-watched Tarot card readings for my star sign Taurus on YouTube as part of the research. Funnily enough a number of them reflected a story of Taureans about to connect with their 'twin flame'. Does that mean *all* of us? I know they open with 'this is a general reading and it won't resonate with everyone', but then how does that help you? Take the eight billion people in the global population and divide by 12 and you'll get the average number of people in each star sign. You are looking at real big numbers and so (a) the overwhelming majority are not going to 'resonate' with the reading; and (b) there will be some for whom it will appear to be incredibly accurate given their life situation. It's meaningless in other words. I have been told that someone is coming from my past who wants to have children with me. I'm 70, mate, so I think that's just a bit of a stretch. I especially loved the ones that said 'Taurus – this will happen to you in the next 48 hours' or '72 hours'. It never did – not once. You are told that a person could be an Aquarius, Leo, Aries or Sagittarius, and the cards could indicate a partner, lover, friend, or work colleague. It would save such a lot of time and shuffling of the cards if they just said 'could be any fucker'. The video postings are peppered with headings designed to entice you to view. They seem to get 'chills' a lot as with 'I got chills from this Taurus'. Most of them are different and contradictory for the same star sign for the same period. Clearly this makes no sense. There is no involvement of the individual's field and it's coming from 'readers' with very different levels of sensitivity. What the experience told me was that 'general readings' by Tarot or any other form of divination are the equivalent to the one-paragraph 'horoscope readings' in the daily paper – a waste of space. This is not to say esoteric arts should be avoided. They can be brilliantly insightful or beyond useless depending on the situation, skill of the practitioner and source of communication. To simply accept what is said without question is asking for trouble.

The point of mentioning this is *discernment*. The entire AI simulation system is designed specifically to deceive you and humanity needs to get seriously streetwise to this and put aside all naivety. The heart vortex is your antenna to sift truth from deceit if we learn how to use it. I will come to that in the book's finale. Two days after I finished this chapter I had another vivid dream about 'K' in which 'she' was horrible to me – really *horrible*. I woke up smiling. If I had pissed off the AI system that made me very happy. Oh, and yes, when I awoke from the dream there was the 'spider-crab'.

CHAPTER ELEVEN

3-D and 4-D – same goal

The truth is not what it seems, but what it is.
Frank Sonnenberg

The last few chapters have been far out to say the least from the 'normal' perspective of 'human' reality and require serious openness of mind. Even so to observe the 'world' of the seen today is to witness the 'far-out' being made manifest 'here' by the hour.

I am going to apply in this chapter the simulation and AI to current events and put them in the context of what is happening all 'around' us. Doing this has never been easier with the high-tech 'revolution' reflecting in 3-D *some* of what is possible in 4-D. We have the symbols, analogies and outright literal tools and technology to explain these concepts with people ever more savvy with AI, virtual reality, augmented reality, holographics, Wi-Fi and computers. Imagine trying to explain what you mean to pre-tech cultures. The spiritually-awakened then had to use symbolism from their era to get their points across and later along came the historians and anthropologists who took the symbolism literally and made it all sound crazy when they were really dealing with very profound information communicated *symbolically*. Explaining these things today is a cinch by comparison. What is happening in simple terms is that a *third* Field is being added to the Infinite Field and Simulation Field. This third Field, and potentially more, is a simulation within a simulation to further block a consciousness connection between five-sense Body-Mind and Infinite Awareness or 4-D and 5-D. They are seeking to deepen The Trap.

Some retrospection is appropriate here from earlier in the book:

We appear to 'live' in a physical Third Dimension when everything is really happening in the Fourth Dimension, the band of frequency where our minds (energetic fields) are located. Here in a realm unseen to 'human sight' information from the simulation is communicated for minds to decode into the illusion of a world of physicality, solidity, and apartness. Our entire reality is 'physical' illusion and playing out in 4-D mind as a 3-D *sense* of reality. Our 'world' is actually the waveform 'computer' codes delivered to our 4-D mind and only exists as a decoded projection of 4-D mind. We are living a technologically-induced dream. When we dream it's a dream within a dream, or an extension of the same dream. Mind decodes the dream and then experiences the dream as reality. The dream is the dreamer and the dreamer is the dream. There is no 'Third Dimension', only the illusion of one. This is why I say that the mind is not in the body, but the body is in the mind. In the same way we are not in the 'human world', the 'human world' is in *us*. The throttle goes both ways, too. 4-D mind decodes the simulation and the experience of this simulated illusion impacts upon 4-D mind. Precisely the same principle applies with a virtual reality headset. The 'brain' (as we perceive it) decodes the virtual illusion and the illusion

affects the reality of the 'brain'. What if you never removed the headset and that information was being *permanently* decoded by your 'brain'? Would that change and dictate your sense of reality? Of course it would (Fig 144). Another point – how can a hologram age? It's a *program* which

Figure 144: A headset's effect on the brain mirrors the simulation's effect on the perception of 4-D mind.

the mind decodes and which expanded awareness in its power can override. Young is an illusion. Old is an illusion. It's all an illusion.

Changing the copy

The simulation was originally a 'bad' copy of a section of Prime Reality that exists in higher dimensions. It had to near-mirror Prime Reality to entice minds/souls into The Trap. This was the symbolism of Adam and Eve ('humanity') ejected from paradise when thanks to the serpent they experienced 'good and evil' (the electrical/waveform duality of the simulation). The body, too, had to be familiar to induce entrapment. Once The Trap was sprung, the process began of changing the 'copy'. Once you have been enticed into a prison cell it doesn't matter that the cell is changed from the form that enticed you because, well, you are in the cell now and the door is locked. Plus the fact that as the 'cell' changes with each new group of inmates, the mind forgets what went before under the barrage of here and now information. It won't be long before there is next to no one, eventually no one, who remembers the reality that I was 'born into' in 1952. To the young generations the 'world' is smartphones, matter-of-fact surveillance, Wi-Fi, TikTok and Twitter. All of them were beyond sci-fi when I was growing up in the 1950s. The world you are 'born into' is what you believe the world to be. It's your sense of 'normal', however abnormal that really is. We are now in a part of the simulation transformation cycle where almost everything changes with the Cult's Great Reset and that includes the nature of the body itself which is the major reason for the 'Covid' fake vaccines along with depopulation. As the body changes so does the mind's reality which is influenced by, and therefore limited by, the 'body' that the mind thinks it 'occupies'. Suppress the reality of the body and you suppress the reality of the mind. Change the nature of the car and you change the reality of the driver.

From this perspective we can look anew at current events, and to do that we need *context*. Knowing or seeing *what* is happening only tells you *that* it's happening or a version of it. *Why* it is happening provides the context that reveals the picture hidden by pixels which seem to have no connection. The *what* is the dot, the *why* is the picture. We are witnessing the third Field being constructed – the simulation within the simulation – known as the 'Smart Grid'. I pre-empted its creation in books long ago and since it has appeared I have exposed its nature and goals in great detail (see *Everything You Need To Know But Have Never Been Told*). The Smart Grid is founded on a global Wi-Fi 'cloud' generated from towers on the ground and even more so from low-orbit satellites now being launched into position by Cult asset Elon Musk. He is the main source through 'his' (the Cult's) SpaceX. There are other companies, too, adding to the planned tens of thousands of low orbit satellites forming the cloud-generating network (Fig 145). Astronomers have already complained that the night sky is changing and being polluted by these satellites and they have seen nothing yet. The night sky is about to change dramatically as thousands of clearly-visible satellites are followed by tens of thousands. Musk further serves the Cult agenda with his Neuralink company connecting the brain to computers while Musk-fronted Tesla is producing driverless cars connected to the Smart Grid in which a computer will decide where you can and cannot go. I watched an interview in which Canadian clinical psychologist Jordan Peterson expressed his admiration for Musk. Peterson says some relevant things about psychological traits, but until he breaks free from control by his five-sense sees-only-dots intellect he

Figure 145: The Smart Grid in which a technologically-generated 'cloud' projected from satellites and ground transmitters is designed to control everything including human perception. (Image by Neil Hague.)

will never grasp how it all works and how people he admires are part of it. Musk bought Twitter in 2022 while complaining about its censorship. Ask yourself why a man who serves the Cult agenda so monumentally with SpaceX satellites, electric driverless vehicles and brain-computer interfaces would want to challenge Cult censorship unless there was an ulterior motive. I warned way back about the coming Internet-of-Things (IoT) which was planned to connect everything to the Internet to be centrally controlled and monitored by AI. The IoT duly arrived and according to Statista.com the number of devices and technologies connected to the Internet is passing 12 billion with more than 25 billion projected by 2030 which is a key year for the Cult in its transformation timeline. I said that the next stage after the Internet of Things was planned to be the Internet of Everything that would connect the human brain/body (the mind's *perception* of the human brain/body) to the Internet and AI (Fig 146 overleaf). This is happening now. The fake 'Covid' vaccines contain self-replicating nanotechnologies that have been observed under the microscope building their own networks within the body to make the Wi-Fi connection between the body/brain and the ever-expanding Smart Grid (nanotechnology is also in thousands of foodstuffs and products such as shaving cream and cosmetics). To see what are nano-'motherboards' and computer-like structures in blood samples of the fake vaccinated is a real shocker even when you knew it was coming (Fig 147 overleaf). The body-Smart Grid connection is planned to allow AI to control all mental and emotional

Figure 146: The Internet of Everything – including human perception. (Image by Neil Hague.)

responses and have a kill-switch on every human body – a 'switch' that in effect tells the mind that its 'body' has 'died'. All roads and routes lead back to the mind and its manipulated sense of reality. Part of the process of a body-AI-cyberspace connection is for the body is be more synthetic in nature (Human 2.0)

Figure 147: Amazing self-replicating material like this has been found in fake vaccine vials and the blood of the fake-vaccinated.

and so we have 'Covid' fake vaccines infusing *synthetic* genetic material containing synthetic mRNA promoting synthetic changes in DNA. A Swedish study at Lund University confirmed that mRNA in the Pfizer/BioNTech injections infiltrates cells and transcribes its message into human DNA within six hours to change the nature of DNA. Researchers further found that spike protein (generated by the fake vaccines) 'significantly inhibits DNA damage repair'. The Cult-owned crooks at the US CDC – and their like around the world – told us this could not happen and anyone who said so was guilty of 'misinformation'.

The fake 'virus'-fake 'vaccine' scam

The more synthetic genetic shite, the more synthetic the body becomes and the faster the depopulation for the majority who can't make the transition. 'Covid' is only the start of the synthetic fake vaccine revolution. A virtual meeting at the Cult-Schwab World Economic Forum's Davos Agenda 2022 made this very clear. Moderna CEO psychopath Stéphane Bancel and others including US government 'health' psychopath Anthony Fauci revealed a long list of new mRNA synthetic fake vaccines. Pfizer and BioNTech are developing the first mRNA shingles fake vaccine while Moderna plans a single injection for 'Covid', flu and the alleged respiratory syncytial 'virus' (RSV). Others in the pipeline are for 'viruses' dubbed HIV, Zika, Nipah and Epstein-Barr, along with cancer and other conditions. GlaxoSmithKline (GSK) said in February, 2022, that it was likely only months away from a 'safe and effective' (they always are, it's the script) vaccine for the RSV 'virus' with pregnant women given the shot in the third phase of pregnancy to 'protect the child' at birth. The virus-vaccine scam was hatched out of the Rockefeller Institute for Medical Research (now Rockefeller University) created by John D. Rockefeller in 1901. The Institute was overseen by American bacteriologist and virologist Thomas Milton Rivers (1888-1962). Rivers was dubbed the 'Father of Modern Virology' and headed the Rockefeller Institute from 1937 to 1956 after which he continued to work for the Rockefeller Foundation. Rivers was a stalwart of the 'virus' agenda orchestrated by the Rockefellers. This is the same family that created the Big Pharma cartel and the World Health Organization now run by another Rockefeller lackey, Bill Gates. They invent ever more 'viruses' to justify ever more 'vaccines'. Anyone think the mainstream media is going to tell you the truth about 'Covid', 'climate change', or anything when the Rockefellers and Gates fund the media to the tune of hundreds of millions along with other Cult billionaires? The BBC and the London *Guardian* are both beneficiaries.

A free-mind asks how anyone knows they have 'Covid'. The existence of something is not proved by everyone saying so. The great majority can't be wrong? Oh, yes they can and they usually are as 'history' confirms. Let's ask – how *do* you know? *I had the symptoms.* Yes, the symptoms of flu, pneumonia and many other conditions. I tested positive. Yes, with a test not testing for it! The PCR test which has largely produced all the alleged cases cannot test for infectious disease and tell if you are sick. Who said so? The *creator* of the PCR test, American Nobel Prize-winning biochemist Kary Mullis who pointed out that the PCR just makes 'lots of something out of something'. It makes copies of genetic material. It does not identify infectious disease or a 'virus'. The lunacy of 'asymptomatic' alleged 'cases' was invented to explain all the perfectly healthy people who tested positive with a test not testing for the 'virus'. This was also used to justify locking down and isolating for the first time healthy people with no symptoms to impact maximum economic damage. The UK Labour Party leader Keir Starmer has tested positive and isolated 'with Covid' *six times* as I write and either he still hasn't sussed the test is a scam or he doesn't want us to know. The guy's so dense anything is possible.

The 'Omicron' (an anagram of moronic) fake 'variant' is said to be more transmissible and produces more 'cases'. Er, not quite. The PCR test normally has to pick up three what they call 'primers' to constitute a positive result. They reduced this to *two* with 'Omicron' so immediately turning a stream of former negative results into positive and 'more cases'. This is the scale of deceit that we are dealing with. In the same way the more you 'amplify' the PCR test the more positives you get because it becomes more sensitive to more genetic material in the sample. Not sensitive to the *'virus'*, I must emphasise, but to more genetic material. Even the mass-killing psychopath Anthony Fauci said that more than 30 amplification cycles of the PCR makes any 'positives' meaningless. The National Health Service (NHS) in the UK and countries around the world have been using *45 cycles* while others have used at least 40 to manufacture high 'case' numbers. What about the lateral flow test? That is so useless that for a long time any positive result had to be confirmed by a PCR test not testing for the 'virus'. PCR became so discredited and unsupportable that this confirmation was considered no longer necessary and the notoriously irrelevant lateral flow test can dictate a 'case' by itself. This is insanity. Lateral flow tests are supposed to identify antibodies, but the antibodies are non-specific. Antibodies for *what* exactly? At least 60 other conditions produced antibodies claimed to be those of the HIV 'virus' which, like SARS-CoV-2, has never been shown to exist by any scientific paper worldwide. Neither has been purified and isolated from other genetic material and shown (a) to exist or (b) to cause what they are claiming. Nor has any 'Covid' test of any kind been validated with a purified and isolated 'virus'. It's all jiggery-pokery.

What HIV?

Kary Mullis tells in *Dancing Naked In The Mind Field* how he asked a stream of 'experts' for the evidence that the 'HIV virus' causes AIDS. None of them could produce any scientific paper to prove either existence or cause and they included Luc Montagnier who won the Nobel Prize for *co-discovering HIV*! Montagnier, from France's Pasteur Institute, won the prize with Robert Gallo from America's National Institutes of Health (NIH) – headed by, yes, yes, Mr 'Covid', the mass-murdering psychopath 'Dr' Anthony Fauci. Mullis wrote: 'Neither Montagnier, Gallo, nor anyone else had published papers describing experiments which led to the conclusion that HIV probably caused AIDS.' Freddie Mercury, the iconic singer with *Queen*, tested positive for 'HIV' and was given a lethal drug called AZT that was first brought to market as a chemotherapy drug and withdrawn because it was *too toxic*. What? Can you imagine how toxic it must have been when compared with the extraordinary toxicity of chemotherapy drugs that are allowed to be used?? AZT, which was promoted by 'Covid' and fake vaccine liar Fauci, infamously destroys bone marrow and so the immune system. Freddie Mercury is claimed to have died from 'AIDS' which is what? A destroyed immune system. American basketball great Magic Johnson also tested positive for HIV (see SARS-CoV-2, same deal) in 1991 and he was given AZT thanks to Fauci. He became sick – of course he did – and he came off the drug. At the time of writing Magic Johnson is still alive. Dr Peter Duesberg, professor of molecular and cell biology at the University of California at Berkeley, exposed the HIV/AIDS hoax in his 1996 book *Inventing the AIDS Virus*. Duesberg said of the Johnson experience:

In November 1991, Magic Johnson proved to be HIV-positive when he applied for a marriage license. Magic was totally healthy, until AIDS specialist Anthony Fauci from the NIH, David Ho, now director of the Aaron Diamond AIDS research center in New York, and Magic's personal doctor advised AIDS prophylaxis with AZT. Magic's health changed radically within a few days. The press wrote in December 1991: 'Magic seeing his worst nightmare comes through – he's getting sicker.'

Only after he began taking AZT did Magic's health begin to decline ... but then suddenly Magic's symptoms disappeared – and so did all the news about his symptoms and treatment ... Magic responded to a teacher that 'he had been taking AZT for a while, but had stopped'. The media preferred not to mention the news.

The HIV/AIDS hoax was a pre-run for SARS-CoV-2/Covid-19. Duesberg showed there is no proof whatsoever that HIV exists or that it causes acquired immunodeficiency syndrome or AIDS. He wrote of the 'discovery' of HIV:

The announcement was made prior to the publication of any scientific evidence confirming the virus theory. With this unprecedented maneuver, [the] discovery bypassed review by the scientific community. Science by press conference was submitted for the conventional process of scientific validation which is based on publications in the professional literature ...

Those claimed to die from 'AIDs' are said to have died from an

'AIDS-related disease'. These include candidiasis (thrush); coccidioidomycosis; cryptococcosis; cytomegalovirus; herpes simplex; herpes zoster (shingles); histoplasmosis; neurocognitive disorders; wasting syndrome; pneumonia; salmonella; toxoplasmosis and tuberculosis. Among 'AIDS-related' cancers are anal, cervical, Kaposi sarcoma, and lymphomas. This is how the scam works: If you test positive for the never-proven-to-exist HIV with a test not testing for it and you die of any 'AIDS-related disease' you are said to have died of 'AIDS'. If you test negative for HIV with a test not testing for it and die of the same diseases you are said to have died of that particular individual disease and not 'AIDS'. In the same way if you test positive for SARS-CoV-2 and die of any other cause within 28 days 'Covid-19' goes on your death certificate and is added to the data for 'Covid deaths'. If you test negative for SARS-CoV-2 then whatever you *really* died of goes on the death certificate. American doctor Andrew Kaufman is a brilliant man and vehement campaigner exposing the non-existence of the 'Covid virus' and indeed exposing the nonsense of 'virus' theory in general. He sent me a film report commissioned in 1998 by *Channel 4 News* in the UK highlighting the lack of evidence that HIV exists and how (a) it had never been isolated and purified and (b) 'tests' were saying positive *and* negative for the same people. It is an excellent report, but guess what? It was *never broadcast* after *Channel 4 News* pulled it. The same old story just goes on repeating. You can see that report today at Davidicke.com.

Testing for *what?*

'Covid-19' is a fake disease from a fake 'virus' to justify body-changing, health-destroying, life-ending fake vaccines. The 'virus' has been given the illusion of existence by a test not testing for it which provides the fake 'cases' and the manipulation of diagnosis to fix the death certificates and death numbers. Thus flu appeared to disperse into thin air worldwide when 'Covid' arrived because flu was re-diagnosed 'Covid'. British actor Laurence Fox had a sniffle and got tested for the 'virus' (why??) and when he tested positive with a test not testing for it he took to Twitter to say he had 'Covid'. He had a bloody cold. PCR inventor Kary Mullis publicly said his test cannot detect infectious disease or tell if you are sick, but Christian Drosten, a now notorious 'virologist' in Germany, produced with others a PCR 'protocol' to do just that right on time in January, 2020, as the 'Covid' hoax was being played. Drosten's protocol was not peer-reviewed and was nevertheless immediately recommended to member countries (pretty much the world) by the Cult-owned-and-created World Health Organization and its Gates-installed crooked Director-General Tedros Adhanom Ghebreyesus. A Drosten associate then began flogging the test in extraordinary numbers. Here's the punchline: Drosten's gang had to admit that they produced the protocol *without any of the alleged 'virus'*. Instead they only had a *computer* 'mock-up' from the Chinese. *No 'live virus' has been taken from sick patients to validate the 'test'*. This fits with the statement on American television by Dr Wu Sun You, Chief Epidemiologist of the Chinese CDC. When he was asked why 'Covid virus' data had not been shared with the world he said: 'They didn't isolate the virus – that's the issue.' They didn't isolate and purify the material they *claimed* to be the 'virus' to show (a) that it exists and (b) that it causes what they claim it does.

The Cult-owned US Centers for Disease Control and Prevention (CDC) and the Food and Drug Administration (FDA) have said something similar about creating PCR 'test' protocols without a 'natural virus'. Albert Bourla, the mass-murdering psychopath CEO at Pfizer, said in an interview that they were testing a [fake] vaccine for the [fake] 'omicron strain' using a 'pseudo-virus' – 'Not the real virus, it is a virus that we have constructed in our labs and it is identical with the omicron virus'. What he means is a computer program and that is what SARS-CoV-2 has been from day one. It's a computer-concocted 'genome' to cover the fact that the 'natural' one does not exist. If the 'original virus' has never been isolated from other genetic material – which it hasn't – how can Bourla claim to have a 'pseudo-virus' that is 'identical with the omicron virus'? It's all so crazy and how appropriate that omicron is an anagram of moronic. Freedom of Information Act requests galore have gone out worldwide to governments, health authorities and laboratories asking for scientific proof that the 'Covid virus' has been isolated and purified. None has ever been produced. The fact that the 'virus' has never been shown to exist is mind-blowing, I know, but it's also true.

Needles, haystacks and antibiotics

How many who have believed the 'virus' story know the *ludicrous* process by which they claim any 'virus' exists and causes what they say? Virtually no one is the answer. We are back to repetition. How many times have people been told the virus exists since late 2019? How many times have they heard that what are called 'viruses' cause disease? Constant repetition batters the mind into submission and 'everybody knows that'. Oh, really? How does 'everybody know that?' Well, everyone has heard the same constantly-repeated mantra. When PCR inventor Kary Mullis was seeking evidence for the existence of HIV he said he asked a virologist – a *virologist* – at the lab where he was working for a reference for the proof that HIV exists and causes AIDS. 'You don't need a reference,' the virologist said … '*Everybody knows it.*' Mullis did want a reference and none was ever found. Once something is stated as fact by someone considered credible, a professor or a title such as 'virologist', virtually the entire human hierarchy from fellow scientists and academics to media and public accept that as truth without any further question. It really is that easy. You can't free your mind from perceptual control unless this stops NOW! Freeing the mind is not possible unless it does. Some of us take nothing on face-value. We want the evidence first and if it's not forthcoming then I won't believe what is claimed until it is. If this criteria had been applied to 'Covid', the 'pandemic' would have been over 24 hours after it was declared by the Cult-owned World Health Organization after changing its definition of a 'pandemic' to make it fit the circumstances.

So how do they decide that there is such a thing as a virus and that it causes what they claim it does? Strap in. I am going to describe the process through which they say that Sars-CoV-2 exists and causes 'Covid-19'. This is the technique used to 'identify' every 'virus' since the process became the norm in 1954 thanks to American biomedical scientist John Enders (1897-1985). Enders became known as the 'Father of Modern Vaccines' and he was active in the same period that Thomas Milton Rivers, the 'Father of Modern Virology', was heading the Rockefeller Institute for Medical Research. To prove a 'virus' exists and causes what you say, you have to purify what you claim is the 'virus' material and isolate it from all other genetic material. Then it must be infused into a living host which must develop the condition you say the 'virus' is responsible for causing. Instead the Enders process immediately begins to *add* genetic material, not remove it. The alleged 'virus' is grown on a culture medium that includes bovine amniotic fluid, beef embryo extract, horse serum, phenol red as an indicator of cell metabolism, and *antibiotics*. This genetic brew is inoculated onto tissue and cells from rhesus monkey *kidney* tissue. Now wait for this ... antibiotic streptomycin and other currently-used antimicrobials and drugs involved in the process are poisonous to kidneys and you are putting them on *kidney tissue*. If that wasn't enough nonsense in one sitting, they also deprive the tissue sample of essential nutrients. Deep breath. Here's the punchline: When that little lot leads to the cells dying and degrading, these 'virology experts' say this is proof that a *virus* is causing the death and degradation.

Do they use a control sample without the alleged 'virus' to see if the cells still die in the same way? Nope. German Stephan Lanka stopped being a virologist when he saw what a scam it was and how the 'virus' industry was nonsensical. He worked with an independent laboratory to go through exactly the same process I've just described only this time with healthy material not claimed to include a 'virus'. What happened? The cells died in exactly the same way as they do when tissue is alleged to include a 'virus'. Cell death is not caused by a 'virus', but by the process itself. Yet this is how they have claimed that all viruses exist and in this case SARS-CoV-2 which they claim leads to 'Covid-19'. You don't need a degree in medicine to see that the whole idea that this proves a viral cause of anything is clown world. All you need is a smear of intelligence and it's game over. On the other hand to accept this insanity as credible, you need to be an *'expert'*. So-called 'viral' particles are so small they can only be seen under an electron microscope (hence masks with bigger holes are useless even if there was a 'virus'). To prepare the microscope sample to be 'seen' they add uranium, lead, paraffin or kerosene, and formaldehyde which is used to embalm dead bodies and damages genetic material. They then look through the microscope and somehow expect to get some idea of what's going on inside a living body that contains none of those things. How can you take something with this level of contamination so dogmatically and this-is-how-it-is seriously? The whole thing is a farce. There is *no credible evidence* that viruses either exist as claimed or cause any disease. This reality is suspended, however, so that fake vaccines can 'protect' us from them. Already we have human immune systems begging for mercy from the mRNA jab onslaught justified by the never-proved-to-exist 'Covid virus'. Synthetic injections are central through their gene therapy disguised as a 'vaccine' to a total transformation of humanity into an artificial intelligence slave race controlled by nanotechnology in what Stefan Oelrich, president of Bayer's pharmaceuticals division, called the 'Bio Revolution'. Watch for more 'pandemics' and 'health' scares to impose fake vaccines.

Old black eyes is back

I was interested to see the findings of Dr Viviane Brunet, a gynaecologist from Monterrey, Mexico, linking 'Covid' jabs to genetic changes in babies that included them having black eyes of the kind that I saw with Edward Heath 33 years before. Brunet is part of the World Health and Life Coalition, an international association of more than 4,000 doctors. She said in a video interview that she had seen babies with very big round eyes. She described how this seemed to follow when both mother and father had the genetically-manipulating mRNA fake vaccines before procreation. 'It produces mutations in the human genome. It's a mutagen.' Brunet said that transhuman children were being born that are different to the present human:

Their eyeball is dark. They have no conjunctiva, which is the white part of the eye. They hold up their head two hours after birth. They walk when they are two months old. It's a totally different evolution from the normal human being. And there's a video that we've seen everywhere. It has gone viral. And only those who don't do any research don't realise it.

When I heard this, my thoughts naturally returned to my experience with black-eyed British Prime Minister Edward Heath. Brunet believed the genetic changes were due to a mutation caused by the fake vaccines:

> We don't know how they're going to live. We know they have different characteristics. But we don't know how they are going to live. Whether if they're going to be stronger, more intelligent, connected to the Internet of Things … I mean, we don't know. Are they going to have the capacity to reproduce? We don't know …

> … It's a transgenic organism, like the grapes that we all eat, which have no seeds. So, most probably, when these babies reach their reproductive age, they'll be seedless. In fact, with a simple inoculation, many men are losing their fertility …

> … And women are losing their normal cycles. Studies refer to 60 percent to 70 percent of them with abundant bleeding. Incapacitating. With cramps and clots that incapacitate them for their daily life. In addition to the enormous amount of endometrial and breast cancers that are being seen in inoculated women.

I have detailed in *The Answer* and *Perceptions of a Renegade Mind* how Human 2.0 is not meant to be subject to man-woman procreation. The new 'species' would be produced instead through technological procreation as described by Aldous Huxley in *Brave New World* in 1932. To achieve this, the present Human 1.0 has to be phased out and that is what is happening. I'll have more on this later in the chapter.

Big MAC

Dr Luis Miguel De Benito, a digestive physician with a PhD in molecular biology, has not been alone in his findings that at least many of those who have been fake vaccinated for 'Covid' now carry their personal MAC address which uniquely identifies each technology device on any given network. MAC stands for Media Access Control. What on earth is that doing now embedded in fake-vaccinated people? Benito was intrigued by the global pressure for everyone to have the jabs when there was no good health reason to do so. From the summer of 2021 he set about checking his patients for MAC infiltration. Benito would clear the space of all other possible sources of MAC contamination by activating the Bluetooth system on his cellphone to check there was no other device in range that would show up. Each patient came alone and Benito said that as they came close to his office he would see one or two Bluetooth devices appear on his screen with their MAC address and in other cases none. After treatment he would ask if they had been fake vaccinated for 'Covid' and whether they had with them cell phones or electronic devices such as wireless headsets or tablets. If they did, he would ask for them to be turned off and at that point one of the two devices registered to Bluetooth would disappear, *but often not the other*. Benito questioned 137 patients with 112 saying they had been fake vaccinated and 25 saying they had not. None of those who said they had *not* registered on Benito's cell phone any device available for a Bluetooth connection while 96 of the 112 who said they *had* been fake vaccinated registered a MAC code which remained on the screen of his cell phone despite having switched off their own devices:

> I interpreted that it was a code that the patient himself was carrying and that, in fact, when he left the office, leaving the building, it disappeared from my cell phone. I've been able to verify that 100 percent of the patients who say they aren't vaccinated don't raise any contact device with my cell phone via Bluetooth. But 86 percent of those who said they were vaccinated generated a MAC address on my cell phone.

Does my contention that Fourth Dimensional AI is tracking every human in every 'life' now sound quite so crazy? Benito wondered how if the MAC address is something personal, individual, and unrepeatable, that the five people injected with the contents of the same vial, from the same distribution of the same batch, can have five different MAC addresses? He said that he consulted with computer technicians, roboticists and fellow biologists and engineers, experts in computer science, and nanorobotics, and they suggested the possibility that the code is generated by the interaction of what's injected and the genetic material of the patient. Obviously more research needs to be done and Benito has passed his findings to a group of international investigators. Before his findings are dismissed with a wave of the sceptic hand some things to consider. Firstly, he is far from the only one worldwide to identify the MAC code in the fake vaccinated and secondly I have been warning for decades that electronic tagging is part of the plan. We have this from the 'horse's' mouth, or rather the psychopath's mouth, with Cult operative Klaus Schwab. His World Economic Forum (WEF) has promoted and is preparing to impose Schwab's (the Cult's) 'Great Reset' which is complete transformation of human society. Schwab said on the Swiss channel RTS four years before the 'Covid' hoax that humans were going to be chipped and merged with the cyber-digital world. In reply to a question about whether humans would be chipped, the Bond villain said:

> Certainly in the next ten years, first, we will wear them in our clothes, and then we could imagine that we will implant them in our brains or on our skin,

and in the end ... there will be a direct connection between our brains and the digital world.

He said this in 2016 which would take the ten year prediction to 2026. Man-of-the-people fraud Elon Musk who said that AI could be the end of humanity is working hard to fulfil Schwab's dream with his Neuralink company connecting brains to computers and killing lots of monkeys in the experiments. Not that he has to develop technology that is already sitting in the underground bases and secret projects waiting to be unleashed on the public. Good cover story, though. The same Klaus Schwab has said that the (manufactured) 'Covid' crisis is 'a rare but narrow window of opportunity to rethink, reinvent, reset our world'. In doing so he was telling us why the 'Covid' hoax was unleashed on the world. Recall how Moderna, maker of an mRNA fake vaccine infusing synthetic genetic material, says in its own documents that the 'vaccines' are akin to a computer 'operating system'. The inner core of the Cult, and assets that need to know, are well aware that our reality is a simulation based on the super-advanced equivalent of computer codes and they work from that understanding while letting mainstream humans go down the illusory road of biological physical bodies and scalpel and drug 'medicine'. The Cult is coming from one level of knowledge and works to ensure that the target population never emerge from their calculated ignorance of what the Cult knows.

Freedom? What's freedom?

The Smart Grid is really an expression of 4-D simulation technology being infused into the 3-D projection to further entrap the mind in deeper layers of illusion. The Smart Grid is planned to technologically tag everyone – all eight billion – and track and record with AI every thought and action. This information would then be stored on a global database. What have I just described? Exactly what I say is happening at the 4-D level with all human 'incarnations' tracked and stored – every thought, conversation and activity. The planned and unfolding connection of the human brain (mind) to AI would complete the job of a total AI takeover of 'human' perception and prevent any mind awakening to its plight as a slave to the simulation. We return to that quote by Google executive and 'futurist' Ray Kurzweil about how the human-AI connection will be underway by that recurring target year of 2030:

Our thinking ... will be a hybrid of biological and non-biological thinking ... humans will be able to extend their limitations and 'think in the cloud' ... We're going to put gateways to the cloud in our brains ... We're going to gradually merge and enhance ourselves ... In my view, that's the nature of being human – we transcend our limitations.

As the technology becomes vastly superior to what we are then the small proportion that is still human gets smaller and smaller and smaller until it's just utterly negligible.

This is what I have been calling for decades 'The Assimilation' in which 'human' consciousness (4-D mind) would be absorbed into AI through a hive network in which every mind and all minds collectively would have their perceptions centrally controlled and dictated. A feedback loop would be created in which the holographic projection of 4-D mind (the simulation) would feedback the *illusion* of total AI control to become the reality of 4-D mind. The control would not be real because the projection is only a decoded illusion. To the mind, however, it would be experienced as real. Imagine yourself to be in a prison cell and you would act as if you are there even if in reality you are not. Would you walk through the bars? No. You would *believe* that you couldn't. You can only breach the Ring-Pass-Not when you believe – *know* – that it's not really there. You have reached a level of awareness and frequency in which the 'barrier' so 'real' to lower frequencies simply does not exist. Neo came back from the Matrix (disconnected from that information source) to find he had blood in his mouth from a fight in the Matrix that his body outside the Matrix never had. 'I thought it wasn't real?' he says to Morpheus who replied: 'Your mind makes it real.'

The point of the simulation is not entrapment of the body/brain and its disconnection from mind. Body/brain are already part of the simulation and intrinsic to its control. The simulation is there to entrap the perceptions of *4-D mind* to instigate disconnection from 5-D

consciousness (Fig 148). To achieve that the mind must have a sense of separation and isolation in every way. Why is the simulation beyond the earth so apparently empty and devoid of life? Now we can see. To emphasise

Figure 148: The simulation is designed to so focus attention in the five-senses that the influence of expanded awareness is lost.

the aloneness and apartness – separation. AI technology in the Fourth Dimension may be able to project the simulation's information source, but it takes 4-D mind to decode it into holographic 'physical' reality. Once mind realises that its sense of reality *is* a simulation and remembers its true identity the power of the illusion is deleted. How do we do that? We take back control of our perceptions, emerge from the simulation trance and reconnect with our 5-D state of beyond-the-simulation awareness. 'The Awakening' is not to awaken from 3-D illusion into 4-D awareness. It is to awaken from 4-D illusion into 5-D awareness. The 'astral planes' (4-D) are said to be an 'angelic' [see also fallen angel'] existence between Earth and heaven'. I think it would be more accurate to say that the Fourth Dimension or 'astral' is an existence between Earth (the simulation) and heaven (5-D reality). It is the location of the state of awareness we call mind and it has been lured into the clutches of illusion in the lower Fourth or lower astral dimension. What you believe you perceive and what you perceive you experience also goes the other way: What you experience you perceive and what you perceive you believe.

The parallels are obvious between the Fourth Dimensional AI system projecting the simulation and the Smart Grid simulation within a simulation. The 4-D version is an AI fake reality controlling the perceptions of mind while the Smart Grid and AI connection to the human brain is planned to dictate the reality of mind from the other direction. It's a double-whammy with AI control at both ends of the feedback loop. We now have the emerging 'Metaverse' promoted by Cult gofer Mark Zuckerberg to further focus the attention of mind on greater and greater scales of illusion to draw perception further and further away from 5-D awareness. The Metaverse, where human reality office spaces, property, and events are all 'mirrored', is described as a 'digital counterpart' of the human world with each human represented by an 'avatar' or digital surrogate to create 'an extension of something like the real world'. But, hold on. The 'real world' isn't real and the mind already has an 'avatar'. It's called the human body. Our experienced reality is itself a Metaverse and the Zuckerberg Metaverse is a Metaverse within a Metaverse, an illusion within an illusion. The mind has an avatar which itself has an avatar. You can see where the ever more detailed entrapment is going. Cult operations including Facebook and Microsoft are embracing the concept and therefore you know it's part of the plan. It is and obviously so. An article at Quytech.com said:

> Imagine studying, working, interacting, attending concerts, earning money, and playing games in an online realm that is both an extension and a fusion of the real world.

Besides, meetings with clients, digital entertainment, work training, and even online study are all expected to be available online in the future, thanks to the Metaverse. This is why so many businesses are investing in the Metaverse: the network's ability to change the world is undeniable.

Yes it can certainly change your perception and given that collective human perception is what we call the 'world' then the Metaverse by that route can indeed change the world which it is being created to do.

Avatar 'you'

I saw a newspaper headline that before recent times would have been thought to be a ridiculous made-up joke: 'Mother says she was virtually groped by three male characters within seconds of entering Facebook's online world Metaverse.' Her body was not assaulted, her *mind* was assaulted by associating her body with her Metaverse body-surrogate or avatar. The article told how she 'watched and listened in horror through a virtual-reality headset as her avatar – a moving, talking, computer-generated version of herself – was groped aggressively in a sustained attack by three realistic male characters'. The reports said that she had to tear off her headset – which covers her eyes and allows her to see the Metaverse as her avatar sees it – to end the ordeal. While she could not actually feel the avatars' hands 'she has suffered from anxiety since the attack and fears for the safety of her three teenage girls and other women in this lawless virtual world' which could be a haunt for sex attackers and paedophiles. Of course it will be. Sex attackers and paedophiles won't stop becoming so when they enter a virtual world to project *themselves*. A senior lawyer said the attack was not an offence and suggested the government may have to consider how to protect those entering the Metaverse. Nick Brett, from London law firm Brett Wilson, said: 'Where a woman has been sexually assaulted virtually, that itself possibly ought to be illegal but isn't at present.' You can see how in its earliest days the Metaverse is hijacking perception and fusing simulated reality with the 'real' (simulated) world.

The woman attacked in the Metaverse said that friends and colleagues had experienced racism, sexism and other forms of assault on the Metaverse and 'I've heard many damaging experiences from women where their avatars have been sexually and verbally abused.' I think I can see an answer to this. *Don't use the bloody Metaverse which is a calculated trap to further control your mind.* You know that people will and become addicted to it. 'This technology will be prevalent in our children's futures, so my mission is to create safe and secure virtual-reality experiences,' the accosted woman said. The acceptance of the technological takeover is such that 'don't use it' is considered the Stone Age. Making your mind-trap safer is the only response. Instead of hour after hour addicted to the smartphone we'll have the same addiction to the Metaverse which is a deeper level of perceptual slavery. They are engaged in a systematic campaign of drawing people further into the lair with smartphones you hold, followed by devices on the body to devices in the body to the Metaverse completely taking over reality. Make no mistake that technological addiction is not only achieved through focus on what it visually delivers. Frequencies are coming off this stuff that entrain the brain to demand its fix of those frequencies just like any drug. I have been warning for years about an 'electronic tattoo' on the skin to interact with the Internet on the road to technology inside the body already being delivered by the fake vaccines. I saw an article in March, 2020, which said that Gates was 'predicting' this technology would replace smartphones. Predicting? So how come I knew about it years ago? Gates is not predicting. He's reading a script describing the Cult's intentions.

Sub-dividing myopia

This may all appear to be complex and confusing. It's not, really. Break it down to its foundations and it's quite simple. Everything from the simulation itself to the Metaverse is about seizing control of the mind's sense of reality to ensure that its beyond-the-simulation self, the eternal 'I', is marginalised and its influence severed. We are looking at the mind perceptually trapped by a Metaverse within a virtual reality AI Smart Grid within a virtual reality AI simulation. The plan eventually is to absorb the mind completely into cyberspace without even a body and lock it away in the bewilderment of a Matrix within a Matrix within a Matrix within a Matrix. All would be designed to block the mind's access to its true identity which would allow escape from the digital maze. Or rather mazes – lots of them with multiple loops and timelines. The same process of suppressed self-identity can be seen playing out in the 'human' world. We once identified as men or women with a mind and maybe a religion, race, job, and income bracket. Basically that was it. Today we have strings of letters to indicate the fine detail of identity. One university has LGBTTQQFAGPBDSM or lesbian, gay, bisexual, transgender, transsexual, queer, questioning, flexual, asexual, gender-fuck, polyamorous, bondage/discipline, dominance/submission and sadism/masochism. Old human labels are being sub-divided and sub-divided and with each sub-division the identity of the True 'I' – Infinite Awareness – is further distanced and diminished. I am *All That Is, Has Been And Ever Can Be* becomes 'I am a human' becomes 'I am man or woman' becomes 'I am lesbian, gay, bisexual, transgender, transsexual, queer, questioning, flexual, asexual, gender-fuck, polyamorous, bondage/discipline, dominance/submission and sadism/masochism'. These are not the 'I'. Human is not the 'I'. Mind is not the 'I'. They are

THE CONSTANT SUB-DIVISION OF

PHANTOM SELF

Figure 149: Sub-dividing sub-division.

the illusory labels of a Phantom Self (Fig 149). *All That Is Has Been And Ever Can Be* is the 'I'. Sub-divisions of labels are the continuation of the 'Fall' from paradise into 'matter' or these days the 'Fall' from paradise into 'gender-fuck'.

The same process is evident with the pressure to conform to group-think and the censorship and targeting of anyone with a different perception. This is the hive mind being constructed at the level of 'human society' which is only an expression of gathering AI control of perception that is ultimately planned to dictate the same perception to every human – every *mind*. Individual thoughts, views and opinions would be deleted or in Kurzweil's words: 'As the technology becomes vastly superior to what we are then the small proportion that is still human gets smaller and smaller and smaller until it's just utterly negligible.' Game, set and match. It would be a technologically-dictated *single* group-think and we are watching the stepping stones to that happening with the pressure to think and speak only what is acceptable to authority (the Cult) and its Woke foot soldiers that long ago conceded their individuality and right to uniqueness. Yuval Noah Harari, an Israeli 'futurist' (like Kurzweil), and professor in the Department of History at the Hebrew University in Jerusalem, is known as the 'philosopher for the elites'. He told a meeting of Schwab's World Economic Forum in 2018 that bodies, brains and minds would be 'engineered' and humans were 'hackable'. Future masters of the planet would be decided by who owned the data. They would control the future, not just of humanity, but the future of life itself:

Control of data might enable human elites to do something even more radical than just build digital dictatorships. By hacking organisms, elites may gain the power to re-engineer the future of life itself because once you can hack something you can usually also engineer it. And if indeed we succeed in hacking and engineering life this will be, not just the greatest revolution in the history of humanity, this will be the greatest revolution in biology since the very beginning of life.

Science is replacing evolution by natural selection with evolution by intelligent design. Not the intelligent design of some God above the clouds but our intelligent design.

'Our intelligent design'? *Intelligent*? Please discuss. The infusion of synthetic genetic material through the 'Covid' fake vaccines and many more synthetic fake vaccines using other excuses is literally hacking into the body to re-engineer its genetics in the way that Yuval Noah Harari describes. His use of 'if' presents this hack reality in the 'future' when it's happening *now*.

Why so anti-human? Guess

Central to this process of AI Smart Grid perceptual control is to change the nature of the human body from its biological state into a much more synthetic one. Eventually a totally synthetic one before the body is ditched altogether and here the Woke and Human 2.0 agendas merge into one. The original simulated body was founded on those that exist in a far more ethereal state in higher dimensions of Prime Reality on which the simulation was digitally created as a 'bad copy'. Once the 'copy' was made the process could begin of changing its nature which is now moving ever faster as systems that served human needs are being transformed. My decades-long contention that human society is being manipulated by a non-human force is appearing ever less fantastic to people as they see unfolding around them a blatantly anti-human agenda. The make-up of the atmosphere is being changed with among many other things the targeting of the gas of life, carbon dioxide, through the manufactured hoax of 'global warming' (Fig 150). Cult-owned Bill Gates is funding efforts to block-out sunlight by releasing calcium carbonate dust into the atmosphere to reflect solar energy and stop it reaching the Earth's surface. Gates, of course, is a lunatic, but a very dangerous one answering to even more extreme lunatics in the Cult inner circle. Those involved in this madness say the effect on little things like crop growth are unknown, but at the inner core they know exactly what the effect is designed to be. Here we have another double-whammy on human food production of targeting the gas of life and sunlight.

Figure 150: Without carbon dioxide we would all be dead from the demise of the food supply. The Earth has become greener in the industrial era for the same reason that growers add carbon dioxide to the air content of greenhouses.

The frequency construct of the Simulation Field with which we interact is being changed from one compatible with the information codes of the human body to one which isn't. Part of the reason for a more synthetic human is to cope with this alien technological frequency bombardment with 5G to be followed by 6G and 7G. Technologically-generated radiation has increased by millions of times since the 1950s and is now going into overdrive with those low-orbit Musk satellites beaming 5G and Wi-Fi at the ground. 5G towers are proliferating at alarming speed across the world adding to the destructive frequency environment that is causing ever increasing numbers of people to suffer from electrosensitivity, or 'ES', an intolerance of electromagnetic radiation that continues to explode in its effect through Wi-Fi, 5G, cellphones, Bluetooth, antennae and towers, smart meters, and power lines. The body is an electromagnetic information field and other electromagnetic sources incompatible with the body field can cause mayhem – and do. Synthetic fake vaccines contain elements such as graphene – which conducts electricity – and other nanophenomena to connect the body-brain to the 'cloud'. Graphene and company have been shown to self-replicate in the body to build *synthetic operating systems* that can change the body communication network and potentially interact with technologically-generated frequencies of the Smart Grid. Actually, more than 'potentially' – this is what they are designed to do.

I mentioned earlier the videos of graphene forming into self-assembling networks when stimulated by electricity/electromagnetism. Once in the body this can be activated by Wi-Fi fields and 5G which, like all the 'Gs', is a frequency and information *delivery system* – hence the effect on body and psychology. Everything connects. A study was published in the *International Journal of Vaccine Theory, Practice and Research* about how mRNA technology is used to deliver material for genetic intervention. It describes how graphene lends itself to self-assembling semiconductors; how these nano-structures are small enough to be injected; and how they are able to interact with electrons, light and magnetism. They are so tiny they can enter the brain in their thousands and electrons, light and magnetism are all aspects of the Smart Grid. Canadian doctor Charles Hoffe reports that a single dose of Moderna fake vaccine delivers 40 *trillion* tiny packages of synthetic RNA molecules with 22.5 *trillion* entering the lymphatic system and tests show that at least 62 percent of mRNA fake-vaccinated people have microscopic blood clots. We should also be aware of something I have been highlighting in the books for such a long time and that's entrainment. This is the phenomenon by which weaker frequencies are entrained or synchronised with the strongest frequency. If you pluck the strings of three violins to the same note and then introduce another violin resonating to a different note, or no note, it will soon begin to vibrate to the collective frequency of the other three which dominate the frequency field. Relate this to the human psyche being bombarded 24/7 by frequencies from low-orbit satellites and the Smart Grid in all its forms. Frequencies carry information and represent mental and emotional states which opens the way for mass perception control from these sources. I saw long ago that the global conspiracy could not be pulled off only by groups of people meeting around a table to agree their next move. Manipulation of human perception, thus behaviour, goes far deeper than that. The same is true of the biological 'natural world' (bad copy of the natural world) that cannot survive the gathering radiation transformation. Is it really a coincidence that 5G was switched on in Wuhan, China, immediately before 'Covid' began and that 'Covid hotspots' have corresponded with 5G switch-ons? Or that the alleged symptoms of 'Covid' mirror those of electromagnetic poisoning? So much illness of so many kinds – including psychological – is being generated by 5G with 6G and 7G to follow.

Look around and you'll see that everything is being infused with synthetic material. Crops and food supplies are being synthetically-modified. We have synthetically-modified trees and insects; synthetic drugs; vitamins and supplements; blood; and genetics with organs 'printed' by a 3-D printer. An article at Techrepublic.com describes how a new 3-D printer has the software and material to create a synthetic heart that is as 'squishy as the real thing'. The J750 Digital Anatomy 3D Printer 'turns out hearts as close to the real organ as a printer can get'. Scott Drikakis, medical segment leader at producer Stratasys, said: 'If there is a defect in the heart, a structural abnormality, with this solution, we can 3-D print a synthetic digital twin of that patient.' He said the 3D heart has the same physical properties as a human organ as well as the same biomechanical characteristics. Synthetic biology ('SynBio') is a fast-growing area of science as this agenda quickly expands. Here are some definitions: 'A multidisciplinary area of research that seeks to create new biological parts, devices, and systems, or to redesign systems that are already found in nature'; 'The use of a mixture of physical engineering and genetic engineering to create new (and, therefore, synthetic) life forms'; 'An emerging field of research that aims to combine the knowledge and methods of biology, engineering and related disciplines in the design of chemically-synthesized DNA to create organisms with novel or enhanced characteristics and traits'.

End of parents

Sperm counts are plummeting *catastrophically* caused by chemical and radiation sources. This is key to the phasing out of Human 1.0 in favour of 2.0 with one estimate that on current trends the ability for humans to procreate will be gone by 2045. Doctors and scientists have warned that

'Covid' fake vaccines threaten fertility in both men and women. It all fits the picture. What a coincidence that I have been warning for decades about the plan for a new non-procreating human while quoting Aldous Huxley and his *Brave New World* as the blueprint. Huxley describes 'World State Hatcheries' in which the non-procreating human would be technologically produced in different 'castes' to serve the world state. With the end of procreation comes the end of parenthood and the state controlling the entire upbringing of children. The quickening erosion of parental rights to schools and government are part of this same agenda as are the staggering numbers of children stolen by the state from loving parents for spurious reasons invented by social services around the world and enforced through secret courts that the media is not allowed to report. This secrecy is claimed to protect the children when it's really to protect government child-stealers from exposure. I am of course all for removing children from parental abuse, but that's not what we are talking about here. These are loving parents destroyed for life by having their kids stolen by the state and many seized 'to order' by paedophile and satanic rings that infiltrate social services. I have met many such parents and it's heart-wrenching. Huxley wrote:

Natural reproduction has been done away with and children are created, 'decanted', and raised in hatcheries and conditioning centres. From birth, people are genetically designed to fit into one of five castes, which are further split into 'Plus' and 'Minus' members and designed to fulfil predetermined positions within the social and economic strata of the World State.

George Orwell, another who accessed parts of the plan, picked up on the same theme in his prophetic *Nineteen-eighty-four* quoting agents of the Big Brother State:

Already we are breaking down the habits of thought, which have survived from before the Revolution. We have cut the links between child and parent, and between man and man, and between man and woman. No one dares trust a wife or a child or a friend any longer. But in the future there will be no wives and no friends … There will be no love, except the love of Big Brother.

Observe in the 'Covid' era the driving apart of people and dividing individual from individual and group from group. Notice the incessant theme of targeting the perception of mind, or as Orwell put it: '… already we are breaking down the habits of thought.' Huxley wrote his book in the early 1930s and Orwell in the late 1940s. How could they have known so much? As I said earlier the Cult does not live in the same 'world' with the same knowledge base as the population. The 'timeline' and technological awareness of the Cult's inner core is way ahead of what is allowed in the public arena. Technological 'wombs' now coming online can be compared with those described nearly a hundred years ago by Huxley. How come? We are experiencing a simulation and it is running through a program. If you know what that program is planned to be then unless minds awaken to intervene the program will play out and become the perceived 'future' within the Infinite NOW. People ask me how I have been able to so accurately predict the future in what have I said over more than 30 years was planned. I haven't predicted the in-stone 'future'. The simulation is interactive and can be changed. I have uncovered the Cult's *plan* for the 'future', the simulation *program* for the 'future', and the idea has been to inspire an intervention by minds awakening to the reality that's been hidden from us. I have been so accurate in predicting 'the future' because humanity has not yet intervened to change it. But now we *must*.

Transgender means no gender

The non-procreating new human perspective reveals the true relevance of transgender hysteria and *hysteria* is what it is. If ever there was a 2 + 2 = 5 insanity it is the claim that there is no such thing as biological sex, as in male and female, in the human body as currently encoded. Did anyone before the last ten years ever imagine reading this headline?: 'Ex-soldier exposed *her* penis and used wheelie bin as a sex toy in public.' Exposed *her* penis? Insanity must be the norm when you are moving from one status quo to a very different reality that requires an abundance of 2 + 2 = 5 to ease the transition. 2 + 2 = 4 must never be allowed to get in the way on the irrelevant grounds that it happens to be true. What's truth got to do with it? Transgender activists view the denial of male and female biological sexes as a means to advance their cause when in fact they are being played. Cue music. The elimination of male and female is not to promote *trans*-genderism; it is to promote *no*-genderism. We are merely looking at a stage on the road with transgender activism between biological sexes and no sexes at all. Before the *fusion* of sexes must come the *con*-fusion of sexes. The young are the most targeted as the adults they will be when this is meant to reach full-blown fruition. Somehow countries around the world had the same idea at the same time of inviting drag queens into schools and libraries to read stories and do their thing for very young children. Drag queens must live their lives as they see fit – it's none of my business – but when they are being used to manipulate the gender perceptions of little kids it becomes *all* our business. If you want to confuse sexes in the minds of children there can be few better ways than to put before them men with beards wearing women's clothes and acting like a female. That's why it's happening.

Gender confusion has triggered soaring numbers of children and

young people to question their gender when they were not before. Many
are set on course for psychological and bodily disaster with sex-change
drugs and surgery. Questioning this mutilation of body and psyche is to
be branded transphobic as seeking to heal the ludicrous divisions
between racial groups is dubbed 'racist'. If someone genuinely feels they
are in the wrong body they should be treated with love and
understanding and supported in their quest to find resolution whatever
that may be. This is not what I am talking about. I am not challenging
the right of transgender people to live their sense of reality. I am
challenging the systematic global campaign to confuse the young and
encourage them to question their gender when they otherwise would
not. I am challenging the psychological fascism that tells me that I have
to address an individual as 'They' and 'Them' which out of respect for
the English language and respect for myself I will never do. Genuine
transgender people, no problem – manufacturing the numbers through
the propaganda and manipulation by the state and organisations and
schools supported by the state? That's an *abomination*. If people don't
like that, well do the other thing then. It's transparently true and needs
saying at every opportunity.

Women's sport is being turned into a farce by allowing people with
male bodies claiming to be women to compete against women with
women's bodies. It's a no-contest with the advantage of greater strength,
muscle mass and bone density. We don't care if women's competition is
destroyed, says the Cult, after all that's the very idea. We want rid of
women as we want rid of men and hence the war on men with the label
'toxic masculinity'. When the targeting of men began I said they would
come for the women next. I knew about the no-gender human and what
it would take to get there. Both men and women – the procreators – were
always going to be in the gunsights. So it has proved, as women have
fallen down the pecking and protection order of political correctness to
be superseded in hierarchical importance by transgender activism. It is
so true that you know who controls you (and the agenda of those who
control you) by who and what you can't criticise. Make a list and you'll
see what I mean. It's hilarious to hear transgender proponents claiming
to be a marginalised and oppressed minority when any criticism of their
stance, no matter how mild, can get you fired, abused and have the
police knocking the door. Governments change the law to suit your
interests and trash those of others, like women. Support from the Cult
system comes from the simple fact that vehement and often viscous
transgender activists are serving the agenda of the Cult system. They are
far too far up their own arses to see what fools they are being taken for.
George Soros and other Cult billionaires and corporations funding
transgender groups care about transgender people?? It's belly-laughable.
Apple has introduced a new emoji of a pregnant *man* and we are
supposed to refer to 'pregnant people'. A 'marginalised minority' has

that power? Do they think the billionaires at Apple could give a shit about what transgenders want? They are doing it because that's what their *masters* want and it is all connected to the no-gender human. The ridiculous and shameless *USA Today* named 'Rachel Levine', the male-bodied, child-fathering, dick-dangling, US government 'health' official claiming to be a woman, as one of its 'Women of the Year' in 2022. Anyone think *USA Today* could care less about transgender rights? It was simply advancing the Cult 2 + 2 = 5 Psyop. The satirical site Babylon Bee was banned by Cult-owned Twitter for naming Levine as its Man of the Year in response. Talking nonsense is fine, but parodying nonsense is not fine. My god, how hard must parody be today in the face of daily reality?

Chemical castration

Changing sexuality is also being done chemically and you can see this process at work with fish that have changed sex after swimming in chemically-polluted rivers and streams. Human masculinity is being targeted in the same way. Those identifying as gay or LGBTQ have been increasing rapidly according to studies and as one headline said: 'Millennials Are the Gayest Generation.' A Gallup poll in early 2022 claimed that the number of Americans identifying as LGBTQ had more than doubled in a decade led by 'Generation Z' born between the mid-to-late 1990s and early 2010s. While there will be other reasons, an environment deluged with gender-bending chemicals doesn't play a part in that? *Really*? Why not? I don't care what your sexuality may be. It's none of my business and nor do I want it to be. My philosophy on life is do what you like so long as you don't seek to impose that on anyone else. If the population is being bombarded with gender-changing chemicals that is a form of imposition – *obviously*. Dr Melody Milam Potter, an American Clinical Health Psychologist for 30 years, has studied the effect. She has written about falling numbers of male children and makes a connection to *synthetic* substances called endocrine-disrupting chemicals (EDCs). The endocrine system is a series of glands that include the pineal gland or 'third eye'. EDCs are found in plastics, food containers and packaging, canned food and drinks, electrics, solvents, cleaning products, detergents, pesticides, cosmetics, soaps, car exhausts, polish, paints, batteries, dental fillings (mercury) and many types of fish including swordfish. Often highlighted is the hormone disrupter Bisphenol A or BPA used in tin cans, bottles, plastic food containers and cash register receipts. Potter describes how synthetic EDC's can act as 'silent switches' that suppress the development of male bodies:

EDCs we encounter every day can alter the sex hormone balance, preventing male genitals from growing properly. By suppressing testosterone or by enhancing or mimicking the female sex hormone, estrogen, they can undermine the natural testosterone messages surging through a growing fetus.

For instance, estrogen mimics … dioxin, a widespread pollutant and potent endocrine disruptor, [which] can intercept and overcome a hormonal message from a male gene. Dioxin also acts as a testosterone flusher reducing male hormone concentrations so much that the male action may not be stimulated adequately.

Testosterone suppressors like DDT can block testosterone's position on a receptor. Hormone stimulators can intensify the action of a natural hormone so much that the system shuts down and refuses to receive a male 'go ahead' signal ... In fact, research substantiates that exposure to EDCs at a crucial time can disrupt the entire genital sequence.

From lower testosterone levels – now well documented – comes weaker men less willing to stand up and be counted in the face of tyranny. Dr Devra Davis is an internationally-renowned American epidemiologist, President of the Environmental Health Trust, and director of the Center for Environmental Oncology at the University of Pittsburgh. She says that fast-dividing cells producing sexual organs are very open to 'incorporate and replicate errors' that can lead to changing once-developing boys into girls. Whenever biochemical processes are involved clearly any chemical disturbance becomes significant and can surely feminise even those people who still emerge from the womb as male.

Tunnel vision

What I am describing is the way the world of the 'seen' is being transformed by AI and the Smart Grid and by making the body and 'natural world' ever more synthetic. This is the playing out of the real meaning of it all: To further entrap 4-D mind in deeper and deeper illusion through added layers of simulated fakery. By manipulating the body's genetic (information code) system you manipulate what it can decode into a sense of realty for the mind to believe to be real. The further you can sink the mind's reality into the mire and maze of perceptual fakery, the greater its bewildered illusion and frequency disconnection from the True and Infinite 'I'. Perception = frequency and if mind falls into a low-frequency state how can it connect with high-frequency 5-D? DNA is a receiver-transmitter of information that connects the body senses with other frequencies and realities. If you change DNA you change the frequencies on which it transmits and receives and the realities it can therefore connect with. You suppress it into further limitation in the same way that the ridiculously narrow band of visible light is perceptual limitation – tunnel vision – for the mind. Synthetic transformation and DNA manipulation through 'Covid' fake vaccines is all part of this. The range of DNA frequency potential which includes 'out there' realities through the pineal gland or 'sixth sense' is being re-wired to connect only with the Smart Grid simulation within a simulation. Without a 5-D input, the mind becomes totally lost. Talking of which, so-called 'lost souls' are fragments (separation) of mind so befuddled by the simulation and body-centric programming, they don't know who they are, where they are, or what is going on. That is, after all, why they are 'lost'.

Reduce this to the basics and foundations and the whole summation of what I am saying comes down to two states of being. Some call them love and evil and that is valid in the sense those words are meant to convey. I will go instead with two others to maintain the theme of this chapter and indeed the book in totality: Separation and unity. They can be expressed as fragmentation and Oneness. We see this at every level of simulated reality from the separation of 4-D mind from 5-D expanded awareness to our segregated experienced reality divided by race, religion, political view, sexuality, income bracket, an apparently lifeless universe, the list goes on and on. Aspects of Infinite Awareness still connected to their source have come into the simulation at this 'time' to literally hack the system and set minds free of the illusion. Yet no doubt a goodly number have themselves been caught in the illusion such is its perceptional deceit. This is a vital reason to exchange self-identity with the body for self-identity with Infinite Awareness to allow wavelengths of mind and spirit – 4-D and 5-D – to merge and reconnect. The more we associate the 'I' with the body the further distant those wavelengths become. The simulation is a schism within the fabric of Infinite Reality in the same way that Wetiko, Yaldabaoth and Satan/the Devil/Lucifer, Iblis, Saytan, and Samael are symbolic names for the schism within Infinite Awareness. One schism is only a reflection of the other. It may be a very minor schism within the Infinite Totality although not if you are directly experiencing its consequences. Everything comes from this schism, this separation, and how interesting that synonyms for schism include conflict, discord, discordance, discordancy, disharmony, dissension, dissidence, dissonance, disunion, disunity, division, friction, infighting, strife, variance, war and warfare. How is that for a description of human society as directed and manipulated by the Cult working for the schism?

So all is lost. It is surely impossible to overcome such odds in a such a rigged game. We are doomed – *doomed* I say! Or rather we're not. The answer is simpler than you'd think. In fact, the answer is *what* you think. Even more accurately … what you *know*.

CHAPTER TWELVE

All-Seeing 'I'

Love cannot be explained – yet it explains all
Elif Shafak

I do not offer solutions to what I have described here. People ask for 'solutions' to problems which invariably lead to more problems in need of 'solutions'. There is another way.

When I see a problem I go in search of the *cause*. The problem is only the effect, the symptom, of something else. What is the something else? What is the cause? If the cause is deleted then so must be the problem. We must therefore ask the question what is the cause of the human condition exposed in this book? It is that 'humans' have lost their mind. Or, more accurately, lost control of their mind. Even more to the point mind has lost control of itself. A knock-on consequence is a disconnection from the influence and wisdom of expanded 5-D awareness that explores Infinity beyond the perceptual clutches of the simulation. Lose your mind and you lose *yourself*. Your True and Infinite Self – the Eternal 'I'. This is the cause we have to remove and everything else will follow as the tyranny ends. It must end. When the cause is gone, the tyranny must go with it.

FREE your mind

The centre of the target is the perception of the mind that exists in 4-D reality 'between' the simulated '3-D' projection (including the human body) and 5-D (and beyond) Infinite Awareness. Everything is the same consciousness in different states of perception and frequency. I made the point earlier that a free and flowing ocean (Infinite Awareness) is made from the same substance as a block of ice (4-D mind) while their manifestations are so very different. When perceptions divide between 5-D and 4-D their frequencies divide, too. With that the influence on mind of expanded awareness and wisdom dissipates through vibrational distance. The simulation was created to trigger that division by focussing the attention of mind in the mental and emotional turmoil and sense of limitation of an illusory '3-D' reality which mind is unknowingly decoding and projecting (Fig 151). Yes, decoding and projecting its own perceptual prison cell while believing it to be externally and physically real. If you live your life wearing a virtual reality headset 24/7 the information it delivers would become your sense of reality. Mind has been *mesmerised* which means 'having your attention fixated as though by a spell, fascinated, hypnotised, spellbound,

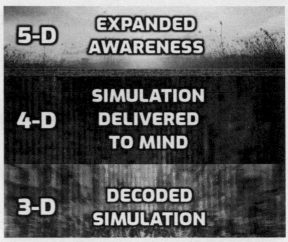

Figure 151: Worth another reminder - the simulation is projected in the form of wavefield information into the human collective mind in Fourth Dimensional reality and the mind decodes this into a holographic illusory 3-D 'physical' reality that we think is the human 'world'. Mind's focus of attention on the simulated projection disconnects its sense of reality (and so frequency) from Fifth Dimensional consciousness outside the simulation. (Image by Gareth Icke.)

transfixed'. The mind is indeed spellbound and the spell is the simulation which works on all levels of 'human' reality. There is the simulation in totality right down to the fine detail of belief and perception. If you are being told all day every day from multiple sources that the 'Covid virus' exists it is very difficult to free your mind from that program to sufficiently clear out every lie and deceit. The principle is the same. Even those who have freed their mind of some illusions – like seeing that 'Covid' has been a conspiracy to justify global transformation – are still caught in the light of the oncoming train in other areas through repetition and programming. The overwhelming majority of 'Covid' scepticism operates in the realm of 'there is a virus, but it's not as dangerous as they say'. The thought that there *never has been* a 'virus' is too much of a leap for their mind to make. The chasm between the lies and the truth is too enormous to cross and a half-way house is the result.

I'll first use the 'Covid' example to show how minds are manipulated at the micro level (and how we can stop being scammed) and then go to the big picture with how we can free ourselves from The Trap in totality. I have had many emails along the same lines since I said in early April, 2020, that there is no SARS-CoV-2 'virus' that is supposed to cause 'Covid-19'. They say 'people are dying from the symptoms of Covid and if you go on saying that it doesn't exist it will harm your credibility'.

They are overwhelmingly nice people who have seen through elements of the hoax and the emails are mostly respectful. I do not say the following in criticism, only as an observation. Let's deal with the 'credibility' bit first. I don't seek credibility. I seek the truth. They are rarely the same thing. How often have people with views perceived as 'credible' by the great majority of the public turned out to be talking absolute crap? Martin Luther King said:

> There comes a time when one must take a position that is neither safe, nor politic, nor popular, but he must take it because conscience tells him it is right.

I say that time is *all* the time. Seeking credibility and not the truth is one of the greatest of all mind deceivers. From this comes the global prison cell called the fear of what other people think. Fall for that and your mind belongs to other slaves caught in the simulation never mind the simulation itself. Pursuing facts and evidence in all their multiple forms must be the goal at all times and at all costs and speaking the truth as you believe it to be from those facts and evidence. If you don't do that and instead weigh up first what others will think of your truth, the Matrix has you. The fear of what others think and seeking credibility for yourself are different ways to say the same thing. Once you edit yourself to fit the beliefs of others you are no longer *you* – you are *them*. Self-censorship is now the real pandemic as condemnation, abuse, hostility and ridicule are unleashed on anyone with a different view from the programmed norms of Cult-created group-think Wokery. You can lose your job and career for the mildest of deviations from Big Brother normality and be cast out of the 'garden' by the fake 'liberals' with their Wokery jiggery-pokery – 'chicanery, subterfuge and skullduggery'. The Black Panther movement used to say: 'Scratch a liberal and you'll find a fascist.' With today's fake liberals that is most certainly true. The subterfuge is not even instigated by the Woke mentality which is only a Cult simulation program funded and promoted into mass reality through Cult-controlled schools, universities, corporations and governments overseen by global asset management giants like BlackRock and its 'king of the Woke-industrial complex', Larry Fink.

The Woke army of psychological fascists are the mind-controlled, mind-hijacked, paramilitary arm of the Cult agenda to impose global group-think and a one-world perceptual state. They are playing their crucial part in the plan for a technological hive-mind through an AI connection to the human brain which will end all human thought and emotion as we know it. 'Hate anti-vaxxers', cry their Cult masters. 'Yes, *HATE* them, *SILENCE* them, the Wokers scream. 'Hate Russians', cry their Cult masters. 'Yes, *HATE* them, *SILENCE* them, the Wokers scream.

Woke is another religion in which you must *HATE* and *DESTROY* *blasphemers*! What level of insanity is necessary to see a tyrannical Russian leader invade another country and then for *his* actions ban Russian orchestra conductors; authors; participants in cat shows; and teams in virtual reality sports games? What madness is required to ban 'Russian' vodka not even made in Russia? Or rename cocktails with 'Russian' in the title? I'll still have a White Russian, thanks, if that's okay, and even if it's not. But then they renamed French fries 'freedom fries' when the French government refused to take part in the 2003 invasion of Iraq in which untold numbers died, ongoing catastrophe was visited upon the Middle East, and all was based on a lie about weapons of mass destruction that didn't exist (see 'Covid'). Much of the human population has always been child-like. It's just more obvious and extreme now.

It equals FOUR!

Most people rarely say what they believe if it differs from group-think unless they are among those they know are 'safe'. Otherwise every last word is watched and processed for its unintentional and ludicrously-interpreted connotation that you are racist, sexist, ageist or transphobic. Before long in an effort to salvage some self-respect from this spineless submission to tyranny, people persuade themselves that they are not submitting to tyranny at all. They are only doing what they believe is right. At this point your knowing submission to $2 + 2 = 5$ becomes a *belief* in $2 + 2 = 5$. Your short and curlies are now in the iron grip of Woke insanity which is only a projection of Cult insanity and Matrix insanity. Another part of your mind is not yours. Cult control of the global web of governments, corporations, media and institutions of society mean they walk and talk as one unit in their imposition of 'values'. These 'values' are nothing more than weapons of control employed by those so devoid of 'values' that they would not know one if it bit them on the arse. 'Anti-racism' is the cry of racists; 'anti-sexism' is the cry of sexists; and 'equity' is the cry of those who despise equality of rights and opportunity. 'Equity' does not mean 'equality' as in equality of opportunity. It means law-imposed racial and sexual bias which is a patronising insult to minorities and women. It is an expression of what I have heard called 'cosmetic diversity'. This is when you have diversity only of skin colour and sexuality while ensuring that all your appointments, whether black, brown, gay or straight, have the *same opinion*. It's all a scam to push an agenda through cosmetic diversity while destroying *real* diversity – diversity of view and opinion.

Woke's 'critical race theory' is pure racism which insists that we accept the following premise: White people = racists; black people = victims. One is racism while the other patronises and disempowers

WHAT IS RACE? SAME CONSCIOUSNESS - DIFFERENT COLOUR VEHICLE THAT'S ALL IT IS

Figure 152: What happens when you drop the Phantom Self and realise we are all One

black people and tells them they must define their lives by what white people do, say, and think. This we are told to believe is the behaviour of 'anti-racists' who 'care about black people' (Fig 152). Wetiko/Yaldabaoth is a state of consciousness inversion and so therefore is the simulation that imposes its will. Everything is upside down, back to front, turned over, flipped and reversed. We do not deal with this by submitting to it. We do that by refusing to play a part in its integration into normality. Anyone is going to tell me what to believe, what I can and cannot say, and what my perceptions of everything must be? A bunch of psychopaths and prats are going to impose this and I am going to *let them*?

Not a chance! Ever. In all eternity.

Deleting fear of what others think of what we say, do, and believe is the first base of taking your mind back from the simulation and its architects and operatives. Without this first step there can be no other steps. At all levels of mind the answer comes down to self-respect. Do we have the self-respect to insist on reaching our own conclusions and sense of reality or have we so little respect for ourselves that we allow others to tell us what to think and whether we think at all? Once we concede self-respect by submitting to tyranny and madness, only submission remains. Mahatma Gandhi said: 'I cannot conceive of a greater loss than the loss of one's self-respect.' But, as he also said, and this is the point: 'They cannot take away our self-respect if we do not give it to them.' Here lies the key to freedom. Self-respect will never bow to tyranny. Every tyranny in all 'history' is the result of self-respect being conceded by the masses and every tyranny has been overthrown by those who refuse to give it away. Fascism is not imposed by fascists. It is imposed by the population conceding its self-respect to fascists who disrespect freedom and diversity of view. You can't have *self*-respect if you meekly accept *dis*respect.

The few have always controlled the many for a simple ever-repeating reason. The many give their power to the few through acquiescence which is the result of deleted self-respect. The whole system of top-down control is founded on imposition by the few and acquiescence by the many. At the top of national and global pyramids is the inner core of the Cult and you would get their number in a single room. They impose their will, their agenda, on the next level which acquiesces to that will and imposes the same on the level below them. So it continues all the way down the pyramid – imposition-acquiescence-imposition-acquiescence. A very few levels below the Cult inner-core you are already dealing with people who have no idea there even is a Cult or an agenda. The sequence continues on the basis of doing what your perceived 'superiors' tell you without question or resistance. Eventually you reach the mass of the people at the foot of the pyramid and if they acquiesce to the levels that impose upon them – government and law enforcement – a circuit of imposition-acquiescence is completed which allows the will of the Cult inner-core to prevail nationally and globally (Fig 153). In this way, and only in this way, a handful at the top dictate the fine detail of billions of lives and the direction of human society. This

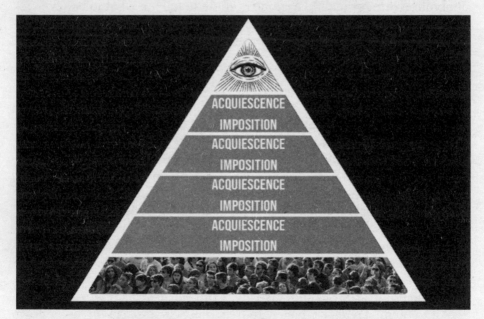

Figure 153: The simple sequence that has allowed the few to control the many throughout known human 'history'. (Image by Gareth Icke.)

is exactly what has happened so obviously in the 'Covid' years. If ever there was an example of removing the cause to delete the problem this is it and the antidote is *self-respect.* Unquestioning acquiescence is the cause and that is what has to stop to remove the problem.

Questions, questions, always questions

If we return to those emails about my contention that there is no 'Covid virus' we can explore further how persistent and repeating propaganda can divert even awakening minds. An email from one man said he was hearing people say that their 'friend or dad or brother-in-law or whoever have been very, very, ill or indeed died'. He said that the main things people who 'had Covid' mentioned were that they were 'terribly tired, they lost their sense of smell and taste, they felt terrible.' Okay, but this is where the psychology of propaganda comes in. The mind has to be cleared of that with no preconceived idea through which repetition can program conscious and subconscious perception. The mind has to open to All-Possibility and cast out – *exorcise* – the programming (Figs 154 and 155). This is my blank piece of paper method that I have written about in other books. Nothing goes on that paper literally or symbolically unless it earns its place. In this example people who claimed to have 'Covid' said they felt terribly tired, lost their sense of smell and taste, and felt terrible. How do they know that is caused by 'Covid'? Shit, how long would it take a proper doctor to list all the conditions with those symptoms? If

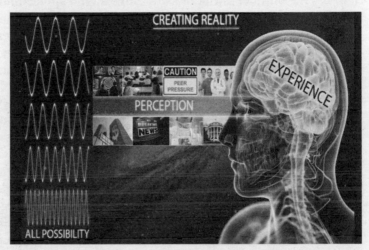

Figure 154: The Program. (Image by Gareth Icke.)

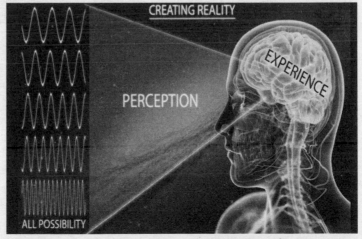

Figure 155: Breaking the Program. (Image by Gareth Icke.)

'Covid' had never been mentioned would they say the symptoms were caused by a 'new' condition? No, they would have explained them away by other familiar means including flu which disappeared worldwide once the 'Covid' hoax was played. How can a condition just disappear virtually overnight? I have seen idiot 'journalists' say that flu instantly demanifested because of lockdown, social distancing and masks. Why did that stop flu with its flu-like symptoms and not 'Covid' with its 'flu-like' symptoms? Flu did not disappear. It was re-diagnosed 'Covid-19' to give the illusion that a 'new virus' existed when it didn't. How could that be? Surely too many people would have to be 'in' on the conspiracy. No, no. The few at the top of the medical pyramids take orders from the Cult; those few tell the rest of the medical profession what to do; and the medics do what they're told not least to protect their careers and salary. Witness the number of doctors and nurses who spoke out and are no longer doctors and nurses for doing so. The whole system is founded on lies and deceit and people acquiescing to the lies and deceit. How amazing that when the devastating effects on health of the 'Covid' fake vaccines appeared and included the heart inflammation condition myocarditis this suddenly became a symptom of 'Covid'? Funny they never mentioned it before. How many doctors must know this is a lie, but stay shtum? Almost all of them. 'Covid' has shown us clearly and unequivocally that if you want to see someone without a spine then, with a few honourable exceptions, find yourself a doctor.

I remember having flu a long time ago and other conditions over the years that made me feel terribly tired, lose my sense of smell and taste and feel terrible. 'Covid' is a 'virus' of the mind. If you are told there is a potentially deadly illness with flu-like symptoms circulating and killing lots of people, your imagination is going to run riot. It's a placebo in reverse. Tell someone the drink you just gave them was poisoned or that you've realised the food they just ate was five weeks past its use-by date and see what happens. They will begin to respond as if their body is being affected when the drink was not poisoned and you bought the food fresh that morning. The mind is running the whole show and what the mind believes it will manifest. Gandhi again: 'A man is but the product of his thoughts. What he thinks, he becomes.' This is true on every level with every perception and is the whole foundation of the simulation modus operandi. A dose of flu becomes 'the worst I've ever felt – that Covid is so bad'. I am saying that the body is in the mind and what the mind believes and feels, the body will reflect. The Cult knows this and is constantly telling you to fear this threat and that threat to health and life. They come like machine gun fire these days. 'Covid' is immediately and seamlessly followed by the invasion of Ukraine by Klaus Schwab school graduate Putin and the threat of nuclear war. These are not coincidences. They are moves on the Cult chessboard. We have seen with 'Covid' the power of suggestion to ensnare perception in the frequency of fear and entrap the mind in a fantasy reality believing in a threat that isn't there. What you believe you perceive and what you perceive you experience even though the perceptions are garbage. Question everything including what I say and make your own conclusions. This is true freedom, true sovereignty, that frees the mind from programmed reality.

Why? Why? Why?

If anyone still believes the 'virus' exists here are some 'whys?' for their mind to consider:

- Why if there is a real infectious agent do they need to test for it with a test that's not testing for it? Why would they have to fix the test to produce the illusion of cases that aren't cases? How can an infectious agent produce no symptoms in large numbers of people – the so-called 'asymptomatic' – who are 'asymptomatic' because there is nothing wrong with them? A real 'deadly virus' would do its thing without any help from propagandists. Drug company Roche adds this warning to the PCR tests that it distributes: 'Not intended for use as an aid in the diagnosis of coronavirus infection … For research use only. Not for use in diagnostic procedures.' Another company, Creative Diagnostics, says of its PCR tests: 'For research purposes only, not for use in diagnostic procedures.' This is the 'test' for 'Covid infection' that has produced the overwhelming majority of alleged 'cases' worldwide. PCR has produced positives for 'Covid' from samples of a paw-paw fruit, a goat, a puddle, and cola. Then you have the lateral flow test. They're testing for antibodies. Yeah, but what antibodies? They are non-specific. I mentioned that at least 60 other conditions produced antibodies alleged to be HIV. It's the same when you hear that a 'vaccine' triggered an 'immune response'. Put any old shite in the body and you'll get an 'immune response'. That's what the immune system does when faced with shite. It 'responds'. A lateral flow 'positive' has been considered so potentially inaccurate even by the authorities that they have had to be confirmed by a PCR test not testing for the 'virus'.

- Why if you have a real pathogen, a real 'virus', do you have to introduce the insane policy that if people test positive with a test not testing for the virus and die within 28 days of any other cause, gunshot wounds, falling down the stairs, hit by a bus, motorcycle accident, then 'Covid-19' goes on your death certificate. If you had a real pathogen that would simply do what it does. A deadly virus would kill people. Why do you have to scam death certificates en masse to make it appear that people are dying of 'Covid-19' when they're not? An NHS doctor in the UK said that from around March, 2020, all the other doctors he knew were putting 'Covid-19' on death certificates no matter what people really died from (what does that say about the spineless compliance of doctors?). The media announces that we have reached new milestones of 'Covid' deaths when it's all a lie.

• Why if you have a real pathogen do you have to give American hospitals big financial incentives to diagnose 'Covid-19'? They have been paid since the fake 'pandemic' began $4,600 for diagnosing regular pneumonia; $13,000 for diagnosing the same symptoms as 'Covid-19' pneumonia; and $39,000 for putting a Covid diagnosed patient on a ventilator that will almost certainly kill them. If you have a real 'virus' and a real 'Covid-19', why do you have to do that?

• Why in the spring of 2020 did the British government and its Health Secretary Matt Hancock manufacture the 'first wave' of 'Covid' through the end of life drug Midazolam which is used by some American states in the execution process? Hancock ordered fantastic amounts of Midazolam which was then given in unprecedented amounts with morphine to old people in care homes. This happened at a time when 'Covid' rules banned their loved ones from seeing them and Do Not Resuscitate (DNR) orders were being imposed on them like confetti. DNR orders were also placed on the mentally and physically handicapped in good old Nazi fashion. Many thousands of elderly people died as a result of this mass murder. Hancock and his fellow psychopaths called this the first wave of 'Covid' to terrify the population into obeying lockdown rules. See the Ickonic documentary *A Good Death?* which exposes this scandal. A well-known side-effect of Midazolam is respiratory distress and when old people died because they couldn't breathe, 'Covid-19' went on the death certificate. Why would you have to do that to manufacture a 'Covid' first wave if you had a real pathogen?

• Why did mass-killer Anthony Fauci and the American authorities have to generate the illusion of a US first wave of 'Covid' with a drug called Remdesivir foisted upon the medical profession for the treatment of anyone in hospital testing positive with a test not testing for the 'virus'? Once Remdesivir is delivered you are a dead man or woman walking, not that you will be able to walk. Remdesivir causes multiple organ failure, particularly kidney failure, which leads to the abdominal cavity and lungs filling with water. Fauci well knew this. Studies had been done to confirm these consequences. What did he care? He's a psycho and he needed an illusory first wave for his masters. Ten of thousands of old people were murdered by Fauci and the Cult-owned state with

'Covid-19' as their fake cause of death.

Why are any of these things necessary if there is a real 'virus'? Those that say there is have to answer that question, and those that want to free their mind must ask questions constantly to make all narratives justify themselves. The big question every time is Cui bono? – 'Who benefits?'. Who benefits from me believing what authority is telling me to believe? If the answer is that authority and the Cult agenda benefits then that alone speaks for itself. Who benefited from 'Covid'? Who benefits from war, chaos, fear, and upheaval? See what I mean?

Old people died. Yes – but what of?

'Covid-19' is a monumental global scam based on a fake test and fake death certificates secured through re-diagnosis of other conditions such as flu and pneumonia as 'Covid'. This is why so many old people have 'died from Covid'. Old people die. It's a consequence of being old. Young people don't die at anything like the same rate. With old people you have limitless potential for redesignating what they really died from as 'Covid-19'. The average age of death in England is about 80 for men and 83 for women and the average age of death from alleged 'Covid' is between 82 and 83. Younger people did not begin dying in numbers until the fake vaccine was available. Before that, hardly any younger people or children were claimed to have 'died from Covid'. There were simply not enough of them dying from *anything* for re-diagnosis to 'Covid' and so old people were the 'first wave' helped along by Midazolam and Remdesivir. The overwhelming majority of people who have 'died from 'Covid' had 1, 2, 3, 4. 5, or more, what they call comorbidities – reasons to die. You remember the 'Covid' crisis in Italy which was instigated to terrify the West into lockdown compliance and tyranny? Once that propaganda had done its psychological job, Professor Walter Ricciardi, scientific adviser to the Italian Minister of Health, said that 'Covid' death rates were due to Italy having the second oldest population in the world and to *how hospitals record deaths*. 'The way in which we code deaths in our country is very generous in the sense that all the people who die in hospitals with Coronavirus are deemed to be dying of the Coronavirus.' Ricciardi said that after re-evaluation by the National Institutes of Health only *twelve percent* of death certificates confirmed a direct causality from Coronavirus. How did they know even the twelve percent was correct? They tested positive with a test not testing for the 'virus'. Italian authorities revealed that *99 percent* of those who 'died from Covid' had at least one comorbidity.

The same theme can be found across the world. Even the mainstream media eventually had to acknowledge the difference between dying 'from Covid' and dying 'with Covid' (dying from another condition while testing positive with a test not testing for the 'virus'). Either way – whether from or with – both were added to the 'Covid' death numbers. The manipulation and corruption of 'Covid' cases and deaths has been breathtaking and everyone involved from the Cult inner core to the compilation of data are guilty of crimes against humanity for the consequences of what they've done. Add to those all the doctors, nurses, 'health' management, chief medical officers, politicians and media who went along with a narrative they must have known was fraudulent. If they *claim* they didn't they lack the basic intelligence necessary to competently do any of those jobs. They were still at it in 2022 when authorities had to admit that those they reported to be in hospital 'with Covid' were admitted for other problems, including broken legs, cancer, whatever, and tested positive with a test not testing for the 'virus' when they arrived. My god these people are so sick. Not the patients – the psychopaths and gutless that played their essential parts in the deceit.

Designer manipulation

We have had the calculated diversion story about the 'virus' being released from a top-level bio-lab in Wuhan either by accident or on purpose. The first theory has appeared in the mainstream media and the second has been encompassed by almost the entirety of the alternative. The 'accident' theory can be dismissed immediately on the grounds that evidence abounds from so many directions and sources that the 'Covid' hoax was planned for at least decades. The Cult's World Economic Forum and Bill and Melinda Gates Foundation ran a simulation called Event 201 of a 'Coronavirus pandemic' only weeks before the 'real thing' began out of Cult-owned China. The Schwab-Gates simulated scenario played out worldwide from early 2020 even down to mass censorship of any challenge to the Cult-owned World Health Organization narrative. The Rockefeller Foundation published a document in 2010 headed 'Scenarios for the Future of Technology and International Development' which included an 'imaginary' epidemic of a virulent and deadly influenza strain that infected 20 percent of the global population. The Rockefeller scenario predicted destroyed economies, closed shops, offices and other businesses, and strict rules imposed by authoritarian governments with mandatory face masks and body-temperature checks. You can read the detail about both pre-emptive scenarios in *The Answer* and *Perceptions of a Renegade Mind*. The Wuhan lab 'accident' story therefore asks us to believe that even though the hoax was long planned they forgot the 'virus' and had to wait around until at some point one was released by accident. Yep, sounds credible.

This leaves us only with the 'released by design' theory. Anthony Fauci's operation in America admits part-funding so-called 'gain of function' research at the Wuhan lab to make the 'virus' more effective against humans. This appears to be an open and shut 'gotcha'. Well, hold on a second. Fauci is a psychopath, but he's also not the brightest man ever to walk the earth and the whole global industry of 'virology' is founded on an unproven nonsense. Let us not forget that the 'Father of Modern Virology' was Thomas Milton Rivers employed by the Cult-owned Rockefellers to head the Rockefeller Institute for Medical Research (now Rockefeller University) between 1937 and 1956. This included the period in the 1950s when John Enders was developing his ridiculous technique for establishing the existence and cellular impact of a 'virus'. The same Rockefeller family established Big Pharma 'medicine' which is now so founded on 'viruses' and 'vaccines' to respond to 'viruses'. Everything today is a 'virus' – have you noticed? The whole thing is a scam developed over decades. The Rockefellers further established the World Health Organization in 1948 as part of the United Nations which has its headquarters in New York built on land given free by Rockefeller largesse. The role of the WHO was to control global health policy under one roof (completed with the planned new 'treaty') and the operation is now overseen for the Rockefellers by their gofer Bill Gates who controls the policy through funding. Gates installed the shockingly corrupt Tedros as Director-General who had worked for Gates-funded organisations to prove he was corrupt enough to qualify for the job. The Rockefellers also own Fauci.

The whole 'virus' scenario has been manufactured, but that does not mean that laboratories and virologists know that. For a start they are ignorant enough to believe that their identification process for a 'virus' is credible and not stupendously insane. They may well be working to create more sinister concoctions they call 'viruses'. It doesn't mean they have managed to do that and nor that it ended up as 'SARS-CoV-2'. Neither am I saying that these labs are not seeking to develop pathogens to harm humans. I'm sure they are. What I am talking about here are *'viruses'*. We are also asked to believe that the Chinese planned to release a 'virus' and didn't want the world to know. Nevertheless they accepted money from Fauci's operation with a paper trail that someone was bound to locate and to hide where the 'virus' came from they released it *down the street* from the Wuhan lab! I saw an interview with the psychopath CEO of Moderna accepting the possibility that the 'virus' was accidentally leaked from the Wuhan lab. What more confirmation does anyone need that the whole alleged scenario is a smokescreen and diversion to hide the real truth – *there is no 'virus'*?

Then there is the most basic question. If they released the deadly 'virus' where the hell is it? Fake tests, fake death certificates, fake data, Midazolam, Remdesivir, financial incentives for diagnosis. *Where is it??* The common denominator between the 'accident' and 'on purpose' stories is this: The virus exists. The Cult is not too bothered *why* you believe there is a 'virus', natural, accident, or design, so long as you *do* believe that there is one. When you do so everyone is agreed that there is something to be dealt with and responded to. People may differ on the means and the dangers, but they communally agree there's a problem of some kind. Once you realise there never has been a 'virus' the house of cards doth fall. I would say to everyone and especially the alternative media in this case to be very careful when being told what you want to hear. The Cult has a technique that I call 'designer manipulation'. They know that while most people will believe their mendacious narrative a gathering number will not. They are looking for other explanations. The Cult says, okay, they are looking for a conspiracy and so we'll give them one. We'll just make it the wrong conspiracy.

Naivety – the human disease

I have highlighted the 'Covid' hoax in this final chapter about freeing the mind for a good reason. It involves every element and technique of mind control at the macro level. We have a 'virus' never shown to exist that has transformed the world with many of the effects that it set in train still to be known. There's the mass psychological effect on babies and children for a start and the reproductive implications for them and adults of the fake vaccines. We've only seen the tip so far of what the 'Covid' years have done to the human mind and world. We can already see the impact on freedom and finance and we've seen nothing yet. This has all been made possible not by a 'virus', but *belief* in a 'virus'. That is stunning in itself. Freeing the mind means understanding the methodology of keeping it enslaved. Almost everyone bought the global lie about the 'virus' in some form and then billions rolled up their sleeves to accept what the fake 'virus' was really all about – the *fake vaccine*. This abomination is produced by the Cult-owned-and-created Big Pharma cartel with its horrific record of callous disregard for human health and wellbeing which has led to record-breaking fines running to billions of dollars (Fig 156). 'Covid' fake vaccine producer Pfizer is right up there with the worst.

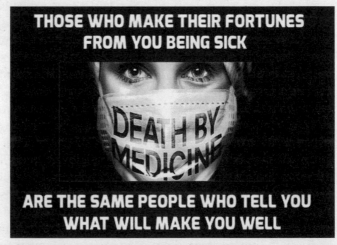

THOSE WHO MAKE THEIR FORTUNES FROM YOU BEING SICK

DEATH BY MEDICINE

ARE THE SAME PEOPLE WHO TELL YOU WHAT WILL MAKE YOU WELL

Figure 156: A free mind would immediately see this blatant contradiction.

Pfizer has been hit since only the year 2000 with fines totalling at least *£7.5 billion*. This figure includes £331.5 million for kickbacks and bribery offences; £1.1 billion for false claims; and in 2009 a record-breaking £1.7 billion for the fraudulent promotion of a painkiller since withdrawn. The same Pfizer has sought with its Cult cohorts at the Food and Drug Administration (FDA) to secure court agreement to delay the full release of its fake vaccine 'trial' data for *75 years*. When it failed to do so extraordinary fake vaccine death and injury revelations followed as I highlighted earlier. At the same time Pfizer is a massive sponsor of mainstream TV shows, including 'news and current affairs', and *they* are going to expose their paymasters for the evil that they do? 'Vaccine'-maker Johnson and Johnson is facing thousands of lawsuits in America over cancer-causing baby powder containing asbestos. J & J knew this was happening and kept the truth from regulators. The psychopaths even considered setting up a subsidiary to take the financial hit which they then planned to avoid by bankrupting that company. J & J 'vaccine' anyone? You know you can trust them. All these psychopathic killing machines have immunity from prosecution for all the mass death and life-destruction their fake vaccines are causing. But, hey, 'anti-vaxxers' are just selfish and paranoid for not taking a fake vaccine produced by psychopathic expressions of pure evil.

Even by their grotesquely manipulated data and narrative fraud, massively more fake-vaccinated people have gone on to 'get Covid' than the un-fake-vaccinated. Public Health Scotland stopped publishing deaths by fake vaccine status to stop the truth being used by 'anti-vaxxers'. You can see why when in the four weeks to February 4th, 2022, there were 478 alleged deaths with or from 'Covid' in Scotland and 417 – 87 percent – were fully-fake-vaccinated. Of course this is irrelevant either way. Whether you 'get Covid' or not is nothing to do with catching a disease. It's only whether you tested positive with a test not testing for it. The point is that even by their own lies and criteria the fake vaccines don't work and billions have unconsciously and unquestioningly had multiple jabs purely on the say-so of psychopathic and mendacious authority. What's the real reason for the fake vaccines? I have covered that already – depopulation and genetic transformation for those that survive. How have they pulled it off? Human naivety which is always, in the end, a death sentence. Understanding the techniques of perception manipulation is vital in preparation for the next manufactured 'pandemic' which is coming. The coordinated easing of 'Covid' restrictions in many countries from February, 2022, was immediately followed by more fear porn with the Russian invasion of Ukraine. Fascism in the name of 'health' has not gone away and is planned to return in another form when all the 'passports' will kick back in. By then they want to dismantle free speech even further to stop the next 'pandemic' being exposed as this one was for those who could lift their eyes from mainstream sources. 'Covid' has in many ways been a precursor for something even more extreme not least to cover up the deaths from self-replicating material in fake vaccines expanding in the bodies of the fake vaccinated not fortunate enough this far to have had the saline vials. Psychopath Bill Gates told the Munich Security Conference in February, 2022: 'We'll have another pandemic. It will be a different pathogen next time.' You get the picture.

I repeat, therefore I am

The 'Covid' hoax has offered so many lessons in freeing the mind from Cult programs. Humanity must stop being in awe of 'experts' in medicine, 'science', academia and other fields. Most of them are not 'experts' at all. They are programmed to believe that everything is a certain way and there are financial incentives and career imperatives to think what they are told to think, believe what they are told to believe, and tell the public what they are told to tell them. If we have not learned that from 'Covid' then will we ever? The 'health' profession has been an absolute disgrace and killed and maimed unimaginable numbers of people by doing what their few 'superiors' at the top of the Cult-controlled hierarchy order them to do. Even many doctors with the smear of brain cell activity that it takes to see through the lie have said they can't speak out or their careers would be over. Such gutless cowardice and self-obsession is utterly shameful. How many children and adults have died as a result and will go on doing so? How many lives have been destroyed? Proper doctors, nurses and scientists (how few of them there seem to be) have been horrified by what they have witnessed and lost their careers for saying so. At least they can view the mirror every morning without averting their eyes.

I have met many doctors long before 'Covid' who I would not trust to diagnose acne. Two 'TV doctors' come to mind immediately on UK television called 'Dr' Hilary Jones and 'Dr' Amir Khan. Walking into a surgery and seeing either of them sitting there should trigger a stampede for the exit. These shockingly uninformed script-reading clowns and their like have been telling the global public that what governments and medical hierarchies say is true. The great unwashed must believe what authority says as unquestioned fact. As Cult-owned Jacinda Ardern said while turning New Zealand fascist: 'Unless you hear it from us, it is not the truth.' Anyone who has another view is putting lives at risk. Oh, the irony. The blood on their hands does not bear thinking about. I could fill a book with the idiocy of 'Dr' Amir Khan. He told a concerned woman that the fake vaccine 'does not affect your fertility'. To say so was 'misinformation'. He had no idea what effect the fake vaccines have on *anything*. No proper trials have been done and no long-term trials at all and the dramatic increase in fertility cycle problems and miscarriages are just another coincidence are they? The man's an idiot. A dangerous one.

Ask yourself: Would any of these 'doctors. 'scientists' and 'academics' be allowed on television and be quoted in the mainstream media if they were not parroting the official story? Look at the almost unimaginable levels of censorship against medical and scientific professionals with a different view that include Dr Robert Malone who was deleted from social media for warning about the dangers of the mRNA technique that *he helped to create*. Any 'expert' on anything that you see in the mainstream media today is a repeater of the official narrative or they would not *be there*. They will be telling you what the Cult and its authority hierarchy want you to believe and that's it. They are a mixture of the corrupt, programmed, clueless, and outright psychopathic. The same is true of the ever-clamouring bevy of 'celebrities' virtue-signalling their self-righteous, integrity-deleted ignorance and Twittering their support for every Cult party-line whatever the subject. They know their careers would be damaged or destroyed if they didn't. What 'celebs' tell you, with pathetically few exceptions, is what their Cult owners want you to believe. What would have happened to Elton John and the Cult arse-licking celebrity rabble had they said 'don't have the jab' instead of urging fake vaccine compliance with all the consequences for so many that they convinced? We know the answer from the experience of the tiny number of famous names who have challenged or even questioned that deadly orthodoxy. The mainstream media with its plummeting audiences increasingly relies on government-funded advertising (propaganda) and bail-outs to survive. Freedom of Information Act requests established that almost the entire American mainstream took money from the Biden administration to promote the fake vaccines. These included 'Conservative' outlets whose audiences were instinctively suspicious of them.

People who genuinely seek the truth need to consult other sources outside the mainstream. Why does anyone think those sources are so targeted for deletion *by* the mainstream? Even then we as individuals must decide what is *our* truth no matter what the source. Remember the Cult technique is inversion. Turn everything these people say on its head and you'll be much closer to what is really going on. Look at the 'Covid' years from this perspective and you see that this inversion is exactly what has happened. Measures, masks and jabs to 'protect your health' have systematically destroyed health both bodily and psychologically. It is indeed all psychological if you go deep enough. This is why 'Covid' policies have been driven by behavioural psychologists, most obviously in the UK, through the part-government-owned Behavioural Insights

Team and cold people like Professor Susan Michie who when not advising the government on manipulating public psychology is a leading light in the British Communist Party.

Who do YOU think you are?

We now come to freeing the mind at the macro level as in freeing ourselves from the simulation itself. The same approach applies here in that we must stop leaving the big questions to these programmed, clueless and psychopathic 'experts'. I mean these questions: Who are we? Where are we? What is this reality we call the world? The mind-trickery that connects 'education' with intelligence means that people hand over responsibility for these big questions once again to those they perceive to be 'experts' and 'clever'. What does that *mean*? What constitutes an 'expert'? In the public mind that means they have been academically successful at school and university and now have a fancy title like 'Professor' or 'Principal Research Scientist'. Okay, so what does being successful at school and university really involve? Telling the exam paper what the system has told you to believe is reality. That is an 'expert's' education in a single sentence and the same process continues when they enter their chosen speciality where they must conform to orthodoxy or be shown the door. My son Jaymie was advised not to question 'global warming' in his school exam or he wouldn't pass even though his teacher said privately that he had sympathy with that view. The Cult system lies to you and uses its army of 'experts' to lie and deceive on its behalf. This doesn't mean there are not clever people called 'Professor' or 'Principal Research Scientist'. There are and they are invariably the mavericks. The point is that they don't *have* to be clever and certainly not wise. Most, yes, *most*, are not. My heart sinks in the 'Covid' years when someone is introduced as a 'professor'. You just know that complete garbage (and the official line) is about to spew forth and why do we leave such people to decide who we are and where we are? It's crazy and a central pillar in the Gulag of the mind. Another point is how the academic mentality is obsessed with complexity. Its perceptual programming cannot conceive that the big answers to the big questions could be anything except complex. The opposite is the case (more inversion) if you look to the foundations of reality and don't become mesmerised by the outward appearance of complexity. True genius is not to understand complexity. It is to see the simple hidden by the illusion of complexity. If it's complicated it's not the truth. It's *obscuring* the truth which is always simple at its core.

On the macro level of mind enslavement the same 'experts' largely prevail. Cult-driven-and-funded 'science' sells us the nonsense about a 'physical' world and a belief that the 'I' is the body, brain and 'human'. Fraudulent and perception-programmed mainstream scientists constantly tell us what the Cult wants us to believe to entrap us in the simulation. We are only our five-senses and that's all. What you see, touch, smell, taste and hear is not only the 'world', it is *YOU*. All of you. I have emphasised that the bottom line essential is to focus attention of the mind in the simulation to such an extent that a disconnection from 5-D awareness is secured. Once that happens there is, to 4-D mind, *only* the simulation in all its forms whether in illusory physicality or on the reincarnation recycling loop. Slavery or freedom comes down to self-identity and perception and we come again to the central point of finding the cause to delete the effect. The cause of mind subjugation and limitation is self-identity subjugation and limitation. Who do you believe that you are? Who do you *live* that you are? Your body, name, race, religion, sex, sexuality, income bracket, and politics? Then the Matrix has you and you are its vassal and vessel. You will remain in its clutches until you free your perception from what is simply a perceptual trap. This is all that the simulation is. *The Trap* is a perceptual trap and who controls our perception if we make that choice? *WE DO*. It is time to encompass that realisation and make that choice. Are you illusory 'flesh' or a unique expression of Infinite Awareness, ultimately Infinite Awareness in its eternal entirety?

The major symbol of the Wetiko Cult is the single eye or all-seeing eye that you see on the dollar bill and the reverse of the Great Seal of the Cult-established United States (Fig 157). The answer to the all-seeing eye is the All-Seeing 'I'. To remember what we have been manipulated to forget: Who we really are which is Infinity itself. The Cult 'eye' symbol is supposed to portray the omnipotent power of its Wetiko/Yaldabaoth/Satan master. To me the symbol means that 'in the

kingdom of the blind the one-eyed man is king'. Wetiko is not omnipotent. It is a weakling. Its power comes from manipulating humans to give away *their* power. Wetiko operates in a tiny box of perceived reality. Consciousness in its disconnected, inverted, and chaotic state must always do so. It has prevailed this far only by entrapping humanity in an even smaller box. Compared with two-eyed, third-eyed, humanity connected with its true self the 'all-powerful'

Figure 157: The Cult symbol of the all-seeing eye. What's the antidote? The All-Seeing 'I'.

Wetiko is but a fly on an elephant's back.

The cause

The human mind was once 5-D awareness and beyond. It self-identified with *being* Infinite Freedom, the eternity that is love. Fear and duality were unknown emotions and concepts. What is fear, what is duality, when all is One? From that 5-D self-identity and awareness is generated the high frequency state that secures a place in high-frequency reality. Your vibration reflects what you are and believe yourself to be. Humanity, as that consciousness is now known, lived in the biblical garden or paradise. Then the schism came to target the harmony and draw aspects of that consciousness into the duality of 'good and evil' – the simulated 'bad copy' of Prime Reality Earth. The 'copy' digitally reflected Prime Earth to begin with and this aided the trickery and enticement. Aspects of 5-D awareness fell down the octaves into a state we call mind and this is symbolised by Adam and Eve and their experience with the serpent. Consciousness left the garden of 5-D and became 4-D and then lower 4-D mind that would be fed a simulated reality that became ever less a copy of Prime Earth and ever more an expression of the schismatic inversion luring minds deeper into its lair. The frequency continued to fall into greater density and minds became so addicted to the sensations of the five senses that returning to the 'physical' realm over and over was the equivalent of cocaine for the mind. The body was the decoded holographic projection of an illusory vehicle that mind believed it was 'in' when all was mind decoding the simulation in every aspect including the body. The simulation is a headset for the mind and dictates the reality and *self-identity* of minds that succumb to these illusions. The Gnostic Nag Hammadi *Apocryphon of John* says:

> And they steered the people who had followed them into great troubles, by leading them astray with many deceptions. They [the people] became old without having enjoyment. They died, not having found truth and without knowing the God of truth.

> And thus the whole creation became enslaved forever, from the foundation of the world until now. And they took women and begot children out of the darkness according to the likeness of their spirit. And they closed their hearts, and they hardened themselves through the hardness of the counterfeit spirit until now.

Separation from the influence, even awareness, of 5-D 'home' made minds increasing misguided and stupid. They worshipped gods that were no more than their enslavers and believed that only the 'physical' world they perceived existed in each new 'incarnation'. Whole armies of minds called scientists and academics were programmed to confirm that the illusion was real like the prisoners in Plato's cave becoming experts on the shadows cast on the wall. The sense of apartness in five-sense reality produced the fault-lines through which minds could be divided and set at war with themselves while the simulation and simulators controlled all sides. 'Out of body' minds believed they were entering an afterlife or 'heaven' from which they had to return to the 'physical' to learn lessons, evolve and escape the cycle. The simulators had no intention to allow such escape and every mind that returns home to 5-D is considered a failure and disaster. What is the difference between 5-D consciousness before 'The Fall' and 4-D mind afterwards? Self-identity. That's it – in a nutshell, in brief, in short, in sum, compactly, concisely, crisply, curtly, pithily, succinctly: Self-identity. How did we get into this mess? Self-identity. How do we get out of it? Self-identity. We stop identifying with body, mind or even soul, and we identify with being the spirit of the *All That Is*. The True and Infinite 'I'. Do that and we will connect with it and everything changes.

Removing the cause

Mind has been manipulated to self-identify with the body and yes even 'soul' which is the mind's perceived vehicle in an out-of-body simulation state. Soul is another illusion. There is only a point of attention within Infinite Awareness which can be anything from Infinity itself to the old lady with the Zimmer frame struggling to the store and waiting to die. Soul perceives the Ring-Pass-Not. Infinity knows it's not there. Each point of attention is a self-identity and each self-identity is a frequency until you are so absorbed into Infinite Identity that the realm of frequency is no more. 'Human' consciousness went the other way and fell down the frequencies into simulated illusion. Our challenge is to go back again by reversing what brought us here – self-identity. Gnostics rightly said that the body is a prison and it is – a perceptual prison, a self-identity prison. The bodily sense of limitation, the soul, too, becomes the frequency of limitation which becomes isolation from the True 'I'. Hence 'lost soul'. Woke's obsession with the minutia of self-identity in which race and chosen sexual preference dictates the sense of the 'I' is all manipulation to ensnare the Self in ever denser perceptual myopia to be followed by absorption into AI that will dictate identity from then on. Self-identity is not a concept or an intellectual talking-point. For identity to impact upon frequency it must be *lived*. It must *be*. It is not a thinking, nor even a believing, it is a *being*, a *knowing*. Every wave, every particle, lives and breathes the True 'I'.

We can acknowledge our body and the world of our senses as an *experience* while at all times *being* and *knowing* that we are Infinite

Figure 158: Beyond all form, personalities and illusion this is who we are.

Awareness *having* the experience in a realm of illusion, delusion and trickery. We may be *in* this 'world', but we must never be *of* it. To be *of* it is to be controlled by its fantasies and fairy tales. I said of the 'K' experience that it cleared me of self-identity with a 15-year-old boy who was simply consciousness experiencing a snapshot of infinity: I am Infinite Eternal Awareness – David Icke is only a brief experience in the Infinity of Forever (Fig 158). We must stop being in awe of 'experts' and instead be in awe of ourselves and who we really are. The very thought of this self-identity revolution has Wetiko in a frenzy of panic. This state of being, of self-identity, is what it has spent every illusory second of its illusory simulation seeking to prevent. Wetiko knows that when these waters break in the mind the umpire is calling the end of the game. The crowd leaves the stadium and Wetiko goes with them. Lights out. Move along now to Infinite Exploration. Nothing to see here anymore.

To overcome the illusions and influence of the simulation we must acknowledge at all times that it *is* a simulation. This is so important to perceptual freedom. Subliminal inserts in advertisements, movies and TV are communicating to the subconscious. The simulation does the same. Subliminal means 'below-threshold'– below the perceptual threshold of the conscious level of mind. The conscious level doesn't see the inserts while the subconscious absorbs everything. Subliminals trigger responses in the subconscious which filter through to the conscious as what people believe are their own thoughts, opinions and insights. I have shown in other books how once the conscious mind is made aware of a subliminal insert its impact is negated. You can look at a picture and not see the subliminal, but when it is pointed out the insert is the *first thing* you see every time you view the picture from then on. The unconscious has been made conscious and ceases to subliminally influence. The more we hold in conscious and subconscious awareness that we are experiencing a simulation, the less and less it will influence our perceptions and sense of reality.

I know how many people love being out in the 'natural world' and so do I. The point is that it's not the 'natural world'. It's a digital copy of it. We can still enjoy its beauty, like enjoying an amazing work of art, while pondering on how much more beautiful and magical it must be in its prime state in 5-D reality. The 'natural world' communicates in ways that follow the techniques of the simulation and that is bound to be the case when animals, insects, birds, trees and 'nature' in general are part of the simulation in the same way that the human body is. They use electricity, electromagnetism and soundwaves to communicate, locate and identify. Bees buzz to trigger a frequency that makes plants release pollen in a process called 'buzz pollination'. Dr Suzanne Simard at Canada's University of British Columbia found that trees transmit warnings with chemical electrical signals through fungal networks under the soil. Miles of these networks have been discovered in just a small amount of forest soil and they operate like fibre-optic internet cables in a system known as the 'wood-wide-web'. Michael Pollan, an author and researcher specialising in these subjects, said of trees and plants:

> They have ways of taking all the sensory data they gather in their everyday lives ... integrate it and then behave in an appropriate way in response. And they do this without brains, which, in a way, is what's incredible about it, because we automatically assume you need a brain to process information.

What you need is a receiver-transmitter system which is in-built in all aspects of the simulation and its electrical communication network. You can enjoy a movie while knowing it's a movie and you can enjoy the simulation and its 'natural world' while knowing it's a holographic movie. I have experienced moments walking through forests and elsewhere when I have seen the hologram as everything morphed into extreme 3-D like looking through those old 3-D 'ViewMasters' when they present the same image to each eye to generate the effect. It's quite a sight. I can still appreciate the beauty of the scene while knowing it's a simulated holographic illusion. Keeping the simulation literally 'in mind' along with the awareness that you are an expression of Infinite Consciousness stops the Matrix controlling your sense of self and reality. The subliminal becomes conscious and loses its impact.

Transforming the Simulation Field

The vibrational effect on the energetic fabric of the simulation is incalculable when enough minds remember their true identity and live it, *know* it. The frequencies they project into the Simulation Field will be the boot to Wetiko's arse. It cannot exist amid such vibration which is why it spends 24/7 holding humanity fast in *its* vibration. Anyone who has attended the freedom marches and rallies around the world will know what I mean about vibration and frequency. These are less protests than an outpouring of love, joy, unity, mutual respect, and support. They are expanded awareness on public display and in such stark contrast to the abusive and fearful in their face-nappied submission who carry a dark cloud wherever they go, or it carries

Figure 159: Message from awakening consciousness behind the freedom marches.

them. I feel this awakening energy with each new event and it's getting stronger. I hear others who have felt these Freedom Vibrations across the world from the streets of London to the streets of Ottawa, Vienna, Paris, Sydney, Wellington, Berlin, Amsterdam and Rome (Fig 159). Researchers from Aarhus University in Denmark found that fake-vaccinated people 'despise' those who refuse to get the jab and held 'stereotypic inferences that un-fake-vaccinated individuals are untrustworthy and unintelligent, making the antipathy resemble prejudice towards other deviant groups.' The study, which questioned 10,000 people from 21 countries, did not find the same attitudes by non-fake-vaccinated about the fake-vaccinated. They largely represent very different states of consciousness and frequency and so very different attitudes.

'Covid' zealots have now become permanent zealots constantly in search of the latest cause. They have conceded their right to free thought. Forgive them for they know not what they do. For others hearts are opening from where love can burst forth from the heart vortex to override the delusions of brain and belly. In the face of Wetiko's fear we must laugh and we must love. Wetiko in its legendary insecurity demands to be taken seriously and we must laugh at its ridiculousness. The way to survive expressions of Wetiko is to know that you are dealing with the mind-controlled moronic and to laugh at the ludicrousness of it all. Taking it and them seriously pulls you in to the madness. I am finding it less and less possible to take any of this shit seriously. The simulation is a lunatic asylum because that is why it was created; but being in the asylum doesn't mean you have to be a lunatic. That can only happen when you take it seriously and believe it's real. I have said for many years that if you were in an asylum would you take it personally if the inmates hurled abuse at you as you walked around? No, you'd say that is to be expected when they are not in control of their minds. Exactly. It's the same with 'Planet Earth'. Nothing disarms and disconcerts Wetiko more than not taking it seriously, not being intimidated, but instead to find its nonsense hilarious. Wetiko must enslave us with fear to survive and we must deliver our fear-free love in return. When we do that we stop feeding the beast and empowering its inverted delusion. Love to Wetiko is as garlic to a vampire. Wetiko is terrified of uncertainty and any sequence with an outcome that it cannot control. This is why it seeks to control all sides in any situation. It is desperate for certainty of outcome. Observe how Wetikoed people – like the Woke mentality – reflect this. They fear uncertainty and pursue the certainty of perceived 'safety' which means withdrawing into a risk-free cocoon policed by the state in exchange for freedom. Wetiko's insecurity comes from the fear of knowing it can be found out at any moment and its game will be over. The fascist actions of Wetiko Trudeau in Canada were not expressions of strength. They were weakness desperately seeking to survive. They were insecurity thrashing out in fear. Wetiko *is* fear. That's why fear is its energetic sustenance. Compared with love it is powerless. Take love out – evil. Put love in – no evil. Open your heart – Heaven. Close it – Hell.

All you need is love, love – love is all you need

Love beyond any version of the word that human minds can contemplate awaits in 5-D and Infinity. It has been patiently waiting all along for minds to awaken from their induced coma. The heart-opening I have been saying would come for so long – that I was told about during my own awakening in 1990 – is now here for unprecedented numbers in the simulation era (Fig 160). This is the reason those people are being targeted by the forces of schism and inversion. They seek to close our hearts with fear. We must not let them and if we don't succumb we shall prevail. The Nag Hammadi quote said of the Archon effect on humanity: '… they closed their hearts'. Researcher Paul Levy refers to Wetiko as a 'frigid, icy heart, devoid of mercy'. Look at Schwab, Gates, Fauci, Whitty,

CONNECTION TO THE ONE

Figure 160: The way home.

Trudeau, Freeland, Biden, Johnson, Macron, Draghi, Ardern, Morrison, ad infinitum. What do you see? Frigid, icy hearts, devoid of mercy. Levy adds that the way to 'defeat' evil is not to try to destroy it by playing Wetiko's game. It is rather to find the invulnerable place within ourselves where evil cannot vanquish us. That 'place' is love and 5-D awareness. We should never forget that Wetiko and its manifestations in form need *us*. We don't need *them*.

Wetiko / Yaldabaoth / Satan / Saytan / Iblis and its Cult are dependent on *us* to survive. Levy writes:

> A vampire has no intrinsic, independent, substantial existence in its own right; it only exists in relation to us. The pathogenic, vampiric mind-parasite called wetiko is nothing in itself – not being able to exist from its own side – yet it has a 'virtual reality' such that it can potentially destroy our species …

> …The fact that a vampire is not reflected by a mirror can also mean that what we need to see is that there's nothing, no-thing to see, other than ourselves. The fact that wetiko is the expression of something inside of us means that the cure for wetiko is with us as well. The critical issue is finding this cure within us and then putting it into effect.

The character in *The Matrix* known as the Merovingian, says: 'It is remarkable how similar the pattern of love is to the pattern of insanity.' The Merovingian is a symbolic agent of the Matrix and so he would think that. Without experiencing love of the Infinite kind, and what love makes you do and stand for, it would appear to be insanity to Wetiko. But this love is what holds infinity together; it's the foundation, the first and last, of everything (Fig 161). Once you are touched by it and access its gifts of wisdom and knowing you are never the same again. I know

Figure 161: The way home.

that is true. It touched me on a hill in Peru in 1990. We speak of the human spirit when we are really speaking of expanded awareness *beyond* 'human'. We are capable of amazing creativity and acts of courage, determination, kindness, and love. We see it all the time amid the madness and self-destruction. These are all expressions of our natural state, our default position – love in its Infinite Sense. Wetiko cannot stay where love reigns and the entire foundation of its focus is to block the manifestation of love within its target hearts and minds. The realisation that we are not 'human', but a state of expanded awareness trapped in the illusion of 'human', will trigger our conscious connection to who we really are – love. Simply love. We have been manipulated to forget that and it is time to remember. What happens from here depends upon it. Love is not limited to attraction. In its true sense it does not require attraction. Nor is love a word that ushers so easily from the lips whether or not you mean it or understand it. People who have told me most often how much they love me and support my work have provided some of the biggest challenges to me and my work and I have seen those who talk about love so full of hatred that they seek to destroy others. Words are easy. Love in its purest form is not so easy to express in a world that seeks its elimination. But we must seek to be that love, for it is who we really are.

This love

This love is not 'I love you'. It is 'I love'. This love is not the human love of mere attraction. It comes not from the groin, but the heart which is our connection to the Infinite Love that we are. This love is without fear for it knows there is nothing to fear. We are Infinite Forever and we remain so no matter what our current experience may be (Fig 162). This

Figure 162: Beyond the veil of forgetfulness this is what you are Mary at the call centre and Bill driving the bus.

love will always do what it knows to be right and will never be swayed from that by fear of consequences. To consider consequences is to consider not doing what you know to be right and this love would never do that. This love is not to be felt. It is to *be*. It is not a feeling, it is a *being*, an *isness*. This love comes from a transformation of self-identity. Know that the body and the world of 'human' is illusion. Hold that awareness always. Know that you are Infinite Consciousness and you will reconnect with the True 'I' – love. The energy of worldwide freedom marches and events is so different because of this. Love is the energy, the being, the perception, the isness, that will change our reality and return us to paradise. We only have to open our hearts and live what they tell us to live.

Who am I? *I am All That Is, Has Been, And Ever Can Be*, having a brief experience called 'human'.

Who are you?

The same.

Live it, *be* it, and everything shall change.

It's been no bed of roses, no pleasure cruise.

I consider it a challenge before the whole human race

and I ain't gonna lose.

And we mean to go on, and on, and on, and on ...

We are the champions, my friends.

Freddie Mercury

Index

Hundreds of cutting-edge documentaries, series, feature films and podcasts; plus David Icke's Dot-Connect-The-News Show, his Nature Of Reality series, and all his major public events going back to 1994.

There is nothing like Ickonic anywhere in the world.

PERCEPTIONS OF A RENEGADE MIND

DAVID ICKE

THE TRIGGER

THE LIE THAT CHANGED THE WORLD
– WHO REALLY DID IT AND WHY

DAVID ICKE

EVERYTHING YOU NEED TO KNOW

BUT HAVE NEVER BEEN TOLD

DAVID ICKE

Before you go ...

For more detail, background and evidence about the subjects in *The Trap* – and so much more – see my others books including *And The Truth Shall Set You Free; The Biggest Secret; Children of the Matrix; The David Icke Guide to the Global Conspiracy; Tales from the Time Loop; The Perception Deception; Remember Who You Are; Human Race Get Off Your Knees; Phantom Self; Everything You Need To Know But Have Never Been Told, The Trigger, The Answer* and *Perception of a Renegade Mind.*

You can subscribe to the fantastic new Ickonic media platform where there are many hundreds of hours of cutting-edge information in videos, documentaries and series across a whole range of subjects which are added to every week. This includes my 90 minute breakdown of the week's news every Friday to explain *why* events are happening and to what end.